Behind the C

Behind the Curtain

Making Music in Mumbai's Film Studios

Gregory D. Booth

OXFORD
UNIVERSITY PRESS
2008

OXFORD
UNIVERSITY PRESS

Oxford University Press, Inc., publishes works that further
Oxford University's objective of excellence
in research, scholarship, and education.

Oxford   New York
Auckland   Cape Town   Dar es Salaam   Hong Kong   Karachi
Kuala Lumpur   Madrid   Melbourne   Mexico City   Nairobi
New Delhi   Shanghai   Taipei   Toronto
With offices in
Argentina   Austria   Brazil   Chile   Czech Republic   France   Greece
Guatemala   Hungary   Italy   Japan   Poland   Portugal   Singapore
South Korea   Switzerland   Thailand   Turkey   Ukraine   Vietnam

Copyright © 2008 by Oxford University Press, Inc.

Published by Oxford University Press, Inc.
198 Madison Avenue, New York, New York 10016

www.oup.com

Oxford is a registered trademark of Oxford University Press

Library of Congress Cataloging-in-Publication Data
Booth, Gregory D.
Behind the curtain : making music in Mumbai's film studios / Gregory D. Booth.
p. cm.
Includes bibliographical references and index.
ISBN 978-0-19-532763-2; 978-0-19-532764-9 (pbk.)
1. Motion picture music—Production and direction—India—Bombay—History.
2. Motion picture music—India—Bombay—History and criticism.   3. Motion picture industry—
India—Bombay—History.   I. Title.
ML2075B66 2008
781.5'420954792—dc22   2008007201

Recorded video tracks marked in text with ●
are available online at www.oup.com/us/behindthecurtain

1   3   5   7   9   8   6   4   2
Printed in the United States of America
on acid-free paper

This book is dedicated to Cawas Lord

Cawas Lord (extreme right) rehearses Latin rhythms with his son, Kersi Lord (far left, on bongos), and Dattaram Waadkar (second from left, on congas). Music director Shankar Raghuvanshi looks on (Famous Studios, ca. 1957). Courtesy of Kersi Lord and family.

Shortly before this volume was completed, the Indian film industry lost its eldest living member. Coming from a middle-class Parsi family in Pune, Cawas Lord began his long musical career playing military drums and bagpipes under the tutelage of various local military bandleaders. He later switched to trumpet and, still later, to dance and jazz drums and played for various bands. In the 1930s he began working in Mumbai's film studios, initially for Imperial Studios, where he played music for some of India's earliest sound films. During World War II he toured India as a captain in the British army entertaining the British troops. After the war, Lord returned to Mumbai, where he joined the band of Mumbai's great jazz trumpeter, Chic Chocolate, as a drummer. The presence of touring dance-band musicians provided Lord an opportunity to learn Latin American–style percussion instruments. He subsequently played a fundamental role in the popularization of those instruments and Latin dance rhythms in Mumbai's dance-band scene. His influence became national when he rejoined the film-music business. Working with composers such as C. Ramchandra, S. D. Burman, Naushad Ali, and others, Lord pioneered the incorporation of Latin musical elements into the music of the Hindi cinema.

Widely respected throughout the film-music industry, Cawas Kaka (Uncle Cawas), as he was known, helped younger musicians to develop their own careers.

Acknowledgments

I express my sincere gratitude to numerous musicians, engineers, music directors, and others of the Mumbai film industry. These individuals kindly put up with my questions and confusion; many offered hospitality and friendship, as well as information and connections. They are all cocontributors to this book and this history; without their generosity this project would not have been possible. I have sought to do justice to their careers and their words; some have been kind enough to read parts of this manuscript and suggest corrections, for which I am grateful. Any errors that remain are solely my responsibility. These people are listed here alphabetically by first name, as is common practice in industry listings:

A. N. Tagore, Abbas Ali, Amar Haldipurkar, Amin Sayani, Amrut Katkar, Anandji Shah, Anil Mohile, Anjan Biswas, Anníbal Castro, Anthony Gonsalves, Anupam De Ghatak, Ashok Ranade, Ashok Shukla, Avinash Oak, Bablu Chakravarty, Benny Gracias, Benny Rosario, Bhanu Gupta, Bhavani Shankar, Bhupinder Singh, Bishwadeep Chatterjee, Bosco Mendes, Cajetano Pinto, Cawas Lord, Charanjit Singh, Daman Sood, Dattaram Waadkar, Deepan Chatterji, Deepak Chauhan, Ernest Menezes, Franco Vaz, Gyan Prasad, Halim Jaffar Khan, Homi Mullan, Indu Mehrani, J. V. Acharya, Jerry Fernandes, Jerry Pinto, Joe Gomes, Joe Monsorate, Joe Pinto, John Gonsalves, John Pereira, Kartik Kumar, Kersi Lord, Kishore Desai, Kuku Kholi, Leslie Godinho, Louiz Banks, Loy Mendonsa, Manohari Singh, Maoro Alfonso, Mario Fernández, Maruti Rao Kheer, Micky Corea, Mukesh Desai, Naresh Fernandes, Naushad Ali,

Nisar Ahmad Sajjad, Omprakash Sonik, Prabhakar Jog, Prakash Varma, Pyarelal Sharma, Ramanand Shetty, Ramesh Iyer, Ranjit Gazmer, Ratna Nagari, Ravi Shankar Sharma, Raymond Albuquerque, Robert Corea, Sanjay Chakravarty, Sardar Malik, Shakti Samant, Shankar Indorkar, Shankar Mahadevan, Sharafat Khan, Shivkumar Sharma, Shreekant Joshi, Shyam Raj, Shyamrao Kamble, Sultan Khan, Sumit Mitra, Sunil Kaushik, Suresh Kathuria, Suresh Yadhav, Tanug Garg, Tappan Adhikari, Taufiq Qureshi, Thakur Singh, Uttam Singh, V. K. Dubey, Victor D'Souza, Vijay Chauhan, Vijay (Viju) Shah, Vipin Reshamiya, Vistasp Balsara, Yash Chopra, and Zakir Hussain.

In addition, I owe special thanks to Alison Booth for her understanding and encouragement of the fieldwork process and for her help with the videos that accompany this book; to Naresh Fernandes for his insights and contacts in the Goan community and Mumbai generally, as well as his collegial support of and interest in this project; to Kersi Lord, for his knowledge and conversation and many highly educational lunches; to Sunil Shanbag of Chrysalis Productions for his friendship and enthusiasm, as well as his support of the filming that was undertaken as part of this project and the production of the video excerpts that accompany this book; and to the University of Auckland Research Committee for its support of the necessary fieldwork.

Contents

Introduction: Who Is Anthony Gonsalves?   3

Part I   History, Technology, and a Determinist Milieu for Hindi Film Song

  1   Popular Music as Film Music   27
  2   Musicians and Technology in the Mumbai Film-Music Industry   56
  3   Changing Structures in the Mumbai Film Industry   87

Part II   The Life of Music in the Mumbai Film Industry

  4   Origins, Training, and "Joining the Line"   121
  5   Roles, Relations, and the Creative Process   154
  6   Rehearsals, Recordings, and Economics   184

Part III   Music, Instruments, and Meaning from Musicians' Perspectives

  7   Orchestras and Orchestral Procedures, Instrumental Change, Arranging, and Programming   225
  8   Issues of Style, Genre, and Value in Mumbai Film Music   255

Conclusion: Oral History, Change, and Accounts of Human Agency   284

Notes   293

References   295

Index   305

Behind the Curtain

Introduction

Who Is Anthony Gonsalves?

Almost anyone who grew up in urban India after 1950, especially in the northern two-thirds of the subcontinent, knows who Anthony Gonsalves is: the middle of the three fictional brothers at the center of the classic Hindi film *Amar, Akbar, Anthony* (1977), directed by Manmohan Desai.[1] The film is a typical 1970s' Desai action film with seemingly endless mixed identities, brothers lost and found, cross-generation revenge, car chases, fight sequences, flashbacks, and a very urban, slang-based dialogue. As a "brother film," a structure that the Hindi cinema has borrowed and modified from traditional epic narratives and modified to suit twentieth- and twenty-first-century India, it is full of narrative and dramatic parallelism at all levels, treating each of the three brothers identified in the film's title (who have been separated at childhood and raised as Hindu, Christian, and Muslim respectively) with precisely the proper amount of attention and respect to establish the hierarchy (Booth 1995). As the middle brother, Anthony Gonsalves is the most colorful. He does most of the fighting, cuts more corners than the others, and has the most exuberant romance.

Anthony, played by Amitabh Bachchan in the early days of the "angry young man" phase of his remarkable career, also generates most of the comedy. Among his famous comic scenes in this film is the song "My Name Is Anthony Gonsalves" (composed by Laxmikant-Pyarelal, with lyrics by Anand Bakshi). In the song, Anthony bursts forth from a huge Easter egg at a Goan (and hence Christian) celebration of that holiday, dressed in a

3

Figure 0.1
Anthony Gonsalves (2005).

caricature of old-fashioned Goan formal dress, in an absurdly large top hat and tails. The scene, the song, and the character are iconic images of India in the 1970s and of the career of India's most famous Hindi film actor.

From a different perspective, almost no one outside the Mumbai film-music industry knows who Anthony Gonsalves is (figure 0.1). Born in 1927 in the Goan village of Majorda, Anthony Gonsalves was the son of a choirmaster attached to the local Roman Catholic church, Mãe de Deus. Anthony was trained in European classical music by his father and from 1943 through 1965 worked in the film-music industry in Mumbai. Although he frequently played violin in the front row of various film-studio orchestras, he made more significant contributions through his arranging and composition work for a long and distinguished list of music directors (composers), including Shyam Sunder, S. D. Burman, and Madan Mohan. This real-life Anthony Gonsalves also taught many younger musicians to play violin, read European staff notation, and understand the intricacies of (European) music theory and harmony (Fernandes 2005).

> ANTHONY GONSALVES: I was known for my willingness to teach. I would
> teach anyone. I didn't mind about religion or caste or any of those things.
> Lata [Mangeshkar, a famous film singer] arranged a hall for me in Bandra

so I could teach there. I taught them how to play for the films because mostly they had not done this kind of work before.[2]

One of Gonsalves's young students in the 1950s was Pyarelal Sharma, who, along with Laxmikant Kudalkar, went on to become one half of one of India's most famous composing teams, known publicly as Laxmikant-Pyarelal and within the film industry often as simply L-P.

Anthony Gonsalves had left Mumbai and the film-music industry behind more than ten years before Laxmikant-Pyarelal started composing the songs for *Amar, Akbar, Anthony*. Because the film required three names, preferably alliterative, representing three different religions, Manmohan Desai settled on Anthony for his Christian hero but had originally thought of his surname as Fernandes, also common in the Goan Christian world. When Laxmikant-Pyarelal met with lyricist Anand Bakshi and Desai to start working out the songs, however, the title "My Name Is Anthony Fernandes" simply did not appeal to anyone. On a whim, Pyarelal Sharma suggested that the name be changed from Fernandes to Gonsalves, consciously recalling the name of his own real-life violin teacher and naming Bachchan's soon-to-be-famous film character for an important, if largely unknown, film musician.

Pyarelal Sharma is not a man on whom irony is lost. To name a character played by India's most famous actor for a musician totally unknown outside the small circle of the Mumbai film-music industry was a gesture that no doubt appealed to him as both a sincere gesture of affection and a humorously ironic reflection on film-musicians' anonymity. Nor is the irony lost on Anthony Gonsalves, who explains the film-music business as a life of invisibility: "We were always hidden, always playing behind the curtain. No one knew."

The image of "playing behind the curtain" came up more than once in the research leading to this book, sometimes in similar language, sometimes in precisely those words; hence its place in my title. Although he comes from a different sociocultural and musical background and from a different time, *tabla* player Sharafat Khan, who began playing on Hindi film scores in the 1970s, has used almost exactly the same imagery as Gonsalves to explain the nature of the musical life in the film business:

> SHARAFAT KHAN: You know the thing about being a musician in this line is that people never know what happens. We do such good work, but the public never sees behind the curtain, so they never know what we've done. It's like that even today. [🔊 Video 0.1]

The musicians of the Mumbai film industry have always understood their own anonymity. They were working at jobs in which many earned substantial amounts of money, but some at least would rather have been playing jazz or classical music. A number encountered the results of their work in theaters or on the radio; others had no knowledge of the names of the songs or films they were working on.

In one sense, these are conditions that Mumbai's film musicians share with many film and studio musicians throughout the world. How many viewers watching *Lawrence of Arabia,* for example, are actively paying attention to the musical score or wondering about the composer's identity, let alone the name of the musician who played the oboe solos? Anonymity is a fate shared to a greater or lesser extent by musicians in many narrative traditions.

There is one significant difference, however, between the music of *Lawrence of Arabia* and that of *Amar, Akbar, Anthony.* The songs that were part of the latter's score were naturally composed to be integral components of a feature film, but because of the specific circumstances of the popular culture industry in India after 1947, they were simultaneously items in a uniquely dominant popular music repertoire. Not only, then, does almost everyone who grew up in independent India or lived in the northern two-thirds of the subcontinent from 1977 onward know who Anthony Gonsalves (the film character) is, most would also recognize the song in which that name was made famous. Unlike the musicians who played for Hollywood soundtracks, those of the Mumbai film studios were simultaneously performing songs that were also the major components of India's popular music culture. They were the men and women who played the hits heard and sung in homes and on the streets, as well as the music to which Hindi film stars mimed and danced on the screen. They contributed to what has been arguably the most important and widely received non-Western popular music of the twentieth century.

This dual identity of Anthony Gonsalves is at the heart of this book. As a film persona he embodies the enormous cultural presence of both the Hindi cinema and its music. As a real but almost unknown music performer, composer, and arranger, he embodies the anonymity of his profession and his many colleagues. Perhaps more than in any other film-music industry, Mumbai's film musicians were participating in the production of their country's most popular songs. Moreover, perhaps more than any other popular musicians, they remained anonymous throughout their careers.

An Oral History of Mumbai's Film-Music Industry

This book offers a view of the professional lives of musicians who played in the Indian, Hindi-language film industry located in Mumbai. I contextualize the stories they tell with a consideration of the fundamental cultural, technological, and industrial issues that shaped Hindi film-music production and the place of that music in Indian culture. The book is constructed largely through and in the words of the musicians, which were spoken to me in interviews and conversations conducted between 2004 and 2007. Well over half of the interviews were conducted in English, which is widely spoken in the film business and is the principal language spoken by most Goan musicians. The remainder of the interviews were conducted in Hindi. It is thus an oral history.

Although musical performances often accompanied silent Indian films and were consistently present in sound films from 1931 on, this volume focuses on the period that has recently been termed "Old Bollywood" (Virmani 2004, 77). "Bollywood" is a somewhat contentious term for a variety of reasons (I discuss my use of this term in detail in chapter 3). Briefly, however, Old Bollywood refers to the period in which Mumbai film production was characterized by an independent-producer industrial system and by a series of technological processes that ultimately required the synchronized rerecording of sounds and images onto a single strip of celluloid film. These two processes dominated Mumbai's film-production processes from the late 1940s on and persisted throughout the late 1990s.

When younger, more technically sophisticated filmmakers and technicians finally introduced digital sound and filmmaking techniques and computers became widely available, a new era began that I call "New Bollywood." Many aspects of New Bollywood are in fact new: The various features of digital technology, multiscreen theaters, the increasing economic power of the Indian diaspora, and the globalization of music television are the most important ones here. New Bollywood has offered a range of positive outcomes for Indian filmmakers, including the wider international access that comes with world-class production values and legible English subtitles, but the introduction of digital, computer-based sound recording marked a drastic and less positive change for film musicians. New Bollywood has also seen the advent of a new breed of professional film producers, as Virmani argues. One consequence of these new developments has been the collapse, in effect, of the musical life that I describe. New Bollywood, of course, is an ongoing phenomenon in which musicians are still active; as its history becomes its present at some point, it is necessarily incomplete. In one sense, history becomes less satisfactory the closer it comes to that imaginary line between it and the present.

Nevertheless, there is a sense among the musicians (even the younger ones) in Mumbai's film industry of something that began rather gradually around the time of Indian independence in 1947 but ended somewhat abruptly just before the beginning of the new millennium. This oral history considers the years both before and after this period but focuses primarily on the musical, professional, and cultural aspects of what I maintain is a remarkably coherent period of roughly fifty years.

History and Oral History

An oral history is a dangerous thing. Michel de Certeau writes that "one type of history ponders what is comprehensible and what are the conditions of understanding, the other claims to reencounter lived experience, ex-humed by virtue of a knowledge of the past" (de Certeau 1988, 35). "Claims to reencounter lived experience" must be deceptive, of course, especially in histories based on documents. No historian can legitimately support such a claim, as de Certeau argues. An oral history, on the other hand, does, in at least one sense, offer readers an encounter with actual experience. The words in this book are, explicitly and inarguably, retellings by those who lived the composition, performance, and recording of Mumbai's film music. Of course, the attraction of such a history is that it provides its read-ers unparalleled and personalized access to fascinating historical phenom-ena. In the chapters that follow, musicians of Mumbai's film industry speak to questions about how recordings took place, how the music was created, how they made decisions about careers, who controlled their pay, and so on from irreplaceable firsthand knowledge. No documents can offer such clear and immediate understandings of these questions. Naturally, as with anything so appealing, one encounters a number of traps having to do with the historical process.

Among other things, oral history seems especially vulnerable to the val-orization of "the relation the historian keeps with a lived experience" (White 1987, 2). This is an inevitable outcome of the ethnographic (rather than historical) method, which effectively requires participant/observation–style fieldwork, the living of at least an ersatz version of the experience that is the object of study. In the collection of oral history, the necessary field-work establishes a relationship between the historian-ethnographer and the people and places that are the objects of the research. This connection provides access to a lived experience that, in some cases (however tem-porarily or artificially), closely resembles the actual experience of the ob-ject. I make no claim to any such resemblance with regard to my fieldwork. The life that most of the musicians describe in this volume is effectively over; I can never claim to have lived that life or even convince myself that I have.

All historical discourse narrates in some form, but the act of *narrativiza-tion*—that is, the construction of accounts of perceived reality in story form—is problematic. The distinctions between history and oral history lie in the difference between "a discourse that openly adopts a perspective that looks out on the world and reports it and a discourse that feigns to make the world speak itself and speak itself as a story" (ibid., 3). Neither the world nor the events of history are capable of speech, of course: In a history that is derived from documentary evidence, "real events should not speak . . . real events should simply be" (ibid.).

In an oral history, however, narrators abound. The musicians in this book are people who have subjectively reported the events of their professional lives. They are narrators indeed. What is more, many of them understand their careers as stories and tell them as such, beginning at the beginning and continuing until they come to the end or to a point after which they perceive things to have gone on without change and therefore as unworthy of (and untellable as) a story. This is not at all unexpected. "Narrative is a meta-code, a human universal on the basis of which transcultural messages about the nature of a shared reality can be transmitted" (ibid., 1). The specific nature of an oral history lies in its ability to more legitimately access the metacode that White proposes and equally in the fact that these musicians, these narrators (and their words) are simultaneously the subjects of the events they recount and the historical objects of my study.

In the context of a coffeehouse, bar, or musician's front room, these words are accounts by actors in the Mumbai film business speaking for and of themselves and the world in which they live; they are the "world speaking itself" as White puts it (above). In the context of this book, however, they are words spoken to and subsequently selected by me. In constructing a history I not only become the source of subjective narration but also deconstruct the individual narratives told to me. I select some portions of those narratives and not others to weave into the fabric of a new narrative. I place the words of each of these individuals in a new context, alongside the words of their colleagues, interpreting and creating new historical meanings thereby. In the juxtaposition of three narratives about recording sessions, for example, those stories may still appear to be accounts of historical action, but like all such descriptions, they are history because their juxtaposition is the result of my historiographic action. The words and stories of these individuals are inevitably enmeshed in a narrative that, to some extent, goes beyond their own immediate experiences.

Oral History in the Mumbai Film-Music Industry

I had a number of reasons for undertaking this project. First, of course, it is a fascinating subject. The Mumbai film-music industry offers a globally unique instance of an interaction between a film-production system (with all its aesthetic, commercial, and industrial associations) and a popular

music–production system. The musicians of the Hindi film world composed, arranged, and performed film music as part of a self-organized
method that combined technological, aesthetic, and industrial aspects of
filmmaking with film-music and popular-music production in a cultural
context where the identities of film and popular music were effectively synonymous. Under the constraints of this technique, creative roles and socioprofessional structures interacted in specific ways with economics and
technology to relegate particular creative musical tasks or different types
of recording to various locations on the long path to film completion. In
other examples, musicians were separated from the composers they
worked with daily not only in terms of the sources and nature of their payments but also through distinct professional bodies.

As popular music, film songs benefited from being embedded in a film-
production system, even one as chaotic as the Mumbai film industry. Songs
and their narrative contexts were often mutually reinforcing in terms of
publicity, reception, and emotional impact and meaning. Ironically, song
production in this environment was at times only partially or loosely con-
strained by budgetary limits in both the short and medium terms. As long
as films were hits, it appears as if film-music production was sometimes
funded from a seemingly bottomless pocket. These stories relate the conditions of this impossibility, which is then thrown into less rosy relief by stories of limited budgets and late wages. At the same time, no amount of
money could overcome the physical limits of sound technology at any
given point in the history of that fascinating subject or the barriers created
by the Indian government to the acquisition of such technology. Human in-
genuity and an enormous amount of hard work, together with the socioprofessional organizational skills that Indian culture possesses in great
measure, overcame these obstacles. The result was a sophisticated, if time-
consuming, song-and-picture production process that generated one of the
world's most famous and most distinctive popular-music repertoires.

My second reason for embarking on this book and adopting its particular structure is that, although much ethnomusicology is based on oral history, there are very few oral histories in ethnomusicology. Oral history lies
at an important confluence of ethnography and history as fields, a place
where the current broad trend toward subject-centered ethnography meets
head-on ethnomusicology's and anthropology's concerns with the political
implications of essentialist representation. These were initially called to our
attention by Edward Said (1991). As I have noted, it offers the potential for
a more direct connection with the object of our inquiry than does a history
based solely on documents. While this volume is as much a subject-centered
work as any other (and with all of the aforementioned caveats in mind), I
suggest that an oral history provides access to the words of musicians

themselves and offers the possibility of a desensationalized, demystified, but essentially human understanding of this music-production culture and process.

The Mumbai film-music industry is an excellent choice for such an approach. Although there were the usual professional, personal, and communal jealousies and tensions, the world of Mumbai film music, throughout its history, has been quite small, tightly knit, and remarkably collegial. The Cine Musicians Association (CMA), the professional union for film musicians, has rarely (if ever) had a membership of more than eight hundred musicians. Probably fewer than three hundred of those were playing music in the studios on a daily basis at any point in time. Roughly two hundred more were working regularly but not daily.

Although every individual's story is different, most are familiar with others' careers; in many professional aspects, those careers were quite similar. More than in some musical traditions and professions in India, the musicians of the Mumbai film industry can and do speak of "the industry" as a collective, homogeneous unit. Most have a sense of its history and of changes over time, as well as a perception that developing technology and business practices were driving much of that change. Musicians are aware of their own place and that of others in the broader narrative of the profession. One of the most consistent comments musicians make about the film line, as most musicians call their business, concerns the pleasure they had in meeting on a regular, if not daily, basis. They understood themselves as a group and, for the most part, recognized their common perceptions of its divisions and subdivisions.

In the comments of many of these musicians, an enjoyment of the work and their pride in the quality of their performances are evident. This is especially so because, although these were recording sessions, most recordings sessions were explicitly performances. Even if they did not like the music all that much (and some did not), a sense of shared musical accomplishment and camaraderie stands out.

Musicians often express their feelings in these respects in language that appears to be nostalgic. Nostalgia as such is a concern in any oral history and for any oral historian. As with matters of narrativization, nostalgia is peril in which both the historian and the informants can participate. A romanticized longing for a "better," "purer," "happier" past that was somehow more authentic, more diverse, and so forth is prevalent among members of any elder generation in any context. The romanticizing or orientalizing tendencies of ethnomusicology have themselves been a concern within the field. In a volume that focuses largely on a musical past and uses the words of the musicians who lived that past to represent it, the dangers of nostalgia are considerable.

The distinction between accurate and nostalgic representations in this context is a very difficult line to draw. I have no doubt that at least some of the comments in this volume are nostalgic. I address this issue specifically at the conclusion of chapter 8, but I note at this point that, in empirical terms, the professional lives of film musicians *were* better in the 1970s and '80s. Work was plentiful, pay rates were set by negotiated settlements, wages were paid largely on time, and the future seemed certain. Sons followed their fathers into the film-music business with no expectation that musicians who began the 1990s working forty- to sixty-hour weeks would, by the end of that decade, be working forty-hour months if they were lucky. Thus, a longing for a lost (better) time is very much part of the mindset of many musicians in Mumbai, although it is usually tempered by a sense of resignation to the inevitability of change. Part of the value of this volume is that it captures the beginning and the end of a distinct period in world music history that lasted roughly forty years and almost inevitably instills a sense of wistfulness among those who experienced it.

Many of these musicians are very aware of having participated in something quite special. It would not have been possible to live in Mumbai or anywhere in India after 1940 and not be aware of the cultural importance of the music they were playing. Musicians in the film business have always understood that they were making the popular music of the nation and doing so in a fashion significantly more anonymous than film composers, whose credits in the opening moments of a film are normally located prestigiously just before the names of the director and producer. Musicians worked daily with the stars of that music, the composers and the singers, but were completely unrecognized outside of the industry. The extent to which they contributed to the construction and development of this highly syncretic music was also generally unknown. Part of the justification for the format of this volume is that it provides a forum and some degree of recognition in the academic arena for the voices of these musicians who were "playing behind the curtain."

Scholarship on the Hindi Cinema and Its Music

This book can also be seen as a response to the nature of the West's reception of Hindi film music and the scholarship to date on this topic. Until very recently there have been major gaps in our understanding of the ways this music has been created, produced, and received.

Ethnomusicology's initial concerns with authenticity and the confusion that characterized the field's early relationship with popular music and the media resulted in a dubious silence regarding film music in the scholarship of the 1970s and early 1980s. Hindi film music also had the problem of being intensely hegemonic, obvious, and blatantly commercial. These characteristics no doubt made it a relatively unappealing object of study in a field that, as we all now understand, was initially fascinated by the exotic, the endangered, and the authentic. The echoes of India's officially negative midcentury position on film music (as exemplified in the 1952 ban on the broadcast of film songs by the state-owned All India Radio) still resonated in many circles in which foreign scholars traveled.

Unlike the classical traditions, which could be approached through literature, classical texts, and performance training, there was no specific methodology for the study of film music. The partial applicability (at best) of existing popular music theory to Hindi film song (chapter 8) added yet other obstacles. Furthermore, while there has always been an enormous popular press devoted to the Hindi cinema and its music, there has been little in the way of documentation of this industry and still less of its music—and literally none in English until the 1980s.

Prior to the advent of the digital age, only those who spoke Hindi could productively watch Hindi films since the addition of English subtitles using videotape technology was not cost effective and rarely undertaken. Even with the language, viewing Hindi films in the 1970s and 1980s most commonly meant watching pirated videos of highly variable quality and choosing films in what was a more-random-than-usual guessing game at the local (but often invisible) video rental store. The export of films was a government-controlled activity until 1992, "subsidiary to the policy of exporting 'art' films" (Rajadhyaksha 2004, 120). Finally, the "sheer gigantomania of India's film factories"—close to seventy thousand commercial Hindi films and roughly half a million songs—was intimidating (Rajadhyaksha 1995, 10).

As a result, if we talked about Hindi film song at all, it seemed that the invocation of Lata Mangeshkar's name three times and the recitation of the popular formula "six songs and three dances" was sufficient. Ethnomusicologists could then go back to a consideration of serious (that is to say, classical or sometimes folk) music, which was viewed as worthier of attention. As with so many other things, I have Zakir Hussain to thank for suggesting to me that film music deserved serious attention. That notion and my own experiences in India—where the cultural importance of film music is inescapably impressed on even the most casual visitor—have led to my efforts to improve my understanding of Hindi film song and ultimately to this book.

Ethnomusicologists generally, and South Asianists especially, have been aware of Hindi film music for a long time, of course. Whether we knew about playback singer Lata Mangeshkar and her former place in the *Guinness Book of World Records* for the most songs recorded by a single artist or about "the biggest film industry in the world" or simply that "all Hindi films are musicals," most have been at least dimly aware of the behemoth that is Hindi film and film-music culture. Despite this general awareness, film music took quite some time to appear in published research. Wade's 1979 text is limited to the classical traditions and does not mention film music. Neuman's ethnographic study of classical musicians similarly ignores the topic and notes only that film music "is a social phenomenon of great but unstudied significance" (1980, 21). On the very first page of his musical ethnography of a Bhojpuri village, Henry states that "shrilly amplified film songs, the popular music of India, have for decades been a part of the urban ambience" (1988, 1). Henry also refers to the presence and use of film songs in village life.

The first direct approach to film song production and the people involved in the business was made not by ethnomusicologists but by a filmmaker-journalist pair riding the crest of the "world-beat" phenomenon of the mid-1980s. Their documentary film, *There Will Always Be Stars in the Sky*, and accompanying book chapter presented a sensationalized and sexualized view of the Mumbai industry, in which terms such as "hotchpotch" and "conveyor belt" were combined with tales of corruption, antiquated equipment, and general incompetence (Marre and Charlton 1985). The appearance of references to Hindi film song in the growing "world music" literature and ethnomusicology's awareness of the phenomenon ultimately led to serious study of the phenomenon by a small group of foreign scholars.

Ironically, film music also received little attention in Indian writing, although studies of Indian cinema inevitably mentioned music. Firoze Rangoonwalla's considerable expertise and fondness for film music are both apparent in his early study of the Indian cinema (Rangoonwalla 1983). Barnouw and Krishnaswamy (1980), on the other hand, did little more than reinforce the formulaic nature of the genre's "six songs and three dances." Dissanayake and Sahai (1988) noted song's expressive power in the films of Raj Kapoor. More recently, Rajadhyaksha and Willeman (1995) have produced a valuable source of information on Indian films generally, which includes biographical information about some important Hindi composers, lyricists, and singers. Rajadhyaksha suggests that many Indian readers of the *Encyclopedia of Indian Cinema* will be familiar with how, in the 1970s, "cinephilia relating to mainstream Hindi cinema became an important source for celebrating 'indigenous' cultural populism while mounting a free-market attack on the Nehru–Indira Gandhi socialist model of state institutions" (ibid., 10).

The more recent Indian scholars of Hindi cinema are the children of those times. As such, they have engaged with Indian cinema from a position of cinephilia while, for the most part, rejecting the almost compulsory expressions of embarrassment that most Indians of their parents' generation seemed to feel was obligatory in conversations (at least with foreigners) about the Hindi cinema. Primarily scholars of film rather than music, they offer interpretive analyses that include at least the mention of song in relation to politics, cinematic structure, or aesthetics and semiotics (e.g., Aziz 2003; Chakravarty 1993; Gopalan 2002; Mishra 2002). This research is long overdue: Aziz focuses exclusively on Hindi film song, while Mishra has devoted a full chapter to its consideration. Most others at least mention the importance of songs or the scenes of which those songs are a part. This scholarship, however, has been based largely on film, media, and/or cultural studies models; it has resulted in a broad focus on cultural meaning, reception, and an explicitly subject-centered interpretive approach.

In addition to this research, a handful of Indian authors have addressed film music outside its cinematic context. Ashok Ranade published some early essays (1984), as well a 2006 volume that he describes as "paying his debt" to the Hindi cinema; the latter work is an important account from a musical and stylistic basis of the earlier periods of Hindi film music. Manek Premchand (2003), very much a film song fan, has also published the results of his interviews with many of the major figures of Mumbai's film-music world, an additional, if not always consistent, source of information. Along more obsessive lines, Harmandir Singh's six-volume *Hindi Film Geet Kosh* [Hindi film song dictionary], which lists the entire output of films, composers, songs, lyricists, and singers, is an indispensable research tool, written in Hindi, that has made possible much of the statistical foundation for studies in this field.

Until recently, the Hindi cinema and its music have not fared well in Western perception and scholarship. Based on the scantiest of sources but with some apparent familiarity with the genre, Skillman published an early historical study in 1986. A more extended ethnomusicological study of Hindi film song was produced by Alison Arnold, who took a relative unfamiliarity with India, along with standard ethnomusicological methodologies and concepts, with her to Mumbai in the late 1980s. The resulting doctoral dissertation (1991) is part standard music history and part musicological analysis that focuses on music directors (i.e., composers) and, to a lesser extent, singers. There is justification for this approach, both from Indian and foreign viewpoints, but the scope and the complexities of the project were perhaps broader than Arnold realized.

As it is, the document provides irreplaceable information about individuals and music in the industry. The interviews that Arnold conducted in the late 1980s are an invaluable resource at this point since many of those she spoke with are no longer living. The comments of Anil Biswas and Salil Chaudhuri that appear in this book have been transcribed from Arnold's original interview recordings.[3]

Peter Manuel's study of cassette culture in north India (1993) helped re-orient ethnomusicological attention toward the popular and industrial side of world musics. Despite his industrial focus on the cassette industry generally and his interest in (and preference for) nonfilm genres, his research set out some key issues in film music, including the distinctive relationships between the recording and film industries and the control of popular music production by film producers and distributors. Manuel's research provides valuable information about the cassette industry, which, from the 1980s on, radically increased the consumption of film music outside the theaters and broadcast media. Manuel also implies the unique ideological and aesthetic nature of Hindi film song content when he notes the explicit presence of "extra-musical values and associations" (ibid., 48).

There is a unique relationship, a tension in fact, between musical style and genre ideology in Hindi film song (see chapter 8). This has, I believe, contributed to the relative paucity of scholarship (especially foreign research) on film song. I suggest that this relationship, in which musical style elements appear to be randomly deployed in a repertoire with a high degree of ideological uniformity, makes Hindi film music less amenable to the kinds of analysis that have informed much ethno- and popular musicology (e.g., Waterman's excellent 1990 study of popular music in Nigeria).

In coming to grips with these issues, Arnold resorts to an explicitly evolutionary and ultimately comparative paradigm and states that "the evolution of film song . . . has progressed remarkably slowly in comparison with the development of Western pop music" (Arnold 1991, 227). Although Arnold does not make this clear, her conclusions implicitly equate the history of film song with the series of ideologically or musically distinct styles or genres that characterize Western popular music. Manuel also bases much of his analysis of film music on what is effectively a Western (if not American) popular music model.

Arnold's consideration of production is largely in musicological terms; she problematizes the creative process through a concern for the production of autonomous, "unique" songs. Manuel more profitably recognizes the distinctive nature of the Hindi film-music production process, but he does not appear to fully consider the consequences of that uniqueness for the validity of the comparison with Western popular music. While Arnold provides information about the creation of songs (largely as melodies) and Manuel offers a wealth of facts about the production of cassettes, this research does not help us understand these aspects as part of a single cultural and industrial process. There is very little material on the actual production of music in the Hindi film industry, the ways in which that music was arranged, performed, and recorded, and who organized and undertook those tasks. Given the intensely syncretic content of Hindi film music

(Arnold describes it as eclectic), in which Indian classical and folk musics were routinely combined with both Western styles and the distinctive orchestral sound of Mumbai's film orchestras, we have little real information about how this amalgam was achieved.

More recently, Anna Morcom's 2007 study of film song begins with Arnold's and Manuel's research. As the first study written by a foreigner familiar with ethnomusicology, India, and Hindi cinema, however, Morcom's ethnographic approach and her results offer a more integrated view of the key issues in Hindi film song. Significantly, its production and meaning are placed in the aesthetic and industrial contexts of the film industry. Morcom considers industrial production, style, meaning, and the commercial life of film songs, as reported by the producers, directors, and composers of the Mumbai film industry. Hers is consequently a rather rarified view of the film business from the top, at least in comparison to my sub-altern focus on musicians and arrangers.

The more recent time frame of Morcom's research (and much of the content as well) places her work in the transitional period between Old and New Bollywood. She also avoids earlier implied expectations that film song should, in one way or another, be analyzable in a way similar to analyses of Western popular music. Like Morcom, I argue that Hindi film music's uniqueness must ultimately be understood on terms that extend beyond repertoire to include uniqueness as a music culture.

The exceptional nature of Mumbai's culture of film-music production comes out clearly in this oral history. The inclusion of and focus on all of the roles involved in the creation of film music—the musicians, arrangers, and engineers, as well as the star singers and composers—generate a culturally and industrially complete understanding of the conditions of production under which this music developed. From this perspective, we can begin to develop a broader understanding of the music of the Hindi cinema.

Structuring a History of Mumbai's Film-Music Industry

No history of any single language-based film industry in India can be complete without a consideration of the others. The influences among the major and minor players (not only Hindi, Bengali, Tamil, and Telugu but also Panjabi, Gujarati, Bhojpuri, and Malayali) have fluctuated over the years but have never been completely absent. Nevertheless, films in Hindi have been the largest single component of the national output for the vast majority of years since 1931. In stylistic terms, Hindi films have frequently been leaders in fashions for stories, costumes, music, and so on. Finally, within the context of the linguistic politics of South Asia, Hindi has been the closest thing there is to a national language; Hindi film songs are thus the closest we can come to a national popular music. With these justifications and because of the level of detail that I assess, my focus remains exclusively on the industry that produces films in Hindi. Since the early 1950s that industry has been located wholly in Mumbai and, in an Indian play on the colonial name of that city (Bombay), has increasingly become identified as Bollywood (cf. Prasad 2003). I suggest that there is considerable scope for future research in the musics of the regional cinemas, especially by those fluent in Tamil or Telugu.

When I first discussed this topic with Kersi Lord, who has played, arranged, and composed music for Hindi films since the late 1940s, his response was, "You've come ten years too late." He was right. An oral history developed in the twenty-first century cannot begin at the beginning (leaving aside completely the matter of beginnings as a theoretical concept). There is hardly anyone still living who was working in the business before the late 1930s. Even since I began this research, that population has dwindled. There is, furthermore, little documentation that gives us any sense of the working realities of the 1930s; a detailed history of music production in the early years of the Indian film industry is beyond our reach. For these pragmatic reasons, this history begins in the late 1930s, which is after the development of what is called the *playback system*. As I explain in chapter 1, playback represents a significant shift in the limits of the possible; it laid the foundation for the processes that later became the norm. For the most part, the stories in this volume take place from the 1950s through the present.

At this point, astute readers may already be experiencing some historical discomfort. I have proposed an Old/New Bollywood historical framework but have made little reference to playback. As an important technological and cultural phenomenon that began in 1935, playback clearly imposes a level of historical difference on the films and the music made before and after its advent. However, it does not align with (or even directly relate to) the Old/New Bollywood distinctions. This tension is built into the nature of cultural/industrial change and into my approach to writing about it.

Toward the conclusion of his monumental economic history of civilization and capitalism in the fifteenth through the eighteenth centuries, Fernand Braudel questions the notion of historical change (and hence periodization) in the context of the Industrial Revolution:

> [The Industrial Revolution] was certainly not on account of progress in some
> particular sector . . . but on the contrary as the consequence of an overall and
> indivisible process, the sum of the reciprocal relations of interdependence
> and liberation that each individual sector as it developed, sooner or later, by

accident or design, had helped to create for the greater benefit of the other sectors. Can "true" growth . . . be anything but growth which links together, irreversibly, progress on several fronts at once, creating a mutually sustaining whole which is then propelled on to greater things? (Braudel 1984, 539)

As always, Braudel accurately identifies the key historiographic issue. In writing this volume I have dealt with nonsimultaneous change on "several fronts at once," change that was, what is more, nonsimultaneous for different reasons in different instances. The developments that have taken place in Mumbai's film-music industry are the result "both of a rapid sequence of events and of what was clearly a very long-term process: two different rhythms were beating simultaneously" (ibid., 538).

No period of seventy years (1931–2001) can be defined as long-term processes, of course, but advances in Mumbai's film and film-music worlds happened both relatively suddenly and more slowly. There were always (to paraphrase Braudel) developments that demanded or allowed innovations and systems of cultural value and social organization that inhibited them. As the first three chapters explain, no single periodization satisfactorily encompasses the history of the Mumbai film industry.

Structure and Usage

In confronting this problem, I have chosen not to organize this book as a series of strictly chronological chapters. Instead, I have structured the material as a combination of industrial/technological and ethnographic chapters, organized into three parts, not all of which rely equally on oral interviews. In the first part I address directly and repeatedly the matter of periodization. Each of the first three chapters presents a different view of the subject, such that the same issues resurface in the context of three slightly different chronological models of the Mumbai film industry.

I begin with a consideration of the industrial and cultural systems of music production and consumption as these were created by playback, the phenomenon that gave rise to the life of music that most of the musicians I have interviewed have actually lived. Playback (chapter 1), in which prerecorded songs were played back while film actors mimed their words for the cameras, also produced the stars and music that have typified Hindi films from that point on. The ways in which playback has structured Indian popular culture is broader than the limited discussion I offer here, which provides only the necessary contextual and historical background.

Chapter 2 effectively picks up the largely technological story once playback had been introduced. It identifies major advances that allowed or imposed significant innovations in film-music production. Although it may seem quite early for such a detailed and specific chronology, that chronology and the technological developments that define it form the foundation for other, more commonly advocated chronologies of Mumbai film song.

In chapter 3 I directly confront the matter of periodization and propose three broad periods based on industrial and cultural practice. This exercise examines the outcomes of the technical changes described in chapter 2. Industrial structures and interactive responses to social, economic, and professional processes all play a role here.

The second part of this volume begins with chapter 4, which draws on the musicians' perspectives to develop a descriptive understanding of music production in Mumbai's film studios. I should note at this point that I made an early decision not to discuss the choirs and chorus singers who contributed to many film sound tracks. It seemed to me that while many of the issues affecting their professional lives were similar to those of their instrumentalist colleagues, other aspects of the choral world would require enough additional discussion to warrant separate treatment. This is a topic that remains to be explored. As do all the chapters in this section then, chapter 4 examines matters of training, identities, and the pathways by which instrumental musicians found themselves playing in the film business. In these stories we hear echoes of the collapse of music drama forms and, later, of the touring dance-band trade as well. This chapter also offers important insights into the sources of the foreign musical styles that found their way into Hindi film music.

Chapters 5 and 6 examine the roles and tasks of creating and recording music in the film industry. Initially I consider professional roles in the context of the structure of the music production process, the composition, arrangement, and approval of songs, as well as the fees and salaries that drove the industry. The vast bulk of musicians' incomes came from playing at recording sessions; I subsequently look at the recording process and its financial aspects. How did music directors and musicians structure this procedure?

Chapters 7 and 8, which form the final part of this book, are more directly concerned with musical sound. Chapter 7 addresses the growth and eventual demise of the studio orchestras in Mumbai, which was due in part to the role of electronics. I consider musical matters that in other contexts would be called *style* or *genre* and relate how the musicians thought about sounds and the technology (in some cases) that produced it.

Chapter 8 discusses matters of style and value in Mumbai film music from a theoretical and a musical perspective, as well as through the ideas and comments of the studio musicians and composers. This is a large and complex topic that should no doubt be a book in itself and may one day be so. In this chapter I limit my consideration to the ways that musicians conceptualize style, the stylistic expertise they brought to the creation of this music, and how those sounds and concepts interact. This chapter also examines the musicians' expressions of the value systems at work within their profession and the ways in which their specific attitudes have interacted with those of the broader movie-going public.

English/Indian Usage and Structure

For the aforementioned reasons I have chosen to use extensive quotes from the musicians and others involved in the Mumbai film industry. Like all popular culture enterprises in my experience, the film line is full of nicknames and abbreviations. Perhaps the most famous in Mumbai is the name "Pancham" (literally, fifth, often used to indicate the fifth degree of a musical scale), which still routinely refers to R. D. Burman (reported by Valicha 1998 to have been coined by actor Ashok Kumar). I define nicknames on their first appearance in musicians' comments.

Another idiosyncrasy in musicians' talk revolves around pairs of composers. In the film business composers are called music directors; I use these two terms synonymously. Many composers work as individuals, but Mumbai's film industry has had numerous pairs of composers who have worked together for much, if not all, of their careers. Teams such as Shankar-Jaikishan, Shiv-Hari, or (in a much more obscure example) Vipin-Bappu are common. In recent times the number has occasionally increased to three, as with the trio Shankar-Eshaan-Loy. Musicians talk about teams as unitary identities but also recognize that they are made up of individuals. Especially in English, this sometimes leads to a rapid shifting between singular and plural constructions.

When speaking in English, Indians routinely use two numbers that are specific to Hindi and the Indian system of counting. These are most commonly written in English as "lakh" and "crore." One *lakh* is a one followed by five zeroes (or one hundred thousand); one *crore* is a one followed by seven zeroes (or ten million). When used in multiples (e.g., ten lakh, or one million; two and a half crore, or twenty-five million), the same principle applies, but as can be seen, these constructions cut across the system used in the West, which are based on thousands and millions.

I have spelled the names of Indian cities according to contemporary practice (e.g., "Mumbai" rather than the colonial "Bombay," "Kolkata" rather than "Calcutta"). However, when the old name is part of a specific (and usually historical) institution (e.g., Bombay Talkies or the Calcutta Symphony) or is used by musicians in quoted material, I retain the older forms.

Another idiosyncratic usage routinely encountered in Mumbai involves the music-industry giant that was originally the Gramophone Company of India, Ltd. This was the first overseas production subsidiary of EMI (London), of which the British parent, the Gramophone Company, was also a part. The company's primary label was the widely recognized His Master's Voice (HMV), with its reproduction of the phonograph horn and attentive dog Nipper. As fascinating as it is, the Gramophone Company's history is beyond the scope of this book, although some of it is available in the work of Kinnear (1994) and Manuel (1993). As an Indian record label, His Master's Voice was retired at the end of the twentieth century and replaced by the more appropriately Indian label Sa Rē Gā Ma (as in Do Re Mi Fa). Nevertheless, most film musicians, especially when talking about the past, still refer to the company exclusively as "HMV," regardless of what its actual name was at that particular moment or which label might have released a particular song (there *were* other labels in India). In the context of this volume, I have followed the musicians' practice, although when I refer specifically to the post-1998 company, I use the new name, Sa Rē Gā Ma.

Early film-music recordings were often made on film sets—the large spaces in which films were shot—rather than in recording studios. Musicians routinely refer to any such space as a "set," whether in fact it is a film set or not. The changing nature of recording spaces in Mumbai is discussed in chapter 2; regardless, a musician who says "I was sitting on Nayyar-saheb's set" means he was at a recording studio, recording a song composed by and under the supervision of O. P. Nayyar. Less unusually, musicians frequently use the word "take" as both a noun and a verb, to mean "recording session" or "to record."

Finally, as in the preceding example, common Indian discourse routinely attaches a range of suffixes to people's names to indicate levels of social or family relations and usually respect. The suffix "ji" is widely used in the northern, Hindi-speaking regions. When one says "Pyarelal-ji," one says, in effect, "Mr. Pyarelal" or "Pyarelal-Sir." Some of those speaking English out of habit or politeness to me will routinely use a person's full name (e.g., Mr. Pyarelal Sharma) simply to maintain the respect in a language woefully devoid of such structures.

"Ji" is most commonly used either toward those for whom one has respect and with whom one's relations are somewhat formal or in formal situations (which for some can include interviews with unfamiliar foreigners). "Ji" is not a gendered suffix. One can say "Lata-ji" with the same effect as "Pyarelal-ji." However, in referring respectfully to women, some musicians in this part of India use the suffix "bai" instead (e.g., "Lata-bai"). "Saheb" is a still more formal and respectful Hindi term, with explicit connotations of social distance and the "superiority" of the person so called. It is a bit too formal and distant for common usage in the tightly knit and relatively informal world of Mumbai's film-music culture and indeed is used almost exclusively for especially esteemed members of the older generation of music directors (such as O. P. Nayyar).

More commonly, musicians who are speaking Hindi may use "bhai," which means "brother"; the term is often used affectionately not only among social and chronologic equals but also by juniors in addressing or referring to seniors. It may indicate a degree of respect and seniority and also suggest a closer personal friendship than does "ji." Because so many Bengali musicians have been part of the film industry, the common Bengali suffix "da," which has a slightly more respectful connotation than the word "bhai," is also often heard in Mumbai. Usually it is used by or in reference to those with Bengali connections. Thus, R. D. Burman is frequently referred to by his nickname, Pancham, accompanied by the suffix "da" (i.e., Pancham-da). His father, on the other hand, might be referred to as Burman-dada; the second "da" here adds still greater respect and often a generation to the distance in the relationship.

Dates are always a matter of concern in history; in oral history they are vulnerable to the inconsistency of people's memories. In most cases, the experiences or insights in this book are more important than whether the year was 1959 or 1960. When dates and sequence are especially significant, I have located events in relation to larger developments (pre- or postpartition, for example) or by referring to films. Sometimes it has been impossible to completely sort out sequences; chronologic inconsistencies thus appear in some of the comments included here. For much of the history of Old Bollywood especially, people were simply too busy to keep track or were merely unconcerned. With some exceptions, Mumbai musicians are, in my experience, at best mediocre at accurately specifying the year in which something happened.

An additional factor in the matter of dates is musicians' tendency to refer to specific films as time markers. In many cases, however, and especially in the case of songs, recording sessions (which is what musicians most consistently remember) sometimes occurred well before a film was finally released. The only consistently verifiable date in the Hindi cinema, however, is that on which a film's censor certificate was issued (which happened immediately prior to its release). These are the dates reported in Singh's *Encyclopedia of Hindi Film Songs* and those that I use in all circumstances. Readers should keep in mind that these dates are always later than the experiences the musicians report for those films.

Background music may have had a less demonstrable public impact than songs, but musicians spent a great deal of time in background sessions, which were consequently an important part of their lives and their income. Background music production and recording are therefore important but slightly slippery parts of this study. The same technological processes were involved, as were most of the same individuals. Aesthetically, however, and in direct contrast to song recordings, to which actors and camera people responded, background music was composed in response to the images that had already been filmed. It was recorded after the filming instead of before, usually on a very tight schedule, and was often composed by assistants. I specify comments and discussions that apply specifically and exclusively to either songs or background music; all other comments apply to both processes.

Finally, it is not my intention in this book to report gossip or stories that reflect badly on individuals. I mention this since certain stories in the film-music industry have little to do with the construction of an oral history and do not aid our understanding of this music culture. Where I feel that comments can contribute to a productive understanding of the Mumbai film-music culture, however, I report them. In so doing, I intend no disrespect to anyone.

The oral history and historical context that I present here offer one perspective on the music of the Hindi cinema. It is not the only viewpoint, but given the general lack of information and understanding about this industry, I consider it the best place to start. The majority of this volume is based on the interviews that I have conducted with musicians, music directors, arrangers, recording engineers, and others connected to the film-music industry in Mumbai.

Part I

History, Technology, and a Determinist Milieu for Hindi Film Song

No one works in a vacuum. As I have already suggested, the musicians who are the focus of this volume were significant contributors to and thus part of India's popular music culture. As more or less anonymous musicians for hire, however, their role in that popular culture was intimate but limited. Part I is, in effect, my first approach to the central historical period that I approach again in parts II and III. It is also the most circuitous in that it focuses on not only the industrial and technological milieu that shaped Old Bollywood but also the early years of Indian cinema leading up to the very beginnings of that period.

Part I reflects on the historical and technological factors that produced the conditions under which musicians worked and argues that musicians acted under a set of constraints imposed by the cultural and economic structures of filmmaking in India, which themselves functioned in the context of the technological limitations of sound recording for film. This section outlines those structures and limitations and adds input from those musicians whose experiences provided them with perspectives modified by time, individual perceptions, and professional roles. Not all musicians attended to or were able to perceive the structural nature of the system in which they worked. While some were interested in and able to participate in technological decisions, others spared only an occasional thought for the ways the music they were playing was being recorded. While some participated in musicians' attempts to influence the economics and working conditions of their industry, others took their pay, complained (or not) as they felt appropriate, and went about their business. Overall then, part I offers the broadest perspective of Mumbai's (and India's) film/popular-music industry and its role in popular culture. My focus remains the musicians, but this section contains less input from fewer musicians than those that follow; their comments are supplemented by those of composers, recording engineers (called sound recordists), film directors, producers, and other music-industry figures who were better placed to understand the structures and limitations under which they all operated.

Part I is more history than ethnography. Specifically, aside from the technological information in chapter 2, the section eschews ethnographic detail for the broad outlines of cultural/industrial structure and of the large-scale changes in them. Since I have already argued that those developments were interactive and nonsynchronous, I would normally not need to repeat that chapters 2 and 3 each offers a distinct chronology of the same period. However, I do need to emphasize this, given the vulnerability of the Mumbai cinema to attempts at periodization. Hardly anyone who has written about the subject has failed to organize it into various "early periods," "golden ages," and so forth, as I discuss later. These many historicizations all confront, knowingly or unknowingly, the problematic that Braudel sets out (see the introduction). I confine each of the three chapters of this section to a single historical perspective and approach covering the same years, and I separate the various strands that determined the history of Mumbai's film and film-music industry. In doing so, I inevitably expose myself to the charge of repetitiveness. Nonetheless, only by focusing on each perspective in turn am I able to proceed to a more comprehensive perspective in succeeding parts of the book.

I argue later that the technology and practice that India calls "playback" is one of the primary determinants in a determinist history of film song in Mumbai. Playback is a technological practice that occurs all over the globe. The cultural and industrial practices that developed around it in India, however, have often been unique and had significant repercussions for everything that followed.

Other determinants of more immediate importance to film musicians arose from this most fundamental component. In combination with film song's role as popular music and other factors, playback has had a profound impact on the entire range of Indian public-performance culture. The three chapters of part I examine these causal factors: playback as such, film-music recording technology in general, and industrial and cultural structures. I argue, in effect, that determinism, whether technological or economic, can at best paint the broad strokes of cultural practice that ethnography's more bricolage-style approach must necessarily flesh out.

1

Popular Music
as Film Music

The interaction between music and film begins very early in the history of cinema and the music industry. In the United States it extends into the sheet-music industry, which published music for the accompaniment of silent films. The record industry, however, has had a much longer-lasting and widely distributed set of relationships to cinema around the world. In this chapter I briefly examine the interaction between music (and more distinctively, song) and film in India. In the particularly intense and symbiotic relationships between popular film and popular music that developed, the careers of the musicians whose stories appear in this book were made possible.

The depth and breadth of the Hindi film song's impact on popular Indian culture is a book or more in itself, as Morcom (2007) suggests and as a forthcoming study of the "transnational travels of Hindi song and dance" by Sangita Gopal and Sujata Moorti (2008) no doubt demonstrates. An enormous range of cultural behaviors and content owes its existence to the specific ways in which Indian popular music was produced exclusively (for much of the twentieth century) for commercial narrative films. My concern here, however, is only with ways in which that impact and the industrial relationships that were part of it affected and contextualized the professional lives of the musicians who are at the heart of this study.

More specifically I offer a basic historical and contextual consideration of the practice of playback as a technological, industrial, and cultural process. This generic term refers to many things in the recording process. In the Indian film industry, it commonly defines a method of filming in which a song is recorded and then played back over loudspeakers while actors mime, dance, and act for cameras. The term and the technology are based on separate audio and visual recordings that are subsequently combined into a single finished product. The careers of the musicians who are the focus of this book were shaped by the technological constraints and possibilities of playback and by India's cultural response to that system of music production.

The relatively simple technology that made playback possible and the practice of playback were hardly unique to Indian filmmaking; a wide range of miraculous cinematic musical performances, in all national cinema traditions, owe their existence to the flexibility that was possible once the production processes for music and image were separated. The way in which that simple technology was implemented in India and the extent to which its demands defined industrial practices of popular music, however, are unique.

Finally, playback as a cultural and industrial system stands out quite clearly in India, in contrast to the practice of filmmaking from 1931 to 1935. The importance of this historical context lies in the specific changes in industrial logic that developed after 1935 and formed the basis for most of what followed in Indian popular culture. In effect, the industrial history of what would later be called "film songs" begins before the advent of sound films. To this extent, it is crucial to consider a song in its role as a commercial, industrial product, a saleable artifact. This chapter, then, provides the essential framework for the stories that appear in the following chapters. I suggest, however, that it also provides a background (although at greater and lesser distances) for all considerations of Hindi film song.

Popular Music and Music Drama before Sound Film

Most foreign scholars (e.g., Arnold 1991; Manuel 1993; Morcom 2007) address the reason for the inclusion of songs and song scenes in Indian commercial films, but this is of little concern to musicians and others who work in the film industry. Prakash (1983) offers a useful summary of the rationales most commonly advanced and notes the tensions around commercial film music's influence on India's noncommercial "new cinema." Despite the quarter century that has passed since Prakash's summation, fundamentally new explanations have yet to be advanced.

I have not addressed this question here and discuss it only briefly in this chapter in a purely historical manner. In the period of my primary concern, from the mid-1940s through the early 1990s, the question was effectively moot; almost no commercial Hindi films were made without songs during those years. In my conversations with musicians, industry personnel, directors, and others in the film-music industry I have routinely encountered variations on the phrase "films must have songs" not as a statement of principle or even an assertion of aesthetic norms but as a simple and unquestioned explanation for behavior or events, somewhat similar to the law of gravity. In his description of the workings of the record and film industry, Abbas Ali, who began his music-industry career in the 1950s with All-India Radio before working for the Gramophone Company of India and later the cassette giant T-Series, mentioned songs, along with film stock and other items that one must accumulate in order to make a movie:

> ABBAS ALI: You are producing a film. So that means you are fulfilling all the requirements for a film. That means the makeup, the raw stock, and that means you are making the songs also. Song is a part of the film.

The cultural expectation of music scenes in films was never subjected to substantive internal critique within the mainstream film industry, although alternative or parallel filmmakers raised the issue from time to time, even if only through their sometimes nonmusical movies. The "first Hindi film ever made without songs or dances" was K. A. Abbas's *Munna* (1954), but despite international critical success, it failed at the Indian box office (Barnouw and Krishnaswamy 1980, 139). In most of the years this book covers, the primacy of song in film was not seriously challenged or even examined by those who were making commercial films. It appears to have been accepted along with other aspects of precinema popular drama and continued because it was well received. Only India's recent and newly competitive appearance in the mainstream global film market has suggested that there might be a viable commercial alternative to the assumption that "song is a part of the film." Regardless of the explanatory models, however, the fundamental assumption that "films must have songs" is a key understanding for almost everything that happened in Indian popular culture after 1931.

Historical Precedents

Prakash (1983) and Ranade (2006) are among those who suggest that the live music drama forms that were prevalent in India in the early twentieth century are the basis of the cultural assumption that films will have songs. The range of these forms in India and the cultural and industrial motivations in the transition from the stage to the screen are among the many things that are beyond the scope of this book (see Gupt 2005 and Ranade 1986).

Many early Indian films were adaptations of stage music dramas (as indeed were some early American films). From 1931 to the late 1940s, composers, singers, and musicians who had been working in live theater were finding new jobs in the film-music industry. Of the sources of influence in Mumbai, the most important were the rather classically oriented, Marathi-language Sangeet Natak and the urban, popular music–hall theater form called Parsi Theater. Tamil-language music dramas in Tamil Nadu were influential in that region, while in Kolkata and Bengal generally, the Bengali form called *jatra* played a similar role.

Music-drama traditions occupied a major place in popular or light classical public culture that films gradually usurped. Similarly, the growing relationship between music dramas and India's incipient record industry (largely as a source of popular content for that industry) was threatened and finally replaced by the association between films and the record companies. In western India, the music of Sangeet Natak attracted the Gramophone Company's attention; Marathi songs and singers were recorded on disc from the earliest days of the Indian record industry and constituted one regional genre of popular, light-classical music (Kinnear 1994). Historical recordings are still available in Marathi-speaking parts of India on CD and cassette. In Chennai, 78 rpm recordings of excerpts of dialogue and songs from Tamil stage plays were produced by the Gramophone Company's main international rival, Columbia, in the 1920s and 1930s. These compilations were known as drama sets (Hughes 2007).

There is little information about industrial relationships in the 1920s, but it is instructive to speculate about the relationships between recordings as mediated commodities and the dramatic productions that were their sources. These issues were crucial to the development of the film-music industry. Hughes's (ibid.) research shows that drama sets were recorded and released *after* the success of the stage plays from which they were taken had determined which dramas, scenes, and songs were popular. The logic in this sequence is based on the production process and the value of the component parts in the overall profit-making system.

Songs that were excerpted from stage plays and later released on disc were initially produced by a method and an economy that were completely independent of the record industry. They were part of the aesthetic and economic demands of creating a music drama for the stage and would have been produced whether the recording companies existed or not. Companies such as the Gramophone Company of India or Columbia thus had access to ready-made content (songs) that had been, so to speak, market-tested for audience response.

I can only speculate as to whether the producers working for early Indian record companies came to some financial arrangement with the dramatic producers who had paid for the production of the songs they wished to record or whether the songs were recorded without agreement. Because there was no copyright agreement applicable to Indian intellectual property in 1930, both scenarios are possible. Any fees that the record company might have paid to a music drama's composers, producers, or singers/actors added to these individuals' incomes, making their dramatic careers more successful overall. Regardless of whether such fees were paid, it is significant that the interaction between the recording companies and the stage drama content was economic, as well as cultural. It made all aspects of the commercial activity of operating a drama company at least slightly more viable in both direct and indirect ways. This kind of historical speculation is justifiable only to the extent that it emphasizes the fundamentally symbiotic relationship between the economics and the content of music dramas (staged or filmed) and India's recording industry. This connection existed from the very beginning of the latter's history.

In releasing songs from the popular stage, early Indian record companies were following international practice; European and American stage songs of all kinds were released on record after their introduction through live commercial performance. With the introduction of sound film, film producers and recording industries also established various types of relationships across the globe. The patterns that were created in India were naturally specific, but they persisted throughout the entire twentieth century in a way that was unique to South Asian industry and culture.

Because of music's flexible and indexical sources of meaning, songs with origins in dramatic narrative have the ability to act as standalone aesthetic, emotional, and commercial objects but also enhance their meanings via the narrative context (cf. Turino 1999; Morcom 2001). A song that might be played on a gramophone or broadcast over radio could reach a larger audience than the music drama for which it was originally composed and also require neither the staged context nor the other songs from the drama to constitute an attractive commercial package. The consumption of an individual recorded song required less time and less attention than did dramas and was not dependent on whether the song's consumers had seen the drama. Songs could form a pleasant background to social activities in a way that even drama sets (which routinely included dialogue) could not. In effect, songs could live an independent existence and take on personalized emotional meanings that might supersede or simply ignore their dramatic context. For these reasons, their potential audience exceeded the size of that for the staged drama. In the music drama/record industry nexus, a song's potential commercial value consequently came in two ways. First, it was an attractive, expected, and expressive component of the dramatic, narrative experience; second, it was an independent recorded commodity.

At the same time, and in a way that has had distinctive implications for live and filmed music dramas, those who *had* seen the stage play (or later, the film) would have memories of the physical realities of the actors and the emotional content of the dramatic context, both of which could potentially contribute to the song's affective and contextual content. Therefore, the relationship between a music drama, whether on stage or screen, and the mediated song that might have come from it is both flexible and complex. In the case of the Mumbai film-music industry, individual music producers (that is, filmmakers) entered into a range of relationships with record (and cassette) companies; both expected to benefit economically from the increased consumption of each others' products. When sound films appeared in 1931, the producers of India's popular recordings and much of its "popular" music had already been confronting the complexities of the situation in which popular music had been located in dramatic forms for some time. It was not only the content of the songs or the films that maintained a degree of continuity between stage dramas and films. The industrial relationships between music and dramatic narrative of all types also demonstrate a similar degree of conceptual continuity.

Musicians before the Advent of Sound in Films

Of more immediate relevance to the content of this book was the human continuity between musicians of the presound era and those of the film industry. Early film musicians were often drawn from drama troupes, but those who had been accompanying silent films also crossed over to the new medium.

Prior to the arrival of sound-film technology in India, many theaters showing silent films had live musical accompaniment. Outside the main urban centers, issues of literacy (especially in English, but also in Indian languages) made music and live narration essential. These elements were crucial for Naushad Ali, who was growing up in early twentieth-century Lucknow. Naushad-saheb was one of India's most important film-music composers and an early fan of silent (and later sound) films:

> NAUSHAD ALI: Before [sound film], there had been some one in the theaters
> to play the music, maybe on tabla or harmonium. If there was a fight scene,
> they would play music for that, or if there was a chase, they would play
> differently. That was very good, and people liked it very much. Then they
> also had one boy for singing. And so if there was a love scene, he would
> sing a *ghazal* [a romantic poem, usually in Persian or Urdu]. And also on
> the side would be one announcer who would give an accounting of the
> scene. "This girl has fallen in love with this boy, and her parents do not
> approve, and now they will meet to decide what to do."

While harmonium and tabla were suitable for theaters that showed Indian films or attracted an Indian audience, those for the colonial classes often used Western instruments (piano, violin, etc.,), as was the practice in theaters in Europe and the United States. A small handful of musicians such as composers R. C. Boral and Pankaj Mullick, who both directed and conducted for silent films (Arnold 1991), later worked in Mumbai's film studios but began their careers before sound film.

Born in Goa in the first years of the twentieth century, cellist Alphonso Albuquerque was a well-known figure in the film-music industry. Before he began playing in the film studios, however, Albuquerque spent some years as a musician in the silent-film theaters of the British Empire not only in India but also in Singapore "around the time of the Great War," as his son relates. Those who played tabla, harmonium, clarinet, or bowed lutes such as *sārangi* or violin often accompanied silent films as well, especially those produced in India. In western India, some of this group, who had been working in music drama troupes, also transitioned first to silent films and later to sound films.

Early Sound Films

In the remainder of this chapter I examine the fundamental production conditions under which sound films were made in India and consider, at least briefly, how they structured both the relationship between the film and music industries and the role of film music in Indian culture. These topics deserve separate books and considerable additional research, but an overview establishes the necessary foundation for an examination of the more specific ways that technology and industrial structures influenced the lives of Mumbai's film musicians. India was one of many countries experimenting with the organization, technologies, aesthetics, and ideologies of sound film; in that context, Indian popular culture and its associated industry developed their character. To that extent, I offer some comparative analysis in relation to the dominant Hollywood industry, as well as to early French cinema. In this discussion, some consideration of early sound film technology and production is inevitable.

Until the development of digital media, sound films were strips of celluloid on which both visual and aural information were recorded: images of actors, settings, speech, background sounds, and any added music. In different parts of the world, however, those two sets of information arrived on the completed filmstrip in different ways. In Hollywood, sound and image were recorded separately on two different strips of film and subsequently mixed on what became the completed film strip. In Hollywood, "by 1929, music and sound were being recorded separately [music was recorded in music studios], then the recorded music was played back while the scene was being acted and its dialogue recorded" (Altman 1985, 46). Given the limitations of the condenser or carbon microphones of the 1930s, which were nondirectional, hard to use, easily broken, and sensitive to all kinds of ambient noise, this separation was desirable. Nevertheless, the separation of soundtrack from image in the production process was "a primary factor in the constitution of film ideology" in Hollywood films (ibid.).

In France and India (among other countries), on the other hand, sound and image were recorded simultaneously on one strip of film for at least part of the 1930s. Thus, the songs and music heard in early Indian films were sung by the performers, who acted and sang simultaneously, just as if they had been on a music drama stage. Accompanying musicians played directly into the same microphones the singer was using but arranged themselves so as to remain out of view of the camera. Like the French film industry of the 1930s, early Indian films retained "the aesthetic practice of conceiving a scene as if it were a theatrical performance" (O'Brien 2005, 54). Early Indian sound filming entailed the recording of an event: in this case, the complete performance of a scene (or a portion of one) from what was effectively a music drama that was being performed in a film studio instead of on stage. This practice was diametrically opposed to Hollywood's practice of fashioning a composite, postperformance narrative from discrete recorded elements (Lastra 2000).

In India the network of attitudes and practices that determined the use of sound-film technology was structured by the technological demands of simultaneous recording, as well as the aesthetic and narrative conventions of music drama performance. In this network, music and song were central, and those songs continued and gradually enlarged their role as the staple product of Indian record companies. The first recording of songs from a film *(Madhuri)*, sung by actor/singer Vinayakrao Patwardhan, was released in 1933 (Ranade 2006, 111). Increasingly thereafter, the source of popular music recordings was the cinema.

For the record companies, film songs were another source of prepublicized, market-tested content. Although HMV and others paid direct production costs (for recording facilities, musicians, singers, engineers), they did not pay the indirect costs of artists or repertoire development. For the use of the songs themselves, recording companies sometimes paid straight fees and at other times offered royalties (percentages of sales) to the film's producers. They thus enjoyed access to a steady stream of content that was relatively risk free and inexpensive. The symbiotic relationship that HMV, Columbia, and other labels had enjoyed with the music drama tradition was replicated in intensified form with the film industry. There were industrial, as well as aesthetic, reasons, therefore, for the continued use of songs in films. Again, this is apparently in contrast to industrial developments in the U.S. film industry. Although recorded popular songs were commonly found in Hollywood films of the late 1920s, "they had largely disappeared by 1931 . . . when the American film industry curtailed the production of revue musicals and began standardizing the making of orchestral scores for films. By 1933, music no longer functioned as a special attraction *a la* the recorded pop song but instead became integrated into a film's overall formal design via a romantic symphonic score" (O'Brien 2005, 29).

In Indian sound films, on the other hand, producers adhered to a version of the music drama model in which recorded pop songs continued to be prevalent. Indian film production thus offers a unique trajectory characterized by its retention of songs at the heart of the form even after the constraints imposed by simultaneous image-sound recording were lifted in 1935. Although Ranade argues that "Indian film music sets up an auxiliary but alternative musical structure" (2006, 146) and Morcom (2001) accurately suggests that Hindi film composers adopted stylistic features and content from Western symphonic soundtracks, in the end it was song—not the symphonic score—that was integrated into the formal design of Indian films.

Technological and Industrial Structures
Supporting Film Song

The need to record sound, including music, during filming carried with it a range of challenges for the actual production of film, but it also prioritized an experience of filmmaking (and film-music making) in which the resultant movie was a holistic product rather than something constructed from discrete components. Simultaneous recording encouraged the seamless integration of music into the story and a comparatively flawless transition between music-oriented and dialogue-oriented scenes. In early films, many items now considered film songs were in fact "non-prose . . . recited or partially 'sung' items [that] registered a movement away from prose but . . . stopped short of becoming 'songs.' 'Film song' as such emerged later on the Indian film scene" (Ranade 2006, 110). In addition to this aesthetic integration, however, songs were physically and technologically inseparable from the images they accompanied.

Despite the limited technology and the ambiguous nature of film song in this period, many early song scenes possess characteristics that became the industrial standard. These defined a distinct type of narrative scene both technically and aesthetically. In films such as Prabhat Films' 1932 release, *Ayodhya ka Raja,* a musical spectacle begins in the opening scene. This famous story—originally taken from the epic *Mahabharata* but also a Marathi music drama—recounts the trials and tribulations experienced by

Raja Harishchandra, the king of Ayodhya and his family. The film opens with the entry of members of the royal court into the throne room, singing the praises of the king and his family. The scene then shifts to the courts of heaven, where a dancing girl performs for the gods' entertainment. The scene moves between close-up shots while this unidentified performer sings and longer shots as she dances and thus demonstrates the challenges inherent in the simultaneous recording process.

The musicians do their best to maintain continuity, but the breaks in the musical line are inevitable. This early, slightly erotic spectacle is followed by the entrance of the gods' musical messenger (Narada), who sings a solo before the heavenly throne. As the scene shifts back to Earth, the queen (Taramati) is found in her boudoir, singing as a servant combs her hair. In all, fifteen of the film's first twenty-five minutes include four discrete songs. These are more musical than Ranade's "non-prose" items; later in the film, however, nonprose items also appear. Collectively the songs set the scene, provide spectacle and narrative commentary, and introduce major characters. In music dramas, music routinely performs these functions, while song scenes do the same for the Hindi cinema in the early twenty-first century.

In the production of a recorded sound film from 1931 to 1935, sound, song, costumes, sets, dialogue, and action were all prepared and rehearsed, the cameras rolled, and the scene was recorded. Although postfilming editing took place, this consisted largely of splicing together the separate scenes. For the record industry, however, the most significant implication of simultaneous filming was that, once the song was recorded onto a strip of film, there was no way to remove it. Apparently sometime in the 1920s the Gramophone Company built a recording facility in Mumbai. It became normal practice for the musicians and singers to spend a day recording the song on film in a film studio and subsequently, while everyone still knew the parts, to record the song again for the company's disc cutter. This required them to travel down to the heart of the city's business district, an area called Fort, where the Gramophone Compay studios were located on Pheroze Shah Mehta Road.

The orchestras that recorded at the HMV studios were smaller than the film orchestras in many cases, especially in the 1940s and '50s. What is more, the personnel were not identical; HMV had its own group of staff musicians, but those who participated in this early process suggest that HMV's musicians played only for "private" (that is, nonfilm) recordings. Despite that separation, many of HMV's studio musicians made the transition from HMV to the film studios.

Even in the earliest years of the film and music industries in India, then, two parallel technologies existed for sound recording (sound cameras using optical film and disc cutters using acetate or lacquer discs). I examine this dynamic in detail in the next chapter, but the importance of film songs in HMV's output and the long-term existence of parallel recording formats had enormous implications for the way sound recording technology developed in Mumbai and the ways that those involved conceptualized the processes from these very early years into the early twenty-first century.

Two years after HMV released its first film song recording, the industrial and cultural dynamics among the film and music industries and their audience changed significantly. Those developments led to the gradual emergence during the late 1930s and the 1940s of a distinct form: the film song in Ranade's (2006) terms. That came to mean a standard three- to five-minute song with two major melodic sections, a number of instrumental interludes, and lyrics that included a series of related verses; this was incorporated in a specially framed narrative context and accompanied by suitable instrumental music. The factor that led to this development, I argue, was the arrival of playback technology and the industrial responses to it. In large part, it was playback technology that led to the long-term dominance of film song in both the Mumbai film industry and in Indian culture.

Playback: New Technology and a New System of Use

As filmmaking practice, the separate and the simultaneous recording of sound and image stand in contrast to one another. "In the United States . . . instead of the recording of actors' performances, sound-film work in 1930s' Hollywood was understood in terms of a process of assembly, whereby scenes were constructed from separate bits and pieces" (O'Brien 2005, 1).

In India, simultaneous recording was abandoned slightly later than in the United States, but that discontinuance had different implications because of the ongoing importance of song in the commercial Hindi film. While dialogue was still recorded simultaneously, songs were now recorded by the musicians and the actors, in their role as singers, before a scene was shot. It was then played back over loudspeakers while the singers, now in their role as actors, mimed the singing of the prerecorded song. The technology and the practice were pioneered at Kolkata's innovative New Theatres Studios, apparently at the suggestion of the studio's sound recordist, Mukul Bose (Ranade 2006). Rangoonwalla (1983, 84), however, specifically credits composer R. C. Boral for this development. This may be a reflection of the traditional focus of most early writing on film music to attribute all musical innovation to film-music composers.

The first Hindi-language film to use this technology is reported to have been New Theatres' *Bhagychakra* (1935). This was a Hindi-language re-make of the Bengali-language film *Dhoop Chaon,* also released in 1935 and widely reported as the first movie to use playback (e.g., Arnold 1991; Barnouw and Krishnaswamy 1980).[1]

With regard to the phenomenon called "the cinema," "the *device* never fully embodies the practices and institutions"; instead, the cultural system of use "refers not simply to a device but to an entire network of attitudes and practices determining the use of that device with the goal of producing im-ages that render the world familiar and explicable through a structure of rep-resentation" (Lastra 2000, 135). Lastra maintains that the notion of the cin-ema encompasses such a network; I propose that playback itself was another device that led to specific cultural outcomes. Indeed, an engagement with the outcomes of playback technology might be said to be at the heart of almost all Indian popular culture in the late twentieth and early twenty-first cen-turies. Many of these consequences, such as the careers and stardom of mu-sicians identified in India as playback singers or the role of film song in In-dian culture are beyond the scope of this book. My work here focuses on the specific industrial (and partly musical) system that playback technology en-abled and the musicians whose careers, working conditions, and even pat-terns of socioprofessional organization were defined by that development.

Technically, it had always been possible to record sound and image sep-arately on two or more strips of film, but simultaneous recording had been the only filmmaking process available in India that would ensure a final product (strip of film) in which sound and image were synchronized. That changed, apparently in late 1934, but ironically the new technology was hardly a major innovation. There were no new microphones or film print-ers, and no sudden change or improvement occurred in either the record-ing medium (35 mm celluloid film) or the recording format (variable area). Sound cameras were still doing the recording. All that changed in 1934 was that Indian filmmakers began using a new mechanical mixer, the optical dubber, which allowed two strips of exposed film—carrying whatever in-formation (sound or image) had been recorded on them—to be mixed onto a single new strip, as recording engineer Daman Sood explains:

> DAMAN SOOD: The final audio print was placed on a special double projector that was also a recorder, but it had a synchronous three-phase, 220 volt/50 Hertz motor. The "synch point" was established, and the two were run simultaneously. That made the release print; sometimes we also called it the "married print."

The new strip of film, the release print, had both sets of information on it, as one would expect, but the absolutely critical factor was that the two sets of information were synchronized.

The synchronous mixing process was mechanical: A technician set the starting point on both strips at the desired frame by locking the sprocket holes in the two strips of film—one with music, one with images—onto the sprockets on the mixer. Once a physical starting point had been established for both strips, sound and image would be synchronized in the final copy. Any changes in the electrical current (which could affect the speed at which the motor turned the sprockets) would affect both strips equally. On the screen, the resulting film would show images of physical movement that corresponded to the words and sounds of the speech, sound effects, songs, and music. The changes in film-production practice that this simple piece of equipment enabled were entirely disproportionate to its simplicity.

Fundamentally, playback technology allowed Indian filmmakers to participate in a more sophisticated version of "sound film's fundamental lie, the implication that the sound is produced by the image" (Altman 1985, 46). More important for this study, playback changed film musicians' lives and careers. In 1931 film musicians were part of a unified filmmaking studio staff; they, along with almost everyone else, worked on the sets daily, while the camera recorded their unseen performances along with those of the actor/singer. From 1931 to 1935 the history and experiences of film musicians and other film-production staff were the same in this fundamental sense. From 1935 on, however, the processes of sound and image recording and their histories were separated. And, beginning in 1935, the technological story of sound recording and the film industry's use of that development are significantly distinct from the history of film production as such.

The song-recording practice changed almost at once. From 1935 on, a song was recorded before the scene in which it was to be featured was filmed; acoustic conditions improved when musicians no longer had to station themselves out of the cameras' visual range and when recording spaces could be at least marginally adapted to improve the acoustic conditions. Musicians could sit comfortably in one place, and singers/actors could concentrate on their singing without having to act simultaneously. The film with the recorded song was sent for processing, and the recorded song could then be played back on an optical camera, while the actors, now in costume, mimed the lyrics they had previously sung as their actions were recorded on a separate strip of film. As long as the actors mimed to a recording whose master was made on a format synchronizable with 35 mm film, filmmakers would be free of concerns about synchronicity. That fundamental condition defined the recording process in the film-music industry and consequently the careers of the musicians who are the subject of this book.

In India, the cultural and industrial response to this wide-reaching technology and the system of use that grew up around it produced India's distinct film culture. In a theoretically unrelated circumstance, however, HMV's growing dependence on film songs for its popular music content meant that films and film songs came to dominate popular music culture.

Playback technology encouraged the continued development of two symbiotic industries. Music dramas, both live and mediated, had already demonstrated their value to HMV as a source of preproduced, demonstrably popular songs. The advent of playback technology exacerbated the interconnectedness of the relationship because it separated the production of songs (physically, chronologically, procedurally, etc.) from that of films, thereby enhancing the identity of the former as standalone commodities and the record industry's access to them. Playback also changed the relationship between a film's songs and the film itself. "On account of Indian aesthetic decisions, because of the nature of conditions under which film music is composed, recorded and propagated, and [because of] the unqualified acceptance of singer-speaker differentiation (due to playback), Hindi film song . . . leads an independent existence—a free musical monad owing its initial life to a cinematic impulse" (Ranade 2006, 146). However independent film songs may have been in the 1950s (which represents the end of Ranade's critical focus), Uberoi implies an increase in the independence of film and song in the 1990s. Based on a 1996 article in the *India International Centre Quarterly* by Doraiswamy, she argues that "it is well-known that even exceedingly popular song-and-dance items cannot redeem a film otherwise destined to 'bomb' at the box-office; or rather, with the expansion of cable and satellite TV, the films and their songs increasingly follow an independent trajectory of popular appeal" (Uberoi 2001, 310).

Despite the separation of musical and cinematic popular response, however, playback and the physical separation of song from film established a hegemonic industrial structure that Indian popular culture has yet to completely overcome. Playback is a key explanatory factor for the regularly noted absence of an independent music industry and a popular music culture in India. Playback became the central concept and key process in the system of use, the interwoven sets of attitudes, practices, and cultural values that defined the Hindi cinema and its music.

The separation of sound and image recording changed filmmaking in India from consisting of the recording of what were effectively well-planned live performances to the subsequent assembling of independently produced elements. Although this moved Indian films closer to the film ideology that Hollywood was asserting worldwide, the continued incorporation of the recorded song into the formal structure of the cinematic narrative affected the impact of that globalizing tendency. Ironically, Mumbai's composers and film directors carried this ideological separation of sound and image to greater extremes than did many of their colleagues in Europe or the United States. At the same time, the relationships between the film and the music industries created a popular culture that more thoroughly integrated the musical products of that split and in fact was possible only because of it.

New Industrial Relations

Two factors that contributed to the particular industrial structure in which film musicians (and others) worked are, first, the continued importance of the recorded song in India's commercial cinematic form and, second, the linguistic content, which limited the distribution of Indian films to India. Although both the Indian and French cinemas began the 1930s using simultaneous recording, that similarity ceased in 1935 with the advent of playback. In yet another instance of the multiplicity of cultural responses to similar technology, however, the film industries in both countries were "producing films mainly for the domestic film market." O'Brien maintains that "recorded songs continued to permeate the mainstream cinema through the mid-1930s, featuring in operettas and other types of musicals but also in dramatic films" (2005, 31). In yet another variation on this theme, I argue in chapter 3 that O'Brien's characterization of the 1930s' French film business as a "cottage industry" is more applicable to that in Mumbai after 1947.

Although the recorded song remained central and in fact increased in both cultural and industrial importance, in the late 1930s and the '40s India began its engagement with the movie industry by seeking to replicate the industrial, factory-like notion of the self-contained and vertically integrated film studio.

The symbiotic connection between the recording and the film industries continued to develop after the advent of playback, but the nature of the relationship changed, most of all in the way songs were conceptualized and created. In the new system, a recording of the song was necessary before the actors could mime the singing for the cameras. Songs were composed and recorded well before the shooting even started. Shooting might take place within days of the recording of the music, but it could also take place months later (and sometimes did).

In the new process, the film's director, scriptwriter, music director, lyricist, and occasionally the choreographer had to meet to agree on how many songs a film required and where they would fit into the story. Specifics then had to be decided about what Mumbai calls "the situation." A song situation includes an enormous range of considerations, such as the identities of the actors and their characters, the location of the scene (e.g., indoors or outdoors), the nature of the actions or dancing in it, and the scene's emotional context. Is the setting a fancy-dress party or a farmer's field? Is the song meant to be a song of love in bloom or of heartache? Once the situation was clarified, lyrics and a melody would be developed and ultimately approved, and the song would then be rehearsed and recorded. (Chapters 7 and 8 discuss situation, as a determinant of musical style and arrangement, in greater detail.)

In the conceptualization of Mumbai's filmmakers, the song became an object that was then visualized; to identify this process, those in the industry invented a new verb, "to picturize," and an accompanying noun, "picturization." A song composed by S. D. Burman would be recorded and subsequently "picturized on" actors Madhubala and Kishore Kumar, for example.

The ready availability of completed, recorded songs, often months before the release of the film in which they would appear, also led to a process in which the songs were released beforehand (most of the time by HMV) on disc. This industrial response to technological change appears to have been completed more promptly than the cultural change from actor/singers to playback singers. Nevertheless, Arnold notes that, "not until the 1940s did record companies start the practice of releasing records before the film's release" (1991, 116). It also appears that songs, which had originally been made popular by the films in which they appeared now became a means of advertising upcoming films by the early release of their songs. This relationship between the two products ultimately had the effect of bringing HMV and the film industry closer together.

Actors, Singing Actors, and Playback Singers

After 1935 the advent of optical dubbers resulted in more sophisticated soundtracks; the practice of using singing actors, a requirement in the days of simultaneous recording, was more gradually transformed. Many available recordings and films from this period demonstrate that not all singing actors were selected for their vocal ability. Ashok Kumar was a leading actor of the late 1930s and 1940s (and beyond) who starred in many hit films of this era (e.g., *Achhut Kanya,* 1936; *Naya Sansar,* 1941; *Kismat,* 1943; *Mahal,* 1949). Despite his enormous box-office appeal and his many song recordings for these films, he was not known for his talent for singing. As Ashok Ranade rather backhandedly suggests, it was only in 1943 that "Ashok Kumar's musicality became recognizably adequate" (2006, 120). The date Ranade suggests is crucial. Three years earlier, a letter to one of India's film magazines had requested "Ashok Kumar to stop singing in pictures" (Majumdar 2001, 167).

Radio broadcaster Ameen Sayani, who hosted Radio Ceylon's extremely influential Binaca Geet Mala film-song program, reinforces Ranade's point. He suggests that some singing actors had difficulty with the new musical challenges from the very beginning. He also reports an intermediate stage in the industry's progression toward playback, in which actors' singing voices were used for film soundtracks, but other singing voices were used on the recordings:

> AMEEN SAYANI: When sound came in, it was necessary for the actors and actresses to sing their own lines. But even in the early days, there were some music directors who realized that this was not going to work. And they started changing.
>
> After his first few films, Ashok Kumar started singing, but Anil Biswas, in a film he was doing, took another actor called Arun Kumar, who was a fairly decent actor, to sing for Ashok Kumar. [For the song] "Gangan dhire dhire aa rahe baadal," Ashok Kumar sang it for the film, but for the record, Anil Biswas, who was one of the founders of film music, took Arun Kumar instead of Ashok. Very often it used to happen that the record version was not the same as the film version.

As filmmakers gradually worked through the implications of playback, it became evident that it was no longer necessary to settle for such uneven skill sets, as composer Naushad Ali points out:

> NAUSHAD ALI: Once playback came in, it was no longer important that the actors could sing. They could do their work [acting], and somebody else could sing.

Despite the accuracy of Naushad's observation, however, it took more than fifteen years for total structural separation to develop. Apparently the "radical potential" of this new technology was initially suppressed by the industry; as Brian Winston suggests, "a technology's commercialization becomes likely only when established economic powers are confident of controlling the commercialization's potential disruption of the economic status quo" (1996, 8). Although this was not precisely a matter of commercialization, the film and music industries approached the technology's radical potential cautiously.

During the 1930s and '40s, many stars still did their own singing. Some actors based their careers more on their abilities as singers than as actors. The famous Kundan Lal Saigal might fit into this category, as would great vocalist and sometimes film heroine Noor Jahan. Suraiya, who became a very popular actor, actually began her film career as a singer.

As figure 1.1 shows, singing actors outnumbered playback singers through the early 1940s. In the ten years following the introduction of playback, however, this chart also reflects a steady growth in the number of specialist playback singers that, with the benefit of hindsight, appears inexorable. The data on which this chart is based are taken from Singh (1984, 1988) and concern only those films produced by Mumbai and Kolkata studios (although together those two cities produced well over ninety percent of the released films). The chart takes into account the songs recorded by playback singers and those recorded by singing actors, per film, for all of the movies released in the years shown for which information is available (Singh's data appear to be based on HMV listings, so the singers of songs that were not recorded are apparently not listed).

The most obvious (and expected) change shown in figure 1.1 is the complete reversal that takes place over the years depicted. In 1936 the ratio of recordings by playback singers to those by singing actors was one to three; by 1946 it was more than three to one. The rise in the number of recordings by playback singers is relatively constant over this period, but recordings by singing actors grew significantly in 1938, especially given the decline in film output. Singing actors appear to have held their own through 1942, when they still slightly outnumbered the playback signers on disc. A minor increase in the number of recordings by playback singers in 1944, however, contrasts with the sharp decline in the number by singing actors (down from 114 in 1942 to 59 in 1944). Singing actors are present on disc at stable levels between 1944 and 1946, but in that period the number of recordings by playback singers almost doubled (as it did between 1938 and 1940). See Arnold (1991, table 7) for a listing of some of the playback singers in this period.

The late 1940s witnessed a series of largely coincidental personal events that nevertheless must have tipped the scales away from the singing actor. Perhaps the most prolific and popular singing actor, K. L. Saigal, died in 1946, the same year that Lata Mangeshkar first appeared as a playback singer in a Hindi film *(Jeewan Yatra)*. Two years later, with the partition of India, Noor Jahan, one of the great singing actresses of her day, left Mumbai for Pakistan.

Finally, in the last two years shown on the chart, there begin to appear the musicians—composers and singers—who would become the founding members, so to speak, of the generation that would dominate the Mumbai film-music industry for the next thirty years: playback singers Muhammad Rafi and Mukesh and composer C. Ramchandra (working as a playback singer) in 1944 and composer S. D. Burman (in addition to Mangeshkar) in 1946. Roughly three decades later, Rafi and Mangeshkar were still the dominant playback singers in Mumbai. Burman died in 1975, as his last films were just being released. Mukesh's last film song was released in 1976. Only C. Ramchandra had more or less retired from the film industry.

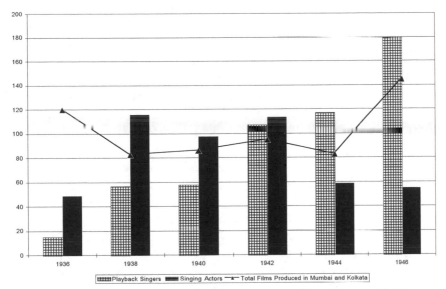

Figure 1.1 Changing dominance: playback singers and singing actors in the studio period. (Compiled from information listed in Singh 1984 and 1988.)

The term *playback* became an adjective that was applied to the new breed of specialist singers. These playback singers, selected exclusively for their vocal abilities, gradually took over more and more of the singing for films, while film actors, chosen for their appearance and acting skills, were limited to acting. Film culture in India became the embodiment of an extreme version of Altman's "primary ideology." In human terms and in the structures of the industry, sound (the singing voice) and image (the actor's physicality) were separate.

Although "Hindi cinema studios [in the 1940s] used voice casting, or the use of a singing voice that matched both the speaking voice and personality of the actor" (Majumdar 2001, 167), this practice appears to have been overwhelmed by the popularity and commercial success of a small group of singers in the late 1940s. The 1949 hit *Barsaat* exemplified the possible exacerbations when a single playback singer (in this instance, Lata Mangeshkar) recorded songs mimed by two different actors in the same film. For successful playback singers, however, the practice represented a potential gold mine.

In the Hollywood system, the dubbing of another's voice onto an actor's image was not unknown, but generally the singers remained anonymous. Similarly, "singers and composers of Indian popular music [i.e., film songs] are not stars themselves. There is no aura of fantasy and glamour woven around the leading singers, who remain invisible voices singing for the actors. Lata Mangeshkar is not a pop-culture idol" (Manuel 1993, 48). Srivastava offers a similar, although more historicized, assessment: "In India singers are not necessarily stars in themselves and, till quite recently, commercial music was sold in the market under the banner of the film with which the songs were associated" (2006, 123).

These "singer-as-invisible" paradigms (Srivastava refers specifically to Lata Mangeshkar as "relatively invisible") appear to have accurately reflected the position of playback singers in the later 1930s and 1940s, but thereafter it is more accurate to suggest a different category or type of stardom. The appearance and subsequent popularity of Lata Mangeshkar and her small group of colleagues (well described by Manuel 1993, 51–53) in the late 1940s and '50s led to a change in the status of playback singers. As the concept of playback singing became fully divorced from that of acting and wholly institutionalized, playback singers did indeed become stars. Certainly, the notion of stardom did not involve the same kind of physicality (charisma, visual attractiveness, stylishness, etc.) that film actors cultivated. In Mangeshkar's career at least, there appears to have been an intentional effort to project a carefully nonphysical, certainly nonsexualized public persona. Nevertheless, as the 1950s progressed, the leading playback singers (and especially Mangeshkar) became stars in their own rights (cf. Majumdar 2001).

Ranade's assessment of Mangeshkar's career makes this clear: "Her extended influence is felt all over the country and outside Indian borders. Lata has become a national symbol" (2006, 408). That she was a national symbol even in the 1960s is evident from the manner in which the Indian government routinely resorted to Mangeshkar's voice and physical presence for demonstrations of patriotism and national solidarity, as, for example, in the national public events connected with the 1962 war with China and the 1971 war with Pakistan. Mangeshkar's live performances at concerts in New Delhi outside the Lal Qila (Red Fort), another symbol of Indian nationalism, presided over by the prime ministers of those years, were broadcast via radio and embodied a nation united, so to speak, by her voice. In an article celebrating her seventy-fifth birthday, a journalist wrote that "till September 1979, we merely had Lata as the undisputed topmost female voice" and also that the post-1979 period led to Mangeshkar's "curtailing her recordings progressively and yet dazzling us when she did go in front of the mike. This was the phase that simply saw Lata finally acquire the status of a living legend" (Vijayakar 2004, 24).

Despite the specific and delimited nature of their stardom, playback singers were the dominant musical voices of Indian popular culture. Mangeshkar and colleagues such as her sister Asha Bhosle, Muhammad Rafi, or Mukesh all had large fan bases. The vocal presence of a major playback

singer or a particular combination of male and female playback singers attracted their fans to film showings. Although the empirical impact of playback singer stardom on a film's performance at the box office is difficult to
determine, producers clearly believed in that influence. That belief kept a
very small group of playback singers in an exceptionally dominant position
for many years.

Mangeshkar has been the iconic figure in the Mumbai music industry
for both Indians and foreigners, although in recent years her sister has been
more active in developing a postplayback career and personality. The central
period of Mangeshkar's popularity could be said to run from 1950 through
1980 in conservative terms, although she recorded many hit songs through
the 1980s and early '90s. Any comparative suggestion, however, that a
single vocalist might have occupied a leading position in American popular music from the period of Frank Sinatra and Patsy Cline through that of
Michael Jackson and the Clash is preposterous. That a singer might actually have been the dominant voice for such a lengthy period is unimaginable. That Mangeshkar did so is a tribute to her vocal and political talents
but is also a result of the industrial and cultural system in which she found
herself and of which she took advantage.

The musicians who are the focus of this book were, like those singers,
playback musicians. In their conversations, musicians refer to the famous
singers with the combination of collegiality and respect reserved for seniors
or superiors; they normally add appropriately respectful suffixes as well.
Prabhakar Jog worked as a song violinist (see chapter 6) from the mid-
1960s through the late 1980s. His comments here refer to a number of important issues that I develop in this volume. His story involving Lata
Mangeshkar (whom he respectfully calls Lata-bai) helps us understand his
perception of the socioprofessional relationship between himself and
Mumbai's star playback singer:

PRABHAKAR JOG: One song I played, that was for R. K. Films, *Henna* [1991].
Ravindra Jain gave the music for that film. And one music [interlude] was
ālāp;[2] that means "without rhythm." But in this ālāp, there was rhythm
going on and also ālāp going at the same time, but they were separate.[3]
And Lata-bai was singing that song, and this ālāp also she was supposed to
sing. So when Ravindra Jain gave the ālāp, I wrote that down.

Then Lata-bai came, and she sat down next to me, and I was a little
worried. I thought, "Why she is sitting here?" And she said to me, "You
heard that ālāp, and have you written it?" And I said, "Yes, certainly." So
she said, "Come in the [singer's recording] booth and play one time for
me." And then I was even more nervous. But she didn't know it really, so
I had to play it so she could learn it. I was sweating, let me tell you.

Neither Jog nor I relate this event with any intent to belittle Mangeshkar's musical skills. What is important to note, however, is the seriousness
with which Jog treats her interaction with him and his sense of responsibility to her—to accomplish the musical and transmissive task accurately. At
the same time, he is clearly aware of fortunately having written the music
down (in Indian style, *sargam* notation).

Although he joined the film line much later than Jog, Viju Shah's response to the presence of the leading playback singers also demonstrates
the respect with which they were treated:

> Viju Shah: I remember times we had Lata-bai singing or Asha-bai singing,
> and you paid very much attention and tried very hard because you knew if
> anything happened, then everything would stop.

Mangeshkar's star status, at least within the musical world, is also implied in the unusual, if appropriately Indian, juxtaposition shown in figure
1.2. The photograph was taken at a multifaceted benefit concert held in
central Mumbai circa 1953. Mangeshkar, whose career had assumed a
significant level of success only four years earlier, sang and posed afterward
with a group of musicians who were performing Anthony Gonsalves's clarinet quintet on the same program. The five musicians and other major
figures of Mumbai's film and classical music worlds stand grouped around
a young Lata-bai. However, despite the extensive talent, education, and experience in this group and the fact that she is younger than many of the
accomplished musicians in this picture, there is no question as to who the
star is.

Far from being celebrities in any sense, the musicians who are the focus
of this study were virtual unknowns to the general public. Only within
their own very small professional circles were instrumental virtuosity and
creativity acknowledged and respected. Naturally, musicians were rarely
involved in the picturization process. Even when musical performance appears on the Hindi film screen, as it frequently has, extras have usually
been employed to mime the playing. There are exceptions to this practice,
of course, which are often sources of interest and even pride to film musicians. In the 1951 film *Albela,* the famous Goan bandleader and trumpet
player Chic Chocolate (Antonio Vaz) appears with some of his band members in the song scene "Deewana Yeh Parwana." Although Vaz was miming along with the other actors, his image and music are presented in an
alignment that is rare for the Mumbai cinema. Ironically, perhaps, this is
the only film footage that exists of one of Mumbai's best-known and most
successful early jazz musicians.

Some musicians derive a particular kind of pleasure from their association with the more glamorous settings of the shooting sets and stars.

Figure 1.2 The Gonsalves Clarinet Quintet poses with Lata Mangeshkar and other musicians (ca. 1953). Mangeshkar stands in the center in her already trademark white sari. From her right, Italian cellist Edigio Verga, clarinetist Dennis Vaz (wearing a tie), and the highly respected Goan musician and teacher Micael Martins. From Mangeshkar's left, pianist Lucila Pacheco and violinists A. P. Dourado and Anthony Gonsalves. Courtesy of John Gonsalves.

Others see the irony in the situation. Drummer Leslie Godinho appeared only in shadow, so that viewers might associate his drumming gestures with actor Shammi Kapoor, the star of the 1966 hit *Teesri Manzil*. [⬤ Video 1.1]

Violinist Joaquim Menezes, known in the industry simply as Joe, is to my knowledge the only film musician to be formally introduced by name within a film, as reality and fantasy merge. In the context of a nightclub scene, after his introduction by his bandleader, the filmed image of Joe Menezes the musician is aligned with the sound of his actual performance, playing what the band leader calls "a popular Viennese melody" (figure 1.3). Although the choice may seem unusual, it was apparently a favorite melody of director and actor Raj Kapoor; the melody figures prominently in both the story and the scene:

> ERNEST MENEZES: My uncle [Joe Menezes] played many famous [violin] solos. He played first for *Barsaat* [1949]; he is actually picturized there. He recorded the solo and played it in the film as well. [Actor] Nargis falls at his feet because she thinks Uncle is Raj Kapoor.

The image of studio musician Joe Menezes, appearing as Joe Menezes in a fictional film story, miming to his own performance, adds only slightly to the interaction of reality and fantasy that embodied the Hindi cinema (and other cinemas for that matter). Raj Kapoor routinely played characters named Raj; his film romance with Nargis was widely understood to have been paralleled by a real-life romance as well. In the comments of Ernest Menezes, however, the overwhelming sense is that his uncle's participation is a matter of prestige. Despite the fact that few Goan musicians ever watched Hindi films for pleasure, the image of Joe Menezes playing on screen contributes to the substance of Joe Menezes the musician in his nephew's mind.

Like the musicians, although in different fashion, the industrial structures of Mumbai meant that music directors, or composers were quite dependent on the success of the films they composed for. Credit for a movie's success could be claimed by a composer, as well as a director or an actor. In a 1985 appreciation of composer Naushad Ali's music, for example, Nadkarni lists "Naushad's jubilee hits," those films whose first screenings lasted for 25, 50, or 100 days. One of the great paradoxes of the Hindi cinema and its commercial logic is that there is no empirical way to show that Naushad's music was a significant (let along the determining) factor in the success of the films Nadkarni lists, which could, of course, also be listed as jubilee hits of their directors (Nadkarni 1985, 44). The importance of hit films in the success of composers is equally demonstrated in the comments of mandolinist Nisar Ahmad, whose father, Sajjad Hussain, had a

Figure 1.3 Joaquim (Joe) Menezes in a still from the 1949 R. K. Films release, *Barsaat*. Courtesy of R. K. Films and Studios.

much less successful career as a film composer than did Naushad Ali. Nisar Ahmad attributes his father's difficulties to the failure of the films whose songs he composed rather than to the quality of the songs:

> NISAR AHMAD: My father always wanted to do things in a distinctive way, but it was his bad luck that he got films that were never hits. His songs were hits, but the films flopped, so people didn't give him much work.

Film producers nevertheless assumed that the ambiguous and indeterminable impact of songs in the film-song interaction was highly significant in terms of public reception. Narrative and music have a distinctively long-standing and intimate relationship in South Asia, but the assumed importance of songs in commercial films was part of the attitudes and the cultural and industrial dispositions that grew along with playback. That importance kept film musicians working steadily in Mumbai from the mid-1940s through the mid-1990s.

A Professional Geography of Mumbai

Films in Hindi were produced in Lahore, Kolkata, Pune, Lucknow, and even Sindh and Kolhapur, in addition to Mumbai. Of these, Kolkata was the only one to offer any serious competition to Mumbai's dominance. The early studios belonging to the Madan brothers and to B. N. Sircar (New Theatres) both had considerable impact. Nevertheless, Mumbai's dominance in the output of Hindi films was never really in question (see chapter 8). Whether the Hindi film industry would have found itself in Mumbai in any event is a matter for speculation; the strength of the music and narrative professional traditions, communities, and audiences must have been an added factor in the industry's growth. Mumbai was also routinely exposed to all manner of cultural and business influences from all over India:

> VISTASP BALSARA: In those days, Bombay was a cosmopolitan city. People came from Bihar, and from Panjab, from Assam and all those places.

Keyboard player, arranger, and composer Vistasp Balsara is speaking of Mumbai in the late 1930s, the last decade of the British Raj, a period in which the city's cosmopolitanism was enhanced by the presence of many foreigners, British and otherwise. Although Kolkata, the imperial capital and major port for many Indian import-export industries, may have been still more vibrant and diverse, Mumbai's importance as a center for finance and nightlife all increased after 1931, when the capital of British India was moved from Kolkata to New Delhi. The latter achieved an appropriately important political status, but it was not able to match either Kolkata or Mumbai in terms of cultural production. Although the Gramophone Company's primary production facility was located just outside Kolkata, it was Mumbai that became the de facto center of India's popular-music industry, which was subsumed within the film culture.

The city of Mumbai consequently forms the center of the professional geography in this story. With the exception of a handful of retired musicians in Goa, the United States, and Australia and those who have sought professional opportunities elsewhere, Mumbai's film musicians, past and present, are still in that city. They spent their time moving from studios to HMV to the music offices (called music rooms or sitting rooms; see chapter 5) of various film composers.

Mumbai as a city is oriented on a north-south axis along a peninsula created by the joining together of seven islands. Figure 1.4 shows the lower two-thirds of the city, along with the locations of some of the major recording studios between which the musicians commuted. The map omits the northern suburbs of Mumbai, where some film-productions centers have been located (e.g., R. K. Studios in Chembur, Filmalaya in Goregaon). These were film-production facilities that had basic, if any, music-recording facilities. Although some music was recorded in such locations in the 1930s, the vast majority of sound recordings were made in central and south Mumbai. Places such as Chembur or Goregaon were of little interest to most of the musicians in this book.

One exception was Naushad Ali, who joined the film business in early 1937, when music recording routinely took place in film studios as op-

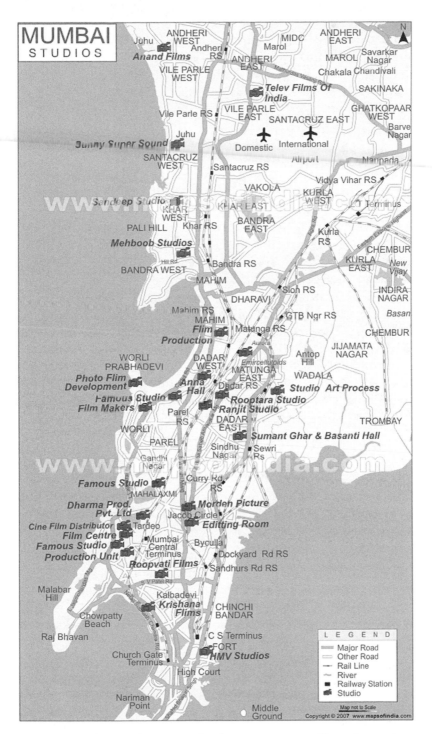

Figure 1.4 The Mumbai peninsula, showing important film-industry sites.

posed to music-recording studios(see chapter 2). Although he was living in central Mumbai, in Dadar, he landed a salaried job in a studio much farther north, in Chembur, then a distant and lightly populated village roughly twenty kilometers outside the urban center of Dadar:

> NAUSHAD ALI: I used to go out to Chembur to work; it was a jungle at that time. No restaurants or hotels were there. I only had *chai* [tea] at the studio. I went on the local train to Kurla Station.

By the end of the 1940s, music was rarely being produced or recorded in north Mumbai; musicians had increasingly little reason to travel that far north.

As a city, Mumbai is also divided into east and west by the major north-south roads and the two railroad lines, all of which create some degree of physical or structural separation between eastern and western suburbs. Many areas of the city have both an eastern and a western version of their designations (e.g., Santa Cruz West, Andheri East). Film musicians spent most of their time commuting from home to studio and from studio to studio along the north-south axis, using buses, cars, and sometimes trains, depending on their economic situation, those of their friends, and the instruments they played. Taxis were often used, especially by musicians with larger instruments or by groups who shared the ride. Violinist Ernest Menezes lived in Mahim, a neighborhood that faces the Arabian Sea and is traditionally home to many Goan families. Because family friend and cellist Alfonso Albuquerque found his instrument awkward to carry, they shared the costs of their journeys:

> ERNEST MENEZES: I knew Mr. Albuquerque very well because he was playing until quite recently. I used to take the taxi and pick him up because he had his cello. And we used to share the taxi because Tardeo was far. Alfie DaCosta also used to come with us.

Tardeo, farther south down the western side of the peninsula, was the location of two of Mumbai's major recording studios, Famous (Tardeo) and Film Centre. For Maoro Alfonso, who lived in Byculla in southeastern Mumbai, travel was in the opposite direction. He, however, had a car, which not only made his trips easier but seems to have helped him get work as well:

> MAORO ALFONSO: Some of the directors were good to me. I had a car, so they would say, "Come for my recording tomorrow," and I would take them. So they were happy.

Overall, the film business often involved a great deal of travel.

As the structure of the industry and the nature of work changed, musicians might spend days or weeks largely in one location or be spread out

across a considerable distance. In twenty-first-century Mumbai, as guitarist Ramesh Iyer points out, sound recording increasingly takes place in
and around the suburb of Andheri (mostly western Andheri) and its own
suburbs such as Lokhandwala or Mahada. These days musicians rarely
have reason to travel to south Mumbai. Given the difficulties created by
Mumbai's (and especially south Mumbai's) increasing traffic problems, this
is no doubt a good thing:

> RAMESH IYER: All the recording has shifted to Andheri and small places with
> room for five or six musicians. And the musicians won't go too far, either.
> It's too hard to travel. If somebody called me for a recording in, say,
> Churchgate, it would take me so long to come and go, by the time I was
> done I would spend five hours going and coming and have nothing. All the
> action has shifted to Lokhandwala.

The southernmost landmark in the professional geography of the Mumbai film industry was the HMV recording studio, where film musicians also
recorded for discs. The studios and the recording equipment were also part
of a technological environment in which film musicians worked. I describe
that environment in chapter 2, which focuses on the development of sound
technology after the introduction of playback.

2

Musicians and Technology in the Mumbai Film-Music Industry

In the years between the beginning of sound film and Indian independence, the initial integration of songs into the formal design of sound films was transformed into a seemingly permanent cultural and industrial convention. More gradually, the roles and images of playback singers and actors became fully separated in industrial and cultural practice and representation. Playback singing took on the appearance of still another permanent cultural convention.

Once songs and playback singing were thus established, everything else that happened in the film-music industry was a matter of the ways in which Mumbai's film-industry musicians, composers, directors, and technicians implemented those conventions and the music industry made use of the resultant songs. The availability of specific technologies was the result not only of actual technical options but also of economics, cultural choices, and Indian government policy in a range of areas. In this chapter I outline the changing "limits of the possible"—as Braudel (1972/1973) has so famously described the ways that technological and economic structures impose barriers to what one can achieve on an ongoing basis—within which Mumbai's film musicians, recording engineers, music directors, and film producers operated. Such obstacles do not define the absolute limit of what is possible, however. Mumbai's musicians and engineers here also recall the exceptions, the instances in which (sometimes through monumental effort and sheer persistence) they exceeded the technological limitations of their environment. Braudel's notion defines what one can routinely accomplish easily enough to do again. In this way, technology has been the ground on which the professional and social structures of daily life were constructed and the primary determinant in a determinist history of this music culture.

As an account of the availability of sound-recording technology from 1935 through the early years of the twenty-first century and (secondarily) of cultural responses, this chapter runs the greatest risk of any in this book of becoming a chronology of dates and facts. This arrangement is an essential backdrop for the chapters that follow, however, inasmuch as these developments directly affected the lives of Mumbai's film musicians. This account also gives voice to some of the recording engineers (called recordists) in Mumbai, who operated the recording equipment and in some cases drove the processes of change. A dismaying number of the key players in the Mumbai recording world passed away before I began this research. Nevertheless, as the men (exclusively in this period) who maintained the borders, so to speak, between the possible and the impossible and often sought to extend them, the voices of Mumbai's recordists add significantly to an oral history of film song.

A history of sound-recording technology in the Mumbai film industry is clearly an oppositional history in reference to those commonly proposed by historians of film music (e.g., Arnold, Bali, Premchand; see chapter 3). For these histories, the major rupture was fundamentally stylistic; it occurred at some point in the late 1940s, when film song was being musically and stylistically redefined by a small group of playback singers. The collective appearance of this group of immensely influential musicians and their rise to dominance was quite sudden, especially compared to the subsequent duration of their importance. In conservative terms, the collective voice that this group represents—in terms of songs, sounds, and stylistic developments—dominated Hindi film song for roughly twenty years.

As I discuss in the following chapter, this sudden burst of creative energy and stylistic innovation aligns roughly with changes in industrial structure, although I cannot be optimistic about the significance of this correlation. Industrial change and musical innovation in Mumbai, however, took place almost halfway through a long period of technological stability. Morcom, quoting various sources and without specifying the changes she means, stipulates that "around 1950, the quantity and scale of background music in Hindi films significantly increased. . . . This is easily traceable to direct Hollywood influence and also to technological advances around 1950 that made the recording of large ensembles more feasible" (Morcom 2007, 138). I argue later that these changes were more properly attributable to the presence of new figures in the music production system and to changes in recording infrastructure, rather than technology.

It is true that the quality of available microphones gradually improved, as did the availability of mixers that could accommodate more than one or two microphones. More important, in the late 1940s and early '50s Mumbai began to see the development of specialized music-recording spaces. In the actual recording process, however, the signals from any and all microphones continued to be recorded on single-track optical film. The technological limitations of what could be recorded and how those recordings could be used in the film and music industries did not change significantly between the late 1930s and the late 1950s. In the mid-1950s those limits began shifting incrementally as studios became able to accommodate greater numbers of microphones and as magnetic tape (and later multi-track tape) made its appearance. Nevertheless, if we look for technological change that had the potential to significantly alter both the music-recording process in Mumbai and the lives of the city's film musicians, we must wait almost thirty years—until the mid-1980s.

This period, enormously long in terms of twentieth-century popular culture, was defined by two technological practices that remained constant throughout these years: first, the recording of live performances of entire songs by the full ensemble stipulated for each song (although later excluding playback singers); second, the need to master the final audio version to optical, monaural film. Those fundamental practices began to grudgingly disintegrate after 1985, but a total transformation took another ten years to complete. When hard-disc and computer-based music composing and recording technology finally became a reality in the mid-1990s, the final remnants of the system that began in 1935 vanished—and with them the livelihoods of many studio musicians.

Recording Technology, 1935–1985

In the recording process that was established in 1935, film songs were recorded first, and scenes were filmed later. Although he was not primarily a film-music recordist, Daman Sood was one of the first graduates in sound engineering from the Film and Television Institute of India (FTII) in Pune to have a major impact on sound recording in Mumbai in the 1970s:

> DAMAN SOOD: Recordings were done mono. The mics increased, but that depended on how many channels the mixer had. Everything was mixed to a single track that was recorded directly on optical film. The negative film was sent to the lab for processing and returned for listening. The music director and the producer would listen and say "okay" or "not okay."

Sood is highly respected throughout the music industry for his work in developing the recording facilities at one of Mumbai's most advanced sound-recording studios, Western Outdoor Advertising (usually referred to more simply as Western Outdoor). As he notes, one of the drawbacks of recording sound optically on film was that the sound could not be heard until the film was developed and the negative image transformed into a positive print. As Kersi Lord explains, recordists in this period almost always made two or three "insurance" copies:

> KERSI LORD: That time, recording was directly on the negative. We'd record one take, and then the engineer would say, "Let's do one more," and then they would process the film. Mostly they would find some wow and flutter. So again we'd have to record it.

Optical film also offered a relatively limited recording range. Even when magnetic tape appeared with its improved recording capabilities, the limitations of film defined much of the final product:

> ANANDJI SHAH: The film could only go to six thousand cycles; it was limited. So you can say we were cheating because we would play the takes back for the producers from the tape itself, which had a higher frequency, and then when it got made for film, it would come down.

What Shah does not mention here is that impressing producers (by any means) was a constant focus of almost everyone's attention.

Another major drawback of optical film was that editing, the physical process of cutting a strip of film and splicing it to another, usually required some kind of musical pause or change that would mask the edit. Although films after 1935 were assembled from component parts, song recordings were still recordings of live musical performances.

Once an approved recording of the song was acquired, a copy—also on optical film—was printed and given to the film producer, who was the owner of both the recording and the song. The original was retained for safekeeping. The film's director used the copy as the soundtrack for filming the song scene. Once the song scene was filmed, the film and the original recording of the song were used to create the final synchronized release copy.

Although the number of microphones a recordist could deploy in a recording session gradually increased during the late 1940s and the '50s, recording technology and processes remained very much the same. In the private sector and especially in the film industry, technological change actually slowed somewhat after 1947. While India remained part of the British Empire, the flow of new film and music technology into the country had been a relatively simple matter of economics in the 1930s and '40s, interacting with distance and various forms of political and corporate colonialism. The policies of the Indian government, however, that limited foreign investment also made access to filmmaking materials and new technologies difficult for Indian filmmakers, musicians, and recording engineers. Governmental policy in independent India erected bureaucratic and economic barriers in matters of foreign exchange, import, and export. The "license Raj," as the system has come to be called in India (e.g., Das 2001; Guha 2007), created a range of impediments in the acquisition of raw film stock, the construction of new theaters, access to broadcast media, and content.

Sometimes the effects of government policy were by-products of common governmental needs to produce income through taxation, protect currency against negative exchange relationships, and define a desirable national identity. In other instances, governmental policy was specifically formulated in response to a largely negative view of the film industry as unproductive in a country vitally concerned with increasing basic production of food and raw materials. In addition to the famous disappearance of film song on the government-owned radio network in the early 1950s, for example, this attitude was clearly shown by the Indian government's persistent refusal to define the film industry as an "industry" (Rajadhyaksha 2004, 124). Such a designation would have provided significant tax and import/export benefits to filmmakers but was, astonishingly, not awarded until 1998. The barriers set up by this policy were enormous in many cases, and the resulting industrial structures were often quite distorted.

Gradually, beginning in the late 1980s, "import restrictions on many items were liberalized, and many regulation and controls were eased" (Manuel 1993, 61) by successive Indian governments. While they were in place, however, they affected many musicians, especially those who played Western instruments, as well as those building recording studios. In one extreme instance, it took personal intervention by his sister and a local mayor somewhere in the American state of Oregon before Kishore Desai could secure his first Gibson mandolin in the 1950s. Drummer Leslie Godinho was one of many musicians who built his own instrument in that period. [● Video 2.1]

Even in the 1970s, guitarist Ramesh Iyer, who fortunately had a degree in electrical engineering, also had to construct his first instrument:

> RAMESH IYER: My first electric guitar I built. I had studied engineering, but I really wanted to do music. So I got the wood and the materials for the pickups, and for the frets I used bicycle spokes, and I had to study very much to understand the fret positions and how pickups worked and how many turns of copper wire I needed.

Those seeking to purchase electronic keyboards or synthesizer equipment also faced many challenges. Moreover, import regulations and exchange rates created difficulties for engineers and the development of new recording technologies.

Twenty years after Ramesh Iyer built his first electric guitar, the obstacles to importing foreign technology began to disappear, but recording engineer Bishwadeep Chatterjee still had trouble getting equipment when he was hired to set up the new Spectral Harmony recording studio in the mid-1990s:

BISHWADEEP CHATTERJEE: We did have a lot of problems. I wanted to get a one-inch recorder, but somebody had put in a regulation that you couldn't import one-inch tape because India was manufacturing tape. But we weren't manufacturing one-inch tape. We had to prove to them that one-inch was a different thing, and 35 mm tape was a different thing. We paid 25 to 30 percent import duties on that stuff. So a lot of foreign exchange restrictions meant that it wasn't easy to get the work done. It's still true today, but it's much better than it used to be.

Advancement in sound technology was not uniform everywhere, even in a single city. In the 1940s some studios were still recording with a single microphone and balancing by physically moving musicians:

KERSI LORD: When I started [1948], there was only one microphone. The singer would be on one side, and we would all be on the other. If you wanted the maracas soft, you just moved the maracas player a little back from the mic.[1] There was only a fixed volume.

Filmistan, which had been created as Mumbai's rival to Kolkata's technologically advanced New Theatres, had two mics in the early 1940s:

VISTASP BALSARA: When I started at Filmistan, there were two microphones, one for the singer and one for the musicians.

Some music directors and engineers strategized carefully to get the most sophisticated effects with the basic equipment at hand:

KERSI LORD: When we were recording *Pyaasa* [1957], I was playing Chinese temple blocks, but I had no mic. They just put me in the middle of all the mics, so the sound was going into this mic and that mic. It made a good effect. So they were always experimenting with the sound and the recording.

Thus, by the mid-1950s, many studios were using multiple-microphone recording systems, although they were still recording on single-track optical film. Arnold (1991) also reports the elaborate measures some music directors took to place their musicians so as to achieve the best balance.

Recording Technology and Studios: Film and Nonfilm

Some of the most significant changes in sound recording in the early 1950s had to do with recording spaces. In the 1930s and '40s, sound recording was not done in acoustically designed recording studios but in the same barnlike spaces where films themselves were shot (chapter 3). Because these were multipurpose sites, no specialized sound treatment or recording equipment was installed. Instead, the producing studios of the 1940s and early 1950s invested in mobile vans that were large enough to house a recording machine, mixer, and other necessary equipment and still accommodate a recordist and perhaps his assistant. The sound van would be accompanied by a generator van so that recording was independent of the electrical power supply and could take place just about anywhere. Microphones would be placed appropriately and connected to the recording van by long cables:

> KERSI LORD: Sometimes we'd just record in a small rehearsal room; there was no recording room or recording booth. We had a mobile recording van with cables going from here to there.

In the 1950s, recording engineers began developing acoustically suitable recording spaces. Many of those who worked in vans helped build or run the first recording studios. Robin Chatterjee was one of the first generation of recording engineers. Growing up in the years before India established FTII, Chatterjee had studied recording in Germany and the United States:

> KERSI LORD: Mr. Robin Chatterjee was recording in the van at Rang Mahal Studio at Dadar. In the van would be a small mixer and a speaker and a recording machine. Before the outdoor shoots, one recording van used to go, and one generator van used to go [to the filming location]. First, Mr. Robin Chatterjee was there in those vans. Then later he was at Mehboob Studios.

Before examining these important recording facilities, I want to make clear the two different technological streams that make this history so complex.

Throughout the history of film music, the need to record on synchronizable formats distinguished recording practice in the film-music industry from that in the music industry (i.e., the recording of music for film as opposed to disc). In the 1930s and '40s this distinction was embodied in the differences between recording on optical film or on wax or acetate discs. After World War II, it meant the difference between film and magnetic tape, which quickly became the global recording medium. Later it meant variations in tape format and diverse rates of technological development.

As developed in the United States for the music industry, magnetic tape came in quarter-inch to two-inch widths (hereafter the "inch system"). In general, the wider tapes allowed greater densities of magnetic particles and thus better sound quality. Synchronizable magnetic tape (i.e., tape with sprocket holes) was also developed in the 1950s but was made to correspond to the size of celluloid film and measured in millimeters: The thirty-five-millimeter width (called "thirty-five em-em" in Mumbai; hereafter

35 mm) was most commonly used. The inch system that was used by the record industry developed more sophisticated technology more quickly than the "em-em" format used for films; what is more, the two were not compatible.

In the history of the Mumbai film-music industry, any reference to magnetic-tape technology must specify which system is under discussion to avoid confusion. When Arnold (1991), for example, reports that magnetic tape recorders began to appear in India between 1948 and 1950, she refers (whether she knew it or not) to inch-system tape recorders that had no major impact on the film-music industry. The unbridgeable duality of this system leads Arnold into a dilemma when she comments on the recording of film songs for HMV that "until the advent of magnetic tape in the early 1950s, songs had to be recorded twice . . . since there was no means of directly transferring the film soundtrack recording to a gramophone record" (1991, 115). While she is correct in stating that HMV was recording film songs for discs on quarter-inch magnetic tape for at least part of the 1950s, it was almost the end of that decade before the need to record songs twice (once for filmmaking on optical film and once for discs) disappeared. That change ultimately took place when HMV acquired an optical transfer machine that transferred sound directly from celluloid film to an acetate master disc:

> V. K. DUBEY: Film songs were recorded in a studio on sound film. After that, HMV had no way of transferring the music from the film, so they [the musicians] used to come to HMV studio and record the song again. That's how it used to be. In 1958 or so, HMV acquired that transfer machine, and then they could transfer the sound from the film to a lacquer.

Dubey was HMV's national vice president for artists and repertory. The transfer machine that he mentions here bridged the gap between two different processes and industries. Because of the close symbiotic relationship between the film and music industries, however, the extent of that separation is not always readily apparent. This remains one of the most challenging conceptual issues in providing a clear account of sound-recording technology in Mumbai; there were actually two different technological systems in place for recording sound: one for the nonsynchronous world of music recording for discs and cassettes and one for the synchronous world of film-music recording. Developments, formats, and studios were aligned with one or the other but rarely both. Bishwadeep Chatterjee reflects on the situation and describes the results of Western Outdoor's early efforts to develop inch-system technology:

> BISHWADEEP CHATTERJEE: Nobody got into the whole business of [inch-system] machines except Western Outdoor. Music for us [India, Mumbai]

was largely film. An independent music industry was largely not there. Everything we did for music was with film in mind.

Although this is a relatively precise technical statement, Chatterjee's comments also casually reinforce the dominance of film, filmmaking, and film music in the minds of those involved in the production of India's popular culture.

Avinash Oak, another FTII graduate, worked for twenty-nine years at Western Outdoor (almost from the time it opened). He makes clear the separation between film recording and what was tellingly called "nonfilm" recording. Like Chatterjee, he highlights the hegemonic status of the film industry and the film-recording process and explains why early efforts to cross over were unsuccessful:

> AVINASH OAK: [Western Outdoor] was a nonfilm studio. That means we were called nonfilm, an album-work studio. The film studios were having 35 mm equipment. For people who were having an optical transfer machine— optical recorders, bulky machines also and very costly—that is more like a qualification; [it means that] you are a film studio.

To be a film (music) studio required a specialized machine, such as the one HMV acquired in 1958 or so, to enable the transition from the "em-em" system to the inch system.

Despite the superior audio quality and flexibility of Western Outdoor's inch-system recorders, they and the other nonfilm studios could not compete for film-music recording work, which represented the vast majority of all recording work in Mumbai in the 1970s and '80s, for the simple reason that the resultant recordings would not be synchronizable. For most of its history, Western Outdoor did "album work;" the company recorded music for what musicians often call "private recordings," that is, recordings that were not connected to the film industry. The phrase is used rather oddly in this context since private recordings are commercial products like other recordings.

Western Outdoor also recorded advertising jingles for radio and television. This was one way in which the film and nonfilm worlds interconnected in the person of the musicians who composed and played for both jingles and films. Jazz pianist, arranger, and composer Louiz Banks joined music director R. D. Burman in 1979 but was soon distracted by the advertising business:

> LOUIZ BANKS: Then the advertising industry discovered me [circa 1980]. And I got so busy with that, I had to make a decision; I couldn't do both. So I chose advertising. It was very lucrative, with quick turnovers, and well, I got hooked for a while.

Film musicians who did jingle work at Western Outdoor were well aware of the benefits of nonsynchronous recording formats. Nevertheless, there was no way to connect these worlds. Even when music directors in the 1980s finally began recording at Western Outdoor and then transferring tracks to 35 mm, the superior quality of the original recording would be significantly diminished and irrecoverable once transferred to a synchronizable format:

> AVINASH OAK: People who joined the nonfilm studios from FTII, like me or Daman [Sood], could see the problem. We insisted on shooting [recording] in multitracks, but then once we transferred that onto a synch kind of a format, like a Nagra [see below] or 35 mm if we had that, then we could not go back to the multitrack format because that [Nagra or 35 mm] is the synching point. And then they transferred that onto 35 mm mono [i.e., single track]. And that is the version for cutting and making the negative [i.e., release print].

Oak's phrase "synching point" is quite telling in that it identifies the initial creation of a synchronizable recording. For filmmakers and their technical assistants and recordists, nothing that came before the synching point was relevant or usable.

The perils of ignoring the technological divide were spectacularly demonstrated as late as 1981, when music directors Shiv-Hari were recording the songs for *Silsila* and were seduced by the technological sophistication of a new tape recorder at a new HMV/ EMI facility:

> AVINASH OAK: HMV/EMI had a multitrack studio, a very new one, at Cuffe Parade in the World Trade Centre. They were having a one-inch, eight-track tape recorder from EMI. It was a very nice machine.

Despite its attractions, however, the EMI machine had the usual problem: Masters made on this inch-format machine could not be synchronized with film:

> DEEPAN CHATTERJI: That machine [at HMV/EMI] was basically for album work. It was a nonsynch machine, not meant for film work. So what happened was that Shiv-Hari recorded the songs on that, and then they mixed down and recorded the songs on a Nagra, and that Nagra tape was sent for shooting. [But] there was no way they could synchronize that machine [at HMV/EMI] with the Nagra, so when they went back to the original, it wouldn't synch.

Sound film negatives for the final release print were made from the original 35 mm recordings because that method produced no loss of sound quality and (even more important) the sound and the images would be in synch. In this case, however, the original recordings were on nonsynchronous one-inch tape. The technological solution to this dilemma did not exist in India in 1981:

> DEEPAN CHATTERJI: What I heard was that they took the quarter-inch Nagra tape to London, along with the original tape, and they took the pulse from that [Nagra] and locked a one-inch machine and played back the one-inch tape from that machine.

The history of sound recording in the Mumbai film industry, then, as experienced by the film studio musicians, is the chronicle of recording on film and subsequently on synchronizable 35 mm magnetic tape. In some studios, that remained the master recording format for more than thirty years after its introduction in 1960.

Film (Music) Studios

Around 1950 four new recording spaces were developed and became the home of the film-music industry:

> ASHOK SHUKLA: There were four main places where people recorded music for films, four film studios you can say: Film Centre, Bombay Sound, Famous, and Mehboob. They're all closed now.

These "film studios" were the opposite of the "nonfilm studios" such as Western Outdoor:

> KERSI LORD: The first was Famous [Tardeo]; they also had a black-and-white [film processing] lab at the back. Minoo Katrak worked there as recordist; that was the place most music directors started recording. But even Film Centre was a lab for film processing. The first floor was a lab; then on the second floor they built the sound studio. Bombay Sound was also part of Bombay Labs. So it seems to me that all the lab people, they were also building sound studios; that's what it looks like to me.

Although he is hesitant to make the connection unequivocally, the development of new technical spaces in independent India's film capital addressed the need for film processing and for sound recording in three of the new spaces. The only exception was Mehboob Studios, which had been built as a film-production facility. Chatterjee reports rather negative descriptions of Famous (Tardeo) as "practically a godown [warehouse], but glorified beyond all proportions to be described as a sound studio" (1992, 128). Nevertheless, as Lord explains, the development of new spaces was followed by changes of venue by many music directors:

> KERSI LORD: Mehboob was the only sound studio that wasn't part of a lab. It was part of the whole studio setup. Anil Kaushik was the recordist there. Kaushik shifted to Film Centre [in 1964] as did Mr. R. D. Burman and

Kalyanji-Anandji. But L-P, who had shifted from Famous [Tardeo] to Mehboob, stayed on, as did Naushad.

Each of the four studios had a characteristic sound that resulted from the combination of its acoustics, the skills and interests of its chief recordist, and the studio equipment. Throughout the 1960s, a single chief recordist managed all of the recording that took place in "his" studio:

> DEEPAN CHATTERJI: A setup like Mehboob studios, they had their own in-house recording engineers [who] would be responsible for recording whatever is there for the film: songs, background, dialogue, effects, whatever.

One recordist and his assistants did all of the sound for the film; only in the mid-1960s did different kinds of recording tasks become specialties. In some cases, long series of recordings, which lasted for many years in some cases, connected specific music directors with particular sites. This was evident in the work of R. D. Burman and Laxmikant-Pyarelal, where the "sound" produced by specific spaces and technological systems contributed to those composers' musical styles.

Famous (Tardeo) was operational at the end of the 1940s, but the other sites opened for business slightly later. The change from "shooting floors" to recording studios, however, was gradual, as Lord explains:

> KERSI LORD: We used to record in many places, not just one place. In And heri there were so many places: Natraj Studio, Mohan Studio, so many places. But those were shooting studios, not film studios. Even *Nagin* [1954] we recorded at Filmistan on the shooting set.

Confusingly, at this time three different film-production sites in Mumbai were all called Famous: Mahalaxmi, Tardeo, and Mahim. Only the first two were sites of musical activity, however. Famous Film Studios and Laboratories on Dr. E. Moses Road in Mahalaxmi was not only a film-production studio but also the site of Shankar-Jaikishan's rehearsal room. Many musicians went there for rehearsals, but Mahalaxmi was not a music-recording space. Famous Film Laboratories (Tardeo) was also originally a filming location but was redesigned specifically as a film-processing center with a recording studio attached. Musicians still use these place names parenthetically in conversation to distinguish between the Mahalaxmi and the Tardeo sites.

Film Centre and the Bombay and Famous labs were film-processing spaces with recording studios built in or added on; after the 1964 death of its founder, Mehboob Khan, Mehboob Studios became a rentable production space like the others. Since processing (i.e., converting the negative print into a positive one) was necessary before a recording on optical film

Figure 2.1   A portion of the now-empty grounds of Mehboob Studios (2007). The covered stairs at far right lead up large recording studio at the far left of the building. Mehboob's famous diesel generator was on the ground floor below.

could be played back, the proximity of the two activities made considerable sense in the early 1950s. These facilities were available to all comers on a per-hour or per-day rental basis. Most film musicians working between 1950 and 1990 spent most of their professional lives in these four spaces. Only Mehboob remains standing today (figure 2.1); as one of the very few large sites remaining in the Mumbai film-music world, it is used for the occasional orchestra rehearsal. The recording facility has been dismantled, although Pyarelal Sharma's piano still sits in the control room.

Magnetic Tape, Tracks, and Live Performances

Magnetic tape appeared in Mumbai's film studios sometime in 1960. Unlike earlier tape formats, the new one used the same width as film (35 mm) and, also like film, had sprocket holes so that it could be physically synchronized with the visual film. It took the industry some time, however, to decide how to deal with this new technology. Suresh Kathuria relates that the integration of magnetic tape was a very gradual process:

> SURESH KATHURIA: Cheaper magnetic machines were coming, and by the end of 1967, direct optical [recording] was gone. But even then, some studios, they would do everything like prerecording, mixing, balancing on magnetic, but the final take, they take on the optical recorder, otherwise feeling that there would be "generation loss." That if we go from tape to tape and

then to optical, we would lose something, so it will better to go directly to optical. But slowly, say by end of 1969, that practice was also given up, and everything was being recorded on magnetic tapes.

Once tape appeared, it began to be divided into tracks. In the mid-1960s Mehboob Studios and Bombay Sound both acquired three-track recorders produced by the German Klangfilm Company. By the early 1970s Klangfilm and Westrex had developed four-track 35 mm tape and recorders:

> ASHOK SHUKLA: They all had three or four tracks, mostly four. And that meant music, rhythm, voice, and composite [which was the other three, plus effects]. And that would all be mixed down to a single mono track for the 35 mm master. That was dubbed to produce the release copy.

Although he knows the difference, Shukla here uses the term *mono* in a common Mumbai usage to mean a single-track tape, not as an abbreviation of "monaural," the opposite of "stereo." In the 1970s A. N. Tagore worked at Mehboob Studios, first as an assistant to Robin Chatterjee and then, from 1976 on, as chief recordist. He also uses the term *mono* in the Mumbai way:

> A. N. TAGORE: When I joined in 1973, we were recording on 35 mm four-track tape. Mr. Robin Chatterjee had just rebuilt the studio. He completely renovated the sound, and at that time he put in the four-track recorder; before that it had been mono. Then slowly we started adding tracks; we went up to eight tracks. Then when I came, we got some magnetic repro ducers so we could go up to twelve or sixteen tracks.

Viju Shah is one of the many musicians who worked through the changes from single- to multitrack recordings. A highly reflective musician, Shah describes the various accommodations and improvisations that engineers and musicians employed as they sought to replicate the sophistication of foreign studios on their transitional equipment:

> VIJU SHAH: I've been very fortunate because I've seen the transition. I've been to recordings where everything was live; we had no dubbing. If there was a cut, then we had to go back to the beginning. It was sixty or one hundred musicians in a big studio, all being recorded live. Then there came a time when there was track recording, four tracks at first. So we had the rhythm being recorded first, then music, then voice. Then we went from four to six, and we had two tapes running simultaneously on two machines [at Film Centre]. They used thread for marking [the synch points]. They would put a thread to the play head, and they used to lock it and then press "play." It was a very primitive way of thinking, you can say. Nowadays you just push a button.

Shah speaks with the benefit of hindsight about strategies that enabled recordists of the time to get more out of their machines than the equipment had been designed for.

By the mid-1970s the tracks in all of the studios had reached double figures but in different ways. In 1975 Film Centre had one 4-channel and one 6-channel recorder. The ten tracks were mixed down to the standard four and in most cases then down to one track for the optical master. In 1977 Film Centre and Mehboob acquired a reproducer (also called a dubber), which allowed them to add four already-recorded tracks to the ten they could record at once, producing something like fourteen tracks (four prerecorded plus ten new), although they were all ultimately reduced to a single track.

Using reproducers that could play back recorded tracks onto new recordings, recordists gradually developed the practice of recording two or three tracks, then dubbing them down to a single track, thus increasing the density of sound on each track. Many arrangers and recordists took advantage of this practice to add more sound to the final mix by condensing more and more music onto the same number of tracks:

> VIJU SHAH: We would add stuff. We were filling tracks to the brim! Wherever there was space, even on the voice track, we would add something because we didn't have [enough] tracks. What happened, we used to take six tracks, remix that to two, again take a new tape, and add two more. This is all the *funda* [rigmarole] we were doing. Because there was no other way of doing it. So we had to do it that way. Today when I think about it, I laugh to myself.

Some recordists took advantage of the inch-system's flexibility by using it for the early stages of "building" a track:

> ASHOK SHUKLA: In the 1980s also I used to record rhythm on a four-track, one-inch machine, then play it back, along with one or two more rhythm parts onto 35 mm. It was like having six rhythm tracks.

The rhythmic and timbral density, rapid shifts in instrumentation and style, and sometimes sheer volume (not to mention distortion) that often resulted from this kind of recording is audible in the sound tracks of many 1980s' films. I discuss these outcomes in more detail in chapter 7.

In the mid-1960s a new development in tape-recording technology reached India. Although it is largely beyond the scope of both this chapter and this book (it affected filmmakers more than musicians or composers), the Nagra recorder also shaped film-music recording somewhat. The Nagra used quarter-inch tape but was driven by what Mumbai musicians and recordists call a "crystal motor":

> BISHWADEEP CHATTERJEE: Nagra had a 50 Hertz signal that was recorded and played back. That kept it [the tape speed] steady.

Nagra's crystal motors ran at a consistent, measurable speed that was independent of the AC voltage. That in turn meant that a recording made on a Nagra or a film shot in conjunction with Nagra playback would be synchronizable. Nagras, which were small portable machines, replaced the use of sound vans and optical film in shooting playback scenes:

> DEEPAN CHATTERJI: The Nagra was a very portable professional recorder that would record and play back in synch with films. Once that came, then the scenario started changing. After the song was recorded, the Nagra guy would come to the studio, and we would transfer from the studio 35 mm tape onto the Nagra, and then the Nagra would be used for playback.

Deepan Chatterji worked as the recording assistant to R. D. Burman from 1970 through the latter's death in 1994. Burman was, to my knowledge, the only music director in Mumbai to maintain a specialist in this kind of role. This is but one example of Burman's exceptional attention to the recording process. It is not unrealistic to suggest that, perhaps more than any other film composer in India (with the possible exception of A. Rahman), R. D. Burman and his music represent a valuable object for ethnomusicological research. This is yet another topic beyond the scope of this book, but the technological adventures of the Burman workshop (see chapter 5) deserve comment here for the extent to which Burman challenged and sometimes broke through the boundaries generally imposed by technology on the sound of film music.

Pushing the Limits of the Possible: R. D. Burman

The presence of a recording assistant as part of the Burman team was the result of Burman's fascination with technology and his use of it to change the way the composition and recording processes worked and the way his music sounded:

> DEEPAN CHATTERJI: When cassettes had just started coming, Pancham-da had just got that Philips cassette recorder. So I thought it was a good idea to record whatever he was composing. I would sit next to him with that cassette recorder and record whatever he was singing. Because sometimes as he would go on he would say, "No, what I did earlier was better, but it's not coming back to me." So I would quickly rewind. That's how it started.

Chatterji effectively created his own role as recording assistant, although with Burman's encouragement.

Perhaps more than many other film composers Burman was concerned with the production of his songs as pop songs. Burman and Chatterji consequently sought to lessen the technological distance between the film and nonfilm systems. Chatterji began to sense the importance of this disjunction when he worked on Burman's nonfilm ("private") recordings, such as the LP *Dil Padosi Hai*. He worked out a way to improve the quality of the film-song recordings that the producers of Burman's films regularly delivered to HMV for release:

> DEEPAN CHATTERJI: Pancham-da would have his private recordings at HMV. Now over there, I saw that we would record the songs on quarter-inch and that quarter-inch would be used to cut the master. So I thought, "Why can't we send the quarter-inch magnetic tapes of film recordings?" So the next song we recorded at Film Centre, when the Nagra guy came, I made the producer buy another quarter-inch tape, and I transferred the song from 35 mm to quarter-inch and took that to HMV.

Part of the significance of Chatterji's comments here is embedded in the notion that a recording assistant could make the film's producer do anything. This was possible in his case because he worked for one the two most sought-after composers in Mumbai throughout the 1970s and '80s. In most other cases it would not have been realistic even if other composers had had a recording assistant.

Chatterji's idea may not seem especially revolutionary, but compared to the older process that Lord explains here, it made a significant difference in the way recordings of Burman's songs sounded on discs:

> KERSI LORD: When magnetic came, once the take is over and the song is recorded, they used to make a copy onto optical and take that only, never the 35 mm original. That [the 35 mm original] never left the studio; that was studio property. And those optical copies used to go to HMV also; they never copied from tape. That's why the original HMV recordings are so bad, you know? On optical there is always a [frequency] loss.

Chatterji's innovation meant that commercial recordings of Burman's songs did not suffer the same loss of quality.

In the mid-1970s Burman and Chatterji undertook the production of the first Hindi film music recorded in six-track stereo for the movie *Sholay* (1975):

> DEEPAN CHATTERJI: That was a great fun film. For me *Sholay* was the turning point of getting involved in other areas of sound. It was basically a learning process for all of us.

Morcom (2007) and Chopra (2000) both offer insight into the popularity of the *Sholay* recordings, to which the sound quality that Chatterji helped achieve no doubt contributed.

Making the *Sholay* recording process even more challenging was the fact that the film's producer and director, G. P. and Ramesh Sippy respectively, had chosen to film on 70 mm (instead of the usual 35 mm) film. Since there were no editing facilities in India that could accommodate 70 mm film, the final editing was done in London. For that matter, there was no multitrack stereo 35 mm tape, to say nothing of 70mm tape of any kind. Every sound had to be recorded separately:

> DEEPAN CHATTERJI: We had no idea of how to go about things using 35 mm magnetic tapes. A roll of 35 mm magnetic tape was like precious gold. And the very thought of cutting that down and splicing it was like unthinkable, but that's how we had to send the tracks to London for mixing.

The recordings were done at the old home of Rajkamal studios, which had become an audio postproduction and dubbing facility. That, in itself, created problems:

> AVINASH OAK: The music was recorded as six-track at Rajkamal; that was basically a rerecording and mixing studio. But there only it was possible to record in six separate tracks [i.e., not on a single machine using a single six-track tape]. So it was a question of having three magnetic tape recorders linked together and then recording on that.

Despite the sophistication of the final product, the Mumbai process of recording live performances was still the only method available:

> DEEPAN CHATTERJI: It was the full orchestra playing in one go; everything was recorded on the six tracks. But then, out of the six tracks, one track was for the monitor. So what we were listening to was mono on the one track. And the other microphones were channeled onto the other five tracks. So really we had five-track mono. And that also was made stereo in London.

Figure 2.2 shows Vasudeo Chakravarty with a contact microphone wired to his cello during the *Sholay* background sessions at Raj Kamal. The eerie sounds that Chakravarty produced became the signature sound of the film's villain, Gabbar Singh, and constituted an important part of the film's (one might even say India's) soundscape. Because it was impossible to produce a six-track stereo soundtrack in India in the mid-1970s (especially one on 70 mm film), every sound and every bit of background music was recorded separately and ultimately compiled in a London studio.

The technical quality of the *Sholay* score stands in marked contrast to anything that had previously been recorded in Mumbai or would be recorded for more than a decade afterward. The effort required to move so far beyond the existing boundaries proved to be prohibitive in the long

Figure 2.2
Vasudeo Chakravarty plays
amplified cello in the
Rajkamal Studios (1975),
creating the eerie music
associated with villain
Gharbar Singh, for the film
Sholay. Courtesy of Sanjay
Chakravarty.

run. Nevertheless, *Sholay* was not the only stereo film produced in the
1970s. The Burman team tried again a few years later with the soundtrack
to *Shalimar* (1977). Unlike *Sholay,* in which a host of discrete monaural
tracks were mixed as stereo in London, Burman and his team recorded the
Shalimar songs in stereo at his usual studio, Film Centre. Ashok Shukla,
another FTII graduate, joined Film Centre just as the recording sessions for
Shalimar began:

> Ashok Shukla: The day I joined, they were recording background for *Shali-
> mar.* Stereo was new to us, but Mr. R. D. Burman was always trying new
> things. That stereo recording took a lot of time and effort. Technically we
> were not prepared. We were not sure how any of it would sound or where
> to put the mics or where to put the musicians. We never thought. Pancham
> just said, "Let's do this," and we all said, "Okay, let's give it a try."

As one might imagine, the problems were considerable, as a close listen
to the *Shalimar* soundtrack reveals. At the time, the novelty of the situation
affected both technicians and musicians. The latter had to play without any
monitors or audible cues, a situation for which they were completely un-
prepared:

> Ashok Shukla: There was no fallback [i.e., headphone monitors for the
> musicians]. You had 100 or 120 musicians, and they had to be coordinated
> by watching the conductor very carefully.

As a result of these experiences, musicians started wearing headphones in the studio, although these were initially unwelcome:

ASHOK SHUKLA: Once we realized that stereo and better sound and more tracks were going to be the future, we started improving and bought the equipment to provide everyone with fallback on headphones. The musicians didn't like this at first and took some time to be able to play with headphones. That took us until about 1981 or '02.

These two Burman soundtracks are the exceptions that made the limits of everyday possibility much more real:

AVINASH OAK: *Sholay* was one of a kind and very much ahead of its time. After that again there was nothing happening on the multitrack side.

Ten or fifteen years later stereo reappeared on film soundtracks right before the 1990s' shift to digital technology:

AVINASH OAK: They jumped directly from that one 70 mm film to suddenly Dolby digital. But you can say after about fifteen years they jumped. But in between, these stereo things were very rare.

Indeed, many of the practices and patterns established in earlier years persevered through the early 1990s. Live recordings of large ensembles were more common than any other practice, 35 mm tape remained the dominant medium for much of this period, and, from the musicians' perspective, the life of music in Mumbai studios seemed a permanent condition. Nevertheless, from the late 1980s on, the technology was changing. Throughout the years that Oak specifies, older and newer systems and people were gradually exchanging dominance.

Recording Technology 1985–2005

One of the most consistent comments film musicians make about "the old days" addresses the professional challenges that resulted from the fact that, through the 1980s and even the early '90's in many cases, film-song recordings consisted of complete performances:

RAMESH IYER: I have been where we were playing live, sixty musicians sitting together in one big hall. Playing together, people could not afford to make a mistake. There was just magnetic tape. You make a mistake, you just rewind, "zero pe jao" [go back to zero]. The whole track you had to play again; the playback singer had to sing again. It was very taxing.

The difficulties of editing sound on film were one reason for the standard recording practice that Iyer describes. Taufiq Qureshi, who played side and electronic percussion from the late 1980s on, still felt the pressure, generated in part by the equipment, not to make mistakes in the live-performance environment:

> TAUFIQ QURESHI: We were recording at Mehboob, they had a four-track with those huge heads, and the person used to have to hold the heads and physically put them on the tape. So there had to be a gap, so the heads could be lifted. I still remember we were playing some song, and I made a mistake [toward the end], so we had to go back. I felt very bad about that. I was so embarrassed. There was no gap in the music, so we couldn't punch it. We had to go back.

Later I discuss in detail the concept of punching; briefly the term derives from modern digital practice and refers to using two different recordings of the same song to compile a single, complete version. Qureshi's use of the term is somewhat premature for the late 1980s.

After India's prime minister Indira Gandhi was assassinated in 1984, she was replaced by her son, Rajiv Gandhi, who continued in that role for most of the years between 1985 and his own assassination in 1991. During his time in power, the younger Gandhi made the first serious efforts to dismantle the entire "license Raj," which had been established by his grandfather Jawaharlal Nehru and maintained by his mother. For film musicians and recordists, this meant a gradual easing of the restrictions on foreign imports and technology. Trumpeter Joe Monsorate was one of the growing number of musicians who were aware that Mumbai's recording technology was increasingly old fashioned:

> JOE MONSORATE: We were very much behind the time. I was in London in 1980, and I saw some recording at BBC, and there, if somebody cracked a note or something, they could punch it, but here, because our machines were not so modern, if there was any mistake, we had to stop and start all over.

In contrast to the relatively stable years through the early 1980s, the years from the mid-1980s on were characterized by increasingly rapid changes, enacted first in one studio and then another, using many different recording systems and formats. While the older studios held out as long as possible in many cases by using the older formats or making relatively superficial modifications, the mid-1980s marked the beginning of a marked increase in the number of studios and a gradual breakdown of the structural division between film and nonfilm recording methods and facilities.

Much of the change was driven by a younger generation of technicians who had excellent educations and expectations heightened by a global perspective. Bishwadeep Chatterjee came to Mumbai in 1987, just as India was taking its first tentative steps toward economic liberalization. Like many of his colleagues, Chatterjee had the advantage of a strong technical education and a broad perspective on the workings of the film-music industry and its place in Indian culture. He and others who realized that the limits of the possible had shifted began to agitate for change:

> BISHWADEEP CHATTERJEE: When our whole generation landed up here [Mumbai], we kind of realized that the whole thing was like that [technologically old fashioned]. The stuff from the West was always the thing, you know, but there was no explanation really as to why we couldn't have that stuff. So finally common sense came in, and we started having our way. And things started changing.

In the mid-1980s things indeed started to change. Programmable synthesizers were one new development that initially altered much about the recording process. Prakash Varma, who has worked as an arranger since the late 1980s, found that they eventually affected composition and arranging as well:

> PRAKASH VARMA: We used to program the song on the keyboard, the song, the harmony, the music, the rhythm, everything, and then dub that onto 35 mm tape, and then run the tape, play it back on the "can" [headphones], and the orchestra would play with that. Then we do a rhythm call and take eight to ten tracks and make a rough balance.

The new machines thus began to break down the "everyone together playing live" model of recording, although, as Varma points out, the early stages of that process made a rather basic division between the melodic instruments (the orchestra) and the rhythm, or percussion, section.

New recording studios installed new, multitrack recording and editing machines rather than the 35 mm, single-track machines made by RCA and Westrex. What was apparently Mumbai's first digital recording system, a two-track machine reportedly made by Mitsubishi, appeared in 1989. A number of major challenges remained as the various systems were gradually modified.

"Track Tuning"

One challenge that affected musicians directly arose as dubbing—as musicians call it—became more common and recordings began to be made in stereo in the late 1980s. Unlike previous "track recording," which normally recorded most or all of the orchestra together (but on separate tracks), stereo recording (and most of the new recording systems, which were being modeled on the those in the West) recorded the orchestra in separate sections: first the rhythm, then the violins, then the cellos, then the solos, and so forth. The machines on which these recordings were made, however, had motors that ran at whatever frequency was inherent in the alternating electrical current in the Mumbai power lines. When track recording began in earnest, musicians discovered that the theoretically consistent frequency of 50 Hertz in those lines actually varied significantly:

> VIJU SHAH: In Film Centre and Mehboob, as well as Bombay Labs, when we recorded the rhythm track in the morning we'd be running at 48.5 Hertz; then when we recorded in the afternoon, say the *santūr* [hammered zither] is coming, then it would be 49.5.

The resulting difficulties were significant. As a guitarist (and one who often played twelve-string guitar at that), Sunil Kaushik felt the results quite acutely:

> SUNIL KAUSHIK: There was a fluctuation in power. It was supposed to be 440 [cycles per second] always, but the speed of the tapes used to vary. So say we had recorded in the daytime, and we had recorded in 440. By the time I came to play solos and different things, it might have gone down to 449 or 448. Then tuning problems, very much! If I have tuned to 440, imagine! Now I have to retune the whole twelve-string. Imagine tuning the whole thing! I used to curse and curse! And by the time I had retuned to 449, maybe the power is back up, and things are running faster again. So again tuning. So those were really tough days, I tell you.

While Shah explains in terms of electrical frequency, Kaushik's explanation (given in more practical—for him—terms of pitch frequency rather than Hertz) appears counterintuitive (i.e., the power going "down" from 440 cps to 449 cps).

Odd as it is, however, Kaushik's way of conceptualizing the problem reveals the intensely pragmatic attitude that he and most of his colleagues brought to any problem. When the recorders were running slow, the musicians would have to tune their instruments higher so that their sharp tuning, recorded on the now-slow machines, would compensate enough to match the tracks recorded when the machines were running faster, which are now sharp. Thus, in their thinking, higher electrical Hertz translated as lower pitch, and tuning up from A440 to A446 meant going down. What is equally remarkable is that there was no way other than trial and error to work out how much compensation was necessary:

> SUNIL KAUSHIK: We used to anticipate. I can't really explain, but usually we were right. See, Film Centre was in a residential area, so if it's the evening time, after six o'clock, the AC, lights, and other home gadgets would start, and the frequency would become 446 or something.

As Viju Shah recalls, it took a few recordings to figure out what was going on:

> VIJU SHAH: We couldn't figure out what was the problem. So what we did first was, we started taking a tone. I had a tuning meter, a Korg, and I used to play that, and we would see that the A was really 444, not 440. That means the tape is running fast. I said, "How come it's like this if we recorded at 440?" Next morning I check again, it's showing 440 again. So then we discovered that this was the mains [utility distribution system]. It took us about two songs.

The solution was to find ways to provide a consistent energy source for the recording machines. Mehboob Studios' chief recordist, A. N. Tagore, bought a diesel generator to provide power during recording sessions:

> A. N. TAGORE: Track tuning came, but that was only for a short period. Then we put one generator in place and used that for the electricity, and then there was no problem.

Film Centre took a different approach. This was where Kalyanji-Anandji (assisted by Kalyanji's son, Viju) did their recording. He pressured the studio owners for a solution that was finally implemented in 1989:

> VIJU SHAH: We were all getting fed up; you would never know whether it was going right or not. I said, "There has to be some solution for this, or we cannot go ahead with stereo recording." So Film Centre got this unit called UPS [universal power supply], so they could generate continuous voltage.

Film Centre solved the track tuning problem in 1989, by which time the problem had been making itself heard in film scores since at least 1985. The difficulty also made for longer recording sessions:

> VIJU SHAH: I was recording as a musician on one song for *Meri Jung* [1985] with L-P. And that song recording went on for five days. I knew everything was going berserk because then Mehboob [where Laxmikant-Pyarelal always recorded] did not yet have that generator. And the trumpets were coming flat, and it was a big mess. I used to have four or five keyboards, and when you have to retune all that all the time, it's too much. I think a lot of songs were recorded wrongly also because you get fatigued, you just can't judge what is happening.

Indeed, the tuning in some of the songs on *Meri Jung* does show the strains of this situation.

New Recording Studios

Track tuning highlighted the disparity between the old technology and the old practices on one hand and the newer technologies and practices on the other. Famous (Tardeo) also invested in a generator, but it appears that Bombay Labs never solved the tuning dilemma. Kersi Lord reports that by the 1980s, recordings at Bombay Labs had largely ceased in any event. However, while the old studios had been coping with the track tuning problem, new ones were being built that avoided the problem altogether.

In the late 1970s and early '80s, the practice called dubbing, which separated the recording of action and dialogue by filming scenes and then rerecording the dialogue, became widespread. A number of dubbing theaters, as they were called, sprang up in the city to accommodate the new practice. Some of these also became music recording studios. Suresh Kathuria was involved in these new developments, supervising the technical construction of a new dubbing studio in Khar, one of Mumbai's western suburbs, called Ajit Recording.

Later in the 1980s Ajit Recording was purchased by Gulshan Kumar, the highly successful and controversial owner of the cassette company Super Cassettes and its primary label, T-Series. Renaming the Khar facility Sudeep Studio, Kumar installed what was by all accounts India's first two-inch, twenty-four-track recorder. Sudeep became an important new music facility as T-Series used its new investments in recording and cassette-production equipment (as well as its new business practices) to overcome HMV's lingering monopoly in the recording industry. Satish Gupta was an FTII graduate who began his recording career in 1971 as an assistant to B. N. Sharma at Bombay Sound. He emphasizes that Sudeep Studios was initially considered a nonfilm facility:

> SATISH GUPTA: That was for music; it wasn't for films. Because the producers used to be very afraid [that] if you record on two-inch and, after mixing onto Nagra, you might get out-synch problem.

What Mumbai's film producers apparently did not realize at first was that the Studer machines in Ajit/Sudeep had crystal motors. When the industry eventually caught on, Sudeep became the center of a new kind of recording:

> ASHOK SHUKLA: When we built Sudeep, T-Series bought equipment like crazy. Everything had crystal motors: the projectors, the recorders, the dubbers, everything. That started in 1989 and went on until 1994 or '95. We did *Qayamat Se Qayamat Tak* [1988] at Film Centre, but *Aashiqui* [1990] and *Betaa* [1992] we did at Sudeep.

At that time, I bought two Studer eight-track, one-inch machines, and I could lock them together, so I had sixteen tracks if I wanted them. And then I would mix those tracks down to 35 mm or whatever was necessary. Everything had crystal motors there. So I could actually punch; there was no problem for pitch or anything. By 1994 or '95 even the projectors had crystal motors, so we could punch background.

Punching refers to the practice of taking a recorded phrase and copying it to produce an ongoing repetitive phrase or splicing it to another recorded phrase. From the late 1980s, the term and the practice, until then relatively unfamiliar, became very important for Mumbai's film musicians. As long as pitch can be controlled and synchronicity maintained, punching saves time and effectively obviates the necessity of recording whole songs in single takes, which had existed until this time.

While these changes were taking place in Khar, Suresh Kathuria had begun another building project farther north in Juhu. Sunny Super Sound also had new recording machines with crystal motors, although these were 35 mm machines:

VIJU SHAH: When Sunny came in, they had that Sondor machine that was crystal controlled, so they didn't have any problem. I worked a lot with [music directors] Nadeem-Shravan, and they were at Sunny. I was playing for them as a musician, harmonium and all that. But that was only possible at Sunny. You couldn't record harmonium at Film Centre because you can't change the pitch. So when we were doing tracks in that time, you couldn't record harmonium.

Sunny was still recording on 35 mm tape at the end of the 1980s, which meant a great deal of dubbing:

SURESH KATHURIA: We never purchased a twenty-four-track, two-inch recorder. What we were doing was recording four tracks on 35,mm, shift it to dubber, record another four tracks, shift it to another dubber, record another four tracks, and that way we used to go up to fourteen and sixteen tracks.

To avoid the problems with distortion that this system produced, Kathuria pursued the solution called Dolby digital noise reduction:

SURESH KATHURIA: Sunny Super Sound was the first studio in India to introduce active Dolby SR cards even on 35 mm multitrack; that was sometime in 1990.

In the late 1980s and early 1990s the new systems at Sudeep and Sunny and the ease with which music could be recorded there began to take business away from the three remaining old studios. Famous (Tardeo), Film

Centre, and Mehboob continued to operate in the old way, recording on 35 mm noncrystal equipment and mastering to optical film, as Kersi Lord explains. When he uses the plural pronoun, he refers to Film Centre, where he did much of his later recording:

> KERSI LORD: We never had Sondor, we had Westrex always. Minoo-baba [Katrak] started with RCA. He had an RCA sound camera at Famous, and we had Westrex sound camera and equipment. Even in the 1990s, when they were recording with Pancham at Film Centre, they were recording on Westrex (six-track).

Deepan Chatterji confirms Lord's description and emphasizes the ongoing conflict between the old system's commitment to optical film and the new sound-recording technologies, which were increasingly available:

> DEEPAN CHATTERJI: Until the late '80s, songs were being transferred onto sound negatives [i.e., optical film], and after the final mix, the song that was sitting on the final negative would be removed, and the footage of the negative would be replaced. Say you have a reel, and there's an acting scene, and there's a song, and then there's another scene. The full reel has been mixed: dialogue, effects, background, the song also. But the song sitting on the final negative is a couple of generations down in quality. So to get back the original quality, the original sound negative would be replaced. And for the final release print it would be printed again. This practice happened until 1986 or '87; even *1942: A Love Story* [1993] was done in this way, from 35 mm, six-track tape to optical.

Until the early 1990s and despite the advances in technology, the majority of the film-music industry remained committed to 35 mm mono tape and the older studios that had been built in the 1950s. Bishwadeep Chatterjee suggests this was largely due to cultural inertia and the prestige of large orchestras and recording spaces:

> BISHWADEEP CHATTERJEE: I came to Bombay around 1987, when these old Westrex and RCA machines were being phased out. But the big studios like Mehboob and all those places still had that RCA and all that. They moved out of optical and got into magnetic, but many of the details were still the same. I think it was largely due to ignorance and not a technical thing. When they changed to 35 mm, nothing else had changed; only the medium of recording had changed. The rest of the infrastructure was pretty much the same setup. So they didn't have a system of playing back and monitoring and these things.

Until Mehboob closed, A. N. Tagore remained its chief recordist. He reinforces the reluctance for change at the older facilities that Chatterjee describes:

A. N. TAGORE: At last we changed over to digital recording, thirty-two track. But that was very late, 1997. That was too late, you can say. The last film we did, *Hello Brother* [1999], was recorded in digital, and the background in Dolby digital and also *Hum Saath Saath Hai* [1999].

In the late 1990s Bishwadeep Chatterjee participated in the construction of Spectral Harmony, a twenty-four-track Dolby studio. Although it was still initially conceptualized as a nonfilm studio, the potential of the technology at Spectral Harmony helped Chatterjee demonstrate that the constraints of the old system had indeed been lifted:

BISHWADEEP CHATTERJEE: I remember in 1994 or so. There was this myth that you need a big, big studio because you had to have the huge film sound. Then that slowly broke up. When I set up Spectral Harmony I could show them, "This is how it can be. You don't have to have a really big space. The size of the studio will be small, but the sound will be big." This was 1996 or '97.

Digital Technology and "Punching"

The conversion of sound into digital (instead of analogue) information began to be a reality in the Mumbai film industry in the early 1990s, but as usual there were various responses:

BISHWADEEP CHATTERJEE: The film studios went from 35 mm onto Hi-8 to an extent and then to hard-disc recorders, the Fairlights and those things.

Hard-disc recording systems were dedicated recording, editing, and mixing consoles that stored recorded sound on hard drives. These were quickly followed by computer and, most important, home-computer, software-driven recording systems. Ashok Shukla was an early enthusiast:

ASHOK SHUKLA: In 1991 or '92 I saw this Pro Tools at Sonic Solutions, so I brought that system back here. At first everyone thought I was crazy. Even Suresh Kathuria told me I was mad, but gradually after that, people started using it.

In 1993 Shukla had been struggling with the difficulties that remained in securing suitable computers to run Pro Tools, but that would also change (see chapter 5). Gradually the nature of composition and recording shifted from the keyboard-and-notation model that had been the norm for many years. Keyboards were now attached to computers that recorded the music as sound and could be directly transferred to another computer. Instead of recording sounds, some engineers found they were simply managing the transfer of data from a home-computerized recording or composition program to the studio's system. When computer software programs became a permanent and dominant feature of Mumbai's music culture, the distinctions among composing, arranging, and recording blurred significantly (see chapter 7). Avinash Oak, however, gives some insight into the changing roles:

> AVINASH OAK: They do all the programming and things at home. Now they come with a Nuendo [a music-composition software program] session, open up the session here, and edit it. Or they come here and record all the acoustic instruments; then they go home with the files and mix at home. So there's an integration of the home studios and the professional studios, but it's causing the studios to go also for Nuendo.

Oak reports a phenomenon that is part of a global trend. In effect, the film-music business in Mumbai is technologically indistinguishable from any other such system in the world:

> BISHWADEEP CHATTERJEE: Today it's different; we're like everywhere else. People started realizing that you had to have quality and that quality translated very well.

Younger engineers such as Chatterjee take considerable pride in the now accurate claim that the Mumbai studios are "like everywhere else." They have played a major role in realizing that goal, which has come about only in the past few years.

For film musicians, however, digital technology had an enormous and not necessarily positive impact. By the early years of the twenty-first century, mastering to optical film had ceased completely, and technological change had forced the closure of Famous, Film Centre, and Mehboob. Attempts to change to the new systems came too late; the buildings were too old, and the necessary infrastructural changes too costly. Film recording moved to new, smaller recording studios such as Sudeep, Sunny, Empire Studio (built in Andheri in 1997–1998; figure 2.3), Krishna (still farther north in Kandivali in 2002), and Blue Diamond (also built in the early twenty-first century in Juhu).

In addition to new spaces, musicians had to get used to unfamiliar ways of playing and recording. Punching became widespread throughout the industry. Digital information could be copied, repeated, and altered with ease. Correcting pitch became a matter of postrecording adjustment. The last vestiges of the live recording practice, in which the whole orchestra sat together, disappeared:

> JOE PINTO: The small guys were dubbing in the early 1990s. It would be the violin section only. Even L-P by 1994–95, they would just have the violins in to dub.

Figure 2.3   Ashok Shukla (2007) in the control room of Empire Studio, which he designed. The original twenty-four-track tape machine is in the center against the far wall, now replaced by the digital recording and mixing console at which Shukla stares with bemusement.

Most musicians reacted badly to dubbing, recording a song section by section, part by part. They disliked the impact dubbing had on their in comes (chapter 6) and also missed the collective music making that the older system had entailed. Dubbing decontextualized everyone's parts, even those of the star vocalists:

> AVINASH OAK: When we first had Asha Bhosle in, we said, "You can just dub this one part that's missing." But she said, "How can I just start right there? I cannot straightaway go to that place and start singing. I'll sing from the beginning, you play me from the beginning, you punch whatever whenever you want." So she wanted to sing the whole song from the beginning. But after a while she began to understand, and now she's okay about that.

Musicians had less say in the matter than singers and have learned to live with dubbing and with "click tracks," but there is a general mourning for the social and musical pleasures of the old system:

> TAPPAN ADHIKHARI: Before we used to sit together. The singer would be there also, and we played. We wore headphones and could hear them singing. Now it's all this punching.

Musicians also objected to the compulsory "click track" in the modern recording process:

> SURESH YADHAV: The click doesn't work for our Indian style of music. If the click is there and you're out of click, then it's no good. But the Indian beauty is in the feel of the rhythm as they accompany the voice. If the click is there, it isn't flexible any more. It kills the beauty.

Ironically, Ernest Menezes, one of Mumbai's most respected violinists, argues that the new technology actually demanded higher standards of musicianship and simultaneously cost people their jobs:

> ERNEST MENEZES: Now the technology has overtaken us. Just like in those days there used to be thirty or forty violins with one mic, now there is one mic for every two people. So the problem is that you have to keep pace. So you have to keep practicing. But in those days they used to call forty violins. Today they call eight or twelve or maybe sixteen violins, but that's all.

The new technology also allows recording engineers to "double track"—record the same eight or sixteen violins on two different tracks simultaneously. This practice is more a matter of economic than musical concern and is discussed in chapter 6.

3

Changing Structures in the Mumbai Film Industry

In the preceding chapters I have outlined some of the technological issues regarding playback and later developments in sound-film recording and argued that these constituted the physical limits of possibility, although it is already apparent that those limits were culturally enforced in some instances. In this chapter I develop a historical model in which overlapping cultural and industrial systems, informed by technology and by economic, cultural, and governmental conditions, resulted in changes in film-music production and the exploitation of music for maximum profit. I continue to use the phrase that builds on Ashish Virmani's quite casual (and noncapitalized) Old Bollywood. "Bollywood" is a contentious, if currently fashionable, term in film studies and popular journalism. Prasad (2003) has examined the term's history, tensions, and meanings and noted the extent to which it facilitates the essentialization of all Indian cinema. The term also tends to highlight, if not exacerbate, the historiographic tensions inherent in the periodization of cultural history and those between popular journalism's casual acceptance of the term and Indian scholarship's problematization of it. This is not the forum for an extended discussion of the term; I use it here only as a name for two specific historical periods and the systems of film and music production that defined them.

I suggest that three rough historical periods emerge from the gradual and seamless process of change in the Mumbai film industry: the Studio Period (1935–1950), Old Bollywood (1950–1998), and New Bollywood (1998–). In doing so, I ignore the first four years of sound-film production, during which sound and image were simultaneously recorded. I also locate transitions at the end of earlier periods rather than at the beginning of later ones.

Earlier research on Hindi films and film music has adopted a range of periodic structures. Writing during the latter years of Old Bollywood, Skillman (1986) notes the importance of synchronous sound recording as a landmark event but proposes two subsequent historical periods: "the formula" (1940s and '50s) and "the trend" (1960s and '70s). Only a few years later, Arnold (1991) organized her study of film song around three major overlapping transitions: from silent to sound films (1930s), from simultaneous recording to playback (1930–1940s), and from the studio system to independent production (1940s). She followed this with a vague post-Independence period (1948–1950s), roughly the first five to ten years of Old Bollywood. A final chapter summarized events since 1955 but offered no theoretical rationale for 1955 as a significant marker of historical difference. Most of Arnold's study focused on aspects of cultural and stylistic transition in the ten or more years that it took for the industrial and cultural responses to synchronous optical dubbers to crystallize into the playback system.

Manuel referred in passing to "the film era" (1993, 54) but largely avoided the pitfalls of periodization. The only chronologic distinctions he made were based first on the dominance of film music and second on the advent of cassettes in South Asia. By the early 1940s, he suggests, "Film music had come to be the predominant popular-music idiom in India, and remained virtually unchallenged in that capacity until the advent of cassettes in the late 1970s" (ibid., 41). In fact, the challenge to film music was minimal; the introduction of cassettes and the new cassette companies led directly to a period of enormous prosperity for the film-music industry.

Writing as both fan and amateur historian, Premchand uses personal preference as the basis of his periodization and states that between 1947 and 1970 "Words, tunes, playback and sound techniques came together in an exceptional, never-to-be-repeated manner" (Premchand 2003, 7). Despite his personalized justification, Premchand clearly defines the period dominated by the first generation of Old Bollywood music directors (e.g., Shankar-Jaikishan, S. D. Burman, O. P. Nayyar, Naushad, Roshan) while de-emphasizing the generation that succeeded them, including much of the work of Kalyanji-Anandji, R. D. Burman, Laxmikant-Pyarelal, and so on, whose careers continued to the end of the Old Bollywood period. Although Ashish Rajadhyaksha resists the temptations of periodization as such, he suggests that "the film industry in India assumed something like its current form" during almost the same years (1946–1975) that Premchand prefers (Rajadhyaksha 2004, 120).

Upperstall, a website that offers one of the Internet's more serious critical examinations of Indian cinema, Hindi and otherwise, provides a highly narrativized "Evolution of the Hindi Film Song," which, like Premchand and Arnold, focuses largely on the biographies of film singers and composers. The detailed account is divided into six parts, beginning in 1931 and ending at roughly 1950, although its author, Karan Bali, describes his history as unfinished. As do most scholars, fans, and even casual listeners, the Upperstall account specifies "the golden period of Hindi Film Music [as] the 1950s and 1960s" (Bali n.d.), the core years, one might argue, of Premchand's slightly longer "golden period."

Morcom's recent study is not primarily historical. Nevertheless, in considering developments in orchestration, she proposes that "around 1950, the quantity and scale of background music in Hindi films significantly increased, with many aspects of Hollywood scoring entering Hindi films, such as large symphony-style orchestrations. This is easily traceable to direct Hollywood influence and also to technological advances around 1950 that made the recording of large ensembles more feasible" (2007, 138).

Ashok Ranade (2006) divides the first fifty years of Indian sound film into early (1931–1947) and later (1947–1980) composers, although he concentrates mostly on those who were active at the beginning of his "later" period. Ranade thus focuses roughly on the same composers that other scholars highlight. He groups preplayback composers with those of the Studio Period, however, and stops rather arbitrarily ten or more years before the end of Old Bollywood as I describe it.

The historical shift about which these scholars most clearly agree is the change that took place some time toward the late 1940s or the early 1950s, roughly coinciding with Indian independence. Bali (n.d.) describes the 1940s generally as a period that witnessed "the collapse of the studio system and the freelance system taking over." The late 1940s and early 1950s are "usually seen as a low moment in Indian film history, when a whole range of independent financiers and producers jumped into the fray" (Rajadhyaksha 2004, 126). Arnold additionally differentiates the years after Indian independence, but throughout these studies, most of the attention centers on Bali's "golden period," the first twenty years of Old Bollywood.

Ashish Virmani also sees a clear break during the late 1940s. He is the only writer who offers the chronologic perspective necessary to suggest a realistic end to the period that all agree began around 1947. "The old days," he suggests, persisted in some parts of the film industry "as recently as 2002" (Virmani 2004, 77). It is a distinctive feature of Virmani's chronology that he defines these periods largely in terms of industrial structure rather than musical style or technological change, but as Braudel (1984, see introduction) argues, each area changed at its own pace.

Figure 3.1 Musicians warming up on the main sound stage at the newly completed Yash Raj Studios (2007).

By 1998, life had changed for musicians. What is more, the two defining music directors whose careers had been perpetuating the practices and styles of late Old Bollywood—R. D. Burman (who died in 1994) and, even more important, Laxmikant-Pyarelal (Laxmikant died in 1998)—were effectively inactive by that point. Sometime near the end of the twentieth century the cumulative changes in sound-film technology seem to have co-alesced as the film industry finally abandoned optical film as its defining reality. As the following chapters show, sometime in the mid-1990s certain musicians began to recognize or accept that things were changing for good.

It may be ironic in this regard that 2005 saw the opening of Mumbai's first new producing studio in approximately fifty years. Yash Chopra's Yash Raj Studios contains six recording theaters, a recording studio large enough for a full orchestra (figure 3.1), and all of the necessary postproduction facilities. Chopra describes the new studio as "a project of a dream, a thing which I have not had for all these years as a producer." However, he also admits the risk of such an investment: "It may not be a viable proposition." Viable or otherwise, Chopra's enterprise embodies the changes in business attitudes (regarding distribution, copyrights, budgets, etc.) and in technology (a fully digital, world-class studio) that define New Bollywood.

The Studio Period

In the 1920s, Indian filmmakers began organizing film production following the industrial patterns of the West. The earliest companies—Madan Theatres, Wadia Movietone, Imperial, Bharat Movietone, and so on—were privately owned, vertically integrated commercial enterprises that invested in the physical and technical facilities (e.g., studios for filming, costumes, cameras, lights, microphones) and human resources (e.g., scriptwriters, actors, composers, musicians, directors, technicians) necessary for film production. Some established private distribution structures as well. Following models in the United States and Britain, as Raina (1983) suggests, these were film factories in structure and practice, as well as name. Mumbai and Kolkata were home to more than 90 percent of these film factories. Many produced multiple films per year and managed their profit and loss as a cumulative result of the sale of their many products, hoping to outweigh the negative consequences of any flops with the profits derived from hits. This characterization of industry no doubt appears simplistic and quite unnecessary, but it has significant comparative implications later.

From 1931 on, the larger studios employed musicians as part of their salaried staff. The size of the musical establishment varied, but the practice was standard. Vistasp Balsara worked as a keyboard player, arranger, and conductor at Filmistan Studios, which was founded in 1942 as an offshoot of Bombay Talkies. As a salaried employee, he oversaw the work of other musical employees:

> VISTASP BALSARA: Filmistan had fifteen musicians; they were the Filmistan orchestra, you can say. I hired them, and they were on salary. They came every day from ten o'clock to five o'clock, whether there was work or no work. That was a good system.

Anil Biswas, one of the most important music directors of the Studio Period, came to Mumbai from Kolkata late in 1933. He worked as a salaried employee at four different film studios: Eastern Art Syndicate, Sagar Movietone, National Studio, and finally Bombay Talkies:

> ANIL BISWAS: For quite some time, until I was in Bombay Talkies, studios used to maintain a complete coterie of musicians [on salary] along with the music director. There was no freelancing at that time or [at] least not very much. All the good ones [musicians] were cornered by the big studios.

Biswas was working as a music assistant and later as a composer in these studios; he left Bombay Talkies, his last studio job, in 1946.

Like musicians, composers were sometimes salaried, but others worked on a more itinerant basis, contracting to act as music directors for a fixed number of films with a series of different studios. Ghulam Haider was apparently traded between Mehboob Khan, who established Mehboob Productions, and S. Mukherjee, the cofounder of Filmistan:

> VISTASP BALSARA: Ghualm Haider had come [to Filmistan] from Mehboob to make *Humayun* [1945]. Mr. S. Mukherjee took Ghulam Haider as a loan from Mehboob-saheb for two pictures. Ghulam Haider normally used to direct four pictures at a time in Bombay.

Haider (who was Sindhi by birth) was working in both Mumbai and Lahore in this prepartition period, when such travel was not a politicized process. Balsara is listed in *Humayun*'s credits as the music assistant (see chapter 5). He also acted as a source of continuity by connecting visiting composers like Haider to the studio's infrastructure. Salaried musicians such as Balsara provided music and support for whichever composer had been hired to work on the film of the moment:

> VISTASP BALSARA: In Filmistan I was the permanent orchestra leader, but the picture director and maybe the scriptwriter would decide about the music director. Whoever would come to Filmistan for music direction, I would be his assistant.

Both Balsara and Biswas (despite his earlier comments) recognized that not "all the good ones" (musicians, that is) were employed by studios. The alternative to working on salary is *freelancing*. Three early and important freelance musicians were cellist Alfonso Albuquerque, saxophone player Ram Singh, and violinist and guitarist Peter Sequeira, who were collectively known by the initials of their first names as "A-R-P." In addition to their performing skills and other significant contributions to early film scores, A-R-P also acted as orchestral brokers by organizing other musicians to perform in the small orchestras of the period. [🔊 Video 3.1]

> ERNEST MENEZES: Mr. Albuquerque started working in the film industry much before partition [1947]. His group was the A-R-P party. They used to call the other musicians and manage it so that everyone would come to the right place at the required time.

Thus, studio orchestras were often reinforced by freelancers or musicians working directly with freelance music directors. In his earlier comments, Anil Biswas seems to suggest that by the time he had reached Bombay Talkies, salaried jobs for musicians were gradually becoming less common. Salaried positions in studio orchestras indeed decreased gradually in the 1940s, but some persisted into the 1950s. J. V. Acharya came from Bangalore to work on salary as a sitar player at Bombay Talkies in 1937. Thirteen years later Acharya, after a stint on salary at HMV and some freelance work with music director Vasant Desai, returned to salaried studio work in 1950:

> J. V. ACHARYA: I joined Raj Kamal Studio. I was a staff artist there. They paid me two hundred rupees per month. But being a music staff artist, I had to work with whoever would come.

Acharya remained in that position until 1954, when he joined composer C. Ramchandra at A. R. Kardar's studio, but began freelance work two years later.

Studio Investments

The fact that both sound and image were recorded on the same medium (celluloid film) may have produced poor-quality sound recordings, but it saved studios from having to invest in two different sets of technology. The sound camera was a multipurpose tool, used separately for recording both image and sound. That separation was a matter of time, however, not space; there were no dedicated music-recording studios in the film industry of the 1940s:

> KERSI LORD: There were no recording studios when I joined the line in late 1947 or '48. We had to record in the shooting sheds, which meant we had to put some blankets or cloth [on the walls] to help the acoustics.

The acoustics in these studio spaces were not always ideal, as Lord points out, and they had other drawbacks as well. Vistasp Balsara regretted the disadvantages of the metal roofing that covered some of the shooting studios in the late 1930s, especially during Mumbai's monsoon season:

> VISTASP BALSARA: They used to record on the shooting floors themselves at that time. We used to have to stop when it rained because of the noise.

Despite their drawbacks, the shooting floors were actually an improvement over the earliest recording spaces for film music, especially background music. Cawas Lord played percussion in some of India's earliest sound films, working for Adeshir Irani's Imperial Movietone studios in the early 1930s:

> CAWAS LORD: In those days, the recording used to happen in the open air. We used to wait for the trains to go by. In the night we recorded, especially background music.

Like other early musicians, Lord grew used to playing all night when the noise of the city had died down. Even though Naushad Ali's first job as a composer of background music was some years later, he faced similar problems:

> NAUSHAD ALI: They were making a picture, *Prem Nagar* [1940], and they gave me a chance in that picture to give the songs and also the background music. We recorded all the songs in one night at the Siri Sound compound [in Dadar]. There were no facilities with suitable acoustic treatment that were big enough, so we recorded in gardens at night. After ten o'clock the traffic would stop and we would record. Around six o'clock or seven o'clock [in the morning] the traffic would start again, and we would stop.

Recording studios—that is, permanent spaces with suitable acoustic treatment and permanently installed recording equipment—appeared in the early 1950s. They appeared, however, not as additions to the infrastructures of producing film studios but apparently as afterthoughts to newly built film-processing laboratories.

The Decline of the Studio System

Film studios in Kolkata may have had an early lead in the production and distribution of films (as Madan Theatres did) or in the technology of playback (New Theatres), but Kolkata's studios and films were outnumbered by Mumbai's increasing dominance of Hindi film production and its high output of films in general. This was clear in 1936, when playback became the dominant song-production model, and it became increasingly apparent as the 1930s and '40s went on. Of the 120 films produced in Mumbai and

Kolkata in 1936, 72 percent were created by a Mumbai studio; ten years later Mumbai was producing 98 percent of all Hindi films. The city's dominance was virtually complete and unequivocally permanent. Mumbai was thus the only place where workers in that industry could be assured of a reasonable income.

Clarinetist Devi Lal Varma was one of many musicians who began their careers in Lahore's film industry, where Hindi films were also being made, as his son, Prakash Varma explains:

> PRAKASH VARMA: Daddy joined the line in 1936, but he joined at Lahore, at Pancholi Studios. He migrated to Bombay in 1944. He came on his own and went from door to door. In those days, there were film companies, and they used to give salary. So my daddy joined Chitramandir as a salaried musician.

Pancholi was the most important producing studio in prepartition Lahore and often employed composer Ghulam Haider.

Figure 3.2 shows a young Devi Lal Varma outside the gates of Chitramandir studios with his friend, guitarist Hazara Singh, who moved from Bombay Talkies about the same time. Singh went on to work on salary at Ranjit Movietone until approximately 1955, as his son explains:

> THAKUR SINGH: My father worked on salary at Bombay Talkies with [music director] Khemchand Prakash. Later he also worked at Ranjit Studios; that was in the 1950s.

Another salaried musician at Ranjit in the early 1950s was a young violinist named Pyarelal Sharma. As he reflects on this early experience with the benefit of his enormous professional hindsight, Sharma distinguishes between the studio system and the procedure that was later adopted in Old Bollywood:

> PYARELAL SHARMA: I joined Ranjit in 1952; I was only twelve years old, but I was getting a salary like everyone else. They paid me fifty-seven rupees per month and later that became eighty-nine rupees. *Rajdhani* [1956] was the first movie I played for. There were three studios all close together: Ranjit (where I worked), Siri Sound, and Rang Mahal. Every day we went there from ten to five. It was different then; everyone was on salary: Dilip Kumar, Raj Kapoor [star actors], everyone. Heroines, side characters, villains, music directors, musicians, lyricists, they would get five hundred rupees, five thousand rupees, something. The producers were real and they had empires. Chandulal Shah, Sohrab Modi, Mehboob, they did the sets; they did the recordings, everything.

The 1940s were years of increasing political tension in South Asia, as agitation for independence intensified. The political struggle, the aftermath

Figure 3.2
Salaried musicians
Devi Lal Varma (left)
and Hazara Singh
outside the gates of
their employer,
Chitramandir Studios,
ca. 1945. Courtesy of
Prakash Varma.

of the Great Depression, the Bengal famine, and World War II all had an impact on film production and content. "Film productions were 'licensed.' A maximum length of 11,000 feet was imposed. . . . The inordinate number of songs that had gone up to nineteen and twenty came down to five or six" (Abbas 1985, 239). The wartime shortages and regulations surrounding access to film stock were lifted briefly after the war, but were reimposed in 1948 by a newly independent but impoverished Indian government due to "the limited availability of foreign exchange" (Dayal 1983, 55).

From 1935 to 1948 the Mumbai industry averaged 112 releases per year, but the number varied greatly—from 73 films (in the war years 1941 and 1945) to an exceptional 183 in 1947. The biggest single-year increase occurred between 1945 and 1946, when production more than doubled to

155 films. In 1947, one of the last good years for the producing studios, the three most prolific (Ranjit, Mohan, and Filmistan) produced 18 films among them. Overall, 1946 through 1949 were enormously productive years for the Hindi cinema; output reached heights that would not be matched for forty years.

Figure 3.3 shows the importance of the Indian producing studio in the production of Hindi films. The relatively low percentage of producers (56 percent) relative to the huge spike in film production stands out in 1947. In other words, more films were being turned out by fewer producers; in the usual way of corporate capitalism, the big were getting bigger. Despite the apparent success of the studios in 1947, ten years later the number of producers had climbed to 72 percent of films; after another five years, the ratio of producers to films had reached 99 percent. It has rarely dipped below 90 percent since that year.

A number of factors are responsible for the decline of the producing studios after partition. The "falling value of the rupee and the escalation of Mumbai land prices" made the maintenance of a studio's infrastructural investment more burdensome than it had been (Kaur 2004, 169). Hindi films and their music, explicitly hybrid forms, were viewed quite negatively by early Indian governments, who taxed both producers and consumers excessively, as even I. K. Gujral (minister of Information and Broadcasting, 1969–1971 and 1972–1975) has agreed (Gujral 1985). In addition, during and after World War II, Mumbai was awash in money earned illegally by profiteers who had benefited from the wartime shortages. The war "brought sudden wealth to speculators and black marketeers. This was not legal money that could be officially declared or openly invested—except in film where no concrete proof of the amount invested is required" (Dayal 1983, 55). As the Indian government sought to control its foreign debt by severely limiting the exchange of Indian rupees and the importation of foreign goods, wartime profiteering was replaced by various forms of smuggling and other criminal activity. Bhanu Gupta explains how the film musicians participated in this "laundering" process:

> BHANU GUPTA: The moment the song is recorded, everybody is paid, but white money only.

"White" and "black" are the terms used in Mumbai to differentiate between legally and illegally acquired funds. "Black money helped financiers [i.e., producers] to do competitive buying of stars whose prices soon skyrocketed from rupees 50,000 to rupees 500,000" (Abbas 1985, 240). As Gupta notes, regardless of the category to which money belonged, once the musicians were paid and once they declared it on their income taxes, it automatically became "white":

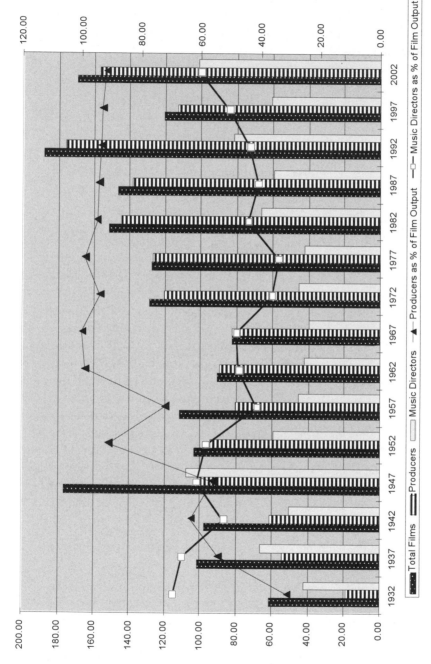

Figure 3.3 The Mumbai film industry: total films, film producers, and music directors, with producers and music directors shown as percentages of total films produced. (Compiled from information listed in Chatterjee 1991, and Singh 1980, 1984, 1986, and 1988.)

BHANU GUPTA: The moment you sign for it, it becomes white. We didn't know where it came from. But we have to give [account of it] to our lawyers, for taxes, that this is the production we got our money from. So wherever the money came from, that was not my business. I had to prove from where I received it.

Investment in filmmaking came to be recognized as a relatively convenient means of transforming illegal into legal income and remained so until the early 1990s.

Finally, the emerging "star system" contributed to the decline of the producing studios. As Pyarelal Sharma stated earlier, in the 1930s and '40s salaried employment was the norm. Actors, composers, and most others involved in filmmaking worked for a studio, and most of them went to work every day "whether there was work or no work" as Balsara has described it. "Actors who worked for a monthly salary, like Nargis, who got rupees 35,0000 for her role in *Andaaz* . . . now started to work for independent filmmakers" (Kaur 2004, 169) and found they could negotiate much higher fees on a film-by-film basis by pitting producers to bid against each other. The increasingly outrageous financial demands that actors began to impose on film producers was also one of the Indian cinema's two biggest problems (Abbas 1985).

Land prices, high taxes, increasing star fees, and the presence of illegal money may well have been the primary causes of the collapse of the producing studios. In the early 1950s the struggle to survive had already proven too much for some, but the process was gradual. Some continued to exist well after they were economically insolvent: Ranjit Movietone, which had been enormously prolific in the 1930s and '40s, survived as a producing studio into the 1960s, but it was almost alone by that time and had long ceased to be a competitive production unit. As Mumbai filmmakers and musicians worked through the implications of this mid-1950s' collapse, Hazara Singh, Devi Lal Varma, and Pyarelal Sharma were all forced to join the increasing number of musicians who were working freelance.

Unlike the freelance musicians of the 1930s and '40s, however, there was no overarching permanent industrial structure into which a handful of freelance musicians could fit. They were now working with music directors who were themselves freelancers, on contract for producers who were also freelancing and owned no physical infrastructure of their own. These independent producers, as they were called, had relatively few employees and often quite short careers; they rented space and production facilities and contracted all aspects of film production on a film-by-film basis. The infrastructure itself, much of which was built by the last generation of producing studio owners, passed into separate hands, business families who hired out their spaces and facilities. This became the standard model of production in Old Bollywood.

Old Bollywood

Old Bollywood is the period of the independent producer and freelance musicians and composers. As a cultural and industrial system, this gradually becomes evident through the equally gradual disappearance of the producing studios in the late 1940s and early '50s. Partition and the decisions made by the new Indian government contributed much to the bedrock conditions under which Old Bollywood and its music developed. Due to these import-export policies, the convertibility and value of the rupee, as well as changes in nightlife, the variety of foreign popular music available in India declined after 1947.

Indigenously produced popular music increasingly meant film music not only because there were fewer alternatives but also because the entire industry seems to have focused on the production of film songs and music. Ashish Rajadhyaksha has noted the remarkable accomplishments of the first years of Old Bollywood in terms of significantly increased national output and the construction of both a "national market" and a dominant and distinctive "narrative mode" (2004, 127). Later I suggest that the musicians' views of Old Bollywood help explain that increase in production. They confirm this in their recollections of the amount of work available in Old Bollywood. Instead of going to the same studio every day "whether there was work or no work," musicians, if there was no work in one studio, went to another one where there *was* work. The totally freelance system of Old Bollywood, as chaotic as it appeared, made maximum use of the industry's human and physical resources. Musicians, along with everyone else apparently, worked very long hours:

> BENNY GRACIAS: [Recording work] used to go on for such a long time that if we got even one day off, we used to run like puppies who have got free. Run to enjoy ourselves.

Gracias's brother-in-law felt the same way:

> ERNEST MENEZES: When I was about twenty-seven or twenty-eight [i.e., the mid-1960s], I was thinking of leaving the line altogether. Because what used to happen, we would work from morning to night, morning to night, and we'd not have any entertainment or recreation, nothing, Sundays included. But then I thought, "What will I do [instead]?" So I stuck with it.

Like many of his colleagues, Menezes discovered not only that film music's dominance made it a remunerative field but also that its dominance had made it the only realistic musical career.

Although it did not directly affect musicians, another reason for the dominance of film music was the unique industrial dynamic in which music production costs and much of the risk were borne by independent producers. Producer/director Yash Chopra is quite blunt about the process:

YASH CHOPRA: We were making the music, and we were paying for the music, and then we were giving it to HMV free [whether] there was royalty or there was no royalty.

Because Columbia (as an independent company) and other major labels had abandoned independent India, the Gramophone Company of India (GCI) under its various labels (the Odeon label, for example, was especially important for film music) enjoyed a de facto monopoly on record production after 1947. Polydor established itself in India in the 1960s and made some effort to move into the film-music line, especially in the 1970s. Even then, however, Polydor's output never exceeded 20 percent of recorded film song. As holders of a virtual monopoly, GCI had little need to pursue innovation in popular music that would have been both more expensive and less reliable than the film songs they and their audience had already grown used to and for which, as Chopra notes, they had to offer only royalty agreements (cf. Morcom 2007).

Film music was thus both profitable for GCI and debilitating to its need for innovation. "Gramophone Company of India historian Michael Kinnear estimates that the number of film and nonfilm music releases [not including rereleases, second pressings, and so forth, which heavily favored film songs] were roughly equal during most of the film era" (personal communication, quoted in Manuel 1993, 54). Manuel also cites Ojha's claim that 58 percent of record releases between 1974 and 1984 were film songs and V. A. K. Ranga Rao's estimate that more than 90 percent of HMV's total output was film music (ibid., 54–55).

In terms of revenues, Manuel suggests that "the actual percentage of film-music *sales* [emphasis in the original], however, is undoubtedly much higher" than the 50–58 percent ratios suggested earlier (ibid., 54). It appears that his assertion was correct. Additionally, V. K. Dubey, who oversaw much of the recording in Mumbai's HMV Studios, offers a perspective—also based on revenues—that positions film music in a remarkable light. Adding to the irony of the situation, it appears that HMV did not even pay the film musicians who were recording the film songs that HMV would release:

V. K. DUBEY: In the 78 [rpm] period, about 90 percent of sales were film music; maybe the beginning is 85 percent, but still very high. . . . They [the film musicians] used to come to HMV studio at Pheroze Shah Mehta Road and record the song again. That's how it used to be. They were coming to our studios to record, but we only paid if they were the recordings of

HMV. In our language, those were basic recordings. If basic recordings
were being done, then HMV paid. If film recordings were being made, then
the producers paid [the musicians].

The term *basic recordings* was commonly used by HMV staff to identify nonfilm recordings. Although I do not pursue the issue here, the idea
that a company could identify as "basic" a product that was generating less
than 25 percent of its revenue speaks volumes about HMV's ideology and
its relationship with film music.

"In commercial terms, [film songs] were insignificant compared to the
film [i.e., sales of tickets], and largely dependent on the film for their success (Morcom 2007, 190). Morcom also suggests that "songs issued on
gramophone records and played on radio constituted valuable free market-
ing for the film, and a small amount of extra money for the producer"
(ibid.). The consumption of films must certainly have generated more income for film producers than the royalties they sometimes received from
HMV (see chapter 6). In reality, the success of a film song, both as such and
as a popular song, was uniquely intertwined, to a variable and impenetra-
ble degree, with the reception of its film; as a result, HMV's industrial decision making was bifurcated in nature. In addition to considering the composers' and singers' popularity, the company also paid attention to the film
producers' success rates. In his explanation of this process, Abbas Ali—
formerly a recording director at HMV—argues in effect that the film's reception was key to the song's popularity:

> ABBAS ALI: If you are producing music for your film, [its success] is totally
> dependent on each film subject, how your music, your songs are fitted in
> each situation. And sometimes, almost 80 percent of the time, when the
> film is released and it is a hit, then the music will be a hit. Because people
> see the songs, they see the picturization, so they understand the real mean-
> ing of the song. If people see the film and they like that, then they will like
> the music. But you can't predict it.

Ali cannot resist adding a final caution regarding the industry's ultimate
unpredictability and the complexity of the dynamic he is describing.

Independent Producers and a New Funding Model

The complexity of the independent producer system in Mumbai and the
transition from producing studios to independent producers transformed
India's film industry into what I call (following O'Brien) a "cottage industry." Based on an artisanal rather than an industrial model, the Mumbai
cinema resembled nothing so much as "the French industry's decentralized,
artisanal 'mode of production'—its patchwork of small and mid-sized

companies, craft-like methods, [and] ad hoc contractual arrangements" (O'Brien 2005, 37–38). O'Brien also notes not only that this system predominated throughout the 1930s but also that filmmaking in France later moved to more "industrial" practices after World War II. At the same time, India moved in precisely the opposite direction. Musicians' descriptions of Old Bollywood are full of ad hoc contractual arrangements, composer workshops, and a professional patchwork of recording work. These descriptions are considered more fully in chapters 5 and 6.

Of the French film industry during its artisanal period, commentator J. G. Auriol wrote in 1934 that "our cinema (production in particular) is in a state of anarchy. There exist nearly as many companies as there are films produced. Each film is an ad hoc endeavor. Each member of the crew is hired as needed, by the week, day, or hour" (quoted in ibid., 38). The preferred word in India was "chaotic," as the Indian Film Enquiry Committee found in 1949 (reported in Raina 1983, 12), but otherwise the same film by-film structure existed in both Old Bollywood and the French film industry of the 1930s.

As the studios were collapsing, sitarist Halim Jaffar Khan joined the film industry in the early 1940s and worked steadily throughout the 1950s. As figure 3.3 shows, at that time there were (again like France) almost as many film-producing companies in Mumbai as there were films produced. He also reports the extemporaneous nature of the independent production-company structure:

> HALIM JAFFAR KHAN: There were so many companies. They would open a new picture company and find some office somewhere, and they would rent studio space. Then they would start one film. If they brought the film out and that was a success, then they would make another film. If it was a flop, they would close the company and start again as a different company.

Khan's causal qualifier, "if they brought the film out," suggests the normalcy of such projects never reaching completion. Kersi Lord offers a similar perspective:

> KERSI LORD: The organization is not very good, and the banks never support. It's like, you're sitting here, and the next day shooting will start. You have to organize who will be hero, heroine, who is doing what, plus payment to pay them. What bank is gonna give you like that?

The chaotic nature of planning in Old Bollywood made financial planning difficult, to say the least. "Film scripts were being written on the sets and shooting wastages due to fuzzy script or shootings cancelled due to the absences or unpunctuality of the stars were *de rigueur*. Everything was based on gut feel. . . . Films were financed under the debt model of shoot now, pay later" (Virmani 2004, 77). What Virmani calls chaos is one of the defining characteristics of the Old Bollywood period.

One industry journalist states that the situation persisted throughout the 1980s and into at least the early 1990s:

> INDU MEHRANI: This is the most disorganized industry in the world. In old Bollywood, there were no budgets; the producers did not know what was going on. The director would say to the producer, "I need 15 lakhs tomorrow or the star won't show up for the shooting." And then the producer calls up some funding people or a money lender and gets the 15 lakhs. And the shooting takes place. But maybe eventually the film is never made; something happens. Then what? Nothing. There is no guarantee, there is no paperwork.

In other words, any association with the film industry has always been a form of cultural capital (see Pinto's comments in chapter 7). Mehrani argues, in effect, that the cultural capital that could result from involvement with the film industry was sometimes enough to generate funding regardless of the financial profits. According to Mehrani and based on popular media coverage generally, star actors have the highest value in this value system:

> INDU MEHRANI: There is an endless supply of people who will provide money just to meet the stars. Some businessman . . . has so much money, he decides he wants to make a film; he wants to meet the stars. So he comes to Bombay, and he meets some producer, who takes him to a party, and he meets Amitabh Bachchan, and [then he] takes him to another party, and he meets Sri Devi [both highly popular actors of Old Bollywood], and it's all so glamorous, that's all he can see. So he puts in 40 lakh or 100 lakh or more, and even if the film is a complete flop or never is made, the memory of shaking hands with Amitabh Bachchan is enough for him to go home happy. For us, there's God, then film stars, then cricketers.

These industrial issues were not enough to prevent the production of highly successful, creative, or entertaining films and in fact encouraged the continued production of a profusion of very popular film songs. Naturally, some production companies produced relatively long series of quite successful films; many of these companies were family enterprises (e.g., Navketan, as well as the productions of the Chopra family; see Dwyer 2002). The nature of work in Mumbai's cottage industrial system is made clear in the musicians' comments in the coming chapters. The recognition of the unique nature of the Mumbai film industry, however, problematizes comparisons with Western industrial models and Hollywood's film factories.

A Transition from Studios to Music Directors

In the 1950s musicians were increasingly aware of the demand for their music. Although salaried work declined, J. V. Acharya suggests, the demise of salaried positions in studios, which took place at the beginning of Old Bollywood, was something of a two-way street and at least partly due to the musicians' decisions:

> J. V. ACHARYA: It [salaried employment] stopped. Because people, when they got some work outside of the studio, they left it. They said, "We don't want service; we'll play freelance." They wanted to be paid by the recording, rupees fifty per recording, something like that.

Although many of the production companies were precisely the kind of off-the-cuff entities that Halim Jaffar Khan and others suggest, the collective amount of money (legal and illegal) available to the industry appears to have been quite high. The demand for successful films and songs (and musicians) was equally cultural and financial. It gradually became apparent to musicians that, depending on one's skill (as well as luck and connections), monthly salaries actually amounted to less—sometimes significantly less—than the amount a good freelancer could make by working hard. When musicians began working freelance, as more and more did in the late 1940s, they were trading the security of a salary for the potential profits to be had by working from recording to recording. Growing demand made this a realistic strategy. In chapter 6 I describe the economics of this process for the musicians themselves.

The freelance system that all musicians were part of by the mid-1950s contributed to the artisanal nature of the film industry, in which everyone, from the last violinist in the last row of the orchestra to Lata Mangeshkar herself, was an independent contractor. Nevertheless, both the development and the recording of songs required socioprofessional structures through which those processes could be managed. Musicians sought to organize the recording process by forming a labor union, the Cine Musicians Association (CMA; see chapter 6). But a less formal socioprofessional structure was in place alongside CMA that managed the composition and development of songs. Instead of organizing their careers around salaried work for specific studios, some Old Bollywood musicians centered them around their association with one or more music directors. Although the structure and finances were all different, music directors (some more than others) replaced studios as sources of continuity in the new system.

This organizational change in Old Bollywood was precisely the mix of professional and social relationships that the artisanal mode embodies. The chaotic quality of the Old Bollywood film industry, especially in the transitional period from the mid-1940s through the early 1950s, was never overcome but instead held together by a complex of social and professional relationships and the consistent demand for films. No one was guaranteed work beyond the next film or the next song; yet most people worked regularly. For musicians, that employment was organized around the orchestras' being called to make recordings with various music directors:

ERNEST MENEZES: I first played in 1958 for O. P. Nayyar, then for
    Shankar-Jaikishan. I was booked two or three days in advance, but
    as the work became more, later, then we used to get a week or fifteen
    days in advance. That was some time around 1960 that things became
    very busy. Mostly I played with Roshan, Naushad, Kalyanji-Anandji,
    O. P. Nayyar, Madan Mohan, R. D. Burman, and Anna [a nickname for
    composer C. Ramchandra].

As I discuss in more detail in chapter 5, connection to a specific music director or group of directors replaced the steady employment that had been available through the salaried studio work of the 1930s and '40s. Collectively, an enormous amount of recording time was, in effect, shared among the musicians based on perceived musical skills and performing ability and also on social relationships in some cases.

Many musicians understood themselves as belonging to one camp or the other, as Menezes implied earlier. There were no formal agreements that specified membership or continuity, but many musicians worked throughout the 1950s and '60s on an almost-daily basis with a handful of highly successful music directors. Most notably, musicians speak of the "Shankar-Jaikishan orchestra" as if it was a permanent, fixed group.

Robert Corea came to Mumbai in the early 1950s with his brother Louis. Their father, Lino Corea, had managed a family-based hotel orchestra in the later years of the British Raj. In Mumbai, Robert worked routinely with Shankar-Jaikishan and speaks as if, in fact, the duo actually had an orchestra:

ROBERT COREA: They had a great orchestra. I went nearly every day. We
    didn't rehearse every day, but most days we did.

There were no formal arrangements between Shankar-Jaikishan and "their" musicians, but the consistency nevertheless extended beyond personnel as such to seating plans in some cases. Because the best violinists were widely known within the small circle of film musicians, one knew who would be in the front row of the violin section in the "Shankar-Jaikishan orchestra":

ERNEST MENEZES: In the beginning I sat in the second row, but by 1963 I
    was in the front row. The front row was Uncle Joe, Jerry Fernandes,
    A. P. Dourado, Martin Pinto, Oscar Pereira, Francis Fernandes, and

another Mr. Pinto. They were all ex-Lahore, Karachi, Rawalpindi, except
Jerry and Dourado.

Jerry Fernandes, however, whom Menezes names in this list of front-row
players, distinguishes between the common understanding that both Menezes and Corea express and the theory that I have explained in which nothing was fixed:

> JERRY FERNANDES: But we never had the musicians fixed for one music direc-
> tor; some people might be busy some place else. We were like freelancers.
> Whoever called, if we were free, we went.

Although Fernandes is absolutely correct, he also admits that he indeed
played in the front row of almost every Shankar-Jaikishan song recording
of the 1950s and '60s.

The uncertainty Fernandes notes and that existed at the heart of the industry was further obscured by the clarity of roles and the work that continued day after day with no formal contract. Musicians working with a
high demand music director could easily be forgiven for forgetting that
nothing was permanent. Drummer Franco Vaz, who worked extensively
with R. D. Burman, offers a perspective on an increasing sense of stability
from late Old Bollywood:

> FRANCO VAZ: He [Burman] used to do sixty recordings a month sometimes,
> so my drums were always set next to the piano in the studio at Film Centre
> Sometimes for four or five months I wouldn't move my drum set. And the
> mic-ing was also set because, if he wasn't recording, Kalyanji-Anandji
> would be recording.

Thus, in addition to the normality generated by the daily routines that
some musicians experienced in composers' music rooms (see chapter 5),
the regularity of rehearsals and recordings similarly produced a sense of
permanence for a much larger group of musicians:

> VIPIN RESHAMMIYA: With L-P we were doing four recordings a day some-
> times. I was with them from their first film.

Four songs a day was closer to the exception than to the rule, even for
the prolific Laxmikant-Pyarelal, but that sense of working all of the time
and the manner in which keyboard player Vipin Reshammiya suggests that
he was "with" Laxmikant-Pyarelal from the beginning of their career are
remarkable features of Old Bollywood.

Late Old Bollywood

For musicians, the film-music industry remained relatively stable throughout much of the 1960s, '70s, and '80s. Some film musicians retired or left

the business, but most of them continued the daily round of rehearsals and recordings, playing for the composer of the moment. Musically, various stylistic elements from assorted forms of rock 'n' roll were incorporated into film sound tracks, along with folk musics and other Indian forms (such as *ghazals),* but the necessity of film orchestras continued to be assumed. If anything, both the sheer size of film orchestras and their instrumental sophistication increased in the 1970s.

Two major changes occurred in the 1970s and '80s that distinguish late Old Bollywood. First was the appearance of a new generation of composers who built their reputations throughout the late 1960s and effectively took over in the 1970s. Film-score production in this period was increasingly dominated by Kalyanji-Anandji, Laxmikant-Pyarelal, and R. D. Burman, as well as Sonik-Omi (Manoharlal Sonik and Omprakash Sharma), Ravindra Jain, Rajesh Roshan, Usha Khanna, and the inimitable Bappi Lahiri. The appearance of this new generation of composers and their workshops consolidated the cottage-industry system of production, which had been developing over the previous ten to fifteen years, in conjunction with the collapse of the producing studios.

The 1970s also marked the coming of age of the first generation of Indians born in independent India, who had grown up with autonomously produced Indian films, and of film musicians who had joined films directly without the training in classical music (Indian or Western) or jazz that had characterized Old Bollywood's first generation. The period from the mid-1960s to the mid-1970s also witnessed the transition from Jawaharlal Nehru to Indira Gandhi, the gradual consolidation of an explicitly youth-oriented pop music in the West, and other broader changes. Among the later of these, the introduction of cassettes and the steady appearance of new cassette companies and labels were perhaps the most significant. Led by Gulshan Kumar's innovative business practices and aided by the inexpensive nature of cassette production and consumption, these companies finally broke HMV's monopoly in popular-music production in the early 1980s.

The Costs of Song Production in Late Old Bollywood

More than their elders, the second generation of film composers achieved a degree of celebrity status and the freedom to make music as they chose. Celebrity brought with it a measure of creative freedom that resulted in some of the Hindi cinema's most elaborate film scores. Ultimately, however, its cost was one of the many seeds of the collapse of Old Bollywood in the 1990s.

Music directors charged producers a fixed amount per song. These professional fees covered the song's composition and the music director's oversight of the work leading up to and including the recording of that song. Significantly, they included neither the cost of arranging, rehearsing, and recording nor the fees paid to the playback singers, musicians, recording studios, and lyricists. They also did not cover background music, which was a separate fee. Not only were these other expenses separate, but the decision-making process sometimes left producers vulnerable to costs incurred by music directors as well.

There had never been a formal mechanism whereby a film's producer could automatically assume control over all of the aspects of the costs involved in recording a song. The size of the orchestra needed was partly a stylistic and situational decision made by the music director (see chapter 7). If the recording took longer than the standard four hours that a session was expected to last, it went into overtime. Costs would then begin to increase on an hourly basis.

With his uncle Manoharlal Sonik (universally called Master Sonik or Master-ji), Omprakash Sharma formed the younger half of the music-director duo Sonik-Omi. Despite their skills, Sonik-Omi routinely found themselves composing music for relatively low-budget films; they provided their producers with a budget indicating what they expected the recording of a song to cost. In films with tight budgets, it was especially important for them to ensure beforehand that the producers had enough money to pay for the recording:

> OMPRAKASH SHARMA: We always gave a budget; it was necessary. He [the producer] was giving the money; he was paying. Our songs usually cost between 10,000 and 20,000 [rupees].

At this level, the cost of recording was a matter for negotiation. Although even twenty thousand rupees was not excessive for a song , a Sonik-Omi proposal for a large orchestra might be rejected because the producer could not afford it:

> OMPRAKASH SHARMA: It didn't happen very often, but it happened. They would say, "I don't have this much in my budget; please make it less, and let me see it." They were the ones paying, isn't it?

Music director–producer dynamics changed as one moved up the ranks to work with more stable and often prosperous producers, who had access to more funding. Furthermore, in the 1970s and even more so in the 1980s, the importance of the most popular music directors in the filmmaking process appears to have given them considerable freedom in decisions that they made about time and personnel, which nevertheless affected the budgets of the producers who had hired them.

Ravi (Ravi Shankar Sharma) produced two or more film scores per year for much of the period from the late 1950s through the mid-1980s. He fits between the relatively low-budget work of Sonik-Omi and the big-budget extremes that I discuss later. Nevertheless, Ravi suggests that his general approach to orchestral decision making was purely musical. Under normal conditions, he gave no thought to the costs his decisions would incur for the film's producer. "Whatever I need, I take that. If I want thirty violins, I take thirty."

These variables were primarily fees paid to the playback singer (which was often a producer's decision), the number of musicians hired, and the number of hours it took to achieve a satisfactory recording. In Ravi's thinking, a producer would not know about the latter two until the music director had decided on instrumentation and the recording had actually taken place:

> RAVI SHANKAR SHARMA: How can he know? Some songs need many violins and also soloists, and other songs need less, so how can he know? There can't be any budget.

Having said that, however, Ravi also points out that if the costs are highlighted ahead of time as a matter of concern, efforts were made to reduce the recording expenses:

> RAVI SHANKAR SHARMA: Once a man came to make a Panjabi film, and he didn't have much money, and he said to me, "Please, you try to be careful with the music because I don't have much money." So I said okay, I would use only a few musicians. So sometimes you try to adjust. If it's a regional film and the producer is poor, then you do what you can. And we had [top-ranked playback singer] Mohamed Rafi in that film also. I told him, "This guy is a small guy and has not so much money. Can you help this guy out?"

Rafi was helping Ravi out, of course, because a song sung by Mohamed Rafi would attract more attention and generate more sales than the same song sung by a lesser-known playback singer. Ravi also states, however, that at the very upper echelons of the profession, costs were automatically greater because of the ways in which some music directors worked. Although he names no names, his description corresponds with musicians' accounts of Laxmikant-Pyarelal sessions:

> RAVI SHANKAR SHARMA: There were some people who did very much work, and they would have forty, fifty musicians that they always had with them. And maybe for some of them that day, there would be no work. They would just say, "You can stay home today."

Pyarelal Sharma himself describes a rather costly approach to orchestration and to the way he and Laxmikant-ji developed and composed music. He is also much less emphatic about who made the decisions:

> PYARELAL SHARMA: Our system was like this, that however much those things cost, the producer had to pay. But see, we did big films. Like if you go to a restaurant and have a meal, no one says, "Okay, the rice will be so much, and the *dāl* [spiced legumes] so much, and each thing so much." You just pay the price. Our system was, whatever should be there, it was there.

Of course, in the "restaurant" of Hindi film song, some of the producers were forced by their funding situations to order à la carte and to negotiate the cost of each item. Sharma makes it clear that he was working primarily for producers who had the luxury of hiring "the best."

Regardless of the cost, there was clearly a significant demand for Laxmikant-Pyarelal film scores. In twenty of the years between 1963 and 1993 their scores represented more than 10 percent of all those released. A producer who had signed Laxmikant-Pyarelal for an upcoming film could expect to have an easier time raising the necessary capital than one who had signed a lesser-known composer:

> JOE MONSORATE: You know Pyarelal was that kind of person that nobody opened their mouth in front of him.

However, despite his claims and his reputation, Pyarelal-ji himself admits that, while budgets were rarely discussed, there was a limit to the amount they were expected to spend. It was one, however, that allowed for any contingency:

> PYARELAL SHARMA: Usually it was 2 lakh for the song. For that you can get 125 to 135 musicians. We usually used between 90 and 105 musicians. By the end, maybe it had gone up to 2.5 lakhs. So the producers knew [that] if there were six songs, then 12 or 15 lakh they would need for the songs. It was always like that, but it could be less. That's no big thing.

Sharma goes on to note that background music cost "maybe 125,000 [rupees] per shift." Since background music conventionally took ten to fifteen days (more commonly the latter) to compose and record and since Pyarelal-ji's methods involved the orchestra and the studio for the entire period, a background score might easily cost a producer 18 lakh, nearly two million rupees.

The expenses seemed enormous to musicians, who were observing this process from below, so to speak:

> LOUIZ BANKS: The producer was shelling out a lot of money! Because the songs used to go three or four days, just for one song. So you have to pay

studio time, and the producers could see that the musicians were just sitting down doing nothing, and "Here I am paying by the hour!" But then everything would be forgiven once the film became a hit. Then the producer made his money, and then he forgot about all that.

In their accounts of the process, many tend to focus on the star status of Laxmikant-Pyarelal:

BOSCO MENDES: Whatever it was, the producer paid. Because they were happy with the man. He gave the best, and producers paid the money. "I've got Pyare-bhai, and I've got his orchestra, so I've got the best. I've got his name. That's all I want." They had his name; that's all that mattered. And his music. That's it.

Musicians also recognized Pyarelal Sharma's willingness to support musicians regardless of the circumstances. They (and I) interpret his behavior as that of a musician making sure that others could benefit from his success. Nevertheless, this sometimes cost producers unnecessarily:

SHANKAR INDORKAR: After my father died, Pyare-bhai called me, and he said, "You are like my son. You just come every day now to my music room. And you work with me; you sit there." He called a lot of people every day. Whether there was work that day for oboe or not, I came and sat there.

Thus, Pyarelal Sharma, due to the demand for film songs and L-P's success in that field, could effectively replicate on a grand scale the studio system that older musicians have described. Indorkar's description of the arrangements echoes Vistasp Balsara's word; the musicians came every day "whether there was work or no work." Joe Monsorate includes Indorkar in a group that acted as Pyarelal's personal orchestra within a larger orchestra:

JOE MONSORATE: Even I got caught in that period from 1988 to 1996. Pyarelal kept me as a permanent member. Me, Shankar, Rakesh Chaurasia, and other guys. Whenever they were recording, whether there was work or not, we went and sat down [i.e., they were in the recording studio and were paid regardless of whether they played]. That means usually alternate day take.

Despite the costs Pyarelal-ji incurred for film producers as a result of his concerns and his system of working, he insists that these were negligible in the context of a film budget:

PYARELAL SHARMA: But this is all nothing. They could lose forty lakh in a day if something went wrong with the shooting. The budgets were very big.

In fact, the conventional understanding was that all of the expenses for a film's music normally came to roughly 10 percent of the total outlay. One of Mumbai's most successful producer/directors, Yash Chopra, agrees:

> YASH CHOPRA: The music was very cheap, probably even less than 10 percent of the budget.

The epitome of stardom for a music director came with Bappi Lahiri, who also used a very large orchestra:

> TAPPAN ADHIKHARI: Bappi-da was a star; he had a special style. No one else was a star like him.

Percussionist Tappan Adhikhari considered Lahiri a family friend and worked with him from his first film, *Nana Shikari* (1973). Lahiri, whose career peaked in the mid-1980s, along with the disco fad, indeed affected extreme and colorful costumes as part of his persona. His workshop was immensely prolific (perhaps the most prolific in the history of the business), but his style of production was equally expensive. Keyboardist Benny Rosario joined Lahiri in 1989, when Lahiri's pretensions could be said to have been at their height. During his rather short heyday he could afford to have the orchestra assembled in the studio waiting (and being paid) from nine o'clock on, although he himself usually arrived four or five hours later. Among other things, Rosario points to Lahiri's late arrivals as a sign of his status:

> BENNY ROSARIO: See, at that time, Bappi was a big star. He would come to the studio around two o'clock in the afternoon. And he'd be dressed all in white clothes, and he would have a top hat and a tailcoat on and every-thing.

Lahiri is the somewhat absurd extreme, however, in a profession that was generally much more subdued. Sanjay Chakravarty, whose family lived with the Lahiris when they first came to Mumbai, illustrates the extent of Lahiri's sense of his position:

> SANJAY CHAKRAVARTY: Bappi believed in the situation, he believed in being a star. We went to one Durga puja celebration, and Bappi-da came there. This was after I was married, and we were there also, so we went to see Bappi. But he had come with one hundred men, they had machine guns, commandos, and they said, "Does he know you?"

Whether they were motivated by concern for their own status or the welfare of their musicians, the excesses of the last generation of Old Bollywood composers contributed to the downfall of that system.

New Bollywood

The transition from Old to New Bollywood was as gradual as that from the Studio Period to Old Bollywood, but it began to be perceptible by at least the mid-1990s. As far as the lives and careers of film musicians go, it is not too dramatic to describe what happened after 1995 as outright collapse, which implies a structural weakness that has spread from the inside out. Ernest Menezes made these comments in 2004:

> ERNEST MENEZES: It became less about eight or ten years ago, or you can say maybe twelve years ago. But it became very bad in the last two years. We used to go daily, and then it became something less, but still we worked most of the time. But in the last two years, we're not going even once in a month. Now our day is over. The present generation has no future.

As always, the change was the result of technological, economic, and cultural conditions. Technology was changing relatively rapidly throughout the 1990s, as chapter 2 recounts.

Bishwadeep Chatterjee argues, not surprisingly, that it took the industry and the individuals in it some time to work through the implications of that change. Orchestral size, which had been a sign of prestige for some film producers ever since Raj Kapoor's *Awaara* (1951), and the huge, visually impressive spaces of the old studios finally came to be seen as unnecessary expenses:

> BISHWADEEP CHATTERJEE: Like, if the music director is trying to impress a big production house by having a huge space, so many people, all these things. A lot of it was showbiz, but the wrong kind. (Cf. Arnold 1991, 175)

Chatterjee is speaking as a sound engineer, of course, and argues for a particular kind of inertia generated by industry figures, including musicians, who wished to protect the status quo. As I have already suggested, by the 1990s that state of affairs was sometimes costing film producers more than it should have:

> BISHWADEEP CHATTERJEE: People started realizing that they could do without these huge places and this old equipment. And also you can say that people started going to the smaller places anyway because they couldn't afford to go to these huge setups. Then you had all these musicians hanging around, sometimes all day, without doing a thing. And you started realizing that the whole point was that these musicians could earn overtime. The whole thing was deliberately done so that they could earn more money. So I don't think it was a technical limitation as such.

I have already posited the advent of New Bollywood in the context of changes to governmental policy that had been keeping technological developments in check. But Chatterjee (and Joe Pinto) also suggest that patterns of investment changed and that, by the mid-1990s, the cultural capital or prestige with which any association with Bollywood had been invested was replaced by a more businesslike approach to film investment and production. I cannot help but believe that the stronger and more immediate impact of the globally dominant Hollywood culture may also have contributed to these changes:

> JOE PINTO: When I was courting, it was very busy. I used to work seven days sometimes. I never got time to see my fiancée. That was about until '92, when all the black money disappeared. It didn't actually disappear, but it went down.

Ironically, economic liberalization seems to have removed some of the motivation for many of the illegal activities that had been generating the funds that the film industry had been laundering. However, there were fewer investors as well—fewer "businessmen" who wanted to "meet the stars":

> JOE PINTO: A lot of the smaller producers also disappeared around that time. There used to be a lot of small, small producers who would give us work when Pyare-bhai's dates got cancelled, but they also went away, especially after the bomb blasts [1993]. I can't remember their names [because] they were so small. It all came crumbling down quite fast. When you look at how long it took to come to that, it was very fast.

Indeed, this rapid change had at least something to do with the persistence of the old system into the early 1990s. One might almost say that as long as Laxmikant-Pyarelal and R. D. Burman were in business, Old Bollywood (and the musicians' jobs) would continue. Shankar Indorkar was one of the L-P regulars:

> SHANKAR INDORKAR: We never thought it would stop. We never thought this kind of change would come. When disco came, I wondered. But that was just songs. In 1980, '81, about then, with *Disco Dancer* [1981] and all that, the violins were a bit down and used mostly for effects. But lots of instruments were still there. Then *Aashiqui* [1990] came; the style changed again, and things seemed okay.

Joe Pinto may have been a bit more farsighted, but he distinguishes here between the final years of the old system as practiced by Laxmikant-Pyarelal and those of Laxmikant's life, when the duo's compositional activity decreased significantly because of his poor health. Laxmi-ji passed away in 1998, the year that Pinto finally left the film line and subsequently India, as well:

JOE PINTO: Even by 1993 we could see it going, and after 1995, '96, it was definitely going down. I finally decided in 1998 that I had to get out of films and Bombay. I did try Bangalore and Goa.

Bangalore, with a smaller regional film industry and a strong Christian community, may have appeared to be an alternative for a Goan musician, but in the end Pinto left India permanently. Bosco Mendes, who left Mumbai about the same time as Joe Pinto, also tried alternatives such as teaching before emigrating overseas in 2002:

BOSCO MENDES: In the last three or four years before we left, it was one take a week or so. So I was taking tuitions and worked in the school conducting brass bands. It got very sad.

The last word in this section goes to Joe Pereira, whose cousin, arranger Sebastian D'Souza, warned him, as long ago as the 1960s, not to give up his night job as a hotel musician:

JOE PEREIRA: I also had a night job here in the Taj. My cousin said, "Keep your hotel job; don't give that up. This [film work] might stop, but the hotel is safe. Keep that." And he was right! See what's happened now. Now everyone is starving in the film line, but I have a good job.

Sebastian D'Souza was an individual to whom I (and others) attribute partial agency in the development of Mumbai's large studio orchestras. He nevertheless seems to have viewed their viability with some skepticism.

New Systems of Production

It was not only technology and investment that changed the system. "The New Age corporate producer is as far removed from his traditional money-bags counterpart as cappuccino is from cutting *chāi* [tea]. . . . Corporate work culture, discipline and professionalism predominate" (Virmani 2004, 77). The professionalism Virmani describes and the businesslike attitudes of younger producers is possible, of course, only because of the changes in the valuation of film culture. Although still the focus of the popular culture, it is India's (and, most important, Mumbai's) new conceptualization of film culture's identity and value—in a new global market where Indian producers can finally compete with their Hollywood counterparts—that facilitates this attitude. It was the new technological developments that allowed producers and music directors to act on that outlook.

Louiz Banks's career has moved from jazz to films to advertising and finally to composing for films; he has seen enough of these systems to recognize the changes:

LOUIZ BANKS: Now you sit across a table, and the producer says, "This is
   my budget; that's it. This is what I've got. Make it work using this amount,
   and the film is yours." So you go and cut corners and use electronics.
   There's no way you can bring in a hundred-piece orchestra in that budget.
   So there's no other way but to use electronics to simulate that sound. So
   this whole world is of simulated sound.

Banks here is describing the decision-making process associated with
what Mumbai calls the "lump sum" payment system, the complete reversal of the Old Bollywood method. In New Bollywood, the relationship between music directors and musicians has finally been made directly and explicitly economic. Unlike the old arrangement, under which the decision to
hire forty extra musicians had no effect on a music director's income, in the
New Bollywood, the cost of those forty musicians comes directly out of the
music director's pocket. The results are inevitable, as Banks concludes:

LOUIZ BANKS: Economics. Yeah, it boils down to that. In the end it's economics that rules. It's very unfortunate; the orchestras are no more, and that's
   very sad. Somebody wanted an orchestra the other day. I said, "Orchestra?
   Where's the orchestra? It's gonna be very difficult now to put together an
   orchestra."

Banks's comments are an appropriate conclusion to the first part of this
volume. In his remarks he specifies two fundamental determinants in
Mumbai's musical life: economics and technology. The historical courses
of these factors have been the focus of part I, but as Banks indicates, human
decisions enact both the unifying patterns and the cultural and individual
variability of these explanatory systems:

LOUIZ BANKS: The younger generation is fascinated by this technology. "I
   alone can be an orchestra, I don't need anybody!" So now you have a lot
   of people working alone. They are sitting in their small studios and creating
   music all by themselves. You have pockets and pockets of that all over
   Bombay. It's the new world. Orchestras have become history.

To say "history," of course, is to mean the past. In part I, I have offered
three different versions of that past, which I have labeled Old Bollywood,
its own past (the Studio Period), and the present, New Bollywood. If I have
not precisely aligned these three stages, each concerned with and defined
by slightly different factors, I have at least argued that they need to be examined as part of the same overarching process of gradual cultural and industrial change in the Mumbai film industry.

The "new world" of lump sum payments, digital music-making and recording technology, carefully planned and managed film budgets, and an
increasingly global place for the output of the Mumbai film industry is not

entirely new, of course, but the collective impact of the changes that began in the late 1980s has been extreme. In India's new transnational perspective, cultural and industrial responses have diminished the role of song in film, finally bringing to fruition the occasional complaints about the "six songs and three dances" that once seemed a permanent feature of the Hindi cinema. I have more to say about the musicians' responses to these changes in chapters 6 and 7 and mention here only that the composite outcomes have relegated Old Bollywood and its life of music to the past.

The industrial and technological structures of the Mumbai film industry that I have described constitute the environment, the professional ecology in which film musicians lived. I argue that they are also core determinants in the development and dissolution of the cottage-industry system of Old Bollywood. In their various ways, the musicians who describe their professional lives in part II offer nuanced visions of both behavior and causality. Many have their own explanations for why things happened as they did. Nevertheless, as people who lived through the period, their remarks offer a hidden view of those professional lives.

Part II

The Life of Music in the Mumbai Film Industry

Daniel Neuman's (1980) fortuitous phrase "the life of music" emphasizes for ethnomusicologists the reality of music not just as an expressive act but also as a complex of economic, political, social, and transmissive actions. The second major section of this volume considers the ethnographic detail of musicians' professional and social experiences in their role as musicians. With varying degrees of awareness and attributions of agency, part II relates and analyzes individual and collective responses to the determining conditions of the Mumbai film business as set out in part I. Historically, this section begins with the actions and decisions that helped construct the cultural and industrial system that became Old Bollywood in the late 1940s and early '50s; it concludes with the transformation of that system more than forty years later. Here the musicians explain their reasons for and method of joining the line, the musical production and recording processes, the industrial negotiations into which they entered, and the pay they received.

In this section, history takes on a much more personal quality; it becomes the account of an individual's career or of groups of musicians and their relationships with specific music directors. Unlike part I, which offers a more impersonal, systemic perspective and in which producers, recordists, and composers all provided equal input, this section prioritizes the lives and views of the musicians regarding their own experiences in the business. It is obviously oral history; the musicians are uniformly the experts. Part II is in this sense the most descriptive section of the book. The multiplicity of viewpoints and experiential knowledge comes out here quite clearly, and so does the uniformity of the life that most musicians live.

4

Origins, Training, and "Joining the Line"

In this chapter I consider the social identities of the musicians in Mumbai's film industry and the pathways by which they came to be part of this musical-professional group. Because social identity often has a direct impact on an individual's choices of occupation in South Asia, it fits neatly into my notion of beginnings.

In one sense, the backgrounds of musicians who joined the film line reflect the film industry's place within the broader national context, as well as the impact on the industry of historical events after 1930. In this regard, one of the most distinctive features of this volume is the very visible presence of Goan musicians (and proportionally, Parsi musicians as well). It is productive to compare the visibility of these communities to their almost total absence in previous research (e.g., Arnold 1991; Morcom 2007). I do not suggest that these rather different representations of cultural (or in Indian terms, communal) identity in the film line necessarily reflect discrepancies in research or analysis. I do suggest, however, that they demonstrate the variability of representation at the two very different levels of music production that have been studied in Mumbai.

Both Arnold and Morcom examined music directors (and singers as well in Arnold's case); at this level, Goans and Parsis are conspicuously absent in the industry. At the level of the musicians, arrangers, and assistants, however, they have been much more visible. I suggest that at both a collective and an individual level, Goan and Parsi musicians have been significant

121

agents in the process of music creation and music-culture interaction to a degree that has been underrepresented in earlier research.

Musical skills of various types were prerequisites for joining the film line, so I also consider the sources, natures, and processes of musical training. In a more specific fashion, each of four basic pathways shows a slightly different aspect of film music and the musical styles that contributed to it. In the very earliest years of sound, musicians came to the film-music industry from both music drama and classical music backgrounds. In some cases they were simply incorporated directly from a premediated context into a film-production system. This continued throughout the late 1940s at least, when the famous music-director duo Shankar-Jaikishan shifted from being musicians for Prithivi Theatres stage productions to working as assistants to film-music composers such as Ram Ganguly.

Another pathway led from the regional cinema industries (especially Kolkata and Lahore) to the more prolific one in Mumbai. This process began almost as soon as sound came to the cinema, but musicians were still leaving Kolkata twenty-five years later to work in what was plainly the heart of India's film business.

In the late 1940s musicians who had been playing in jazz and Western-style dance bands and in the classical trios and quartets of the colonial-era music culture began making economic choices in favor of Mumbai's film-music industry. This became a last resort for those who could see their nightclub and hotel jobs vanishing in the newly independent nations, both of which had reasons for taking a dim view of alcohol consumption, social dancing, and nightlife in general and for establishing their independence from the colonial power's cultural norms. By the mid-1950s, neither country offered a viable national level of patronage for such bands.

The vast majority of dance band musicians in British India had been Goan Christians. Shope (2003) describes the involvement of Anglo-Indians in the cultural world of dance bands, but very few of this community appear to have joined the film line. In addition to Goans, Parsis and Jews were also involved in the production of western music in colonial India. Goans represented the majority of those who joined the film line from live Western music-performance traditions after independence, but we will see that, as late as the early 1970s, the rare, successful nonfilm musician (such as pianist Louiz Banks) was still being recruited.

Finally, by the late 1950s, a pathway that can be described as traditional and more typically Indian emerged. Increasing numbers of second-generation film musicians joined the business because their fathers were playing in films. As the economic and cultural system of Old Bollywood settled down, many musicians began to treat that stability as a matter of course; they came to view their jobs as part of a permanent, reliable industry. Many encouraged their sons to acquire the skills necessary to work in it also, and they routinely introduced them to the music directors, messengers, and others who could ensure their futures. This was true not only for individuals and families but communities as well.

Communities in Film Music

> KERSI LORD: Everybody is communally minded in India; every community
> is communally minded. At first, Daddy had great difficulty to come in
> the line.

Communalism is the commonly used Indian label for tensions between linguistic, religious, and ethnic groups, "caste politics," as Sanjay Chakravarty later calls it. As Parsis and therefore members of a minority group in India, the Lords (three of whom—Cawas and his two sons, Kersi and Burjor—had significant careers as film musicians) were perhaps better placed to judge the situation than many. Communal friction has played a role in determining both the identities of musicians working in films and the control of various economic niches within the industry. I argue, however, that it has played less of a role in the film-music industry and done so at a grosser level of distinction than might be found in other musical traditions in South Asia.

The film-music industry was quite heterogeneous, especially in its earlier years, but cultural identity was at times a factor in determining individual decisions for or against participation. When brothers Kalyanji and Anandji Shah sought to join the film line, they had to buck family opposition to do so:

> ANANDJI SHAH: We are not from a musical family, so it was very hard in the
> beginning to convince our parents, but our uncle helped us convince them
> that it was okay.

Vistasp Balsara's career choice reflects a combination of personal and communal factors. As a member of Mumbai's Parsi community, Balsara belonged to a group that had few direct connections to Hindustani music but a strong orientation toward Western music and a notion of culture that comprised South Asian and Euro-American components. Thus, while it was personal inclination that led Balsara to pursue music, his cultural background directed him toward Western popular music rather than Indian music:

> VISTASP BALSARA: I joined the film industry in 1938. I had a very small
> orchestra for entertaining private parties and these things. And there

was a musician; he requested me to play for one recording. The Goanese
musicians were not available that day because it was Christmas or some
other festival. So for that I went, and the music director liked me, and so
I joined then.

Here Balsara makes an assumption about the identities of the musicians
that would normally have been playing for this film recording session. Had
it not been a Christian festival day, he believes that many, if not most, of
the musicians recording would have been Goans. Goan arranger and composer Anthony Gonsalves suggests that this might or might not have been
the case in 1938:

> ANTHONY GONSALVES: Bombay was the center for music and for finding
> work in the film line. I went to Bombay in 1943; at that time there were
> very few Goans working in the industry.

Relatively few Goans may have been working in films in 1938 or 1943,
but as the 1940s turned into the 1950s, Goans came to form the backbone
of Mumbai's film orchestras. They are the largest community in what is
otherwise a largely noncommunal business.

The history of Goa, its long connection with Portuguese colonialism,
and the relatively successful (from the Christian perspective) importation
of Catholic Christianity into the region make it possible to use the labels
Goan, Christian, and Catholic more or less synonymously, as musicians in
the film line sometimes do. This is especially because there are no other
Christians to speak of in the film-music line. Of course, the majority of Goa
has always been non-Christian. Dattaram Waadkar was in fact born in
northern Goa. As a Hindu, however, living in what is almost Maharashtra,
he also makes distinctions along these lines:

> DATTARAM WAADKAR: We did so much work. And the orchestra that was
> there, that was 99 percent Goan musicians. Indian instruments that were
> there—sitar, dholak [a barrel-shaped hand drum]—those things were
> played by Indians, but the rest were Goan.

Although they were social groups with radically different histories, religions, and places in their communities, Parsis and Goans both had a cultural connection to Western music, both classical and popular. Consequently,
members of these groups in general had more training in those forms than
did other groups in India. This sometimes worked to everyone's advantage.
Although Goan violinist Maoro Alfonso once worked in the film business,
he has had a long career playing European classical music, sometimes for
a Parsi audience:

> MAORO ALFONSO: Parsis were the people who wanted that [Western] classical
> music. They wanted the music for their weddings. They would have such

Figure 4.1 Maro Alfonso teaching a young violinist in his home in Goa (2006).

weddings, and they would give you a lot of money and very nice food and so much brandy. They treated you nicely because they wanted classical music.

Retired now to Goa, Alfonso was still taking the occasional classical music student in 2005 (figure 4.1).

The film orchestra that Dattaram Waadkar referred to earlier and in which Maoro Alfonso played, was the quasi-permanent ensemble that regularly played for Shankar-Jaikishan. Because of the coincident timing between Shankar-Jaikishan's success and the end of the (largely Goan) dance bands widely found in colonial India, the Shankar-Jaikishan orchestra benefited from the many musicians who were seeking work in the film line. The ensemble was perceived to be distinctly Goan in its makeup. This situation sometimes produced tension, as Sanjay Chakravarty's father discovered in 1957. At that time, cellist Vasudeo Chakravarty (figure 2.2) had recently arrived from Kolkata and was trying to establish himself in the film business:

> Sanjay Chakravarty: Caste politics is always there. Especially in Shankar-Jaikishan's group, non-Catholics were, you can say, not appreciated. But Dourado-saheb [violinist A. P. Dourado] heard Daddy playing cello, and he

said, "Vasu, you play very well, no doubt, but you will have to get used to this place. It is always like this when someone new comes. [At first] it seems like there's no room, but eventually people make room."

A sense that orchestral musicianship was dominated by Goans may have contributed to the teaching efforts of Ramprasad Sharma. In addition to his son, Pyarelal, Ramprasad began teaching many other students free of charge in the 1950s and '60s. Most of these musicians learned violin or viola. Many people in the film line view Ramprasad's teaching positively, but it is significant that most of his students were Hindu/Indian rather than Goan/Christian. In the late 1950s the film business was increasingly being recognized as an established economic niche for musicians, but communal control over orchestral musicianship was never really possible.

The one community (if I can use that term in this context) that did maintain almost total control over the film line was a gendered one. Not unusually for India then or now, the film-music line was almost exclusively male, with the major exception of chorus singers. Two female composers have acted as music directors in the film line, but Khursheed Manchershah (who used the professional name Saraswati Devi) and Usha Khanna were the exceptions that proved the rule. Equally exceptional were the handful of women who, for one reason or another, ended up playing for films.

Most of the women who worked as instrumentalists in films belonged to the Goan community, where the notion of female instrumentalists, inflected as it was by the Portuguese culture, was much less radical than it was in the Hindu and Muslim communities. Many young Christian women learned to play musical instruments—most commonly piano or violin—as did their contemporaries in Europe, where music was readily considered a ladylike accomplishment. Bridget Carvalho and Lucila Pacheco both played piano in the film industry, mostly with Shankar-Jaikishan, but with others as well; Pacheco is shown in figure 1.2. Myra Menzies (now Shroff), a well-known violinist in the classical world of Mumbai, sometimes played for films as both a section violinist and a soloist. Her solo recordings are heard mostly in films for which Naushad Ali was music director. This connection was the result of the work of her husband, Josique, as an arranger. Myra and Josique also taught violin. She and Carvalho were still living at the time of this research, but both have repeatedly declined to be interviewed. Violinist and keyboardist Isobel Menezes, the daughter of the famous violinist Joe Menezes, also played from time to time in films.

The only other female instrumentalist in the film line of whom I am aware is Zarin Sharma, who was born into a Parsi family (Daruwalla) and became an accomplished performer on the classical *sarod* (an unfretted, plucked lute). At the age of fourteen she played for the title music of a single 1960 release *(Maasoom)* but began a much longer association with film music four years later, when her professional acquaintance with sitarist Ustad Imrat Khan led to her being called for the classically oriented score for *Chitralekha* (1964), composed by Roshan (Roshan Lal Nagrath). As was appropriate for the time and place, Imrat Khan approached Sharma's father:

> ZARIN SHARMA: They wanted a sitar-sarod duet for the title music, and Imrat Khan Saheb told them, "Look, I don't know if she will play because she is a lady, but if she will, it will be good." He didn't know if I'd do it. But he came to see me with one Mr. Varma, who was Roshan-ji's assistant. They came to speak with my Daddy. But my Daddy didn't think that classical would come in the films. He said that we didn't really have any interest or knowledge about that thing. But they said, "No, no. Just classical we want; nothing that you don't know about. We're recording tomorrow morning at Mehboob. You come there." We went the next morning, and there was only one sitār and one tanpura—and me. It was just like a classical program. Abdul Karim was playing tabla.

Remembering that these events took place in 1964 but that Sharma had been playing classical concerts for some time, I find it instructive to note that neither she nor her father knew what to expect from film work. Nevertheless, Sharma was invited to return the next day to play with the full orchestra. The long story is interesting in itself but justified as well because of the rarity of the female voice in this history:

> ZARIN SHARMA: As we were leaving, Roshan-ji said to my daddy, "Look, I'm recording background for this film tomorrow. Why don't you come and play on that also?" So Daddy said to me, "Do you want to play?" And I said, "But I don't have any idea about how I should play or what I should play." And Roshan-ji said, "Look, you come and see what you think, and if you want to play, you play; if not, don't."

Sharma's first experience with a studio orchestra proved to be daunting not only in consideration but also in the actual experience:

> ZARIN SHARMA: So we went. That was the big first-floor studio [see figures 2.1 and 6.4]. This time there was brass and all blowing instruments and violins, full orchestra, plucking instruments, everything. It was packed. And my daddy was very surprised. He said, "Good grief, what are we going to do in the middle of all this?" He wanted to go back. But I said, "We've come; it won't look good if we just go. Let's see what happens." Roshan-ji said, "Please come, have a seat, and listen and see what you think." So we listened, and I said to my daddy, "This is very different from the music we do."

As a composer, Roshan was especially known for his many classically oriented film scores. It is not clear whether or how carefully he planned Sharma's initial experiences in the film studio, but the outcome was one of gradual acclimatization to a new music culture and an unfamiliar set of musical practices. In the conclusion of her story, Sharma characterizes her gendered uniqueness specifically in terms of her choice of musical instrument rather than in relation to Indian classical instrumental music in general:

> ZARIN SHARMA: It got to be five-thirty P.M., and they had recorded two
> or three pieces, and then Roshan said, "Okay, this piece I would like you
> to play, you and Imrat Khan-saheb. Not duet, but one after the other, so
> we agreed about the *ragas*—it was Bhairao and Bhairavi—and what we
> would play.
>
>   When I began to play, all the musicians who were standing around were
> very surprised. Because I was a lady, no? And lady players of sarod were
> very, very rare. And also there were very few ladies in the film line, so they
> were all astonished. It seemed to me as if they'd never seen a sarod before.
> And people came to know about me because here I was—I was just this
> eighteen-year-old Parsi girl playing in films. But mostly they didn't know
> my name. I was "that Parsi girl."

The sarod is less commonly encountered in film scores than is the sitar, which has acquired a somewhat traditionalist identity in film scores, but the instrument was by no means unused. It is unlikely that anyone at Mehboob that day had actually never seen a sarod before. Since Sharma was the only woman playing the instrument in public in 1964, however, the combination of the instrument and the gender of its player was indeed an unusual sight.

The gendered nature of the film-music community (and of the classical world of instrumental music, for that matter) was largely the result of broader forces in Indian society. In other respects, the relatively novel medium, the syncretic nature of much of its music, and the industry's ultimate location in a highly diverse and rather Westernized city collectively weakened the viability of communalism. In the end, the factors that mattered in the film line were training and expertise.

Coming to Mumbai and to Films

Almost from the beginning, Mumbai was attracting aspiring and established actors, musicians, directors, and composers to its film factories. Manohari Singh was one who came to Mumbai from Kolkata, but he was not the only one:

MANOHARI SINGH: Many Western musicians came here from Calcutta—
  Johnny Gomes, Louis Corea, all those people. One time, Calcutta was
  the capital of India, and best musicians used to be there. And most of the
  nightclubs were there: Grand Hotel, Firpo's, Greens, 300 Club, Dionysus
  Club, also private clubs.

As I have already suggested, however, musicians came to Mumbai with
varying skills and under different circumstances.

Classical Music and Music Dramas

Especially in the early days of the film-music industry, many struggling musicians arrived with no connections, willing to work in any capacity to be
part of the industry:

NAUSHAD ALI: I loved going to the cinema. I went every day; sometimes I
  would go two times in one day. And so, because I loved the music and the
  cinema, I left home and came to Bombay in 1937.

Naushad Ali came to Mumbai from Lucknow, where he had already
had some training in Hindustani classical music. He would eventually become one of the most important music directors in the history of the Hindi
cinema, but initially he took whatever work he could find, even if it was a
low-paying position playing harmonium:

NAUSHAD ALI: One Russian had built a studio. He was making a Hindi picture, and Jhande Khan-saheb was giving the music. I had heard his name
  because he had also given music for stage plays in the past. He was very
  knowledgeable. So I got work with him. He was like my *ustad* [teacher].
  I learned very much from him.

An early and important music director, Jhande Khan was one of the many
who switched from staged music dramas to the cinematic version.

Naushad later graduated to working as an assistant to other music directors. At the same time, he moved from the "jungle" (as he called it) of
Chembur toward the center of Mumbai:

NAUSHAD ALI: After I left that place, I went to Ranjit [Ranjit Movietone in
  Dadar]. Manohar Kapoor was there. I was his assistant, and then I was
  assistant to Kemchand Prakash.

Sajjad Hussain also had both classical training and film-music aspira-
tions when he came to Mumbai in 1937, but with less success (see chapter
1). The small princely courts near Jaora (in Madhya Pradesh state where
Hussain's father made his living), in conjunction with an important Muslim shrine, apparently supported a flourishing, if limited, classical and light
classical music culture in the early twentieth century:

NISAR AHMAD: Our father was born in a village near Jaora; he had learned sitar from his father. He came to Mumbai in 1937 because he wanted to become a music director, but when he came, he didn't know anybody, so people said, "Who are you to be coming like this? Maybe you can be someone's assistant, and after some time we'll see." That kind of thing. After some time, he got a job as a musician with Minerva Studios at thirty rupees per month.

Compared to Naushad's sixty-three released sound tracks, Hussain managed only seven, but eventually he established a parallel career for himself as a classical mandolin player.

Another classical musician who followed the family tradition, Pandit Shivkumar Sharma was becoming one of India's most renowned classical performers in the mid-1950s when he was caught up (albeit temporarily and coincidentally) in the film industry:

SHIVKUMAR SHARMA: I never meant to be in the film line. I came to Bombay for a classical festival. [Film director] V. Shantaram's daughter was part of that festival, so she mentioned me to her father and to [music director] Vasant Desai. Shantaram was making *Jhanak Jhanak Pyal Baje* [1955]. So Vasant Desai called me and asked me would I play in one scene. I remember it had boats in it; it was background music.

Classical music was also a starting point for sitar player J. V. Acharya, who initially found work as a staff artist in the small orchestra that HMV kept on salary. Arnold reports that G. N. Joshi recalled a clear structural separation between HMV's studio musicians, who were "reserved for non-film song recordings" (1991, 116), and the film musicians who may have been hired for specific film recordings.

Musicians who played in the rerecording period (such as Kersi Lord) recall that personnel were a mix of HMV's staff musicians and selected musicians from the film line. To impress music directors with his playing, J. V. Acharya certainly did his best to mingle with the film musicians:

J. V. ACHARYA: I first started playing *dilruba* [a bowed, fretted lute]; then after that I took up sitar, and in 1946 I joined HMV. My career started there, but it was a delicate learning situation. All different types of people were there. Everybody there had his own style, you can say. Everybody was composing in a different way. When the music directors would come to record their compositions, I used to ask them, "Please, you give me a piece; I will play it." Then after that, I came in the film industry.

Training in Indian classical music continued to be a pathway to work in the film industry, but, to use Acharya's expression in a different way, playing for movies could be a delicate situation. Another sitar player, Kartik

Kumar, who joined the film line in the 1960s, notes the changes in economic conditions that led classical musicians to films:

> KARTIK KUMAR: Classical music was maintained by aristocrats, rich people.
> That was the old time. But once our India came, there was some problem
> for the classical musicians. Rich men were still there, but no *rājas* and those
> things. So there was problem, economic problem. They couldn't maintain
> that traditional system. So that problem came to the classical musicians. So
> that is why the classical musicians went for the films.

Kumar implies here, as other musicians later state explicitly, that film work was, in some undefined sense, a second choice, remunerative perhaps, but less preferable. What it offered that other forms of employment could not after 1947, was a relatively consistent income:

> KARTIK KUMAR: The film line was easy money, comfortable money. And it
> was cash money. You went in the morning, played the music, and in the
> evening, you took the money. So you could support your family that way.

There was, nevertheless, a sense of unease about how film work would affect a classical musician's reputation.

Some quite famous classical musicians today are reluctant to talk about their film careers, although most of those who played in Mumbai films know that their contributions to the movie industry were significant. For others, of course, such concerns are of little or no importance. Ustad Sultan Khan has made a career as one of India's masters of the bowed lute, the *sārangi*. In addition to his classical performances, he has played on film scores for much of his career. Implicit in his comments, however, is the notion that he considered the wisdom of his becoming involved in films:

> SULTAN KHAN: I came to Bombay in 1969 and saw that many respected musi-
> cians who played classical music were playing in the films: Ustad Halim
> Jaffar Khan, Shivkumar Sharma, others as well. So I thought it would be
> good if I joined them.

Sultan Khan-saheb feels it necessary to explain his decision based on the precedent set by others. Ustad Halim Jaffar Khan, to whom Sultan Khan here refers, did not have the luxury of such reflection:

> HALIM JAFFAR KHAN: I joined when I was sixteen. My father died when I was
> fifteen, so I had to earn the money. There was one Natthu Ram; he played
> trumpet. He had known my father. So he introduced me to [music director]
> Datta Goregaonkar.

Halim Jaffar Khan later made a significant name for himself as a classical soloist, but his understanding of the two fields is complementary rather than oppositional:

HALIM JAFFAR KHAN: You can say that classical music is like a pure rose; film
music is like a hybrid rose. But both are roses.

Shyamrao Kemble grew up in a village in southern Maharashtra state in
the 1930s. Life in a music drama troupe was both more interesting and
more rewarding than life in what seems to have been a poor village, but his
career suggests that the viability of Marathi music drama was shrinking in
the face of film's growing popularity in the 1940s:

> SHYAMRAO KEMBLE: Food was scarce in the village, and water also. So, when
> I was ten [circa 1940], there was a drama company that came to the vil-
> lage, a children's group with children from seven years up to thirteen or
> fourteen years. They told devotional stories from *Ramayana*. My father
> thought that I would be better off with them because of the difficulties in
> the village, so I went with them as a singer. But then after three or four
> years, my voice went bad; it changed. And I was very sad because I had
> liked to sing, and I didn't know what I would do. I heard the Balmohan
> Sangeet Company [a Marathi Sangeet Natak troupe] about that time. So I
> joined Balmohan, but I didn't get any money. They just gave me food, and I
> stayed with them for three or four years. I learned harmonium there.

This series of what were effectively apprenticeships ended in 1946, when
Kemble left Balmohan for Mumbai.

Kemble used his contacts in the world of Marathi music drama to find
work as an accompanist for classical and light classical music, but employment was intermittent and hardly lucrative. Marathi music dramas were
gradually losing their market to Hindi and Marathi films. Eventually Kemble chose to back the winner:

> SHYAMRAO KEMBLE: One day after I had been in Bombay for a year or so,
> there was an advertisement in the paper for a harmonium player for Jyoti
> Film Studios. So I went to audition, and they gave me a job. That was my
> new career. I didn't know anything about the film business then!

One of the industry's most famous percussionists, Lala Gangawane, also
began his career playing in Marathi music dramas, in his case the lighter
form called *tamāsha.* Gangawane played *dholki,* another barrel drum slightly
smaller than the dholak. Music director C. Ramchandra initially encouraged his move from Pune (a center of tamāsha performance) to Mumbai,
but it was a combination of Raj Kapoor's dissatisfaction with a song's
rhythm and flute player Sumant Raj's habit of eavesdropping that secured
Gangawane his introduction to film work. Dattaram Waadkar describes
the circumstances in video 4.1. Lala went on to form one half of a drumming duo known in the industry as Lala-Sattar. They were the first choice
of all music directors throughout the 1950s and '60s. [🔊 **Video 4.1**]

Roughly thirty years later, still another drummer, Vijay Chauhan, was also playing dholki for premediated Marathi music, accompanying his mother, Sulochana, who was a leading vocalist in the style of a traditional/popular Marathi song form called *lavani*. Chauhan grew up in a household fully and professionally engaged in the light music of Maharashtra:

> VIJAY CHAUHAN: I would play on school benches or anything else. My father played harmonium to accompany my mother on the stage. His name was Shyamrao Chauhan. He was from Kolhapur, and in the evenings he would sit to practice. and he would say, "Look. Vijay, in this song, Pandit-ji would accompany using this pattern, so you try like that." Nobody taught me face to face—just listen and play. And I started playing on tours for lavani and things, and then I got into the cassette line in 1980. This was T-Series, and also Tips, and many different companies.

As Manuel (1993) has noted, the emergence of new Indian cassette companies in the 1980s improved the economic fortunes of many regional and folk music forms. Chauhan moved from lavani to the regional forms of music that the new cassette companies were recording and from there into films a few years later—Marathi films first and then Hindi movies in songs that required a folk music feeling:

> VIJAY CHAUHAN: My first film recording in Hindi was with Mr. Anu Malik; that was *Mard* [1985]. I played *dhol* on "Buri nazarwale."

Folk music, staged music drama, and Hindi films were all quite separate entities, however, and had been for some time. Like the forms of which they were a part, the stage and film musicians had developed distinct cultures and ideologies. Among other things, while drama musicians continued to play "by heart," film musicians were increasingly dependent on notation.

Attractions of a Growing Field

Despite the important contributions of Kolkata and Lahore, there was never any question about where the industrial center of the Hindi cinema was located. These cities, along with Chennai and Hyderabad, focused more and more on regionally important languages (such as Tamil, Bengali, and Telugu). Localized cinema was both important and productive, but even in the years before independence, Hindi was the indigenous language understood by the greatest number of Indians. For musicians working in the "regions," Mumbai was a step up, a place where one might find work in what had always been the biggest film industry in India. Some musicians came on their own, while others were part of a small group centered around a specific music director:

VISTASP BALSARA: Actually, some musicians came [to Mumbai] with Master
    Ghulam Haider from Lahore. I don't remember their names, but they were
    quite wonderful. One I remember was a violin player named Ghias'uddin,
    but then he didn't know notation.

Movement from Lahore to Mumbai continued through 1948, after which
time rank-and-file musicians could no longer do so. Relocation from
Kolkata, on the other hand, began very early and lasted for a much longer
period of time. In 1933, director Hiren Bose, then living in Kolkata, accepted a contract to direct films in Mumbai and brought with him his
friend Anil Biswas as his music assistant:

ANIL BISWAS: We brought four musicians with us when we shifted to Bombay.
    Because we needed musicians who knew staff notation.

Bose and Biswas did not remain in their first studio position for very long,
however:

ANIL BISWAS: Sagar Movietone was a very popular film concern. They offered
    us better salaries. So in 1935 we shifted [to Sagar], but after one picture we
    left them also.

Kolkata was producing Hindi- and Bengali-language films when Bose
and Biswas left, but Biswas was just the first of many musicians and music
directors who moved from Kolkata to Mumbai. The trend remained strong
especially throughout the 1940s and '50s and continued into the 1970s. In
addition to Biswas, music directors Hemant Kumar, Salil Chaudhuri, Kemchand Prakash, and Sachin Dev Burman were significant composers in the
Hindi cinema who moved from Kolkata. Kumar and Chaudhuri spent
some time moving back and forth between the cities, and it seems as if
every time they returned to Kolkata, they encouraged other musicians to
make the change to the bigger industry.

Manohari Singh is one of a small group of Nepalis, originally connected
to British military bands, who found themselves in Kolkata after World
War II. Singh worked in Bengali films and at the HMV recording studios
in Kolkata for some time; he also had a gig at one of Kolkata's remaining
nightclubs (the famous Firpo's, which retained echoes of its postwar glamour well into the 1980s):

MANOHARI SINGH: Salil Chaudhuri was very fond of me, and also Hemant
    Kumar. They both used to do film work on both sides; they would go to
    Bombay and then come to Calcutta. And they said to me, "Why don't you
    come to Bombay? In Calcutta, slowly, slowly the work is going down. Par-
    tition has happened; the market is becoming very bad. Come to Bombay!"

The creation of Pakistan had made irrevocable the various British partitions of Bengal as a cultural unit. When East Bengal became East Pakistan in 1947, the political tensions between Pakistan and India made it first difficult and then, after 1962, impossible for Indian films to be distributed in the eastern half of what had been a single linguistic zone (eastern and western Bengalis all spoke the same language). The market for Indian films in Bengali was consequently cut in half:

MANOHARI SINGH: When my contract was over at Tipu's in 1959, Salil-da said, "Come on." So I went with Mr. Salil Chaudhuri.

In the late 1950s Salil Chaudhuri seems to have been especially interested in having Bengali musicians available in Mumbai:

SUMIT MITRA: Mr. Salil Chaudhuri called me to Mumbai in 1958. He had just given the music for *Madhumati* [1958], which was very big hit and had won the Filmfare award. He was very popular as a music director. So I went, but his house was full of strugglers like myself. At night his wife used to put all the beds down in the hallway for us to sleep.

Chaudhuri's somewhat ambiguous enthusiasm for the Mumbai industry and for Bengali musicians seems to have reached its height between 1957 and 1959. Just before Singh and Mitra came to Mumbai at Chaudhuri's urging, cellist Vasudeo Chakravarty had appeared at the music director's house in Mumbai. According to Chakravarty's son, however, it was music director Naushad Ali who was behind this move:

SANJAY CHAKRAVARTY: There was a huge show in Calcutta, some big film show. Naushad-saheb and many other top musicians from Bombay had come to Calcutta for that show. They brought some orchestral musicians from Bombay as well, but they also used some musicians from Calcutta. Manohari-da and my father were hired to play for that show.

Film shows, in which playback singers performed live on stage with orchestral accompaniment, sometimes with dancers and film stars as well, have a history of their own in India. As such, they deserve serious consideration. Although they are beyond the scope of this volume, such concerts uniquely sought to translate a studio art into a live performance art. Since the singers and orchestras were recording live in any event, the transition to stage musician was easier than it might have been. In this case, Naushad was impressed by some of Kolkata's musicians but engaged Salil Chaudhuri (again) as a cultural or industrial ambassador:

SANJAY CHAKRAVARTY: Naushad-saheb heard my dad playing and liked it very much. When he came back to Bombay, he called Salil-da, and he said, "You should bring these two boys here to Bombay." But Salil-da said,

"They won't come. They're different than these guys here [in Mumbai]. They won't like the food or the place." But in the end he talked them into it. So the credit should go first to Naushad-saheb and then to Salil-da for bringing us here.

My father used to stay in Salil-da's house for months together. And Salil-da's wife would cook for them morning and evening. After he came, my father went and met Naushad–saheb, who recognized him, and from then he started working.

From these stories, it is clear that Salil Chaudhuri's wife made her own contribution to the Bengali presence in Mumbai.

By the time these musicians came to Mumbai, Old Bollywood was in full swing, but it was not just the industry that was getting bigger. Music directors, especially Shankar-Jaikishan, Naushad, and O. P. Nayyar, were creating increasingly complex, often very Western sound tracks calling for large orchestras. There was a need for more trained and experienced performers, especially those who played Western instruments and could play from notation, whether Indian or Western. Regardless of instrumental fluency, notational skills were important. Musicians acquired these from a range of sources.

Notation and the Transmission of Musical Knowledge

Some film musicians were effectively self-taught, especially those whose orientation was toward Western popular music. The importance here of recordings in the transmission process is clear. Jerry Fernandes was a principal violin soloist in movies from the 1960s to 1994, when he retired, but he still considers himself primarily a jazz musician:

> JERRY FERNANDES: I went to Bombay when I was twelve or thirteen [circa 1935]. My father died when I was very young, and we were very poor, so there was no way I could afford to take tuition from anybody. So I used to listen to the musicians and see how they played, what they played, how they did it.
>
> I used to listen to the [Western] classical musicians and to the jazz musicians also, but nobody was playing jazz music on the violin at that time. But then one day I entered Portado's music shop, and I heard one recording by Mr. Stéphane Grappelli, and he was playing jazz. I remember the song was "Lady Be Good." So I asked the price of the record, and he told me twelve rupees. And I hadn't got twelve *paise* in my pocket. But I collected money, and I started buying the records. So I'm a self-made musician. It's a God gift.

Fernandes was fortunate, in a sense, that violins were common and easily acquired in the Goan community and that music was a well-regarded occupation. He was also lucky to have been undertaking this self-teaching in the 1930s, when there was a strong foreign presence in Mumbai and music from the West was relatively easy to find.

In the 1970s Ramesh Iyer was teaching himself electric guitar but had to contend with parental and community disapproval. In addition, foreign exchange laws in independent India made imported musical instruments and LPs both rare and expensive. Nevertheless, like Fernandes, Iyer used Western recordings as the basis of his education:

> RAMESH IYER: My first exposure to the guitar was Cliff Richard and the Shadows. I had one LP as a student, and there was a picture of the guitar player, and the guitar was a Mossright; that was my dream guitar. That was in 1973. I picked up from listening to the Shadows and the Ventures and the Beatles and those kinds of things.

Musicians who had training in aspects of Western music (e.g., staff notation, harmony, orchestration, arranging) had something of an advantage over self-taught musicians who played by heart, from memory. In the 1930s there were three subcultural or ethnic groups whose members were more likely than others to possess notational and theoretical skills. Although the explanations were different in each case, Goans, Parsis, and Sikhs were frequently associated with Western music performance. Of these, the former two had the greatest impact on the film-music industry, but the business was a site for the creation of an inherently syncretic music culture. In effect, everyone played a role:

> VISTASP BALSARA: We had two groups of musicians: those who played by memory and those who played by Indian notation and those by staff notation. I was very lucky that I knew staff notation and Indian notation both.

Balsara actually specifies three different systems by which film musicians learned and performed music. Some read no notational system at all and had to be taught their parts orally; they then played entirely by memory. These were usually traditional Indian-style performers with hereditary connections to musical activity who had learned aurally and orally at home.

Balsara's second category includes those who could read various forms of notation, although he further distinguishes between the various forms of syllabic notation (often referred to as *sargam*, after the first four syllables of *sa rē gā ma*, the Indian version of do-re-mi) traditionally used in Indian music and European staff notation. Indian syllabic notation in the film line was written in Hindi, Bengali, Marathi, and occasionally Gujarati scripts; a single orchestra sometimes included musicians playing from memory, along with others who were reading two different notational systems, using three or four scripts.

Anil Mohile, who began working as an arranger in the 1970s, came from a family that was active in Hindustani classical music and thus writes and arranges all his work in sargam. He argues that European and Indian notational systems are equally functional:

> ANIL MOHILE: There is no difference between Indian writing and Western writing. Whatever phrase you can write in staff notation, you can also write it in sargam. Indian notation has this advantage: Say you write in F major, but now you must play in D major. Indian notation, you just play it, just like a scale changer. But Western notation, you write the dots, and that means the pitch, so you must write it again if you want to change the key.

Mohile's assessment is certainly accurate as far as it goes, but despite that equivalence, European staff notation has been more prevalent in Mumbai, although this dominance was never complete, by any means, and is not so to this day.

Musicians learned staff notation and related musical skills from various sources, depending in large part on their sociocultural background. Some brought that training with them when they came to Mumbai; others learned from other musicians in the city, either as children or in the context of their profession. Bablu Chakravarty came to Mumbai in 1959, a year or more after his uncle, cellist Vasu Chakravarty:

> BABLU CHAKRAVARTY: I learned staff notation in Mumbai when I came here. They were all Goans in those days and very, very capable musicians. But because I was very cautious and very careful, they helped me. They taught me things.

Chakravarty was already an accomplished violinist when he arrived, but coming from Kolkata, he only read Bengali syllabic notation.

Kishore Desai notes that demands for notational skills varied both across time and as a result of the arrangers' demands. Trained in Indian classical styles and sargam notation, Desai had to turn to a Goan musician to help him master staff notation.

Despite his Parsi heritage (which would normally associate him with India's central west coast), Homi Mullan, like Chakravarty, grew up in Kolkata in the 1940s and '50s with his mother's relatives. Family connections led him to Vistasp Balsara, who had, rather unusually, moved to Kolkata by that time. Although Balsara was familiar with both staff notation and sargam, he taught Mullan only in Bengali sargam since that was what was necessary in Kolkata, even in HMV's main studios, located just outside the city:

Homi Mullan: Mr. Balsara taught me [notation] in Bengali language. When
I came down here [Mumbai], I learned in Hindi language. I can follow this
manuscript, staff notation, but not so well as I can follow the Indian notation. At that time in Bengal [the early 1960s] everybody was reading Bengali notations in HMV; no manuscript was there.

It appears that in Kolkata, generally speaking, syllabic notation was
more common than staff notation. But Vistasp Balsara has suggested that
overall, notation was more important in Kolkata:

Vistasp Balsara: There was another difference. In Bombay, 60 percent
were notation players, and 40 percent were memory players, but here [in
Kolkata], 95 percent were notation players, either staff notation or sargam.
That was a big difference.

Balsara himself had learned staff notation from a European. During the
colonial period, a number of foreign musicians were living or touring in
India, especially the main urban centers:

Vistasp Balsara: There was a German lady in Bombay, proficient in Western
music; her name was Hilda Friedberg. So I learned staff notation and piano
from her. Actually, when I started playing piano, I was not playing real true
piano; it was more Indian-style piano.

Notational skills were in demand from the 1940s on, as Anthony Gonsalves has also explained; the social and professional dynamics that different skill levels produced were often complex.

Learning notation was one thing, but specific instrumental skills sometimes represented a separate challenge. While violins have normally been
plentiful in the Goan community, cellos are both less common and more
costly. When John Gonsalves's cousin Anthony decided that John should
learn cello, he had to supply the instrument and the teacher before his suggestion could be taken seriously. As it turned out, the teacher, Edigio Verga
(see figure 1.2), was Italian, but he lived in Mumbai for a number of years
after independence:

John Gonsalves: Anthony Gonsalves used to stay in the Delamar Hotel [on
Marine Drive]. One day he called me to his hotel, and he said, "Just see
what is there for you." And there was a cello. He says, "You'll learn, no?
I'll give you a good teacher." So he just went out of his hotel room and
knocked on a nearby door, and one gentleman comes; he was a white man,
and his name was Verga. And Anthony says, "Mr. Verga, you have to teach
this boy cello." "Of course," he says, "if he's interested." And he says to
me, "Are you interested?" But I couldn't speak English like I can today, so
Anthony translated, and he said to me, "Whatever he asks you, you just
say 'Yes.' " So I said, "Yes."

Verga played widely across all kinds of musical styles in Mumbai during the 1940s and early '50s. He played regularly for movies and at the Taj Hotel in a classical quartet that also featured a Parsi violinist named Melli Mehta, the father of conductor Zubin Mehta.

Although he grew up in 1950s' Kolkata, Sumit Mitra also benefited from the presence of foreign musicians:

> SUMIT MITRA: There was one gentleman, Mr. Hamerculus [*sic*]. He was a Hungarian gentleman, and he played accordion at the Grand Hotel. And somehow I heard him playing, and I thought that was a wonderful instrument. I was trying to play harmonica at that time. So Mr. Hamerculus let me sit in his room when he practiced, and I began to pick things up. After some time he allowed me to come to his rehearsals. So you can say I learned from him like that.

Visiting musicians contributed knowledge and sometimes other things as well:

> CAWAS LORD: I was playing with Chic Chocolate; that was strictly jazz, dance music. I had to have my own drums made by hand. Everyone was making their own instruments. When we were at the Taj, a Latin band came there, called Gadimbas [named after its leader, Victor Gadimbas]. I learned from those Gadimbas drummers, and when they left, I bought all their instruments.

Lord proved to be the key figure in the introduction of Latin-style percussion into Hindi film scores by his association with bandleader Antonio Vaz and music director C. Ramchandra. He also taught others, including fellow Parsi Homi Mullan, how to play Latin-style percussion:

> HOMI MULLAN: Mr. Cawas Lord taught me how to play bongo. He was getting older and didn't want to play so much. He was always giving me a chance. He would say, "Homi, let me sit here, you play." So I started playing bongos.

Lord eventually gifted the instruments he had purchased from Gadimbas to Mullan, who continued to play them on recordings throughout the 1990s.

Shyamrao Kemble, with his background in traditional Indian music performance, also had to learn staff notation when he joined the film line. He also sought to understand the harmonic and compositional practices of European music:

> SHYAMRAO KEMBLE: After I joined films [1947], I saw that there were all these different instruments—sometimes saxophone is there, sometimes trumpet, sometimes mandolin, sometimes flute, Spanish guitar, piano. I

wondered how these things worked and why it was that this [instrumental] music didn't disturb the song? This is what I kept thinking, why wasn't the song disturbed?

I understood best about the piano because it's like harmonium, no? So I talked with the piano players. They were very good and told me many things. I'd ask, "What is this? What is the reason for this and for that? How do you know what to play so that you don't disturb the melody?" So they showed me the chord system.

Like Bablu Chakravarty, Kemble learned these things from Goan musicians. In his case, Kemble identifies pianist Robert Corea as his principal source of information about orchestration and harmony. His basic training in notation, however, came from a different source.

Sikh bandsmen and bandmasters had a strong tradition of association with British military bands in the 1940s, but relatively few became involved in films. One notable exception was Ram Singh of the famous A-R-P group. His military band experience and training made him an extremely important figure in the first two decades of sound films.

Very little is known about Ram Singh, whose family I have not been able to trace. In the late 1940s Shyamrao Kemble turned to him as source of music training:

> SHYAMRAO KEMBLE: Ram Singh knew staff notation very well. I asked him, would he teach me about staff notation? I had to travel from Goregaon to Matunga [more than twenty kilometers' travel on two rail lines] because that was where Ram Singh lived. I had to leave at six-thirty in the morning to reach his house by eight o'clock.

Distance was only one of the obstacles Kemble had to overcome as he sought to gain access to the English-language-based world of staff notation and Western music theory:

> SHYAMRAO KEMBLE: Ram Singh told me to go buy the Trinity College books, and he would teach me that. I was very embarrassed, but I finally told him, "I will not be able to read those things because they are written in English. I can't read English." I said, "I will just ask you questions, and you can give me the answers, and that way I can learn." So that's what we did. He wrote things for me in staff notation, and I copied them, and then he would write them in sargam, and I would write them in staff notation.

Students and teachers who wanted to study Western classical music or music theory availed themselves of the Trinity College curriculum in those areas. In the end, although Kemble mastered staff notation, he managed to do so without learning English.

Sikh or otherwise, the military and police bands of British India were re-
sources for learning, especially for the older generation of musicians; Cawas
Lord and Ramprasad Sharma, for example, both acquired some of their
Western skills in military-style wind bands in various ways. Manohari
Singh's Nepali family had an established connection with the Gurkha units
of the British military and their associated bands:

> MANOHARI SINGH: My parents came from Kathmandu. My grandfather came
> first to Kolkata in 1941 as a trumpet player in the army band. After he
> came, he decided to stay, so then my grandmother and father came to join
> him. He joined the police band. He used to play bagpipe, but basically he
> played clarinet. I picked up instruments because they were all around in
> our house. My father played flute at home and would practice at home, so I
> heard all that. But also my maternal uncle, he was in Burma in an army
> band. He was giving me lessons alongside my schooling.

In the 1940s Singh also benefited from the presence of another Hungar-
ian musician:

> MANOHARI SINGH: There was also one Hungarian there, Joseph Newman,
> from Budapest. He finally went to Australia and settled there, but he gave
> me very good training in music. His father used to play xylophone.

Singh's early training took place in an industrial town in West Bengal
called Batanagar, after the famous shoe factory that was built there. Singh
and his family played in the factory's brass band, conducted apparently by
Joseph Newman. Later, Newman and the Singhs all moved to Kolkata in
search of better-paying work. There Manohari Singh encountered other
foreign musicians and received more training:

> MANOHARI SINGH: In Kolkata in that time, only British were allowed in there
> [Firpo's Restaurant]. But there was a Spanish band, and Francisco Casanova
> was flutist; he was the leader. He became fond of me. I was really quite
> young then, so he gave me lots of coaching and training at Calcutta School
> of Music.

Lallu Ram Indorkar began his career as a member of the royal band of
the maharajah of Indore, for which he is named. Indorkar was the film industry's primary oboist from the mid-1950s through the mid-1980s; almost any oboe heard on a Mumbai film score from that era is being played
by Lallu Ram. As his son explains, Indorkar did not begin his musical profession on oboe; his introduction to that instrument was rather summarily
dictated by the foreign (British?) leader of the royal band:

> SHANKAR INDORKAR: My father was in the band, the maharajah's band in In-
> dore; that was a military band. My father played very nicely on flute [bansi,

Indian bamboo flute] in the British time. One foreign man, he was the bandleader—I don't know his name—he called my father and said, "Okay, don't you play flute anymore. Now you play oboe." And the man who had been playing oboe there in Indore, he showed my father how to play.

Western music, played by Indians of all kinds (including Goans), as well as the British and other Europeans, was a profitable trade in colonial culture. For some, the prestige that accompanied association with the ruling culture was also significant. Military or brass bands played a general role in making Western music visible, but for the film industry, they were probably less important than the classical and jazz/dance ensembles of colonial India.

The Decline of Colonial Music Culture

The very existence of Euro-American music in South Asia was a result of colonialism. During the 1930s and '40s, when colonialism was a physical presence, the physicality of music (e.g., performances, musicians, instruments) was also relatively powerful. Shope argues, however, that Indian understandings of African American jazz musicians (at least) changed during this period, regarded as "progressive" in the 1930s: "By the early 1940s, their image became somewhat of a novelty, symbolic of the initial development of jazz, but marginalized as increasingly antiquated" (2007, 97). Shope also argues that the marginalization of African American jazz musicians in Mumbai created opportunities for local popular musicians, including Goans, "to pioneer new styles of jazz-influenced popular music in the domestic public sphere, especially Bombay cabaret music and early film songs of the 1940s" (ibid., 98).

After 1947, the physical presence of foreign musicians decreased significantly, but their cultural legacy was developed and transformed, as suggested here, through local forms, especially film music. Colonialism and colonial influences had constructed a myriad of paths by which musicians in the Hindi film line could learn something at least of the Western music.

The inhabitants of the central west coast, Goa, may have had the longest and most intimate experience of European colonialism on the subcontinent. Goa served as the administrative center of the Portuguese colonies in Asia from 1510. The Portuguese did not develop a local infrastructure comparable to that of the British, but their 451-year stay there ensured that Portuguese was widely spoken and that the conversion to Catholicism of many local inhabitants survived the end of the colonial era (1961).

A lack of local industry left young Goans with very few choices in terms of nearby employment and thus encouraged them to look for employment elsewhere in India and abroad. Because of the impact of the Catholic Church and its educational system, many Goans found work as musicians.

Christianity had helped a strong tradition of Western music to develop among the Goans. Many of them seem to have valued the elementary education provided by the Catholic schools, which included at least the rudiments of European staff notation and choral singing and quite frequently violin as well:

> JOHN PEREIRA: In every village in the church, there was a choirmaster who used to teach music. When you were seven or eight, you went to the church school. And they used to teach a little bit [of music] reading and this and that. And then he used to put you on the violin. So I did my music in the church school, little bit reading the staff notation, then playing violin. So I took my music first. Then I went to Portuguese school after that.

The choirmasters that Pereira mentions were Goans, not Portuguese, but they were part of a transmission system for European notational skills:

> ANNIBAL CASTRO: My brother and sister both learned music in school. They had lessons, but I learned guitar on my own. At that time [1935–1945] music was in the air; it was in the environment for us to learn music. Also, music was a compulsory subject under the Portuguese, and that meant Western music, church music, harmony, theory, all that. So I picked it all up, even the theory, even the music writing also.

Goan musicians traveled throughout the British Empire and beyond, making use of their Western musical skills. Their fundamental training in Western notation made them especially flexible:

> MICKEY COREA: I first played violin. That was in my brother's band. I was sixteen or seventeen years old. It was Corea's Optimists Band in Karachi, led by Alec Corea [circa 1933; see Fernandes 2005 for a photograph of this group].

Corea eventually changed from violin to saxophone, but the switch was initiated by the needs of foreign musicians:

> MICKEY COREA: One American family band came to Karachi, and they needed a replacement for their saxophone player because he got sick. They wanted a young fellow, you see, because the old guys were playing "pooh, pooh, pooh" [military-band style], and they wanted some one who could play jazz. They heard me with Corea's Optimists and called me to a rehearsal. The leader of the group said, "You should learn to play the saxophone!" and he shoved it into my hands. And he showed me this, that, and the other thing. I was very taken by it, so I played it all the time when they were there.

Goans played different musical styles as required and were also mainstays of the many bands that were part of royal musical establishments in colonial India. Trumpeter John Pereira played in military and dance bands before ending up in the movie business:

> JOHN PEREIRA: I came to Bombay in 1936 and decided to learn trumpet. So I learned that. Then I went to work in [the royal band of] Bhavnagar state. They had a lot of money, and they used to get a big music library. Every month new, new music used to come to that library, and I stayed there for two years and learned all the classical music from that library. But after two years I proceeded to hotel jobs.

Maoro Alfonso came to Mumbai as young boy around 1927 from the small Goan village of Talegaon. He had learned from a choirmaster in Goa as usual but continued his study of violin with Dominic Pereira, a well-known violin soloist of the period, who himself played in films. Alfonso won a scholarship for further music study in England, but this plan appears to have become a casual victim of late-colonial-era politicking:

> MAORO ALFONSO: I got my LRSM [Licentiate of the Royal Schools of Music] in 1932, and I was getting a scholarship to go to England. But my father was in a [Goan] bank, and the [Portuguese] bank manager told my father that Trinity College was not so great. So my father told the Trinity College man, "You take him to Vienna instead of England." But they wouldn't do that.

Maoro Alfonso was one of many who worked in British India's hotels, clubs, and theaters, providing popular and classical music for dancing and socializing. Like Bengali musicians in Kolkata in the 1950s, however, Goan (and other) dance-band musicians found that there were fewer and fewer venues for their music in independent South Asia. Although some wealthy Indians and Pakistanis continued to engage in social, Western-style dancing, the market was simply much smaller. Shope (2003) has chronicled the decline of the colonial music culture in northern India (specifically Lucknow). Among other things, his research demonstrates the uniqueness of the situation in Mumbai. Jazz and popular musicians may not always have appreciated film music (see chapter 8), but the film line at least offered them a livelihood. In other Indian cities (outside the film-production centers) the collapse of the colonial music culture meant no work at all.

Like Anthony Gonsalves, saxophonist Joe Gomes recalls that, before the late 1940s, relatively few Goans were working in the film line. Like many others, he was working in a dance band:

> JOE GOMES: Before C. Ramchandra [i.e., before 1942] Goans were there, but they were not such good musicians because they were playing in the hotels and all these things. Good musicians had no time for films.

The Gomes brothers made a very early transition from dance bands to films, but the process, as always, was gradual. Jazz still appeared to be an attractive avenue to some, even in the early days of Indian independence. Some bands continued playing into the 1950s. Leslie Godinho began his career in dance bands like others who had come before him. His career as a jazz drummer lasted less than a decade, however:

> LESLIE GODINHO: I got a job with [bandleader] Tiny Lobo. They were play-
> ing in Ceylon. That must have been 1949 or '50. I was about fifteen or six-
> teen then. Then we went to work at the Savoy [in Mumbai], still with Tiny
> Lobo. Then we went to Delhi. Then I joined Rudy Cotton, and I played
> with him for two years. And then after that, I got married [circa 1957].
> So after I got married, I gave up traveling mostly. I concentrated on the
> film line.

Sebastian D'Souza (1906–1996) became one of the industry's most highly regarded and prolific arrangers (see chapter 5). D'Souza's training came from his experience in dance bands, and his presence in Mumbai was due to the partition of British India, as his son explains:

> VICTOR D'SOUZA: My father was playing in Lahore when partition happened.
> He was playing at Stiffles and the Regal and Faletti's and those places. In
> 1947 he came to Bombay. Then he met [music director] O. P. Nayyar, who
> was also from Lahore and had known about him there. You can say O. P.
> Nayyar gave my father his first break in Bombay.

Nayyar may have given D'Souza his first break (based on their mutual associations with Lahore), but it was with the music-director duo Shankar-Jaikishan that Sebastian established his reputation. This was due not only to his own talents but also to the unreliability of his predecessor in the Shankar-Jaikishan organization, pianist and multi-instrumentalist Sonny Castelino (figure 4.2), who was born in Yangon, (Rangoon) Myanmar, and spent much time in the metropolises of British Southeast Asia.

Trumpeter John Pereira played with Castelino and married the pianist's younger sister. Like most who recall him, Pereira greatly admires Caste-lino's musicianship but notes that he was a rather colorful character:

> JOHN PEREIRA: Sonny Castelino was a very good musician and pianist; he
> used to play in the nightclubs. And when you play music in nightclubs, you
> know, the drinks are always there. And he married some Dutch woman or
> something. Then, after some time, he came back to Bombay, but you could
> not rely on him. Whenever he would come to Bombay, they [Shankar-
> Jaikishan] would take him, but they could never rely on him to be there,
> and people used to come to his house looking for money.

Figure 4.2   Pianist and arranger Sonny Castelino in a studio pose, ca. 1945. Courtesy of John Pereira.

Tenor saxophonist Joe Pereira started out in the dance-band business with Sebastian D'Souza, who was his older cousin. Although he did some work in films, he stayed out of that line for the most part and is better known in India as a jazz musician. He is one of the few of his generation who managed the two worlds successfully:

> JOE PEREIRA: You can say I was always into music; I was crazy about it. Then my cousin heard about my interest. He told my folks, "Send him up here. I'll look after him. I'll train him." So they figured that would be okay. So I went up to Lahore and joined my cousin in 1942; I was twelve. He taught me about harmony and improvisation and all those things.

Much of Pereira's career is beyond the scope of this book. He persisted in the jazz line well after most of his colleagues had switched entirely to movies and did not become involved in film music until the late 1960s:

> JOE PEREIRA: Then things slowly started to get tight, so I went to Bombay. My cousin [D'Souza] was working with Shankar-Jaikishan then, and I joined him.

Friends and Sons

The wide-open nature of the film-music industry in the 1930s and '40s gradually grew more restricted. People found work because their friends or family were already working in the business and could put in a word for them. Kishore Desai began his musical career studying traditional classical Hindustani music as a student of Ustad Kadim Hussain Khan of the Agra style of *khyal* vocal music. Desai was a vocal student and a sarod player, but as a young boy he made a hit playing film songs on mandolin at a number of important public events. His friend Kalyanji Veerji Shah was one member of the music director duo Kalyanji-Anandji, but in the early 1950s he was acting as an assistant to Shankar-Jaikishan. The publicity and the connections his friend provided helped him get work with Shankar-Jaikishan and others. [🅐 Video 4.2]

Eventually film music became very much a family business. During the 1960s, film-musicians' sons began to take an interest in their fathers' profession. Francis Vaz worked as a drummer with bandleader Chic Chocolate and also played with Chic and others for film recordings. Vaz sometimes brought his son Franco to the recording sessions:

> FRANCO VAZ: I used to love to go to the studios with my dad. I'd learn a lot, you know. It was unconscious, but I was learning a lot, just listening. I started from the age of twelve or thirteen [1968–1969]. People would say to me, "You're not playing any instrument? Okay, in this song you play maracas." And after the take was over, they'd put ten rupees in my hand. That was big money for me in those days.

Ernest Menezes was also born into a musical family; four of his grandfather's sons were professional musicians. Although his own father, José, rarely played in the films, his uncle, Joaquim (Joe) Menezes (see figure 1.3), was a principal soloist:

> ERNEST MENEZES: When I was very young, my uncle took me to learn violin. I learned with him for ten years, and for five years I lived with him only, and I used to go to my parents' house on weekends. And when I first joined, he would take me for recordings.

Shankar Indorkar eventually inherited his father's job as Mumbai's principal oboist but began his career playing violin. He had had no practical experience playing the oboe when his father was taken ill in 1985:

SHANKAR INDORKAR: My father got sick at that time, so there was no money at home. My father couldn't work. There were four of us children, no food, lots of problems. And we needed medicine and money for the hospital. So I had to do something. So my father said, "You go to Pyare-bhai [Pyarelal Sharma], and tell him you're my son." So I went. I was very scared. Pyare-bhai said, "What's the matter son?" I said, "Pyare-bhai, you know me. I'm Lallu Ram's son." I said, "I need to play violin in some recordings somewhere because we have all these problems at home. Can you help me?" But Pyare-bhai said, "What's violin? I have all these violins. Your father plays such nice oboe. You must know how to play oboe also. You play oboe. I need oboe."

That day for me was a God gift. Out of everyone in the world, Pyare-bhai gave me that chance; he lifted me up. Just like that.

Of course, the chance to play oboe was a mixed blessing given that Indorkar had never actually played the instrument professionally. There appears to have been a degree of tolerance among Mumbai's musicians for his father's sake, however, and like at least one more famous musician, Indorkar was aided by the woman who had been watching and listening to her husband play the instrument for many years:

SHANKAR INDORKAR: That day I came home in the evening, and I took out my father's oboe. And I took the reed. And I had seen how he fixed it, but I didn't know how to do it. I had just seen him do it. So I was trying to make it work. And my mother came in, and I told her I was trying to do this. And she had a lot of knowledge, you know? She knew how the oboe was supposed to sound and how the reed was fixed and how to blow and many such things because my father had been playing in the house for all those years. So she knew.

Other musicians actually had to go against their family's occupational traditions to join the industry. Like Indorkar, Ramesh Iyer was expected to take up the family business, but in his case that meant being an engineer like his father:

RAMESH IYER: My father was an engineer, and I completed my B[achelor of] Eng[ineering] as well. But I really wanted to do music. I used to get small, small jobs playing for school shows or small traveling groups that would play at roadside places. Sometimes I'd make only five rupees. And my father said, "You have a degree in engineering. You could be having a good job and earning money. What are you doing?" But I said, "This is what I really want to do. Just give me two years. If after that I haven't made a success in this line, I'll get a job as an engineer."

It took nearly three years rather than the two he had stipulated, but by 1976 Iyer was making a good living playing for recordings and for live film-music performances.

Even though it did not happen frequently, the best pathway into the film-music line was an invitation from a music director. Despite his name, Louiz Banks came from the same Nepali heritage as Manohari Singh. He had been playing in the hill station capital of eastern India, Darjeeling:

> LOUIZ BANKS: I finally got into Calcutta as a bandleader in the 1970s. I had my band and gained a lot of popularity in the jazz field. R. D. Burman came into the restaurant where I was playing; that was the Blue Fox. During my break, I got a message that this gentleman is calling me to his table. And he said, "I'm R. D. Burman. I'm an Indian film-music director. I like what you are playing. Would you like to do some work for me?" It was that fast and that quick. So I accepted his offer, but I told him, "I don't know anything about film music."

The practice of recruiting jazz musicians from nightclubs was itself a distinguished practice in the Hindi film-music business. More than twenty years before R. D. Burman lifted Louiz Banks out of the Blue Fox, music director C. Ramchandra was doing the same thing much more casually and on much shorter notice:

> KERSI LORD: Chic Chocolate was a fantastic musician, a trumpet player. My father was his drummer for many years. They used to play at Greens Restaurant. C. Ramchandra used to go there, and he would hear the band, and he used to say, "Okay, come on. Let's go!" My father would ask, "Where?" "Come, I'm recording in Bandra now, and in the night you come and play."

Auditions

In 1952, as demand for film musicians rose, some of the senior men in the business formed a professional union, the Cine Musicians Association (CMA), in order to negotiate payment schedules with producers (see chapter 6). These founding members simply paid their fees and were enrolled. Thereafter, anyone who became a member had to audition. The CMA audition became the formal indicator that a musician had joined the line.

Although he was playing film music and working with film-music directors (in this case) Kalyanji-Anandji, when Ramesh Iyer wanted to play on recordings, he had to join CMA and audition for work:

RAMESH IYER: I started playing in studios in 1976. We had one thing, these auditions for the CMA. You had to play that audition and pass before you could play for the studios. In 1976 I was the top of the audition, and so I was getting calls.

Auditions were also required for musicians who came to Mumbai from other cities and industries, but passing the CMA audition did not guarantee work. It meant that if you were called, you could play. Although he eventually made his career as a trumpet player, Joe Monsorate learned and auditioned on violin because his father (Peter Monsorate, also a famous trumpeter) believed that violinists would have more work:

JOE MONSORATE: I auditioned in 1960—but on violin because all fathers were giving the work to their sons. Because there was much more work. We were a big family, so we needed to work.

Like Shankar Indorkar, this son of a famous soloist followed his father into the line but not initially on the same instrument. Because there was demand for many violinists and the instrument was relatively forgiving (for those in the back rows), the instrument was seen as a good, secure, if not terribly remunerative entry point:

JOE MONSORATE: Actually, my father took me to Pyarelal-ji. And Pyarelal looked at me and didn't say anything, and he told his informer, "Put him in the violins sometime." But you learn that way only. I was put there, but I was not paid because I was not proven.

In chapter 6 I discuss the role of "informers" (as Monsorate calls them). In the late 1950s and early '60s, however, there were ways to become a member of CMA without auditioning:

SUMIT MITRA: At that time [1958] the system was like that—that if you were not a member but got called for a recording, and two music directors provided letters that you were suitable, they admitted you without audition. So that's what happened.

For some musicians, the CMA audition was a rite that they did not necessarily take seriously. Although he began playing casually on recordings at the age of twelve or thirteen, Franco Vaz auditioned six years later:

FRANCO VAZ: Most musicians had to do an audition before they started, you know? But I just had my big family, so I never did an audition. So one day in the 1970s, I think, somebody called me and said, "You don't have a card?" And I said, no, I didn't have.

Tappan Adhikari began his career playing the *khol*, a barrel drum with an extremely small, high-pitched right head that is associated especially with eastern India (Bengal) and that region's religious or traditional music. He auditioned for CMA sometime in the late 1960s, when he was in his teens. Adhikari's father, who also played khol, had developed an instrumental variation called a *chapkī,* in which the instrument's regular loaded heads are covered with pieces of leather, thereby producing an unpitched, muffled percussive sound:

> TAPPAN ADHIKARI: Iqbal-bhai and Ayub-bhai and Sattar-bhai [three very senior tabla players in the film line] took my audition. So I took my khol for the audition, but they said, "If you're going to play khol, then your daddy should take the audition, not us." But I said, "How can my father take my audition? What should I play?" And they said, "You're playing this every day next to us in recordings. Don't play khol; play that chapkī that your father made." And I said, "What, on chapkī?" And they said "Sure, why not? We'll enjoy that."

Adhikari was joining a media/culture industry that was at the top of its game. By the time of his audition in the 1960s, musicians with a wide range of backgrounds had been finding their ways into the film line for thirty years. Indian classical and dramatic music, jazz, classical, and popular Western forms of music had all been incorporated into the melodies that were dominating Indian theaters, radios, and streets. That status quo would continue more or less for more than twenty years.

These accounts give us a more nuanced understanding of the sources of Hindi film music's famed eclecticism, which represented the performance traditions and skills of a range of musicians, as well as the values of postcolonial Indian culture in general. Everything that Mumbai film composers "borrowed" from the 1930s onward was already present in India and being played by Indian musicians. The stories in this chapter suggest that the scholarly and popular accounts that credit music directors with the musical borrowings that defined Hindi film music's eclecticism are telling only part of the story. Music directors were, in one sense, borrowing the musicians who played the various styles and content of eclecticism as much as they were making use of the materials themselves. The musicians came with the repertoires and musical skills that the composers valued almost as much as they prized their instrumentalism per se. Without them Hindi film music would not have been as diverse as it is. I pursue the musicians' views on eclecticism and style in chapter 7.

When they joined the film line, musicians like Zarin Sharma, Shyamrao Kemble, and Maoro Alfonso were in effect exchanging the local audiences who had been listening to them in the theaters, clubs, and hotels for an invisible but vastly larger audience for the Hindi cinema and its music. Where they had been playing for the elite and upper-middle-class audiences of British and "Indian" India or for those who attended music drama performances, stage shows, and so on, they were now playing in total anonymity for an audience that was almost exclusively Indian.

Musicians joined the film line from a range of cultural and musical backgrounds and with diverse motivations. Many came from Mumbai itself; many more came from Goa, but as Mumbai's dominance in national film and film-music production became more pronounced, musicians also arrived from other film production centers. Unlike the music directors, relatively few of the musicians appeared from outside both Mumbai and the film line. They employed a range of strategies to find work and in some cases to acquire the necessary skills as well, especially in the matter of notation. The next chapter describes how, once they joined the line, musicians became involved in those processes that constituted the actual day-to-day work of the film-music industry. It was an innovative, sometimes collaborative, sometimes piecemeal business of creating the music in response to narrative and visual cues.

5

Roles, Relations, and the Creative Process

The production of songs and background music for films was, in a sense, structurally divided into two aspects: the relatively private, asynchronous process of music creation and the more public one of recording, in which time often had greater significance in more than one way. Moreover, these two components had different outcomes and often quite dissimilar economic and industrial structures, especially from the musicians' point of view. In the initial stages, producers invested in a song as a creative work suited to its cinematic context and set to an appropriate lyric (or vice versa). They purchased songs for a fee from music directors, whose names would feature prominently in the film's credits and who were, in effect, doing piecework. In the subsequent recording process, producers invested in the recording of a song along more industrial lines. The music directors oversaw the recording as part of their fee but involved many more participants and incurred a wide range of hourly costs for the producer, who paid participants an hourly wage directly, bypassing the music director altogether.

The two components were not dichotomous, of course, but they were distinct in many ways. The first part of the process, which is the focus of this chapter, was more hidden and involved many fewer musicians than did recording. Those involved in the initial creative stage later formed the musical core of the larger group who carried out the recording. Nevertheless, because of their dependence on indirect payment, social relationships, and so forth, the early stages most clearly embodied the workshop or cottage-industry nature of the system. In this chapter and the following one I consider the industry's socioprofessional organization since the workshop structures did not extend to all of the musicians or to the studios as such. When a song reached the recording studio, a slightly more impersonal and industrial system came into play. Furthermore, recording sessions were the source of the vast majority of musicians' incomes; they were thus subject to different kinds of industrial pressures. For this reason, I have divided the creation and the production process into two chapters. Chapter 6 examines the more industrial side of song production, rehearsals, and recordings, the conditions surrounding them, and the economic structures that organized them.

The present chapter examines the musical, economic, and social relationships of the creative process that took place in the world of music rooms, music directors, arrangers, assistants, and sitting musicians. It focuses on workshops and professional roles and on the organization of the creation of the roughly nineteen songs that Mumbai's musicians were composing every week from the last years of British rule through the early years of the twenty-first century. This prodigious output was the product of a remarkably informal socioprofessional system.

Music Directors at the Center of the Old Bollywood Structure

To the extent that "music director" means "composer," this role was naturally at the center of the creative process. Music directors did not work in isolation, however; nor was their role limited to composition. Although they were technically just composers, music directors connected the various aspects of song production in human, economic, and process-oriented terms. They were the professional centers around which orbited an entire galaxy of individuals playing many different roles. The nature of the music director's role and its informal links to other aspects of the film line was responsible in many ways for the unique characteristics and musical creativity that the best Old Bollywood film scores embody.

Music Directors

As the studio system collapsed, freelance film musicians found themselves reorganizing their professional lives around music directors, although they too were freelance operators in Old Bollywood. When they review their careers, Old Bollywood musicians most commonly define them by naming the music directors for whom they played. The music director that first gave them work is memorable inasmuch as that break marked the beginning of a career:

> SUMIT MITRA: Mr. Sebastian [D'Souza] came to know about me and also
> Mr. Sumant Raj, the flute player. They were doing one film with Buloo C.
> Rani. He gave me my first work in Mumbai. I remember I had to borrow
> ten rupees to get a taxi to the studio.

Vipin Reshammiya has worked in a number of quite distinct capacities in the film industry, including film production and composition. His son has become one of the more successful music directors of New Bollywood. Although he attributes his success to his contributions to a particular hit score, the elder Reshammiya defines that accomplishment in terms of the music directors who were competing for his services in the 1960s:

> VIPIN RESHAMMIYA: I played with Shankar-Jaikishan. *Evening in Paris* [1967]
> was a big hit for me. That gave me a very big boost up. So then I was play-
> ing for all the music directors: C. Ramchandra, Madan Mohan, Roshan-
> saheb, Laxmikant-Pyarelal, R. D. Burman, everybody.

Although sitarist J. V. Acharya's career began much earlier than Reshammiya's, he too describes his career in terms of associations with specific music directors:

> J. V. ACHARYA: First of all, I started with Vasant Desai. But one day C. Ram-
> chandra called me, "Come, you work at Kardar with me." And from that,
> 1954, I started working with C. Ramchandra and also Naushad and
> Ghulam Miya [Ghulam Muhammad]. And I played most of the songs for
> Shankar-Jaikishan and Salil-da and the Burmans, everybody. S. D. Burman
> used to phone me personally; he never used a messenger. "Accha, aaj kyaa
> kar reha hai? Aaj rehearsal ke liye aa ja" [Well, what are you doing today?
> Come today for a rehearsal]. So I used to go there and played so many
> songs with Burman-dada.

"Everybody" is the widely used word that indicates that a musician—usually a specialist, such as Reshammiya (who had early access to electronic keyboards) or Acharya (who was a sitar soloist)—is in high demand.

Music Director: Musician Relations and Perceptions

Relations between musicians and music directors were entirely professional and rather anonymous in many cases but in other instances were quite collegial if not familial:

> SUDHIR KADAM: My daddy was a good friend of Laxmi-ji and Pyare-ji. He
> wasn't in the line, but he was their friend. There was a family relation

between my family and Laxmi's family. So my daddy was going to their house, and they were coming to our house. Laxmi was coming all the time.

Kadam, who had studied tabla, became a regular member of the L-P workshop but began his work in the line quite casually (I later discuss the term *sitting* in detail):

> SUDHIR KADAM: We were all chorus singers in *Satyam Shivam Sundaram* [1977] me, my daddy, my cousin—and after that I became a sitting member. I still go there [but] only to say hello to the family.

Musicians generally understand quite well which music directors are musically knowledgeable and which are not. Most musicians locate Pyarelal Sharma at the top of the former list. Shankar Indorkar is one of a number of musicians who have told me a version of the following story. There may well be some actual event on which it is based, but at this point it appears to be apocryphal. Musicians tell it, however, when they wish to indicate their perception of the usual level of musical understanding among music directors:

> SHANKAR INDORKAR: I played on some recording for another music director [i.e., not Laxmikant-Pyarelal], and my friend was arranging. So, some song we were playing that was in two flats, but it was too high for the singer. So the producer came, and the music director was there, and they were talking, and my friend [the arranger] said, "We need to go half tone lower," so the music director, who knew we were playing in two flats said, "Okay, add one more flat!"

The story emphasizes this unnamed music director's ignorance of the structures of Western music theory. Rather than lowering the melody by a single halftone (or semitone), an additional flat would lower the melody's tonal center by seven halftones.

In his comments about the Shah brothers, Kersi Lord offers one version of the compositional process (although he himself was a composer) while distinguishing between composition and the more managerial role of music director:

> KERSI LORD: Kalyanji and Anandji weren't really good musicians. Once he got that [electronic] keyboard, Kalyanji was just a hit. He could compose songs, but you don't need much for that. They never used to call themselves composers; they always said "I'm a music director," not a composer.

Some music directors were also known for their appreciative attitudes toward studio musicians. Somewhat surprisingly, O. P. Nayyar, who otherwise comes off in accounts as rather aloof, is routinely mentioned in this way. Like Shankar Indorkar's flat-adding story, many musicians who are old enough to have worked with Nayyar-saheb report him taking off his wristwatch to give (as a token of appreciation) to musicians who had played especially well or, as in this version, to his arranger:

> FRANCIS D'COSTA: Once he even gave his watch; it was a golden watch, a Rolex, and he took it off and gave it to Sebastian D'Souza. He said, "I cannot imagine the simple way you have managed that arrangement."

D'Costa played with Nayyar as a violinist in the early 1960s, toward the end of Nayyar's career. Jerry Fernandes has the experience to provide an earlier, more personal version of this story:

> JERRY FERNANDES: Nayyar-saheb had great love for musicians; he used to appreciate art. There was one recording, we needed an obbligato [an instrumental solo countermelody] for that song, and Sebastian [D'Souza, the arranger] gave me the chance to play it. There was no arrangement [i.e., no written music], so Sebastian asked me, "You see the count and then play your own music." And after the recording, Nayyar-saheb gave me one thousand rupees extra in appreciation.

In addition to Nayyar's attitude, Fernandes describes a not-uncommon situation in which instrumental soloists were asked to improvise music for interludes, countermelodies, and so forth.

Regardless of their relationships, however, or their perceptions of music directors, for musicians, the music directors were at the heart of the social and professional network that facilitated the recording process and its infrastructure, as well as the source of everyone's financial support. They were the crucial link, in other words, between the industry's and the culture's desire for film music and the musicians who produced it. In one sense, the music directors kept everyone working.

Creative Environments and Creative Roles

The first steps in the process of getting a song onto film took place in the working spaces—called music rooms or sitting rooms—of individual music directors. These early stages often involved a team of creatives: the composer, naturally; the lyricist; and sometimes a choreographer. Also directly involved at this stage were one or more people responsible for the film in financial and aesthetic terms: the producer and the director. In addition, the early stages of song development often required a number of musicians in a range of active and supportive roles. Largely from the musicians' perspectives, then, I examine a collective and creative production and decision-making process that involved the work and the decisions of individuals in a number of key professional, financial, and musical roles.

Music Rooms and the Creative Process

As the named composers of songs and the individuals paid to compose them, music directors are naturally at the heart of the creative process. Most music directors controlled and managed what were effectively small creative workshops staffed by teams of musicians, usually including at least one music assistant and/or a number of musicians called "sitting musicians." In and around the music room, people were engaged in multiple tasks associated with various songs or films. The number of musicians with whom a music director worked and the regularity of their interactions depended largely upon the number of films the music director had contracted for at any given time and, naturally, upon personal inclination as well.

Music directors and their teams worked on the composition of songs every day, either on contract for a specific film or in anticipation of future work. Their music rooms were effectively "the office," the place they spent most of the day when not in the studio. Although he began his musical career as a tabla player, Amrut Katkar found a niche in the film-music industry playing what is called "side percussion," a term that refers to all manner of handheld percussion instruments such as maracas, wood blocks, and castanets. Katkar became a specialist on the scraped idiophone called *reso-reso* in Portuguese. He worked regularly in R. D. Burman's workshop:

> AMRUT KATKAR: I came to work with Pancham because Maruti Rao knew me. I was going to his sitting room there in Santa Cruz. I still don't know the address; it's not there now. For thirty years I went there every morning and evening. We were making songs and playing and recording. And the producers would come and Pancham would play the songs for them. We were making new songs always.

Katkar's description of the job is quite matter of fact and sounds rather like an office worker or salaried employee, down to the ironic fact that he never knew the actual address (he knew the physical location and which bus he needed to take to get there). This is yet another echo of Vistasp Balsara's characterization of salaried life in the studio period: "They came every day whether there was work or no work."

In some cases, a music room was no more than the front room of a music director's home; for R. D. Burman (as for his father) it was a rented space on the main shopping street of west central Mumbai (Linking Road). Sometimes a music room was part of a film studio to which the music director might have regular access, but the establishment and maintenance of

such sites appears to be another cultural and industrial response to the decline of the producing studios. Vistasp Balsara reports that Ghulam Haider
had no music room as such: "He used to go to Central Studio, Tardeo, for
all his pictures and his rehearsals." This was a common practice in the studio period, when Haider was active, but less common in Old Bollywood,
at least in the way that Balsara stipulates.

The organization of Old Bollywood's physical plant was controlled
largely by the business families that owned the sites and rented them out to
film producers and only indirectly to music directors. Demand for some
music directors, however, allowed everyone to act as though they were permanently installed in particular studios. As demand for spaces for hire increased, most film-recording studios were booked most of the time; many
music directors found that work spaces outside of the studio infrastructure
were both cheaper and more convenient for compositional work. The
Burmans, Madan Mohan, Bappi Lahiri, and others rented private rooms
near their homes. The most convenient arrangement was perhaps that of
C. Ramchandra, who in the 1940s and '50s lived in an apartment facing
the large recreational and sporting grounds called Shivaji Park; he rented
the floor below it for his music room.

As befitting their popularity and consequent high status, the prolific
Shankar-Jaikishan rented a spacious and rather prestigious industrial site:

> DATTARAM WAADKAR: They rehearsed at Famous Studios, Mahalaxmi. It was
> a big music room. Forty musicians could sit there. We were there every
> day. I came around eight o'clock in the morning and cleaned everything,
> and they came around nine o'clock, and we worked there until nine or ten
> o'clock at night. I also practiced there. Recording time, we went to the stu-
> dio, and at night we went home. But this was like school: Go there every
> day. Practice, composition, singing, everything took place there. Lata-bai
> came there; all the singers came there to rehearse.

Despite the impressiveness of Shankar-Jaikishan's music room, the
height of sophistication and luxury (one might say) came in the 1970s and
'80s in the sitting rooms of R. D. Burman and of Laxmikant-Pyarelal, although each version of affluence reflected other aspects of what were, in a
way, different stylistic schools. Burman, who was fascinated by sound and
recording technology, had quite an elaborate technical setup in his music
room, effectively a complete sound amplification and recording system
maintained by his recording assistant, Deepan Chatterji:

> DEEPAN CHATTERJI: We had microphones and speakers and everything. And I
> had that Philips cassette tape recorder, one of the first actually [circa 1972],
> and I used to maintain a ledger, dates and times, and keeping track of with
> whom Pancham-da had sat, what the directors had said, and what the situ-

ations were, which song, all those things. I would note down the counter numbers.

At the time of which Chatterji is speaking, the Burman music room was generating slightly less than 10 percent of all the film scores being produced in Mumbai. As I mention in chapter 3, the Burman and Laxmikant-Pyarelal teams dominated stylistic trends in film music from 1970 through the mid-1980s (conservatively) and remained important through the early 1990s. Despite the technological sophistication of the Burman workshop, Laxmikant-Pyarelal probably surpassed everyone in the sheer size of their standing establishment, one that further blurred the already fuzzy line between creation, rehearsal, and recording.

On a pedestrian level, the duo shared a series of music rooms, first in Vile Parle, then in Khar, and later in Juhu. These were attached to the different homes that Laxmikant owned over these years:

> BHAVANI SHANKAR: Laxmi-ji had his bungalow, Juhu 10th Road. There were four or five guys who went there every day for sittings. Sudhir Kadam was one of his sitting musicians; he played tumba/dholak. Pyare-ji also went up to Laxmi's bungalow, and there were always two harmoniums there, one for Laxmi, one for Pyare. And we would sit there.
>
> There has to be a sitting room for music, no? And it has to be separate from the family part of the house. Laxmi-ji had two gates for his bungalow, one for the family and one for the business. There was one room in the house for sittings. Everybody went there.

Shankar played chiefly tabla but sometimes also *pakhāwaj* (the classical barrel drum of north India) and other drums for many sound tracks from the mid-1970s on. He worked closely with Laxmikant-Pyarelal as he mentions here and also with R. D. Burman; his solo pakhāwaj debut on film can be heard on Burman's groundbreaking background score for *Sholay* (1975). Shankar also notes the importance of the separation between family and business life that was structured into Laxmikant's home.

Laxmikant-Pyarelal's status as one of the most successful (and expensive) composing teams in Mumbai's history, however, demanded more than a single music room. Their solution (oddly in keeping with similar practices developing in Western popular music at the time) was to use the recording studio as a working space, especially when composing background music. When Laxmikant-Pyarelal moved into Mehboob Studios in the mid-1970s, the facility very much became their own personal space. The duo remained there for the rest of their career.

Pyarelal undertook much of his arranging and background-music composing with his orchestra around him on the Mehboob sound stage, which thus became the epitome of music rooms. The orchestra itself became the ultimate in sitting musicians. Since Pyarelal also composed most of the background music for L-P films, the duo's work took up the vast majority of Mehboob's time. The extremely high costs involved in this process were simply part of the price a producer paid for having the most popular music directors in Mumbai providing music for a film. Whether it was Mehboob Studios and an orchestra of fifty musicians or the front room of a composer's house and a tabla/dholak player, a regular space where music directors could sit at leisure was essential in the absence of the industrial infrastructure that producing studios had provided in the 1930s and '40s.

Sittings

In referring to the L-P orchestra as sitting musicians, I use a term whose explanation contributes much to our understanding of the song-production process. The Hindi/Urdu word *baithak* means sitting room or, less literally, a large (public) living room in which musical or other artistic gatherings might take place (Malik 1998, 14). Generally, Indian musicians use the verb "to sit" to mean rehearse, practice, or compose. In the Mumbai film world, a sitting is any kind of creative session or working meeting; film musicians call the place where these activities occur the "sitting room" or "music room." In most cases, sittings were not especially remunerative aspects of the process for musicians, but they were crucial in the production and successful recording of songs. Sittings were also occasions during which musicians sometimes had an opportunity to offer their own creative input.

During more executive sittings, the music director, the lyricist, and the film's producer and/or director establish the requirements for a film and make decisions about specific songs. During the more creative sessions, the music director, the assistants, and the sitting musicians actually compose the music. Musicians do not use the terms "executive" and "creative," although they do make distinctions in their discourse between sittings at which producers and/or directors are present (and thus at which decisions are made) and those whose purpose is purely composition. Pyarelal Sharma explains some of the goals of the former:

> PYARELAL SHARMA: We talk about the timings [the production schedule], who is the director, these things. We listen to the story, and sometimes we say, "Maybe there should be a song here," or "You should not put a song at this point," that kind of thing. Then we talk about the situations and how those will be, and we listen to the songs [lyrics]. "This song should also have dance. What is the atmosphere at this point?" All those kinds of things we talk about.

As Sharma suggests, lyrics were sometimes ready at this early stage, before the songs were composed. Morcom, however, states that "previously, all films' songs were composed on lyrics. It is only from the 1970s and 1980s that lyrics have begun to be composed on tunes" (2007, 39). In reality of course, the process was flexible and could work either way; lyrics frequently came after the melodies as well as before. Guitarist Bhanu Gupta was a sitting musician with R. D. Burman:

> BHANU GUPTA: You see, the producer will come to me as music director and explain what is the situation; it can be happy song or a dance song or a sad song or what have you. Generally it's not the lyrics but the tune that comes first.

Situations were often the places that songs began (see chapter 7), but many, if not most composers wrote songs for future use without even the stimulus of specific situations. In a Sa Rē Gā Ma compilation of the songs of Madan Mohan, this important composer reports that a melody ("Yeh duniya, yeh mehfil") used in the 1970 film *Heer Raanjha* was composed "about ten years before" director Chetan Anand came to him with the story and the situation for which the melody was finally used.[1]

The practice of composing songs as melodies without words seems to have begun around 1960. It became more widely recognized in the 1980s, when it was commonly referred to by the term "song bank." Although the practice clearly preceded the 1980s, the development and maintenance of song banks is sometimes associated with composers Nadeem-Shravan, especially in conjunction with changes in the film and film-song production process initiated by T-Series.

Part of the problematic associated with song banks in the 1980s and '90s was a perception that films were becoming vehicles for songs. Accusations along these lines were routinely leveled against T-Series and other cassette companies, as violinist Joe Pinto recalls:

> JOE PINTO: That's what they would do, T-Series and Venus and all those companies, but especially T-Series. They would make the songs and sell the rights. And then they would make a movie around those songs.

The 1980s, the decade Pinto refers to, were the heyday of music director Bappi Lahiri, who, despite his traditional music background, was most successful as an interpreter of Western pop music, especially disco. Tappan Adhikhari was a sitting musician and a sometime rhythm arranger for Lahiri. He is specific in the sequence of events as experienced in the Lahiri music room in Juhu:

> TAPPAN ADHIKHARI: First comes the melody. First he [Lahiri] would sit with the producer and understand the situations. Then, does he want five or six

or more songs? Then he'd be writing and call the producer to hear the choices, and the producer would pick. Then they'd decide who to call for the lyrics, like Indeevar or someone. And they'd think about who was to be the hero, then who would sing. Then we'd know the studio and go to the studio and call the arranger.

Unlike Burman and L-P, who always insisted on recording in "their" studios (Film Centre and Mehboob, respectively), Lahiri recorded in whichever studio the producer had hired. Whether the songs were composed beforehand or in response to specific situations, most compositional sittings included musicians who were more or less regular members of a music director's workshop. They were known as sitting musicians.

Sitting Musicians

Most music directors kept musicians, at least a tabla or dholak player, to accompany them in the development process (figure 5.1). I use the term "kept" simply because I cannot accurately say "employed" here, for reasons I explain shortly. Many composers also had an assistant to notate songs. The usual minimum requirement for sitting musicians is a drummer to keep the beat and typically a melodic or harmonic instrument:

> JERRY FERNANDES: Every music director has his own musicians who are always with him when he is composing, suppose on tabla, and guitar or something, and they are like a team. That's how they get inspiration, every music director.

Sitting musicians were defined by their presence and participation at creative sessions. Nevertheless, the nature and regularity of that involvement depended upon the inclination and ability of both music director and musician, as well as the amount of work a music director could generate. Anandji Shah offers some insight into the potential importance of the music director–sitting musician interaction:

> ANANDJI SHAH: There were many people in our music rooms. We had all kinds of people sitting with us, every day different, in both our rooms. When you compose something with live musicians, you get a reaction right then. If the tabla player responds and starts playing with more enthusiasm, you know you've made something good. But if he just sits and plays, and there's no response, then you know to make it better somehow.

Film credits and the industry in general treated brothers Kalyanji and Anandji as a single unit; songs were listed as the results of both brothers' efforts. Nevertheless, each one maintained his own music room; in fact, each composed songs individually as a rule, in his own room with his own sitting musicians:

Figure 5.1 A sitting in Old Bollywood. Music director Jaikishan (at the harmonium) works on a song with Lata Mangeshkar. Sitting musician and rhythm arranger Dattaram Waadkar accompanies on tabla. Courtesy of Dattaram Waadkar.

ANANDJI SHAH: There was also some healthy competition between us. Our policy was that we would each present a [draft] for each song, and the producer would choose which one he would use.

Kalyanji-Anandji's sitting musicians seem to have changed fairly frequently. Sharafat Khan was struggling to break into the film line as a tabla player in the 1970s when he got an opportunity to play on a recording session for the Kalyanji-Anandji film *Do Shatru* (1976):

SHARAFAT KHAN: I had my picture taken with Kalyanji and Anandji and with Satrughan Sinha [*Do Shatru*'s hero]. So then Kalyanji-Anandji offered me work. They said, "This boy plays good. Come work with us." At that time they were working a lot, so I became one of their regular musicians.

Sharafat Khan makes it clear, however, that sitting-musician status with Kalyanji-Anandji did not mean day-in, day-out attendance. It might just as likely have been Musharaf, another well-known tabla player, who was called to a sitting instead. Khan's experience of working as a sitting musician was thus different from that of Amrut Katkar or Dattaram Waadkar, both of whom expected that they would be at "their" music director's sitting room each morning as a matter of course.

Sitting musicians were located in the very midst of the creative process, but their actual involvement was often limited to no more than the kind of accompanimental role that Jerry Fernandes describes or the type of passive-reactive testing that Anandji discusses. As a member of the group who sat daily with R. D. Burman, Amrut Katkar makes it clear that, despite Burman's respect for his musicians, sitting musicians were expected to know when to talk and when to sit quietly (as Katkar puts it):

> AMRUT KATKAR: We were sitting there, but only we would sit quietly while Pancham talked with the producer. Pancham told us how the song would go, and we played. And if the song didn't come nicely, maybe the producer wasn't happy. Then we would make it different. Or make a new song.

Katkar's description offers a relatively passive picture of sitting musicians' contribution to the creative process. This no doubt reflects his personal experience and is certainly an accurate assessment for many other sitting musicians as well. However, Bhanu Gupta, who was also a sitting musician with Burman, offers a different perspective:

> BHANU GUPTA: Like if you know *1942: A Love Story* [1993], there's that song, "Kuch na kaho." He [Burman] said to me, "How do you like this tune?" and he sang it to me. Then he stopped, and for some reason, something came to me, and I played something, and he said, "Hold it!" And he picked it up again and kept going. So that's how we used to work, all back and forth.

Although Gupta was a sitting musician, he and Burman were both Bengalis and roughly the same age. In many ways they were colleagues. They had both played harmonica at one point in their lives (apparently even making a duet recording together in the early 1960s) and shared interests outside music as well. Here Gupta describes a creative session, while Katkar recounts a more executive meeting. Finally, Gupta notes very clearly that "that status-wise thing, R. D. never had that; he was down to earth. If anybody had an idea, he would work on it." It is clear that certain sitting musicians contributed ideas, melodies, or phrases to the songs coming out of the music rooms. It is equally evident that R. D. Burman represented an extreme in this respect.

The number of sitting musicians in Mumbai is indeterminate but must have always been quite small (unless one counts the L-P orchestra). Staffing a private workshop on a daily basis required a music director to have at least four or five films in the works but often as many as ten in hand at any given moment. However, it is difficult to imagine more than one hundred musicians working as sitting musicians even in years of peak demand for music (the late 1980s, for example). Nevertheless, sitting musicians included some quite important or well-known musicians, whose impact on film music sometimes exceeded their official status. They had the potential to affect, at least subtly, the shaping of songs and were often featured as soloists in the recordings made by "their" music director.

Arrangers and Assistants

Located between music directors and sitting musicians in terms of status and creative input were musicians called arrangers or assistants. All music directors have employed assistants; most have hired arrangers as well. The distinctions between these two roles are quite fluid and sometimes rather idiosyncratic. The need for the positions at all had to do with the volume of work in some cases and specific technical skills and understandings required in the compositional process that certain music directors lacked (figure 5.2). Kishore Desai summarizes the role:

> KISHORE DESAI: The arranger was second in importance to the music director. The arranger used to give the countermelody, compose harmonies. Their name didn't come on the screen.

Desai's final comment points to a further complexity in sorting out roles and levels of contribution: while many films list a "Music Assistant" in their credits (usually in a list along with other assistants) arrangers were rarely identified in this way.

Figure 5.2 The arranger's role in Old Bollywood. Arranger Prakash Varma in a sitting with composer Nathan in the singer's cabin (isolation booth) at Film Centre (1975). Varma is notating and harmonizing the melodies that Nathan is composing. Courtesy of Prakash Varma.

Arrangers were freelancers in Old Bollywood like everyone else, but some of them established the kinds of seemingly permanent relationships that characterized this period. Cellist Vasudeo Chakravarty worked jointly with Manohari Singh as an assistant and arranger. The pair possessed complementary experience and technical skills with staff notation, orchestration, and the harmonic materials of Western music. The two (who also composed some film songs) often appear in film credits as Vasu-Manohari. [🔊 Video 5.1]

Additionally, J. V. Acharya connects the work of arranging with the facilitation of the increasingly sectional playing of Mumbai studio orchestras (see chapter 7) and the growing importance of notation in that context. He also notes the importance of the arranging work done by the film line's most famous arranger, Sebastian D'Souza. [🔊 Video 5.2]

Arrangers' actual duties could vary quite a bit but normally included more than just arrangements. An acknowledgement of the nature and scope of their contributions to film music is crucial to an understanding of the collective and sometimes anonymous nature of music composition and film-score production in Mumbai. Manohari Singh explains the general concept of the arranger's role in the production of film songs:

> MANOHARI SINGH: It was like this, that the music was the arranger's department, our department. But with that, music portion, interlude music, introduction, sometimes his [Burman's] idea used to be there. It was teamwork. Just like Bhupi [Bhupinder Singh] would have an idea, or I would have an idea.

These comments pursue the film musicians' routine distinction between "songs" and "music." Perhaps more than in other popular song forms, nonvocal, that is to say, purely instrumental, melodies are routinely used as introductions, interludes, countermelodies, and dance sections (cf. Morcom 2007). The word "music," when used by a Mumbai film musician, normally refers specifically to these instrumental sections, not to melodies to which lyrics are set. Singh thus suggests here that he and Vasu-da composed the introductions, interludes, and other additional music necessary for Burman's songs.

Manohari Singh's work as a saxophone soloist has been heard in many Hindi films from the late 1950s through the 1990s, most iconically, perhaps, in the songs S. D. Burman composed for Navketan Films. Soloists sometimes composed their own music, although this varied from situation to situation. The process could at times be quite improvisational, especially in background music. As an arranger, Singh routinely created his own solos, which he would play while conducting the studio orchestra. Assistants or arrangers were often the conductors during recordings. This practice may have begun in the Studio Period (Vistasp Balsara stated that he always conducted the Filmistan studio orchestra during his time there as music assistant). Recording sessions for background music were even more likely to be conducted by arrangers (and sometimes assistants), since it was they who composed much of the background music. The photograph on the cover of this book shows Kersi Lord, in his role as arranger, conducting the background music he composed for the 1968 release *Saathi*. Like Balsara and Singh, Lord states, "I always conducted my own background music."

Overall, the music director–arranger relationship and the level of the arrangers' creative input could vary significantly from music director to music director. Vasu-Manohari arranged many of S. D. Burman's songs in the late 1960s and all of R. D. Burman's songs as well, but unlike the highly collaborative atmosphere that R. D. Burman favored, S. D.'s sitting room was more hierarchically managed. [🎬 **Video 5.3**]

Finding work as an assistant or arranger was occasionally a way for aspiring composers to break into the Mumbai film-music industry. As did many other Hindus living in the western Panjab, Manoharlal Sonik left his home in Sialkot in 1947, heading for India. Blind from birth, Sonik had been a playback singer working in the Hindi/Urdu film industry in Lahore. Traveling with his nephew Omprakash, who acted as the elder man's eyes, Sonik finally reached Mumbai a year later, where the pair struggled to find work in the movie business. They established themselves first as assistants and arrangers and eventually as music directors in their own right. Omprakash, who undertook all of the notational duties, suggests a very broad role for his uncle in the pair's first job as assistants to music director Roshan:

> OMPRAKASH SONIK: Sonik-ji chose all the instruments and chose the players. He used the whole orchestra; he was a composer actually. Those people [music directors] just gave the tunes, one *mukhra* and one *antara*, after that Sonik-ji gave all the rest of the music.

Omprakash makes two standard—if not consistently applicable—distinctions between various kinds of melodies and the related work of diverse members of the song-production team. Hindi film songs normally consist of two principal melodic ideas: the antecedent melody, which often acts as a refrain (most commonly called the mukhra, or sometimes the *asthai),* and the consequent melody (antara), which often functions rather like a verse, with a series of different lyrics in each repetition. These terms are taken from Hindustani classical music and are used with similar, if less consistent, meanings.

Omprakash states that it was Sonik-ji who, like Manohari Singh, composed the introductions, interludes, and other music necessary for Roshan's songs. This is the second distinction: Music directors compose songs (tunes), while arrangers (and sometimes assistants) compose music. Like many distinctions in the film business, this one has a great deal of truth in it, but in fact the proportions of music-director and assistant input in each song varies according to the individuals involved.

When Vasudeo Chakravarty began his career in this field, it was as an assistant to Pankaj Mullick in Kolkata. His son explains what this meant in this case and reflects on the implications of the term:

> SANJAY CHAKRAVARTY: At that time [1940s], the word "arranger" was not really there. If you were a friend, you could be an assistant. After all, an arranger only comes with the harmony. If harmony is not there, then there is no need for arrangement.
>
> Shankar-Jaikishan did some harmonizing; Naushad did some; in Bombay there was some harmonizing. But they didn't know what was correct or not. So you can't say that my father was an arranger for Pankaj Mullick. He was an assistant; he helped him. Brought him *pān* [betel leaf], coordinated things, and organized the musicians.

The younger Chakravarty distinguishes between the role of assistant and that of arranger. These distinctions are important, and in general the arrangers have more creative input than the assistants. Nevertheless, while an arranger can be assumed to have had a relatively high level of creative input, one cannot assume that someone listed as assistant in a film's credits was not actually arranging. Filmmakers have frequently included the title of "music assistant" in a film's credits, often on a "card" (that is, a shot of a fixed piece of paper or cardstock), along with other assistants (e.g., dance, makeup, costumes). The title of "arranger" is much less frequently listed in film credits. But because film credits were arranged by film producers and their assistants, there was degree of imprecision in this area. Those listed as assistants were sometimes merely that; but in other instances, those listed as assistants were both assistants and arrangers. Kersi Lord notes the potential for tension (as well as confusion) around this matter:

> KERSI LORD: When you look at the credits, there is the music director, but there is sometimes also a music assistant. Those people are doing the background music. I was Mr. Naushad's arranger, and people would come and tell me what a good job I was doing [writing the background music]. So I always used to fight for the credit. The money was enough, but I wanted a full card, "Music Arranged and Conducted by Kersi Lord." In a few pictures it came.

Lord was prepared to take credit for his arranging and conducting contributions. Nonetheless, although everyone in the film line knew that he was composing the background music, he argues that, "I could not claim to have composed the background score as I was working for the 'music director', even though the whole thing was done by me." Not everyone was as concerned with precision. Three examples provide a sense of the possible variance:

In 1944 Vistasp Balsara is listed as music assistant to Ghulam Haider *(Chal Chal Re Naujawan)*; Gorakh and Shashikant are listed as music assistants to Laxmikant-Pyarelal in 1980 *(Dostaanaa)*; and Laxmikant-Pyarelal are themselves listed as assistant music directors to Kalyanji-Anandji in 1963 *(Bluff Master)*. In each instance, however, we encounter different responsibilities and levels of creative input and credit.

Balsara had the skills in staff notation and Western music theory and performance that Haider lacked. This distribution of abilities was extremely common; one rarely finds notational skills, especially in staff notation and Western music theory, among music directors. In 1944 Balsara was a staff music assistant and permanent orchestra director at Filmistan Studios. When Haider was contracted to provide the music for *Chal Chal Re Naujawan*, Balsara worked with him as a matter of course (as he did with the rather more obscure music director Hari Prasitra Das for *Begum*, released the following year). Balsara notated the songs that Haider composed, orchestrated them and the background music, provided harmonies as appropriate (there is very little harmony in this film's sound track), led the rehearsals, and conducted the orchestra. He was thus fully an arranger and at least partly a composer. Although Haider undoubtedly composed the song melodies, in the rest of the sound track overall, there is no clear way to determine where Haider stops and Balsara starts.

Musicians Gorakh and Shashikant routinely acted as assistants to Laxmikant-Pyarelal (Gorakh was also Pyarelal's younger brother), dealing with melody and rhythm respectively. Because Pyarelal Sharma had an unusually substantial theoretical and practical background in Western music, he needed no help in arranging or orchestrating. Sudhir Kadam, a sitting musician with the duo, reports that Laxmikant or Pyarelal normally even composed the rhythm patterns. In this workshop, assistants copied parts and performed other organizational or routine tasks but had no creative input. Shyamrao Kemble, who also worked as assistant to Laxmikant-Pyarelal for many years, explains his role:

SHYAMRAO KEMBLE: Pyare-bhai did all that [arranging]. I was their assistant. I wrote out the parts in staff notation for the violins and others, and I made the transpositions that were necessary. I conducted also and organized the rehearsals. But sometimes, if Pyarelal was not well, I composed some of the background music as well.

Among the sound tracks of the many music directors in Mumbai, one by Laxmikant-Pyarelal almost certainly contains the highest proportion of music-director input. Even in this extreme case, however, part of Shyamrao Kemble's creative energy apparently filtered into at least some of Laxmikant-Pyarelal's sound tracks.

Although their first hit film, *Parasmani*, was released in 1963, Laxmikant-Pyarelal's career as music directors is noticeably successful slightly later, beginning with films such as *Dosti* (1964) and *Milan* (1967). In 1962 and 1963 the pair spent a brief period working as assistants to Kalyanji-Anandji. The fact that they had work of their own may have helped them secure the unusual credit as assistant music directors instead of the more common music-assistant descriptor. Formally acknowledged as composers, the duo composed all of the film's background music.

Morcom (2007) offers a detailed description of the production process. However, because she focuses on music directors' perspectives and because she was working in what was effectively New Bollywood, neither arrangers nor sitting musicians appear in her description. Nor, for that matter, do the tensions that sometimes surface between composer and arranger. Anthony Gonsalves, who worked as an arranger and composer in the 1940s, joined Kardar Studios (in Parel, Mumbai) shortly after Naushad Ali. In his characteristically outspoken way, Gonsalves reflects on the sometimes slow process of composition:

> ANTHONY GONSALVES: When I joined Kardar, Naushad would sit at the harmonium with his cigarette, like that, and maybe he would compose only four bars from ten o'clock to five o'clock. And we would write that and play it over, and then we would drink tea and wait. It was hell. It was so frustrating. In those days we'd be called for nine o'clock in the morning, and then the music director would come at twelve o'clock to begin composing.

Significantly, Gonsalves is describing a producing studio (Kardar) in the mid-1940s, but his description is ironically suggestive of aspects of the recording process in late Old Bollywood and even, although in different fashion, the world of programming in New Bollywood, as I explain in later chapters.

In addition to arrangers as such, some composers employed musicians with specific responsibilities for rhythm. Although he describes himself here as a sitting musician (since he was routinely present in Shankar-Jaikishan's music room), Dattaram Waadkar also made a significant creative contribution to their music:

> DATTARAM WAADKAR: When they sat to compose, I sat with them and accompanied them, and we discussed what rhythms would fit with that song. I was a permanent sitting musician, me, and there would also be a guitarist.

Figure 5.3.   Rhythm at Famous Studios (Tardeo), ca. 1956. A lighthearted moment during a Shankar-Jaikishan recording of a Raj Kapoor song. From left: Jaikishan, Shankar, Kapoor (standing at center holding a large, circular frame drum), Dattaram Waadkar, and Sattar, the dholak player of the percussion duo Lalla-Sattar. Courtesy of Dattaram Waadkar.

Waadkar is widely acknowledged throughout the film line for his role as rhythm arranger. Although he is to my knowledge the first musician in the industry to be so called, Cawas Lord was the first to begin notating rhythm parts. As a senior musician, he also assumed the responsibility of organizing (arranging) rhythm players and their parts in the recordings he played and was in this way the prototypical rhythm arranger. Even though Shankar was originally a tabla player himself, it was Dattaram who provided the rhythms and the drumming patterns for the majority of Shankar-Jaikishan's songs (figure 5.3). [🔊 Video 5.4]

> DATTARAM WAADKAR: I arranged the rhythm, the rhythm section, what the drums would play. What instruments would play, maybe tabla, maybe dholak, maybe *tumba*. What patterns they should play. I matched them up like that and made those patterns, depending on the song. I composed all the rhythms until the end.

Many later music directors used rhythm arrangers. Kersi Lord himself worked informally as a rhythm arranger (or perhaps assistant) from time to time, helping to bridge the gap between traditional Indian rhythmic thinking and the measures and starts and stops of the film music:

> ERNEST MENEZES: In those days you had all these tabla and dholak players who didn't know how to count bars. And Kersi used to manage the whole rhythm section, and he would have to keep them together. He used to show them how to count to finish in the right place. And he used to make them practice so they would learn to do it correctly because they were all by-heart players, no?

Kalyanji-Anandji's younger brother Babla worked with that duo as a rhythm arranger for a number of years, performing the same kinds of tasks that Waadkar describes. Tabla player Maruti Rao Keer moved to Mumbai from the costal town of Ratnagiri just before Indian independence. He joined S. D. Burman as a sitting musician in the 1950s and in the 1960s joined R. D. Burman as rhythm arranger. As Maruti Rao explains, he also collaborated in the compositional process:

> MARUTI RAO KEER: After the evening sittings Pancham and I would stay up until very late, sometimes until two o'clock or three o'clock in the morning, composing. Then when everybody came back in the morning we would say, "See what we've done in the night!"

Although many composers used rhythm arrangers, they were especially important in songs that had Indian classical overtones or were meant to accompany classical or classically derived dance. Bhavani Shankar, with his range of knowledge and skills in classical rhythm and classical dance provided both the rhythms and the playing for Anu Malik's score for the remake of *Umrao Jaan* (2006). He has specialized in providing precisely this kind of rhythmic content but emphasizes the collegial aspect of the process:

> BHAVANI SHANKAR: Maruti Rao-bhai, he was with R. D., no? But for some songs, R. D. called me. See, music is such a thing that it demands teamwork. It was like that. There was one film, *Pukar* [1983]. I made some of the *thekas* [rhythm patterns], and Maruti made some. It's not a bad thing. The important thing is, the work should come out well.

Shankar's father, Pandit Babu Lal-Ji, was a dancer and a director in the film business of the 1950s; as members of a Rajasthani performing arts caste known as Kathaks, the family has a hereditary background in the performing arts. Bhavani Shankar converted this hereditary knowledge into a career as a specialist in traditional Indian rhythms (especially those for dance). In addition to his work with R. D. Burman and Anu Malik, Shankar provided these same kinds of services for the Laxmikant-Pyarelal camp.

Although Shankar has managed to create a specialist niche for himself as a provider of traditional and/or classical rhythms in contemporary films, arrangers, whether rhythmic or orchestral, began to experience a decline in demand for their services in the early twenty-first century. This is because of Mumbai's shift to digital scores and what is called programming. The roles that I have described thus far—music directors, sitting musicians, arrangers, and assistants—were all involved in the creative process. The degree of participation and input appropriate to each was broadly understood throughout the film line but was subject to at least some variability in response to individual preferences and skill sets. All these roles, however, changed radically (and even disappeared in some cases) with the advent of new technologies in Mumbai in the 1990s.

Programming and the Creative Process

This is the first of two considerations of electronic musical instruments in this volume, each of which has a somewhat different focus. In this section I examine the growing importance of electronic keyboards in the creative process and the appearance of the programmer, a new role that has come to be part of the process and that has, to a large extent, replaced the arranger's role.

Keyboards were present in Mumbai's film studios almost as soon as they appeared in the West. Initially these were, in effect, innovations in orchestration, but in the late 1980s programmable synthesizers began to be used in the creative process as musicians programmed musical content into their machines that was then recorded directly onto a track, not by playing in real time but by pushing a button that triggered the programmed content. Like arranging in general, programming was a creative act that preceded the actual recording. It allowed time for reflection and was not dependent on the keyboard player's presence in the midst of a live recording orchestra. In both creative and physical terms, programming bypassed both the arrangers and the orchestral musicians; gradually it displaced both groups. Kersi Lord, who has expertise in both technology and composing and who had been playing electronic keyboards in orchestral recordings, introduced the new process:

> KERSI LORD: I brought the first programmable keyboard into the film line. That was an Ensoniq ESQ-1. The film I think was called *Soormaa Bhopali* [1988]. That was different [from earlier keyboards] because for that you programmed some music, and it went straight onto one of the tracks.

After these early efforts, Mumbai's composers and arrangers began to utilize the potential of programmable keyboards and computers. The Old Bollywood model of arranging involved a composer sitting at the harmonium while his assistant sat next to him with paper and pencil, notating the composition. The resultant melodies were then arranged—with harmony, orchestration, interludes, countermelodies, and so forth—also on paper. Parts were copied, and the music was then performed. In New Bollywood, however, this process was replaced by programming, in which melodies composed by a music director were realized on keyboards as complete songs with harmony, countermelodies, rhythms, and so forth, all of the elements that arrangers used to contribute.

Prakash Varma is one of those few who still negotiates between the world of the notated score and that of the programmed one. Varma worked with music directors Anand-Milind from their first hit (*Qayamat Se Qayamat Tak* [1988]) through the mid-1990s. He still writes out parts in abbreviated score form, but because he does not use a computer himself, he then has to sit with someone who does in order to transfer, in effect, the score onto a music program. That electronic version is then either dumped directly onto a track or replaced by a dubbed instrumental part in the recording studio:

> PRAKASH VARMA: We started using programs in 1990 or 1991. We were using keyboards, and we would program the track and then put it directly onto the tape. There were no computers at that time. We had three people to program our songs for us on the keyboard. One was Viju Shah, and then later we had Raju Singh, and sometimes Kersi [Lord] also would help us. Once I've written [the score], I take it to the programmer; I sit with him to see that it is correct. In four to five hours the whole song will be programmed. Then we do [program] the rhythm section. Then they put it on the MIDI Sync; then we come to the studio the next day and dump the whole track onto Pro Tools.

In contemporary Mumbai, one of the global standards in music computing and recording, Pro Tools, is widely available, although as Ashok Shukla notes in chapter 2, the assumption in the early 1990s was that such sophistication was beyond Mumbai's reach.

The idea that an arranger is necessary for the song-production process has yet to completely disappear. The change, like most of Mumbai's many cultural (as opposed to technological) changes, has been gradual (figure 5.4). Anjan Biswas outlines the transition as he has experienced it and the division of labor brought about by the shifting roles. Originally an orchestral violinist, Biswas nevertheless made the changeover directly to his new (and more profitable) role as a programmer.

> ANJAN BISWAS: When live playing was there, there was always an arranger, and even in programming songs, for Nadeem-Shravan at least an arranger always used to be there. That was Naresh Sharma. So whatever was written, we used to program that. The pattern and everything, we used to make

Figure 5.4   A virtual sitting in New Bollywood. Arranger Prakash Varma records a song being sung to him over his mobile phone by a music director. Once recorded, Varma will perform the usual arranging tasks and then take the score to another specialist, who will program the song on a keyboard or computer.

on our own. That means what should be the bass pattern, what should be the "comping"; the arranger doesn't write that. The melodies, the main obbligatos, all that is written [by the arranger]. How you execute that music, what feel you put inside that music—that is very important.

Taufiq Qureshi would have been a rhythm arranger in the 1960s or '80s, but in the 1990s his role was transformed to that of rhythm programmer:

TAUFIQ QURESHI: There came a time in film music here when everything became electronic. So I was programming rhythms for Anu Malik, Anand-Milind, and the new music directors like Jaitin-Lalit. I'm talking about 1994, '95.

As always happens with new technologies and systems of production, however, the musical content changed as well:

ANJAN BISWAS: The music has also changed, so really there is no call for it [arranging]. Nowadays, nothing is written, even in songs, because the music portion has become less. Means you just have a hook line, maybe eight bars of music that just keeps playing everywhere. The actual concept

of arranging is no more there. What used to be there in film music, nobody
is using that kind of music.

Arranging as a necessary skill has, in consequence, largely been replaced
by computer expertise. Bablu Chakravarty began his arranging career in
the mid-1980s with R. D. Burman and arranged many of the large musical
scores of the next twenty years, including films such as *Baazigar* (1993),
Dilwale Dulhania Le Jayenge (1995), and *Kabhi Khushi Kabhie Gham*
(2001). The subsequent decline in the demand for his talent is the result of
the economic pressures brought about by the use of computers and programmers in place of sizeable orchestras and arrangers. Although in 2004
he was still working occasionally, Chakravarty clearly saw that his days in
the industry were numbered:

> BABLU CHAKRAVARTY: The only thing I am asking is, "Give me acoustic." As
> long as I have acoustic, I have some challenge, I can do something. But the
> day that people only want that box [the computer], then I say bye-bye.
> After doing so much work, it's okay.

Chakravarty retired in 2005 shortly after making these comments,
largely in response to his unhappiness with the new system and the lack of
interest in large orchestra recordings. He was at that time the last major orchestral arranger in Mumbai. He now refuses the few calls that come.

Like Bablu Chakravarty, Anil Mohile worked as both a musician and an
arranger. In the early 1970s he and Arun Paudwal formed the arranging
partnership known as Anil-Arun. The duo did much of the arranging work
for the prolific Bappi Lahiri in the 1980s, but their first real break came
when they were employed to arrange a series of S. D. Burman film scores in
the mid-1970s, in what might be called Burman's explicitly Indian phase,
which included films such as *Abhiman* (1973) and *Anuraag* (1972). In the
late 1990s, when the gradual decline in demand for orchestral arranging
set in, Mohile was not in a position to simply retire:

> ANIL MOHILE: You have to change with the times, be a reasonable, forward-
> looking person, optimistic. You must see what is there and be flexible. I am
> working today with all these electronics. If I was sitting and saying, "Oh,
> this classical music we must play and keep to this *rāg* or that rāg," then I
> wouldn't get work.

In this section I have considered the range of creative or musical roles
involved in the composition of film songs in the workshops of Mumbai's
composers. I have also discussed the changes that technological developments necessitated for those roles. Younger men like Mohile realize they
must change with the times if they wish to keep working in a production
process that is now developing very rapidly.

In both Old and New Bollywood, music directors were at the center of song production, as I stated at the beginning of this chapter. They acted as the hubs, one might say, around which the other creative roles circled. Music directors were not only creatives but also conduits and repositories for the artistic suggestions coming from above (from the film director, for example) and below (the music director's sitting musicians). Ultimately, it was the music director's ability to focus that innovative input into a single song that made the process successful. In addition to this, however, the music director was also at the center of the financial aspects of song production. For "his" musicians, he fulfilled an especially important economic role. The final section of this chapter thus focuses on the all-important matter of money. Having described what I call a cottage industry in socio-professional terms, I now depict it as an economic model.

Music Directors, Sitting Musicians, Producers, and Money

Music directors managed workshops (figure 5.5) that routinely multi-tasked, producing compositions, arrangements, and recordings, managing aspects of the process, working on multiple films at once, adding to their song banks, and so on. As managers of a workshop in a cottage industry, they were responsible for finding work. Many expected "their" musicians to be on call or simply in attendance daily. Nevertheless, music directors were not directly responsible for paying their assistants, arrangers, or sitting musicians. Nor did the fees that were negotiated between the producers and the music directors of Old Bollywood include the wages or salaries of the other musicians in the latter's music room. All of those individuals (when they were paid at all) were paid directly by the producer for their work on his particular songs once they were recorded.

Like music directors, arrangers sometimes negotiated a fee directly with the producer. Alternatively, the music director with whom they were working would mention the arranger's fee to the producer. In some instances, apparently the producer simply assumed the arranger's fee with no actual discussion. Vistasp Balsara was arranging for a number of leading music directors in Mumbai in the 1940s and early '50s, especially Datta Goregaonkar and Ghulam Haider; he reports that his move to Kolkata in 1954 was financially difficult:

> VISTASP BALSARA: For one song [in Mumbai] I was getting 150 rupees or more to arrange. But here [in Kolkata], for two songs I only got 25 rupees. But then I am happy up to now.

Figure 5.5
A music director's workshop: R. D. Burman (standing at center in a dark shirt and glasses) poses with the arrangers, assistants, sitting musicians, and others with whom he worked at Film Centre Recording Studio (ca. 1980). Standing from left to right: Chandrakant, Deepan Chatterji, Maruti Rao Keer, Louiz Banks, Manohari Singh, Burman, Ulhas Bhapat, Dakina Mohan Tagore, Vasu Chakravarty. Seated from left to right: Raju, Ranjit Gazmer, Devi Chakravarty, Santosh, Devi Chand, Homi Mullan, Suresh Bhoi, Binoy Singh, Aman. Courtesy of Sanjay Chakravarty.

Arrangers' fees continued to increase after Balsara left Mumbai, but in the cottage model, producers "bought" both arrangements and songs even if they did not directly or personally contract for them:

> MANOHARI SINGH: The arranging rate was somewhat flexible, but the money
> came from the producer. For sittings, there was no money, but I was his
> [R. D. Burman's] arranger, so if I sit for one day or two days, that has
> nothing to do with the producer. That fee is fixed ahead [of time]. And
> for arranging, maybe 600 or 700 or 1,000, possibly 1,200 rupees per
> song. Now, in the last ten years, any amount that is demanded is consid-
> ered, maybe 1 lakh for one song for arranging, or 50,000. The last songs I
> did as arranger, I received 25,000 rupees per song. But that's now. It was
> cheap then.

As one of Burman's two regular arrangers, Manohari-da expected no pay for his presence at sittings. For him, that was simply part of the arrang-ing process. Further, the pay he received came from the producer of the film he was arranging for, not from Burman, although Burman was responsible for securing work for both himself and his arrangers. In the complexities of the cottage-industry model, however, where social, professional, and economic obligations both merged and could often be extended over time, there was a relatively subtle distinction between the manner in which Singh was compensated for his time and the ways sitting musicians were rewarded.

The arrangements for sitting musicians were often quite vague. Produc-ers also paid them directly, but the amounts varied from music director to music director and according to the prevailing rates at different points in the industry's history:

> VISTASP BALSARA: He [Ghulam Haider] used to arrange with the producers:
> "See, these are my musicians."

Although they were not paid by music directors, the fortunes of sitting musicians were tied to those of the music director with whom they worked. Indeed, when the film musicians in Chennai sought advice from those in Mumbai about forming a musicians' union, J. V. Acharya's counsel posi-tioned music directors and musicians in opposition to each other:

> J. V. ACHARYA: We told them [the Chennai film musicians], "You keep your
> association separate from the music directors." Boss and workers cannot
> be together . . . but they didn't listen."

Nevertheless, Acharya states that pay raises for musicians were not ne-gotiated with music directors but rather with the Indian Motion Pictures Producers' Association (IMPPA). This highly volatile system, in which money moved directly from the producers to the different participants in the film and film-music production process, was one of the defining features of Old Bollywood's cottage industry. Sitting musicians, like workers in any production economy, were dependent on the demand for "their" factory's product. However, it was as if the customers came to the factory and, in effect, paid the workers directly for their participation. For sitting musicians, however, the pay was often not good:

> HOMI MULLAN: That time, I'm talking about twenty years ago [i.e., mid-1980s], the producers used to pay four hundred rupees only for the sitting. I'm not talking about for each member, but for whoever was there. Say Devi Chand, myself, and some others are there, we used to divide the money amongst us. Usually there were eight of us.

Sitting musicians were aware that their role perhaps offered more cultural than financial capital, and to some extent they sacrificed earning potential for a form of professional stability. Their jobs may have offered a considerable degree of regularity and at least a limited amount of prestige, but that was mitigated by the relatively low hourly wages. As rhythm arranger, Dattaram Waadkar was a key component of the Shankar-Jaikishan creative team, but the financial arrangements did not work out well for him:

> DATTARAM WAADKAR: I played in the rehearsals and the sittings, so I had a fixed rate for all that. I was paid two hundred rupees per song for sitting and rehearsals. So that was like fifteen days to finish one song by the time everything was done. I just accepted what they gave me. Shankar was like my guru. I had everything because of him. But others were making more.

Deepan Chatterji, who worked as recording assistant for R. D. Burman, notes that the speed of production accelerated considerably in the later 1970s and '80s. He estimates that the Burman workshop produced one completed song every four to five days, much faster than the eleven to fifteen that Waadkar suggests here for the Shankar-Jaikishan workshop.

Sitting musicians were part of the intimate side of film-song production; they had the privilege, if we accept that characterization, of working closely and sometimes collaboratively with the most powerful figures in their world. The sittings that are described here produced film songs. Despite these positive features, the financial implications were often quite negative. Kersi Lord worked closely with R. D. Burman on many of his more adventurous film scores. In addition to his performing skills on percussion and accordion, he developed a special expertise in electronics, developing many of the unusual and innovative electronic sounds that Burman seems to have enjoyed so much (e.g., *Shalimar* [1977]). Despite their close association, Lord never actually became one of Burman's sitting musicians:

KERSI LORD: I wasn't really a sitting musician with Pancham. I didn't have
the time. The sittings didn't pay so much, only two hundred rupees, so I
went for the recordings.

Sittings were, in one sense, the source of the songs for the Hindi cinema;
they were the creative but relatively small-scale workshops in which musicians played a role. In another sense, however, they were only the preliminary activity and not the true focus of the film-music process. Songs were
only potentially parts of film until they were recorded, and recordings involved many more musicians. Recordings were, as Lord points out, the
source of most musicians' incomes. When the songs produced in sitting-
room workshops moved onto the studio floors, these creative roles and
their economic place in the cottage-industry model both changed. Lord's
words on sittings introduce the importance of the following chapter, which
focuses on the more public and remunerative side of the song-production
process: recordings.

6

Rehearsals, Recordings, and Economics

This chapter focuses on the second half of the song-production process, the conversion of a composed song into a recorded song. At this point a song's potential was realized, and it became a product to be sold to HMV, released on cassette, played on the radio, or played back for filming. Recordings produced more explicitly financial and industrial behaviors than the nebulous payment practices of the sitting rooms, where musicians were sometimes paid and sometimes not. Tensions around management and distribution of the financial rewards have been a major concern of musicians from the studio period to New Bollywood. The recording process was also much more clearly informed by available technology, as I have already suggested.

A recorded performance of a song was the end product for which producers paid and which they provided to HMV in exchange for royalties. After 1980, songs might also be sold directly for cash to T-Series or another of the cassette companies. Consequently, recordings were musicians' most direct participation in the popular culture economy. This chapter examines this public side of the song-production process from rehearsal to recording. In addition, because recordings were the primary source of income for most musicians, I discuss the matter of economics and musicians' livelihoods.

Until very late in the industry's history, recording a song meant recording a live performance by the entire ensemble. If anyone made an error, the entire song was rerecorded from the beginning. To produce error-free performances of what were occasionally quite complex songs, musicians naturally had to rehearse. Dattaram Waadkar has described the cyclical nature of this process:

> DATTARAM WAADKAR: If one day the song has been composed, then Sebastian [D'Souza] has to arrange it. Then there have to be rehearsals, maybe two [or] three rehearsals. After that, we record. Then we go back to the music room and compose another song, and after two [or] three more days, we're rehearsing again and going back to the studio for more recording.

Pyarelal Sharma extends Dattaram-ji's description to the film as a whole:

> PYARELAL SHARMA: Once we've made the song, then we record. Then they make the film and the scene, and we see it and make sure everything is okay. Then we do background score. How many pieces do we need, what are the scenes, these things. So maybe that takes ten or twelve days for recording. Then we do solos for four days. When the tracks are complete, then mixing, but in those days mixing was not much. Maybe one or two days.

Relatively few musicians composed and arranged music or worked in sitting rooms, whereas everyone played for recordings. Mario Fernandes suggests that as many as five hundred musicians often worked on a regular basis in late Old Bollywood. From roughly 1980 on, there were, in effect, two standing orchestras (one for Laxmikant-Pyarelal and one for R. D. Burman), plus perhaps the same number again of floating musicians.

New People and Places

A discussion of rehearsals and recordings introduces a number of new professional roles to this study. In each case, these positions are directly involved with ensuring the recording takes place successfully.

Messengers

In the studio period of the 1930s, the salaried orchestras maintained by the major studios (rarely more than twenty musicians) were supplemented when necessary by extra musicians arranged on an ad hoc basis. Musicians sometimes said, "I can call my friend so-and-so," or the studio's music assistant would make the necessary arrangements. The A-R-P trio acted as orchestral subcontractors by recruiting additional musicians that might have been needed for specific recordings.

In Kolkata, a semipermanent orchestral system was also in operation, one that was independent of both the producing studios and the music directors:

VISTASP BALSARA: Previously, Kolkata had different orchestras [for films]. There was one National Orchestra; there was Suroshtri Orchestra, and the Kolkata Orchestra. They were seven to eight musicians in each. But if a musician is in Kolkata Orchestra, he can't play for National Orchestra, and so on. Producers used to enter into a contract for the whole picture with the orchestra, for the musicians.

Kolkata's independent orchestras and Mumbai's salaried studio orchestras were both finished by the mid-1950s. Ironically, even as these musical/industrial structures were collapsing, Mumbai's film and music directors were acquiring a taste for larger recording orchestras.

Two events—the industrial shift from salaried to fully freelance orchestras and the trend toward larger orchestras—exacerbated the organizational challenges in recording. The producing studios had provided an industrial infrastructure (predictable space and a core of musicians) upon which music directors could both depend and expand. After the decline of the producing studios, however, the new film-recording studios, musicians, singers, and music directors were all freelance and were constantly (and sometimes simultaneously) being reconfigured into different combinations for specific recordings. Increasingly busy musicians were traveling from recording to recording in studios spread across central Mumbai; all arrangements were temporary. Neither music directors nor their assistants had time to undertake what was becoming a daily and often lengthy task. For example, someone had to ensure that there would be twenty violins, four violas, eight cellos, dholak, sitar, mandolin, and flute at Famous (Tardeo) on Tuesday at nine o'clock to record a song and that another (or the same) string section, together with a Western-style wind section, would be at Mehboob in the evening for a background music session and that still another forty musicians who had been booked for a session on Wednesday knew that the date had been cancelled.

In response to these complex scheduling tasks, specialist managers appeared to fill the demand. They were most commonly called messengers or informers and, more recently, music coordinators. Like the musicians they organized, messengers were freelance service providers who acted as three-way liaisons between music directors, producers, and musicians:

AMRUT KATKAR: Messengers would just call and tell you, "The recording will be in this place at this time. Please come." The music directors would tell them what instruments were needed, And the messenger would arrange so they all came to the studio at the right time.

In the days before Mumbai's telephone system was widespread or reliable, being a messenger often meant a great deal of to-ing and fro-ing in person, usually on bicycle:

HOMI MULLAN: The music directors and the arrangers used to make a list of
the names, and then the messengers would give it to us. They'd come on
the bike at twelve o'clock or one o'clock at night: "Tomorrow's recording
is cancelled," or "Tomorrow's session is on; you bring such and such an
instrument to such and such a place."

Messengers were a necessary development in the cottage industry that
was Old Bollywood; recordings would simply not have been possible without this important group. However, they gradually came to play quite significant economic roles in the lives of many musicians because they could
sometimes determine who worked and who did not. Ramanand Shetty
joined the film line in the early 1960s:

RAMANAND SHETTY: I worked for all the big music directors from that time
until now. Pyare-bhai would always call me himself; he could call all of his
musicians by name. But most said, "I need so many violins, so many
rhythm, and such and such soloists," and those things. And very often I
would select who would come. I would ask who was available.

Shetty, from a slightly different perspective, reinforces musicians' perceptions of Pyarelal-ji's exceptional concern for the welfare of his musicians, even to the extent of being able to "call his musicians by name."
Shetty represents his role in carefully neutral terms. Although he admits
that he selected the musicians for recording sessions, he implies that his cri-
terion for that selection was musician availability. Although this was the
formal understanding, some musicians felt that actual practice offered
messengers more opportunities to control who played on recordings.

One of the musicians that everyone in the industry asked for by name is
Jerry Fernandes, a first-row violinist and soloist. He suggests that the musicians' own attempts to organize and control access to their work were
countered by the music directors' actions and the introduction of messengers, whom he calls "informers":

JERRY FERNANDES: It was the informers who were the hold on the musicians.
The musicians were supposed to go through CMA [Cine Musicians Associ-
ation], but the music directors went to the informers.

See, suppose you are a very good musician; no informer can say "no" to
you. But for those in the third row or the fourth row [of the four-row violin section], the informer will call whoever he likes.

When Joe Monsorate switched from violin to trumpet, it took a while
for him to make a name for himself—to be noticed, as he puts it. Informers played a role in this process:

JOE MONSORATE: I was sitting on Laxmi-Pyare's set, and the informer comes
from R. D. Burman [to book musicians]. And maybe there are four or five

of us [trumpets] sitting there. The informer will go to Dad or John [Pereira] or even George [Fernandes] but will skip me because that impression was that I was there because of my dad.

In contrast, Amrut Katkar, as one of R. D. Burman's sitting musicians, was protected from the problems of dealing with messengers on a daily basis:

> AMRUT KATKAR: I wasn't part of that. When he [Burman] went to the studio, I also went. If it was somebody else, Kalyanji-Anandji or somebody, then they would tell the messenger, "Please, you get Amrut-bhai." So they would then call me.

Because Katkar was a sitting musician and thus part of Burman's daily entourage, messengers had none of the effects on Katkar's career that Fernandes and Monsorate suggest. The connection between a role as a sitting musician and direct access to recordings (and therefore fees) was one of the advantages of being a sitting musician. Dattaram Waadkar has recalled, however, that even though he was an assistant to Shankar-Jaikishan, it took much practice and good luck before he was allowed to play in recordings. [Video 6.1]

As the demand for live music and large orchestras began to decrease in the late 1990s, the effect of messengers' decisions on individual musicians' careers became considerable. Deepak Chauhan joined films in the late 1980s, following his brother into the percussion field. He plays mostly side percussion, a nonsoloist position that is increasingly under threat from the click tracks and drum machines that inhabit the studios of twenty-first-century Mumbai. Musicians in such roles are readily replaceable by other humans or machines; thus messengers have an increasing power to significantly influence their career:

> DEEPAK CHAUHAN: The messengers have very much power. You must be very polite to them [and] say, "Good day, sir. Is everything okay? How's the wife and family?" All these things. Because otherwise they would call some one else.

Other musicians report that messengers charged weaker musicians a commission for being called to work. Joe Pinto joined the film line in 1991, one of the last good years for most film musicians. He notes that, although playing for films was initially more rewarding than his former job as a salaried accountant for Indian Railways, he soon realized that he had made the wrong choice of profession:

> JOE PINTO: When I started, the money was very good, but it got bad. I could see it coming, you know, but what to do? And, you know, the messengers

were the kingpins. You had to make sure to keep on their good side. That's what made me decide to give up the whole thing. And they used to take a percentage. Officially what happened was, back when the CMA structure was there, you paid the CMA fee, and you paid a messenger fee. That was just two rupees per session at that time. But if you had sixty musicians or so, then it got to be something. They would stand at the door, I remember. They would check everybody going out. As soon as you got your money, you had to pay the messenger.

Eventually the decline in recordings began to affect messengers as well. Ratna Nagari is a music coordinator who began his career as an assistant to Ramanand Shetty in the 1980s. Shetty and another messenger named Jagirdar were two of the most successful ones in Mumbai from the 1960s on. Nagari, however, left Shetty in the mid-1990s:

> RATNA NAGARI: Now the industry is very cold. There is very little work. I mostly provide musicians for jingle sessions these days.

When technical advances reduced the size of the New Bollywood music industry in human terms, those whose careers depended on that size suffered. Another feature of Mumbai film-song recordings that disappeared in the early 1990s was the role of the song violinist.

Song Violin

Film songs had to be sung as composed. With very few exceptions, film ensembles of the 1940s and '50s played the melody along with the singer or played interludes between the singer's phrases. In the first years of playback, musicians and singer were physically located in the same space; the singers had ample melodic and rhythmic reinforcement to ensure that they remained aligned with the pitch, tempo, and melody. During the 1940s, however, isolation booths (often called the "singer's cabin") were implemented to improve the quality of sound recording and ensure that the vocal melody was distinguishable.

In the booths, however, singers were separated both physically and aurally from the orchestra, making it harder for them to maintain tempo, pitch, and so forth. The role of song violin developed in response to this situation: It acted as a musical link between the orchestra in the main studio and the singer in the cabin.

The song violinist sat in the main recording studio, usually next to the rhythm section. This musician, however, played into a separate microphone that went through its own mixer, where it was combined with the rhythm section (whose members were often playing on one microphone themselves), and was then sent directly to the singer's headphones. While the rhythm section's music appeared on the actual recording, the song violinist (on the separate microphone) never did.

The leading song violinists of the Mumbai studios were Harishchandra Narvekar, Gajanan Karnad, and Prabhakar Jog. Their role required a high level of musicality, but the music they performed was never heard outside the studio; it appeared on neither the sound track nor the disc. Technological developments in New Bollywood have obviated the need for song violinists, and this position is thus entirely historical. If the modern singer requires reinforcement or a reminder, the computer-generated melody can be channeled directly to the singer's headphones.

Rehearsals

Rehearsals were naturally part of a salaried musician's daily work in the studio period. Kersi Lord recalls anywhere from two days to nearly a month of rehearsal before a song was recorded in the late 1940s. Some of this rehearsal time was no doubt due to the need to record performances from beginning to end, but Lord suggests the long hours were necessary because of the orchestra members' relatively low literacy skills:

> KERSI LORD: Some songs I remember, I played about twenty-eight rehearsals, so for twenty-eight days we were going and playing that song because the violins were playing by heart, the soloists were playing by heart, trumpets, woodwinds, all those things, so they had to teach them the music one by one.

Twenty-eight days is no doubt an extreme instance, but Anthony Gonsalves points out that "by-heart" musicians sometimes needed weeks to learn and rehearse an entire song.

By-heart musicians no doubt slowed down song production (which in turn slowed down film production), but the rehearsal structure had been built into the process of film production since 1931, when not just songs but whole scenes (including music) required rehearsal. For musicians on salary, as many were in the studio period, the financial outcomes were the same whether they were rehearsing, recording, or simply waiting for a music director to compose a melody. Songs were practiced by the salaried musicians as part of their job. If the recording called for additional musicians, extra rehearsals would take place on the day of the recording, but with a core of musicians who had already rehearsed the song, further players could quickly be integrated, and competent performances recorded. With the collapse of the studio system, the financial and human infrastructure supporting song production disappeared.

The different directions in which developments proceeded in the transition from the studio period to Old Bollywood help us understand the chaotic nature of this music-production culture. Even as the rehearsal structure built into the studio system was disappearing, the trend toward ever-larger orchestras began (see chapter 8), thus exacerbating the need for practice sessions. The influx of literate musicians from dance bands and hotel orchestras (see chapter 4) no doubt balanced these disparate developments to some extent. However, at the same time, that influx must have highlighted the contrasts between the literate and oral/aural processes of music transmission. Mumbai's music and film industry reacted to these challenges gradually through an improvised process of socioindustrial adaptation and a unique combination of cottage industry, unionized labor, and supply-and-demand economics. [Video 6.2]

Participating in the transition, Jerry Fernandes notes the growing importance of rehearsals for both musical and economic reasons. For freelance musicians, practice sessions were no longer precisely part of the job; in Old Bollywood, pay for musicians was calculated on the basis of their presence at recordings, not rehearsals. Adding pressure from the other side, producers were now paying by the hour for the rented recording facilities, which were commonly booked for another recording for a different film the next day or (increasingly) even later the same day. For that matter, many of the musicians themselves might be engaged to play at a different session the following day. To whatever extent orchestras in the studio system rehearsed indefinitely—that is, "until ready"—that practice was not feasible in the new system.

In response to this situation, everyone adapted, and two kinds of rehearsal systems emerged, both of which were compromises and the source of considerable complaint. Some music directors made rehearsal part of the recording session. Others, especially those who were in high demand, began practicing outside of the recording studio. Ernest Menezes describes both systems but suggests (as do others) that Shankar-Jaikishan were the first music directors to implement the latter method in the mid-1950s:

> ERNEST MENEZES: Shankar-Jaikishan started those regular rehearsals, always two rehearsals and then recording. No other music directors were doing those rehearsals. The others used to rehearse at the take itself. Sometimes that would take two or three hours, and then they would record.

What Menezes suggests here is that by rehearsing outside of recording time, Shankar-Jaikishan had more opportunity to work on the recording itself at the "take."

The Shankar-Jaikishan music room was large enough not only for composition but also for the thirty to forty musicians who rehearsed at the remarkably early hour of seven o'clock in the morning. Although token payments were made for these rehearsals, Shankar-Jaikishan encouraged musicians to attend through a policy whereby those who did not attend were not called for the recording session:

> SUMIT MITRA: Shankar-Jaikishan would rehearse two songs usually every day. And the rule was that if you hadn't played at the rehearsals for that song, when the time came to record, you could not play also.

Although Mitra does not put it in those terms, Shankar-Jaikishan effectively sought to parallel the studio system by rehearsing independently. They relied on their control of the recording sessions (and hence musicians' incomes) to enforce their practice. Rehearsals were once more simply part of the job. Whether or not they were the first, Shankar-Jaikishan were definitely not the only music directors to operate a parallel rehearsal structure. Franco Vaz replaced his father in the group of musicians rehearsing with C. Ramchandra in the mid-1960s. Anna-saheb (as he was sometimes called) also had a private rehearsal room in Shivaji Park called Anna Hall:

> FRANCO VAZ: He had rehearsal rooms. He would rehearse the song for one or two days first. Then on the day of recording, there were no changes. If the director made a fuss and said, "I want changes," then Anna was just, "Pack up. Rehearsal is for the rehearsal room!"

Changes on the day of recording, of course, especially if suggested by the director, would not only interfere with the creative process but also require further rehearsal and delay the recording process.

Rehearsals were opportunities for music directors and arrangers to finetune their songs and for producers to give their final approval. Sometimes soloists also experienced a slightly more intimate rehearsal situation in which their melodies were agreed upon. Both musicians and composers treated rehearsals and recordings as part of the same process, and the necessary work was distributed accordingly. [🅰 Video 6.3]

Despite Shankar-Jaikishan's "no rehearsal, no recording" rule, most practice sessions (like studio system rehearsals) involved fewer musicians than those who appeared for the recordings. Neither Shankar-Jaikishan's nor C. Ramchandra's space could have accommodated a fifty- or sixty-piece orchestra. Prakash Varma also recalls that that prerecording-session rehearsals were often not with the full orchestra. Naushad Ali apparently settled for two prerecording rehearsals instead of O. P. Nayyar's three:

> PRAKASH VARMA: When I joined Mr. Naushad [1964], he would do two rehearsals before recording. The recordings used to happen in Mehboob Studio. So the studio was on the first floor, and on the second floor they had a smaller room that was used for rehearsals. They used to only call

some of the musicians, not all. If there were thirty violins, they would call ten, like that. We used to do two rehearsals for the song and then the take.

Sumit Mitra reports the same situation for the Shankar-Jaikishan rehearsals:

> SUMIT MITRA: There were ten or twelve violins, cello, guitars, and mandolin. Some of the violin players were Joe Menezes, Martin Dourado, Jerry Fernandes; we called them the "three musketeers." Also Albuquerque played cello. Isaac David played mandolin. And there was D'Melo and Boney D'Costa on guitar. Sumant Raj played flute. Leslie Godinho and Cawas Lord played drums and percussions, and Robert Corea, who played piano. Most of them came every day. Goodi [Seervai] was the only one who didn't come. Altogether there were thirty musicians or so every day.

Since Shankar-Jaikishan were often recording with fifty or more musicians in the studio, it appears that their "no rehearsal, no recording" rule was somewhat flexible. This is confirmed by one of the "three musketeers":

> JERRY FERNANDES: I went for rehearsals unless I was going for a recording. Sometimes we used to never go to the rehearsals, but then we would go and play for the recording because they trusted us. Because Sebastian was there, and if you had some recording you tell him, and he would say, "Okay, you just come for the recording." That rule was for the average musicians.

Fernandes points to the pragmatic realities of the film-music line. The violinists in the front line were playing in everyone's recordings and were viewed as indispensable. Since Sebastian was arranging for most of the music directors for whom these men were playing, their attendance at rehearsals was much more flexible.

Furthermore, Mitra's special designation of the famous accordionist Goodi Seervai as "the only one who didn't come" every day may have more to do with Mitra's personal circumstances as the orchestra's second accordionist:

> SUMIT MITRA: At that time, Goodi Seervai played with Shankar-Jaikishan, but he would not come to the rehearsals. He had his own band that would play for weddings and such things, so he refused to come. Shankar-Jaikishan did not like this, but they put up with it because Goodi was the only accordion player until I came. Mostly I played background parts.

Mitra was naturally especially sensitive to the comings and goings of the much more famous principal accordionist. In fact, it was in Mitra's interests that Seervai not appear. Dattaram Waadkar's access to recordings was also the result of the absence of a lead player. In Mitra's case, Seervai's unreliability gave Mitra the chance he needed to make a name for himself. In explaining this, Mitra also shows how the private Shankar-Jaikishan rehearsals connected to later practice sessions in the studio:

> SUMIT MITRA: After the morning rehearsal [in the duo's music room], we would go to the studio to rehearse, and then at ten-thirty or so there would be the mic rehearsal. For that, the singers would come, and the recordist would move the microphones and balance the instruments so that the sound would be correct. And one day, [Mohamed] Rafi and Lata [Mangeshkar] had come and were waiting, and Goodi had still not come. That day it was a song of Jaikishan's, and finally he didn't want to wait any more for Goodi. So Mr. Sebastian said to Jaikishan that I should play. So Jaikishan said, "Okay." So I played, and when that was finished, Jaikishan said, "This boy plays well. Now if Goodi isn't coming I can rely on him [Mitra]."

In addition to the kind of professional rivalry that is almost expected, this story offers two additional and final perspectives on the rehearsal process. First, it points to the liminal nature of practice sessions. If there was "real" work—and most of the time that meant recording—or if musicians felt that they were important enough to be able to ignore rehearsals with impunity, they often stayed away. Seervai, for example, led his own dance band in the 1950s (figure 6.1) and had an independent career as a recording artist. Kersi Lord, who avoided rehearsals later in his life as we have seen learned, was happy enough to go when the alternative was a day at school.

> KERSI LORD: Mr. Naushad used to have rehearsals at nine o'clock, and I would bunk [skip] school to go to those at least two or three times a week. They had a car that would drop me at the station, and I would get to school two hours late.

Second, because of the rehearsals that Shankar-Jaikishan instituted and the request for their music, the musicians Mitra lists were in effect the core of what musicians called the "Shankar-Jaikishan orchestra," although everyone realizes that the group was not precisely the same from day to day. The growing demand for films in the 1960s led especially to a semblance of normalcy that extended to a replication of something like the "studio orchestra" model. Theoretically, freelance musicians came only when there was work, but the reality was that there was almost always work. Although the situation was naturally more flexible than salary employment, musicians developed informal associations with a specific music director (at least the major ones). Musicians "belonged" to the Shankar-Jaikishan or the S. D. Burman "group."

Figure 6.1 Goodi Seervai leads his orchestra during a performance at Birla Theatre in Mumbai in the late 1950s. Trumpet player John Pereira stands in the back row. Courtesy of John Pereira.

As I have indicated, Dattaram Waadkar worked closely with Shankar-Jaikishan throughout the duo's career:

> DATTARAM WAADKAR: I was with them until *Sanyasi* [1975]. That was the last picture. Then Jaikishan-ji died, and Shankar was alone, and that wasn't working so well, so I left him. And Laxmi-Pyare called me, so I went with them for fifteen years.

Waadkar found himself in a new environment, however, with Laxmikant-Pyarelal not only because of the physical move from Famous to Mehboob but also because of the process that Pyarelal-ji used for composing and arranging. High demand effectively allowed him to make his own rules:

> DATTARAM WAADKAR: Laxmi-Pyare changed the style. They didn't have rehearsals. They had the orchestra in the recording studio, and they rehearsed there from the morning until late at night, until eleven o'clock or even one o'clock in the night. The composition, rehearsal, and recording—all happened at once.

Actually, Laxmikant-Pyarelal did rehearse, as Waadkar knows full well. What he means is that they did not rehearse outside the studio. The process of composing, arranging, rehearsing, and recording, which could take fifteen days or more with Shankar-Jaikishan, all occurred in one extended session. And, as I explain later, everything took place in the recording studio.

Groups

Despite the presence of industrial organizations, much of the socioprofessional structure that operated in Mumbai was informal. There were what might be called patterns of association even at the music directors' level:

> FRANCO VAZ: My dad was not in the Shankar-Jaikishan group, but on and off he would get a call, and then he used to go there. Mostly he was playing with Madan Mohan-saheb, C. Ramchandra, Naushad, those guys. There were different groups. It was a different family altogether you can say.

Friendships or professional compatibilities among groups of music directors led to parallel groupings among musicians. Those who played for one composer in "the group" were more likely to play for others in that circle. In part this was because such music directors were more likely to cooperate in scheduling so that human resources could be shared if necessary.

The semiformal nature of this kind of socioprofessional organization was crucial to the functioning of Old Bollywood. These orchestral groups naturally included more people than the few who were sitting musicians but fewer than the number of those called for recordings. Like Franco Vaz, Ernest Menezes identifies the "family" with whom he worked most closely:

ERNEST MENEZES: I worked mostly for the Burmans, mostly with the son,
    because they had their own groups, you see. They would call you first, but
    if they needed some very big group, they might call other musicians as well.
    But I really belonged to Shankar-Jaikishan.

The familial complexities of Mumbai's musical "groups" come out quite
clearly in Menezes' statement. His belonging to Shankar-Jaikishan is based
largely on heredity and cultural affiliation (his uncle, cousin, and many other
Goans "belonged to Shankar-Jaikishan"). In terms of actual recordings,
Menezes did more work with the Burmans, who were a different group.

There were also regular associations between specific music directors,
directors or producers, actors, lyricists, and singers. For example, Naushad
Ali worked with actor Dilip Kumar and lyricist Shakeel Badayuni in a series of films throughout the 1950s and '60s (e.g., from *Andaaz* [1949] to
Leader [1964]), often with director Mehboob Khan as well. Because
Naushad-saheb rarely took on more than two or three films per year, however, he did not generate enough work to maintain a "Naushad orchestra"
in the same way that the much more prolific Shankar-Jaikishan were able
to do. The apparent permanence of an orchestral group, in other words,
was dependent on the music director's ability (or willingness) to accept and
produce a large number of scores over a sustained period of time.

Ernest Menezes was a highly valued, front-row violinist, so his career
traces the peaks of the various music directors who were generating the
most work at any given moment:

ERNEST MENEZES: When Shankar-Jaikishan started going down, I was called
    by Ravi, and when his work became less, then I was with Kalyanji-Anandji,
    and then when their work became less, I was with Madan Mohan, like
    that. Music directors would start and go to a peak and then come down,
    and I would go with the next one. I was very lucky, you can say.

Thus, although he saw himself as coming from the Shankar-Jaikishan
group and working primarily for the Burman group, Menezes nonetheless
moved from composer to composer throughout his career.

"Groupism" reached its height in the 1970s and '80s in the division between Laxmikant-Pyarelal and R. D. Burman, although again this was
more a matter of demand than competition. Cellist Benny Gracias emphasizes the sense of mutual support between these music directors and their
musicians, which was part of this socioprofessional structure:

BENNY GRACIAS: Even R. D. Burman, even if the song didn't need cellos, the
    cellos would be there—even for songs [i.e., as well as background music]. It
    used to be like, "These are my musicians. They are depending on me, and
    I'm depending on them." It was that kind of rapport.

As I mentioned earlier, this kind of bond led to the excesses of late Old Bollywood that others found objectionable. At the time, however, Gracias (who implies that he saw himself as part of the L-P string section) suggests that the groups collaborated because their respective music directors were willing to support each other:

> BENNY GRACIAS: R. D. Burman's rhythm section was renowned, and L-P's string section was renowned. So supposing we were called for a recording: "Ah! Laxmikant-Pyarelal's string section has come!" Like that they used to say. And the same if R. D. Burman's rhythm section came.

Kersi Lord offers an explanation for this later groupism based on the way these music directors worked and the amount of work they were doing:

> KERSI LORD: It would take Pyarelal sometimes thirty-five shifts [sessions] to get the background score composed and recorded. This tied up a lot of musicians, who had to sit while he composed. If you called one of his regulars for work, he would say, "I can only come if Pyarelal doesn't need me."

Even someone like Bhanu Gupta, however, who was a sitting musician with R. D. Burman, played other sessions when he could:

> BHANU GUPTA: It's not that I wasn't playing with others. If I had a recording [with someone else], I'd skip that sitting. He [Burman] used to sometimes say, "I need you at the sitting today." And I'd say, "Well, I have a recording in the morning, but later . . ." So then he'd shift to the evening sitting so I could come.

As the preceding series of comments—beginning with Dattaram Waadkar—suggests, one of the reasons musicians were so busy was that certain music directors in the later years of Old Bollywood began to change the way in which they worked. Best known for driving this change are Pyarelal Sharma and Bappi Lahiri, both of whom pursued a practice that blurred the distinctions between sittings, rehearsals, and recordings. This affected not only song recording but even more so the recording of background music.

Background Music and Changing Notions of the Recording Studio

In contrast to song recording, which played a central and early role in the shooting of a movie, the separation of sound and image recording allowed filmmakers to shoot a film and later add background music to desired scenes. Composing background music was less prestigious than writing songs. Unlike with songs, whose composers are always clearly listed in film credits, background music has become an attributed component only in New Bollywood. As I explain in chapter 5, few Old Bollywood films list arrangers. Although those in the film-music line knew who was composing background music, the public assumed that the music directors composed the background music as well. The ambiguity with which both Arnold (1991) and Morcom (2007) treat the topic of background music reflects this largely erroneous assumption. Adding to the confusion, certain music directors did indeed compose some or all of their own background scores (e.g., Master Sonik, Pyarelal Sharma, Jaikishan); many, however, delegated the composition of background music to their assistants:

> KERSI LORD: I started my career with Mr. Naushad, *Dastaan* [1950] and all those films. One day we were going for the background score for *Ram aur Shyam* [1967], and he took me also. Mr. Naushad doesn't do most of the background. He just supervised. So there was one piece, they were going to the cemetery, and he said, "You just write something for this scene. I want a really good piece; you go home and write it for me." So I went home and wrote something.

Regardless of the relative contributions of music directors, assistants and arrangers, background music was composed once the visual and spoken elements of the film had been completed. Those involved watched the film and made decisions about the moods and emotions of selected scenes, and they timed those that required music. The task was to compose and record music that would be in synch with the film's images and last the right length of time. "Changeovers," as the transition from one mood to another came to be called, were marked with crosses on the film as guides for the conductors, who led the ensembles with one eye on the score and one eye on the rolling film to make sure the group began, ended, and shifted musically on the mark.

Shyamrao Kemble was one of those who assisted Pyarelal Sharma in the production of background music not by composing but by timing:

> SHYAMRAO KEMBLE: First we saw the picture. And we, the assistants, would sit in front of the screen and see the timings with a stopwatch. That means fifty seconds for this scene, thirty seconds for that, like that. And after that I would sit with Pyare; he composed the music, and I wrote it. Then the orchestra players would be sitting behind me, and they would all copy out their parts very quickly. Then we would try it three or four times. Then we would go on to the next one.

In this description the entire orchestra would be present while Pyarelal-ji composed and parts were written out. Jaikishan did background music for many of the films he scored as part of Shankar-Jaikishan. Unlike Pyarelal, however, he apparently relied on feel rather than the common stopwatch:

> J. V. ACHARYA: Jaikishan never took a stopwatch. He used to see the full reel, and he used to call Sebastian and give all the music. The musicians would write [out] the music—solo pieces and everything. We would have one rehearsal, and then he used to say, "Reel lagao" [run the film]. So we would put the reel [running] and start playing the music. Not a single frame would be changed.

In recording, the task was to ensure that the timing was flawless:

> PYARELAL SHARMA: Conducting was sometimes very difficult. Suppose there was a scene which was eight bars long, but suppose really it was eight bars plus three beats. I would have to slow down just a little bit very carefully so that we would hit the mark just right.

Background soloists also had to hit the mark. Although some improvisation took place in background solos, in many instances the soloists played music that had been composed ahead of time. Zarin Sharma describes the process in a story intended to demonstrate the perceptiveness of Master Sonik, the blind arranger who composed background music for Madan Mohan:

> ZARIN SHARMA: Master-ji [Sonik] called me for some background session; it was *Rishte Naate* [1965]. And you know they put those marks on the film, and you have to play from the mark to the next mark, that kind of thing. And he had composed the piece that I had to play from the third mark. That was my starting point. And my piece came, but somehow I missed it. I was sitting looking at the screen, but somehow it went out of my head. I was very embarrassed, let me tell you. But he had given me the sign. Even though he was blind, he knew where the mark was that I had missed!

Because the process was trial and error, background recording was often quite slow and the sessions rather long:

> KERSI LORD: I used to work for fifteen days on the background music composing, then come on the set and rehearse for five days. Most of the arrangements were trial and error—one line or two lines at a time.

Pyarelal Sharma was famous for his background music but rarely accepted criticism, especially regarding his enthusiasm for diverse orchestral sounds. He was popular enough that producers seldom complained, even the famous Raj Kapoor:

> JOE MONSORATE: There's that scene in *Bobby* [1977], the swimming pool scene, where Dimple comes to the pool. Pyare-ji called everybody for that scene, the orchestra, and the chorus, everybody. But we expected we would

have nothing in that piece, so we were standing around outside, and somebody comes and says, "Come on, you're all wanted!" And inside Mr. Raj
Kapoor is also there, and he says to Pyarelal, "What is all this? Why so
many musicians? She's just going for a swim!" And Pyarelal looks at him
and says, "Just you listen." He had us playing with wah-wah mutes in that
scene. Raj Kapoor was amazed.

One of the most important aspects of Monsorate's story is the brass
section's assumption that they would not actually have to play although
they had been requested (and would be paid) for the session as a matter
of routine. The production of background music could be both expensive
and slow:

> JERRY FERNANDES: Pyarelal used to record one or two pieces [of] background
> music per day. That was very slow because he did everything in the studio.
> We would work seven hours a day for fifteen days for one picture. We
> would come at nine o'clock, but he would come late always. I used to get
> excited: "Why this man has come so late, and nothing is done?" But as
> soon as he came, and we played the music, then it was all forgotten. "Let's
> forgive this man." The music was so great.

Fifteen days was hardly a record, however. Surender Sodi, a background
music composer, may have set the record in 1999 at Empire Studio:

> ASHOK SHUKLA: For Mela [1999] we had three hundred musicians in the stu-
> dio all at once, all playing live. The background score was by Surender
> Sodi. It took us thirty days.

Bappi Lahiri extended to excess Pyarelal's system of using the studio for
composing, arranging, rehearsing, and recording. He surpassed Pyarelal in
coming late but, unlike Pyarelal, left much of the actual work to his assistants. Benny Rosario worked as one of Lahiri's many electronic keyboard
players and assistants in the late 1980s and early '90s. Rosario offers quite
dichotomous visions of the Lahiri workshop, in which hard work and high
output contrast with blatant abuse of the system (and of producers' budgets). Here, Rosario reports a very efficient system that worked quite well
even without Lahiri's presence:

> BENNY ROSARIO: The arrangers would come in the morning. Anil [Mohile]
> and Arun [Paudwal] and Vincent [Alvarez] would all work on the back-
> ground music. Vincent would mark the film, and then Anil would write
> something for the first mark, and Vincent would copy it, and then Anil
> would record it, and while he was recording, Arun would be writing some-
> thing for the next mark, and again Vincent would copy, and then Arun
> would record, and Anil would be writing something. We never stopped; we
> would work right through to lunch.

As electronic keyboards in Mumbai became more prominent and sophisticated, the nature of background work changed from ninety musicians on a large soundstage for days on end to one, two, or three keyboard programmers in a music room or even a hotel room with a computer system for monitoring the film. Anjan Biswas was eventually hired to program (i.e., compose) the background music for *Hum Dil De Chuke Sanam* (1999), but he worked by himself, following the film director's explanations.

Taufiq Qureshi often worked as a rhythm programmer with Biswas and others as part of a trio employed by background composer Vanraj Bhatia. In effect, the three were composing the music that would be released under Bhatia's name:

> TAUFIQ QURESHI: Vanraj would say, "Okay, from the cross to C2 [change-overs marked on the film], Sanjay, you program this. And from C3 to C5, okay, Sunil, you program this. And Taufiq, you listen to what's going on and put in the rhythms." And the whole day we would be programming, and at the end of the day we would say, "Okay, Vanraj, come and hear the part. Tell us what you think."

In effect, musicians who learned to program the electronics became composers and arrangers themselves because they could manipulate the technology. Among other things, this has changed the way background music is credited. While Kersi Lord had to fight to get a credit for his background music, more and more Hindi films now list the background music separately from the music direction:

> ANJAN BISWAS: These days, [background music] is completely separate. Recently I did the background music for three of David Dhawan's movies, and I got a separate credit for that. This trend has been there for at least ten years.

Background music, whether programmed or composed, however, has always been produced by a somewhat distinctive process in comparison to the songs, which were, after all, the primary income generators for film producers and the music industry. For musicians, recording sessions for background also differed somewhat from those for songs. Nevertheless, recording sessions of any kind were the major sources of income for Mumbai's film musicians.

Recordings

In the Mumbai film-music studios, daily life centered on recording sessions (figure 6.2). Like many work situations, recordings were simultaneously

Figure 6.2 Devi Lal Varma (clarinet), Mohan Bharve (vertical bamboo flute), Goody Seervai (accordion), A. P. Dorado (violin, seated), Boney DaCosta (guitar), Kersi Lord (accordion) recording at Famous Studios (Tardeo). Courtesy of Prakash Varma.

social and professional experiences. The long working sessions often required considerable flexibility, patience, and stamina:

> PYARELAL SHARMA: We went to work with our instruments under one arm
> and a bedroll under the other arm.

Sharma's picturesque description provides one sense of the amount of
work. He continues, however, by distinguishing between song and background sessions. As an industry, Mumbai's film world revolved around
what were in practice two very different parts of the film-music production
system:

> PYARELAL SHARMA: We recorded background from nine o'clock at night until
> five o'clock in the morning. We recorded songs during the day, one session
> from eight to twelve o'clock and one from two to six o'clock. We would
> work continuously for three days and two nights.

Although the timings changed over the years, background music sessions were always longer than song sessions. As extreme as Sharma's description may seem, others reinforce the image of an industry that worked
all hours:

> JOE GOMES: We used to go eight days in the week. We didn't get sufficient
> time for anything. I used to go for my band work, and we would finish at
> eleven o'clock at night, and then I would go back to the studio. Sometimes
> background session would start at six o'clock in the evening, and we would
> go on until six o'clock in the morning or sometimes the other way round.
> There was no time; we were exhausted.

The socializing that went on after the work required different kinds of
stamina. Violinist Maoro Alfonso did not always have that latter kind, as
he explains in his discussion of another famous violinist of the Mumbai
film studios:

> MAORO ALFONSO: He was a good fellow. Sometimes he would come to my
> house and say, "Maoro, there's a take today. Come, let's go." So I'd say,
> "Okay, I'll come in my car." But he would say, "No, you come in my car.
> I'll take you." So we would take the car and go, and then when we had
> finished taking [i.e., recording], we would go for the booze. And from one
> day it would become another day, and we'd still be drinking, and I used to
> say, "When will I go home? I have no car!"

Despite the occasional clash in lifestyle, a strong sense of camaraderie often
developed among musicians who worked together daily.

The remarkable rate at which songs were produced was a result of the
fact that everyone was working all of the time. Equally importantly, everyone understood the task and their role in it. Figure 6.3 shows the persist-

Figure 6.3 Recording session and roles. Two members of the Shankar-Eshaan-Loy music director team (Shankar Mahadevan and Loy Mendonsa, extreme left and right) discuss the score with the recording session's conductor (Inderjeet Sharma) and Shankar Indorkar.

ence of those roles and that understanding even after the demise of the industrial infrastructure that supported them. In addition to playing viola on the session shown, Shankar Indorkar functioned as a kind of assistant, much as he sometimes did as a Laxmikant-Pyarelal regular, checking and distributing parts.

Viju Shah suggests that, by the 1970s, Mumbai had in fact reached the capacity allowed by its infrastructure. More work would have required a fifth studio; the film music industry was indeed working full time:

> Viju Shah: In those days we had four big studios running all the time: Film Centre, Famous, Bombay Labs, and Mehboob. All were busy, two shifts every day. Song in the morning, background in the afternoon, and the jingles after ten o'clock in the night.

The dominance of film music is shown by the relegation of jingle recordings to the middle of the night.

Because of the amount of rehearsing that went on and because everyone was playing all of the time, songs were quickly recorded. Older musicians are somewhat disdainful of modern recording practices that take, as Benny Gracias says here, up to four or five days for one song:

> BENNY GRACIAS: We used to do a song recording within four hours. Mr. O. P. Nayyar could finish a song within two and a half hours. One time we had an emergency with L-P, and we did five songs in one day. That was when Mohamed Rafi was living, and he had to go abroad for some shows. Today with all this technology, the song recording is going on for four days or five days.

In the technological systems based on 35 mm magnetic tape, changes were costly and awkward. Almost invariably, changes had been made before the tape rolled. In most cases, unless technical problems cropped up, the results were accepted:

> VIJU SHAH: Before I came into the line, my dad used to tell me that they'd record two songs in four or five hours. Live, just like that. And by the time I was watching and working with him, one song used to take three or four days.

The speed that these reports indicate was not always the case, of course. Dattaram Waadkar was present for one of Old Bollywood's more legendary recordings sessions, in which the long and complex Shankar-Jaikishan song "Ghar aya mere pardesi" apparently required almost twenty-four hours to record:

> DATTARAM WAADKAR: That recording was something. We started around ten o'clock in the morning, and we didn't finish until the next morning. All day and all night we were in the studio for that sequence. There were 120 musicians that night. We finally had food [finished] at six o'clock in the morning. When we finished, Raj-saheb sent out for *jalebis* [syrupy pastries].

Dissanayake and Sahai (1988) and Chatterjee (1992) examine this sequence in detail. Briefly, the extended music (instrumental) sections depict the various tensions in the hero's dreams (and in the film). This called for musical sections with radically different tonalities, instrumentation, and so forth.

The "Ghar aya mere pardesi" session took place late in 1950 for release in Raj Kapoor's second major hit, *Awaara* (1951). This kind of marathon recording session was about to get more expensive, however. In part because of the increased demand for large orchestras as a result of this song's popularity, film musicians were able demand clearer structures, more regular pay, and better salaries.

The Economics of Film Musicianship

In both the studio system of the 1940s and the independent producer system that replaced it, producers paid the costs of filmmaking either directly or by finding investors:

JERRY FERNANDES: One thing I'll tell you. Who has the money in this line? It is the producers; they are the paymasters.

Pay for musicians could mean a salary, a per-song fee, or an hourly wage. Depending on the musician and the time, the remuneration could vary considerably. Fernandes goes on to report that in the 1940s pay was sometimes organized on a "per song recording" basis. A musician's monthly earnings were determined by the number of recordings that could be squeezed into that period, not how many hours were spent in the studio; rehearsing was not factored into the equation:

JERRY FERNANDES: When I joined (1943–1944), I was getting up to 62.50 for five [to] ten rehearsals. That means, we rehearse for five to ten days and then do the take, and they paid me 62.50. So you can just imagine how hard I had to work.

Depending upon the hours required for rehearsal, working for a studio on a monthly salary could actually bring a lower hourly wage, as Fernandes discovered when he gave up freelancing and joined Ranjit Movietone:

JERRY FERNANDES: I worked for Ranjit. I was getting 225 rupees per month. And there were three or four music directors, so I played for all of them because that was the contract.

After having joined HMV as a staff artist in 1946, J. V. Acharya was being paid what he calls a "decent salary" of 60.21 rupees monthly. When he began doing film work, he became a staff musician at Rajkamal Kalamandir and received 200 rupees per month, but the hours were no doubt longer.

From available information, it appears that Vistasp Balsara, who left his salary at Filmistan behind for a job as a sitting musician with Ghulam Haider in 1945, was one of the best-paid musicians in Mumbai. As a freelance music director, Haider was apparently able to offer Balsara a better financial arrangement than Filmistan. It was certainly much better than Fernandes's or Acharya's contracts:

VISTASP BALSARA: We used to get 400 rupees per month in those days from each producer. For that we gave two hours of fixed service [daily]. Whether there was recording or no recording, we had to attend two hours for each

producer. So I used to get 1,600 rupees per month to work permanently for
Mr. Ghulam Haider.

Balsara was acting as Haider's assistant, which may help explain the
high wages, but he seems to suggest that all of Haider's musicians were
being paid this amount. Balsara's wages, however, were directly dependent
on Haider's having four films in the works at any one time. The figure he
quotes was not an agreed salary; it was an ideal. If Haider was working on
more than four films in any given period, Balsara's salary went up; if he had
fewer, it went down.

It might seem that in comparison to Balsara, Fernandes and Acharya
were accepting a lower salary in exchange for the regularity and security of
a salaried position and a "nine-to-five" job, but even that is hard to assert:

> JERRY FERNANDES: We were never paid overtime. Not only no overtime, we
> never used to get any payment also. I lost so much money that way. Even
> at Ranjit, I would get my salary after many months. After six months, we
> used to get one month's salary. Or they would pay us very late.

The period these men refer to (roughly 1946–1951) occurred during the
transition from the studio system to the independent-producer system,
which may help explain the bad conditions and economic uncertainty.

Only a few years after Jerry-saheb joined Ranjit, a teenaged Kersi Lord
was working at the freelance rate of 62.50 rupees per song recording
(which is effectively what Fernandes describes). Lord, however, who
played mostly for Naushad Ali, could earn that fee in four hours, a unit of
time that was becoming the industry norm:

> KERSI LORD: I was very young, fourteen or fifteen years old when I started.
> We would have a two-hour session for rehearsal, and then the recording
> session would start. At that time we were paid 62.50 for a four-hour
> session.

As the studio system was collapsing, the ongoing need for rehearsals
with the least organizational stress drove many music directors to rehearse
just prior to the recording session. This may have contributed to the idea
of the four-hour song-recording shift that I describe later, even though most
musicians agree that it rarely took four hours to actually record a song
once the rehearsals were over.

It appears from the available accounts that the transition between the
industrial patterns of the film factories and the new cottage industry was
unstable. Studios were becoming harder pressed to continue as viable
financial concerns and were gradually providing fewer salaried positions.
Musicians working freelance had little to fall back on if a particular independent producer failed to pay them or paid them very late. Each individ-

ual's financial situation could be quite different, both from moment to moment and from those of his colleagues:

> JOE GOMES: At that time [the late 1940s], film line was not very good for musicians. There were no musicians' rates. Afterwards, the rates were there, and all these musicians started joining, and the film line started coming up.

Gomes was working mostly in the dance band field until independence; the rates to which he refers were those for recording sessions established by the musicians' union in 1952. Until that time, pay seems to have always been subject to renegotiation, as Sunil Kaushik suggests:

> SUNIL KAUSHIK: Cawas-kaka [Cawas Lord] used to tell us that one time he played maracas for a recording. When the session was finished, the producer told the musicians, "Please come to my office after some time for collecting the money." So Cawas-kaka went to the office, and the producer asked him, "What did you play in this?" and Cawas-kaka explained that he had played maracas. But the producer said, "I can't hear any maracas! Why should I pay for something I can't even hear?"

For everyone in the music line, the issue of when, if, and how much they would be paid was one of serious concern. These financial difficulties, however, were taking place in the context of the growing importance of film music in a newly independent India, the rising dominance of the major playback singers as India's leading popular vocalists, and the growth of the Mumbai film orchestras.

The Cine Musicians Association

Although 1951 was not a good year for Hindi film output, in Mumbai the demand for musicians was great enough that film musicians felt they might successfully form a union and go on strike:

> VISTASP BALSARA: Work had to be stopped due to nonpayment and all that. It was about the rate; the producers were not willing to pay our rate. This was sometime in 1951, just before the CMA was started.

In 1952, flutist Sumant Raj became the first president of the Cine Musicians Association:

> J. V. ACHARYA: Myself and Sumant-ji, Kersi Lord, Parsu Ram—there were about ten of us at that time. We got together and started the association and had it registered. At that time we were playing the recordings, but we were not taking money. After eight days we would get money, but there was no accounting. We lost so much money because of that.

That year was also the beginning of Acharya's long association with CMA. He served for many years as vice president, as well as president, and was instrumental in negotiations with producers regarding overtime payments.

The film musicians in Chennai also eventually formed an association (the Cine Musicians Union). Acharya, who worked in the Chennai studios from 1981 to 1988, states, however, that the Chennai union was a "*khichdi* [mixed stew] formation" that included film musicians but also "music directors, playback singers, chorus singers; everybody is in one."

As the film industry began to sort itself out along the new lines of collective impermanence, CMA became simply one of the many associations involved. Naturally, each organization has its own history, which I cannot address here:

> ERNEST MENEZES: There are eighteen associations—for music directors, junior artists, playback singers, dance directors—all these things, and they are all part of the Film Federation of India [FFI]. And then there is a confederation of industries: Bombay, Calcutta, Madras, and, I think, Bangalore.

For film musicians, music directors and producers were essential to negotiations, but given the indirect nature of the industrial system, bargaining talks rarely involved only two parties. In the 1990s CMA president Menezes found himself negotiating simultaneously with IMPPA (Indian Motion Picture Producers Association), AMMTVPA (Advertisers, Movie, and Music Television Producers Association), and the Guild, a breakaway, high-end producers' group.

In 1952 CMA reached agreement with the producers on the rates per shift, based on expertise as assessed by CMA. Originally there were three grades, A, B, and C, but Special and Extra-Special grades were added later, and finally a grade simply listed as Top. As originally set up, the rate that had been standard pre-CMA, 62.50 rupees, became the bottom level of the pay scale:

> DATTARAM WAADKAR: Then in recordings we were paid by the CMA rates: 85 rupees per shift [for A grade] or 110 for first class, like that. My rate was Special, 120 rupees.

Shifts were technically four hours long, but it took time for everyone to agree to this standard and its implications for musicians and producers. Not until ten years later did CMA address musicians' concerns about the length of sessions:

> ERNEST MENEZES: In those days there was no overtime. My God! If I had had overtime!

BENNY GRACIAS: There was none of that at those times. We used to play for Naushad from morning till night. And still we would be given the basic amount.

ERNEST MENEZES: They used to count the time from when the last musician came. So if you came at nine o'clock and the last guy came at eleven o'clock, they would count the four hours from eleven.

BENNY GRACIAS: So the musicians started saying, "Why is this happening? You can pay us a fixed amount, but you take any amount of time from us at all. Why is this? You pay us overtime." So they had a big meeting with the music directors and the producers, and they agreed that the shift was four hours time, and after the four hours, they had to pay per hour. You have to pay the overtime.

The union also negotiated a cancellation fee and formalized the norm for recording sessions at four hours for song sessions, during which time one song was to be recorded. Background sessions were much longer (often ten hours), with a one-hour lunch break. Because of the length of background shifts, musicians working them were paid for one and a half shifts. Dattaram Waadkar, for example, would have received 180 rupees for a background shift.

Overtime fixed as an hourly wage based on a proportion of a musician's shift rate. The messenger organizing the recording was responsible for keeping track of the rates and the overtime hours for each musician working in a given session. Nevertheless, although messengers were employed by the producer, it was usually one of the producer's accountants who passed on this information to the producer.

Much rehearsing took place within the four hours of a song shift, but CMA also clarified the relation between rehearsals and shifts and established fees for the former as well, although these were very small:

SUMIT MITRA: We got ten rupees per rehearsal. The producers paid, but we only got paid after the recording. So, if there were two rehearsals for the song, they paid you at the same time that they paid for the recording. They kept it written down who had come. Shankar-Jaikishan were very systematic and very punctual. So they knew, and accordingly they put your name down for payment. One day I came late to rehearsal, and Shankar or Jaikishan said, "You must go out and write a letter of apology before coming back." That's how punctual and systematic they were.

There was also some sense of a graduated pay scale for rehearsals:

DATTARAM WAADKAR: They rehearsed in their rooms, and the producers used to only give ten or twenty rupees per rehearsal, per head, maybe thirty rupees.

Having reached agreement on rates, normalized session timings, and established a structure for overtime, CMA next had to ensure that the agreed-upon wages were actually paid. Producers had been in the habit of having the musicians come to their offices a day or a week after the recording. Now CMA leaders argued that musicians should be paid immediately upon completion of the recording, that is, on the set. This was the "set payment" system:

> Jerry Fernandes: Once we founded CMA, then the producers had to bring the money on the set itself. And if they didn't pay, we didn't play. If they don't pay, then we send them a notice, and if nothing comes, then we tell the musicians, "Don't play for this man."

After the initial work stoppage in 1951, CMA resorted to strikes from time to time to enforce its position. Strikes effectively put a stop to the recording process, which then halted the filmmaking process since song scenes could not be filmed without the songs. Although CMA's complaint was usually with the producers, strikes naturally affected music directors also, who could not get their songs recorded. In this way, musicians had considerable power to disrupt the system. Vistasp Balsara was in Kolkata in the 1970s, where he still felt the effects of one of CMA's biggest strikes:

> Vistasp Balsara: When I was in Calcutta, R. D. Burman had a program here. That time, there was a strike in Bombay. So the producers had requested our association, the Calcutta CMA, to play for them. But we did not do that. That strike was for one and a half months. R. D. Burman was telling the musicians, "Please kindly put off the strike because the music directors are in trouble now because producers are not paying because there was no recording."

The strike was actually longer than Balsara remembered. In 1974 CMA was on strike for four months. Although Burman complained about its impact, the 1974 strike gave him, his assistants, and the studio recordists at Raj Kamal the leisure to work out the musical and technical aspects of the recording processes for the technically complicated *Sholay:*

> Joe Monsorate: Four months we were on complete strike. As soon as it was over, we started the background for *Sholay.* We were starved for work by then, and that came as a bumper for us. It was lucky that the strike happened at that time because they [Burman and his assistants] could sit to work out all the details in the music. They had so much time because of that strike.

As an industrial action, however, the 1974 strike was not unequivocally successful:

JOE MONSORATE: We didn't get much benefit from that strike. We got
some benefit, but we expected more. We all had great losses from the four
months we were on strike, but we showed our unity. That was the important thing.

Tabla player Sharafat Khan was not part of CMA in 1974. By that point
Lala and Sattar had dominated drumming in the Mumbai film studios for
more than twenty years. When this duo went on strike along with the rest
of CMA, Sharafat got involved in an attempt to record some songs for
Kalyanji-Anandji. Music directors, after all, were not on strike:

SHARAFAT KHAN: I had met many music directors, but nothing happened.
Lala-Sattar played all the songs; they had the reputations. I would come
with my instruments, but nothing would happen. My friend Aziz came and
said, "You have to come with me tomorrow" [for a recording]. But that
was 1974. Aziz took me in his car. I didn't know about the strike, but when
we went to the studio, there were all these people outside that I knew and
who I said "Salām" to every day. And they looked at me and said, "Yeh
chakar kyaa hai bhaiya? [What's this nonsense, brother?] We're on strike!
What are you doing?" So Aziz said, "I'm just trying to get my two songs
recorded, and I've gotten this chance after a lot of trouble. Please let us do
these songs." So I played on those songs.

The existence of CMA, the regular negotiations with IMPPA and other
groups, and the occasional strikes all contributed to the appearance of a
permanent industry. The session rates gradually increased incrementally
over the years. By the 1980s, B and A grade musicians were receiving
150–180 rupees per shift, while Special to Top grade rates ranged from 375
to 660 rupees.

Bosco Mendes, who played trombone in late Old Bollywood, gives an
idea of the demand for musicians and the amount of time musicians were
spending in the studios:

BOSCO MENDES: I started working in 1986 or '87. At that time people were
pretty much working daily. We had the morning shift starting from nine
o'clock to three o'clock and another shift from three o'clock to eleven
o'clock in the evening. So many people were working fourteen hours every
day. I used to get work usually two or three times a week.

Trombones (and brass generally) were in less demand than strings; three
recordings a week was about as much as brass players could expect.

The rules that were created to protect musicians in combination with
the practices of some celebrity music directors meant good wages for musicians, at least in the short term, but also excessive costs for producers.
Benny Rosario, who was part of Bappi Lahiri's enormous production team,

explains their attitude: "We wasted a lot of time. The producer was paying, so why work hard?"

Joe Monsorate explains that a musician who worked even two hours on a background shift earned the same wage as another who played the whole day:

> JOE MONSORATE: Suppose they're doing some background session, and suddenly Pyare-ji feels he needs brass section, and suppose it's late, it's almost pack-up time, still he says, "Quick, call the brass section!" And we have to come down right away, only for one piece. But still we'd get the whole day's payment just for that one piece. Background was like that. We were paid by the shift.

Bhanu Gupta is one of the many musicians who maintain that the 1980s and early '90s were the best years to be a musician in Bollywood:

> BHANU GUPTA: It was a very good living; we were very well off. By today's standards we were making 3,000 to 5,000 rupees a week. That's good enough. At least 2,000 a day. And we worked all the year. It was totally business, totally commercial. And in addition to films there were ads, jingles, and that was even more money. Out of about nine hundred members, about one hundred were very, very busy, but really, everybody had good work. And for sittings we used to get paid also.

The ten years between 1982 and 1992 were enormously productive. With more than 160 films per year, they represent the highest average output of any ten-year period in the Mumbai industry:

> BHAVANI SHANKAR: It was a very golden period. There was so much work. You'd start a recording at nine o'clock in the morning, and we'd reach home maybe in the middle of the night. Maybe at one o'clock or two o'clock in the night. There were so many days, like that.

Unlike Bhanu Gupta, who is old enough to retire, Mario Fernandes was an orchestral musician who followed his father into the line in 1980, the beginning of this "golden period," and is thus still living through the transition from Old to New Bollywood. Just like the transition from the studio system, which his father experienced, the change has been extremely hard:

> MARIO FERNANDES: We were comfortable at that time [1980s and early 1990s]. You could support your house and save something, all that. I was a regular with L-P; I used to go daily to Mehboob. A few years after I joined the industry I was fixed for life, you can say.

Unfortunately for musicians of Fernandes's generation, the world changed in the middle of their careers:

MARIO FERNANDES: I had about ten good years. The system has changed, and because of that we are not getting work. First it was 50 percent, then 20 percent; now it's 5 percent, and you can't do it. Now we are living here because we worked in the past. We are just surviving on the savings that we made.

Dattaram Waadkar notes that the system threatened producers, who were the source of all income in the film line. The working process with music directors like Laxmikant-Pyarelal and Bappi Lahiri, in which the whole orchestra was constantly present, was inevitably costly, especially because overtime was an hourly wage:

DATTARAM WAADKAR: We got a lot of overtime with Laxmi-Pyare. If a guy earned 1,000 rupees on the shift, he'd get another 3,000 from overtime.

Whatever the excesses of the Laxmi-Pyare set, these were further exaggerated by Bappi Lahiri. It would often be midafternoon before Lahiri arrived to supervise the recording sessions that began at the usual time of nine o'clock. Here Benny Rosario offers the darkly comic side of the highly productive workshop he described earlier:

BENNY ROSARIO: Bappi—sometimes it would be lunchtime, and we were still waiting for Bappi to come. We would be sitting there from nine o'clock in the morning. And we would all laugh and laugh. The whole shift was over before he came. That's why all Bappi's musicians had cars. The shift was just for lunch and a nap.

Lahiri's system represents the heights of excess in late Old Bollywood, but the lesser excesses of many other music directors contributed to the producers' overall costs. Bhavani Shankar summarizes the "golden period" of the 1980s and early '90s:

BHAVANI SHANKAR: I'd go for a month at a time, every morning and every evening, recording. I had, you can say, seventy-five dates in a month many times. It went on like that for fifteen years. After Pancham-da went [1994], it gradually became less. But L-P were still there, and they were doing a lot, so until '95–'96, you can say it was good, but then slowly, slowly, the downfall of the whole film industry began. Now the track system has come; it has killed life for the musicians.

Chapter 2 describes the technological changes that finally made themselves felt in Mumbai in the mid-1990s, as Shankar and others note here. These developments led to new economic alternatives that may have been inevitable, but I cannot help but suspect that the enormous costs and excesses of what Shankar calls the "golden period" provided motivation.

The Lump Sum System

Musicians call the new system the "lump sum" system. Again, it is important to emphasize the different kinds of change that collectively inform particular historical periods. New Bollywood remains characterized largely by independent production companies even if these are differently financed and managed. The lump sum system is merely a change in the way funds are channeled from the producer to the musicians. Together with roughly simultaneous technological developments, however, the impact of this seemingly minor modification has been enough to completely alter the nature of life in the Mumbai film-music world.

More than forty years after CMA introduced its shift rates, weakened demand for film songs and the introduction of new sound technologies offered producers an opportunity to connect production costs to the amount a music director would earn. Not surprisingly, the music industry disapproved; the new system forced music directors to choose between their own profits and those of the musicians:

> RAVI SHANKAR SHARMA: Nowadays the system is different. They say, "Okay, you do six songs for this much." But in that amount comes the studio, the musicians, maybe the writer, maybe the singer. So they have the whole thing in a lump sum. But this is not a good system. Suppose you make one song, and for that you need sixty musicians. But I will have to give the money for those sixty musicians; it will come from my budget. So I will think, "Maybe I can use only forty." I will try to save money. That is not good for the work, not good for the song.

After thirty-five years in Old Bollywood, rarely considering the impact of his orchestral decisions on film budgets, Ravi-ji might believe it reasonable to support a position in which musical integrity is divorced from economic concerns. Throughout his professional life, this position was enabled by technological limits and industrial structures.

In New Bollywood, however, few composers are choosing between sixty and forty violins. A music director seeking to cut costs would hire ten violins and rely on technology to make up the difference:

> PRAKASH VARMA: The producer will say, "You must do it in so much of money only." So accordingly we call ten violins instead of twenty, four rhythm players instead of eight. But we do it multitrack, so we get the sound of double.

By "multitrack" Varma means that the track, recorded by the ten violins, will be copied onto another track, so that two or more of the sixty-four tracks on the final composite will have the sound of violins. Musicians call this practice *double tracking*. To respond to this replacement of musicians with machines, CMA made new rules, but enforcing them was difficult for a number of reasons. The rules insisted that double tracking be done live with the hypothetical ten violins actually playing the same music twice, recorded on two different tracks. From the producer's and the music director's point of view, this defeated the purpose of the rules since it negated the savings the technology made possible in the first place:

> ERNEST MENEZES: If they double track they have to play twice, but still we can't always tell if that happens. There are some who tell us very frankly, "We're going to double track." And then the money is also double. But there's a lot a hanky-panky.

As president of CMA during the 1990s, Menezes was one of those who tried to limit the impact of technology on his colleagues. Even he admits that CMA's efforts at best only briefly delayed the eventual collapse. As demand weakened and technology became more sophisticated, CMA found it impossible to enforce such rules:

> ERNEST MENEZES: Now it's come down so if they double track they pay us 100 percent of the rate for the first take and only 50 percent for the second take. It used to be that you could see if they were double tracking because you could see that they were taking an extra wire and putting it into a second channel. But now you can't tell. They just push a button, and it's doubled.

Sanjay Chakravarty offers a more comprehensive perspective on the range of economic tensions (distributed almost evenly among music directors, musicians, and producers):

> SANJAY CHAKRAVARTY: I started my career at 80 rupees for a song session. Today it is 1,750 rupees, but I'm worse off. The work is not there, and the cost of living has gone up. And before, everything the producer had to pay. Now it depends on what kind of deal there is. If the producer is sensible, he'll say to the music director, "Boss, the costs I'll pay, but results I want." If he does that, he's not gonna spend more, but he'll get better results. But they're thinking they're minimizing the costs [by] giving the music director a lump sum and taking a poorer result. If I say I'll do it for this much, I'll do it all on computer, and I'll get a bathroom studio where the sound is less and use as few musicians as possible so I can save money. The system changed drastically.

As track recording and digital technology took over, four-hour recording sessions became a thing largely of the past, and the CMA rates gave way altogether:

JOE MONSORATE: Today everything is unofficial; the CMA rates don't work anymore. They just call you for one hour or two hours, and you record everything, and they punch it wherever they want.

The collapse of the CMA rates was not bad news for everyone, of course. Soloists could now charge whatever they chose. In financial terms, Ustad Sultan Khan, who no doubt always felt that the CMA rates were rather low for someone of his stature, is pleased:

SULTAN KHAN: The pleasure is less now because you just go in a room and put [on] the headphones. Before you had eighty or one hundred or even more musicians all together in the studio. It used to be a collegial music, but that music is dead now. But the money is much better. Before they only paid according to the rates. That wasn't so much. But now whatever I want, I can ask, and I will get that also because the producers or the music directors are coming to me and asking, "Khan-saheb, please play for my film."

"Star" Programs

In India by the late 1950s and in the United Kingdom, the United States, and Canada (among other places) by the 1960s, concert programs and tours featuring playback singers and film stars had become part of the live-music culture. These programs combined the singers with film stars, dancers, and an orchestra. Leslie Godinho traveled with the early shows of the 1960s and '70s:

LESLIE GODINHO: I used to go for star shows and tours, even out of India. Lots of traveling! For forty years I've been going all around the world. The West Indies, North America, Fiji, Australia, even New Zealand. It was fun to travel then. It was a good group of musicians.

In Old Bollywood star programs were not necessarily a desirable way of earning a living. The travel was attractive in one sense because it offered trips abroad, but it took musicians away from their families and from recordings, which were a better source of income:

BHAVANI SHANKAR: Recordings were very regular. Programs weren't regular; you'd go for two months and then come back. And the recordings would still be going on.

Ironically, the programs that had been second choice for many musicians became an actual source of income in the late 1990s, when recordings began to dry up (figure 6.4). Anupam De Ghatak, a percussionist and self-described film-music fan, was born in Mumbai in 1970. Although he

Figure 6.4 In the former main recording studio of Mehboob Studios a large group of musicians rehearses for a concert (in this case at a wedding reception) (2007). Arranger Prakash Varma conducts. Violinist Ernest Menezes sits listening (center; wearing a white shirt). To Varma's immediate right accordionist Sumit Mitra is seated. Tenor saxophone player Shyam Raj is seated behind Mitra at far right. Many of the men in this picture worked here almost daily through the mid-1990s, recording as the Laxmikant-Pyarelal orchestra.

plays recordings when necessary, he makes more money playing for film-song programs both in India and abroad:

> ANUPAM DE GHATAK: It is my misfortune, you can say, that I have been born too late. People now are making money from shows, not from the studio. This is backwards to what it used to be. I can earn 5,000 or 6,000 rupees for a show here. Maybe 10,000 if it's in the U.S.

For some musicians, star shows were entry-level jobs that they took until they were able to depend on studio work. One of the positive features of these tours, however, was that they represented opportunities to gain access to things that were simply unobtainable in India until the late 1980s and economic liberalization:

> RAMESH IYER: My first jobs were with the shows that used to travel to the U.S. or Britain with Kalyanji-Anandji or Amitabh [Bachchan]. The first time I went was 1976. We had a lot of problems with foreign exchange in those times; by the time you changed your money, you had $8 in U.S. money. So you had a drink on the plane and landed in New York broke. But we used to get some allowance per day for food, something like $20 or $30. I used to save as much as I possibly could and go to the nearest record store and buy LPs.

Tours and shows did have some advantages, but the enormous costs of travel and subsistence in Europe and the United States were barely offset by the favorable exchange of dollars or pounds for rupees when musicians returned. Unless the tour was structured in an appropriately socioprofessional manner, musicians risked losing touch or being replaced in the studios. The tour advertised in figure 6.5, for example, featured singer Kishore Kumar, who at this point in his career was singing regularly for R. D. Burman. His absence from Mumbai reduced (although by no means removed) the risk that the Burman musicians on the tour (both Singhs, Lord, and Devi Chand were Burman regulars) would lose out on too much recording work. That they were all away together would make it harder for Burman to replace them surreptitiously in their absence.

As this chapter has shown, recordings were the key musical, social, and economic feature of Old Bollywood. They were also the final point at which most film musicians were engaged in the process of music production. The life of songs after the recordings is the topic for another volume. The disappearance of the large orchestral sessions described here has been quite hurtful for Mumbai's film musicians in musical, financial, and social terms. The new practices finally made explicit the impermanence of the Old Bollywood system, something that huge demand and the system's lon-

Figure 6.5   Poster advertising a touring show featuring Kishore Kumar in London, 1972. Kumar is shown at center with microphone; below him seated at the drums, Bhuji Lord. From Lord's left, saxophone player Suresh Yadhav and R. D. Burman regular and dholak player Devi Chand. Immediately below Devi Chand is the tour's Indian organizer, Nandi Duggal. At the poster's extreme left is multi-instrumentalist Charanjit Singh, holding a "Hawaiian" (i.e., slide) guitar; above him, also playing guitar is another R. D. regular, Bhupinder Singh.

gevity (both fuelled in part by films and film music's monopoly on Indian popular culture) made it easy to forget.

Certainly most musicians did forget during the generation and a half that the system lasted. Music directors and their entourages were running from sitting to sitting, while many more musicians were spending their days and nights in the studios. Everyone was too busy, as the musicians in these chapters testify, to worry about a hypothetical collapse. The conclusion of this chapter is also the wrapping up of part II's examination of life in Mumbai's film-music studios. As many musicians, especially those in or past midcareer report, there is no more life. As with so many other things, the disappearance of a profession that musicians took for granted has caused them to reflect on the joys and the meaning of that career and the music they recorded in ways they previously had neither the time nor the inclination to ponder. The final section of this book examines their reflections on these issues.

As a way to begin my discussion of meanings and values, the final note on foreign tours belongs to Joe Monsorate, whose comments offer a professional's perspective on the impact of the songs he and his colleagues had been recording in the Indian diaspora:

> JOE MONSORATE: We used to go for shows. So many shows we played in America and Britain, mostly. And we'd go and we'd meet Indian people. Maybe we're standing waiting for the bus or something, and the Indian people would come and say, "Come on, we'll drop you. Where do you need to go? Come sit in the car." So we'd go, and they would put on some tape. And it would always be some old, old songs. And they would know those songs and who was singing and everything. But it was always old songs, not the modern songs.

The musicians' perceptions of the meaning and value of the music they had been recording and the widely felt nostalgia for the music and the times of Old Bollywood constitute the final topics for this study.

Part III

Music, Instruments, and Meaning from Musicians' Perspectives

In this final section I am concerned with changing ideas about orchestration and background music and with developments in film ensembles and instrumentation. Chapter 7 is primarily the story of the studio orchestras as they developed in Old Bollywood and were gradually replaced by synthesizers. Punching and the "track system" (as Bhavani Shankar calls it in chapter 6) also affected orchestral practice and so come in for further examination. Placing this story in the context of musical, industrial, and cinematic factors, I note innovations in background music, arranging and arrangers, and what is now called programming. Although this is not primarily a book about composition, I briefly discuss the interaction of cinematic context ("situation" as Mumbai calls it), orchestration, and style.

I begin chapter 8 by addressing the notion of musical style and focusing on stylistic influence as musicians experienced and produced it. In much popular-music discourse the discussion of style leads directly to a consideration of meaning and identity. The importance of Hindi film music for the construction of Indian and especially diaspora identity is implied by Joe Monsorate's narrative at the conclusion of chapter 6. It is the subject of a small but growing literature and well beyond the scope of this volume.

I am also concerned here with musicians' perceptions of and statements about the meaning and/or value of the music they were making. These topics interact with style and style labels in a number of ways and serve to unite the two chapters. I examine musicians' understanding of the relationships among the various musical styles that make up film music. In a number of different ways, this is quite distinct from discussion of reception as such or of meaning as constructed through this music's close connections to emotional narrative and visual image.

The enormous range of musical styles, procedures, and content in the Hindi film song repertoire remains very much in need of extended musical analysis. Although I refer to specific songs and passages in this chapter and the next, this book is not the context in which significant musical analysis can take place. Vast portions of the immense Hindi film song repertoire are available on disc and electronically. Interested readers can take advantage of this luxurious facet of postmodern life.

Part III, then, offers a third (if limited) perspective on the historical process of change, one that picks up the threads that begin in chapters 2, 3, and 5. Discussions of orchestration also connect to matters of narrative (and semiotic) meaning to the extent that musicians (and composers) understand instruments and instrumental practice to have narrative meaning. Much, though by no means all, of the focus of these chapters is on the transition primarily from Old to New Bollywood. In this section, with these issues at the forefront, the studio period is almost unreachable from the starting point of oral history. Thus, after the detailed ethnographic narrative of part II, in which musicians are the primary actors, part III reverts to the broader perspectives of part I. It does so, however, by using musicians' comments to shed light on their understandings of the place of the music they were playing in their own society and (in at least some instances) the wider "society" of world music.

7

Orchestras and Orchestral Procedures, Instrumental Change, Arranging, and Programming

The length of this chapter's title reflects the collection of topics that revolve around the notion of the Mumbai film orchestra. The size of the orchestra, the orchestral procedures surrounding arrangements and background music, and the introduction of new instruments took place along lines of thought and action that were largely separate from decisions about what stylistic elements to employ. Morcom (2007) has shown that the interactions of style and situation may be complex. Nevertheless, orchestration and arrangement cannot be completely separated from musical style and narrative situation, thus, the rather catch-all nature of this chapter's title. In addition, musical style, instrumentation, and orchestral size were sometimes vulnerable to the interests and attitudes of music directors, film directors and producers, industrial conditions, instrumental fads, and so forth. In this chapter I propose a notion of the Mumbai studio orchestra as an instrumental ensemble not by means of musical analysis but by an examination of the cultural and industrial conditions of orchestral musicianship.

"Situation," the narrative context and/or cinematic setting in which a song takes place, may be a significant factor affecting orchestration and instrumentation, as well as other issues:

> RAVI SHANKAR SHARMA: I did *Chaudvin Ka Chand* [1960]. In that film there's a scene with the *natchni wāli* [dancing girl] in the *kotha* [brothel, salon], and for that kind of scene you don't need violins. There are no violins in the kotha. Just maybe tabla, dholak, mandolin, *sārangi*, harmonium, that's it. Maybe also guitar.

And indeed, the song Ravi mentions (and composed), "Dil ki kahani rang layi hai," uses only those instruments.

Dattaram Waadkar supports Ravi's argument up to a point but also suggests that traditional logic went only so far in the innovative and volatile world of film music:

> DATTARAM WAADKAR: If you have a scene in a kotha, then you have tabla, sārangi, maybe dholak, but you wouldn't have English instruments in that kind of a scene. But Shankar-ji mixed instruments also. So maybe the orchestra would also play for dance, maybe rhythm and orchestra. No one had done like that before. He worked out that orchestras could also play the *tukras* [rhythmic compositions] that the tabla played.

Despite Ravi's assertions, songs in other cinematic kothas inhabited by other dancing girls—Chandramukhi (*Devdas,* 1955), for example, or Zohra (*Muqqadar ka Sikander,* 1978)—do include violins. The remarkably consistent musical conventions of Hindi film narrative interact with a range of variables that are part and parcel of the film industry's aesthetic and industrial structures. Reality is simply one more convention to be adhered to or not as it suits one.

In discourse (if not consistently in practice), however, composers and arrangers make a connection between situation and orchestration:

> OMPRAKASH SONIK: We have to see what is the location. Say if it's an outdoor scene, then violins will have to come [play]. You have to see the setting and the season, sky and all those things.

One has only to listen to and watch the opening seconds of the Laxmikant-Pyarelal/Manmohan Desai song scene "Dekh ke tumko dil dhola hai," for example, in the middle of the 1977 hit film *Amar Akbar Anthony* to recognize the logic of such conventions, as well as the ease with which they can be viewed as stereotype. Of course, there are no violins in Mumbai's harbor (where this song scene begins) any more than there are in a kotha, but in the Hindi cinema, orchestral conventions and ideas about narrative reality are not consistently aligned. Massed violins have come to represent the sound of blue skies and happiness. When "violins" (both Ravi and Omi use "violins" to mean a large orchestra) are employed, however, they require written parts and arrangements.

In Mumbai, "arrangement" means some or all of the tasks necessary from a specific set of musical practices: the notating of a composed melody; the harmonization of melodies and the composition of the musical content that will express that harmonization; the composition of bass lines, rhythm patterns, contrapuntal or polyphonic content; the assignation of various musical content to instrumental voices (orchestration); and often the composition and use of melodic interludes between statements of the song melody. These practices change according to period, composer and/or arranger, situation, and other factors as does the assignment of tasks to various members of a workshop. Given that very early films and stage dramas used quite small musical ensembles, an orchestral concept of narrative music is one feature that probably did not develop from local practice.

With the frequently mentioned exception of Pyarelal Sharma, arrangements were most commonly undertaken by specialist arrangers. Like some of his colleagues, Pyarelal ji was always looking for new and unusual sounds, especially for background music:

> PYARELAL SHARMA: One day I came into the studio, and Hariprasad [Chaurasia, now a famous classical flutist] was practicing, but very quietly. There was hardly any sound coming; only the sound of his breath was coming. I thought, "What is the point of that?" But then we were making one film, *Kraanti* [1981], and there is a scene where Dilip Kumar is in jail, and he's throwing some cloth to reach the keys that are on the table. And he catches them, and they fall to the floor, and he drags them close so he can reach them. So I made the background music, and I used only brass, just trumpets and trombones, and very sudden chords. "Choom!" like that, then nothing, then again, "Choom!" To make the scene exciting, no? And I also used the sound that Hariprasad had been making, very soft, you could only hear his breath. It was very exciting like that.

Unknown contributions of this kind were frequently replicated in Mumbai's sitting rooms and studios.

Anil Mohile worked as an arranger for many music directors, including Bappi Lahiri and S. D. Burman. In his first collaboration with brothers Kalyanji-Anandji, Mohile arranged and composed background music for *Don* (1978), a major hit film starring Amitabh Bachchan, in which the actor—then at the height of his "angry young man" stardom—plays the film's hero, who happens to be the double of the film's villain (also played by Bachchan). Mohile makes clear that he and Anandji Shah aligned heroism, Indian culture, rural simplicity, Indian musical style, and specific (Indian) instrumentation in opposition to a construction of evil that combined criminality, Western culture, urban sophistication, Western musical style, and specific (but this time Western) instrumentation:

> ANIL MOHILE: In *Don*, Amitabh Bachchan was in a double role. One character was sophisticated; one was a village boy. For the village character we used Indian rhythms and village music and these things. But for the sophisticated, three-piece-suit*wāla* [guy] we used brass and all this. That is the good approach. I've thought about this very much and learned quite a lot also from Anandji-saheb.

As Anthony Gonsalves has also suggested, modern brass (trumpets and trombones), more than any other instruments, have come to mean Westernness and/or villainy in Mumbai's semiotic system.

Anandji Shah himself often composed background music for Kalyanji-Anandji movies, but he had no musical training and so required the assistance of people like Anil Mohile or Frank Fernand to develop arrangements and orchestrations. His comments demonstrate a sophisticated and creative approach to arranging, but he also offers a level of semiotic specificity based on the kind of personalized logic through which some Mumbai musicians connected emotion to specific instruments and performance styles:

> ANANDJI SHAH: In *Khel Qismet Ka* [1977], the hero is Krishna, but he must agree to do some crime for money to save his mother who is dying, I think, or some such thing. So when he agrees to this, I put trumpet in the background because the trumpet means *majbīri* [compulsion], means he is feeling guilt from agreeing to this crime.

In what proved to be the last year of his career, Bablu Chakravarty composed and arranged the background music for a Panjabi-language film. Returning from a sitting at which he and the film's director, Manmohan Singh, had evaluated the score's effectiveness, I discussed the music with Chakravarty. His answers reveal the relatively subtle narrative or emotional nuances that he sought to enhance or reflect through music and instrumentation:

> BOOTH: In that scene where the son meets his mother after all that time, first you had the chorus singing in the background, but then, when the camera shifts to his mother, you had sitār playing alāp. How did you know what changes in instrumentation you wanted have?
>
> BABLU CHAKRAVARTY: I know these things because I have the experience. The sitar alāp brings out the sadness of the mother who has missed her son for so many years.
>
> BOOTH: And later, in another scene where the hero flirts with the heroine, as she drives away, you had santūr playing *jhala* [rapid, rhythmic phrasing]. Why is that?
>
> BABLU CHAKRAVARTY: The heroine is a young girl; she is *chanchal*. You know chanchal? It is like "flighty," something like that. She is also innocent, *pavitra*. The santūr is just such an instrument. It sounds pavitra chanchal, just the right sound for that scene. I know this because of all the great musicians who have established these things. They are just like a formula, only it is not a formula. I must think for every scene.

Chakravarty's concluding comments clarify both the conventional and the creative aspects of orchestration in the Hindi cinema.

Pandit Shivkumar Sharma agrees that orchestration in Bollywood responded in a formulaic manner to situations. He attributes this to habit and the need to work quickly. Given his and Chakravarty's comments, it may not be completely unexpected that Sharma specifies the combination of instrumentation (sitar) and performance style (alāp) for sad scenes involving mothers, which Chakravarty discusses (as does Kartik Kumar; see chapter 8):

> SHIVKUMAR SHARMA: It's come to be like that because it's all very fast. Like if there is a sad scene, then there is *shahnāi* or *tār shahnāi* [a bowed lute with an acoustic horn amplifier], or if there is a scene with the mother, then maybe flute or the sitār comes, and it will be just like alāp, or if the scene is happy, then maybe santūr comes. So it has come to be just like a habit or a custom; different composers have created this.

A review of almost any handful of Hindi films will attest to the formulaic qualities that Chakravarty and Sharma describe here (cf. Booth 2007). Many films also reveal the level of musical detail that went into the hectic creative process.

Instrumentation is widely understood as an expressive element in the narrative music of the Hindi cinema, as these comments indicate. While those involved seem to take for granted both the formulaic and the creative aspects of orchestration, few can explain associations they have come to view as obvious. Oral history cannot clarify the developments of the orchestral conventions of the Hindi cinema; remarks such as those here by Sharma and Chakravarty convey only the contemporary musicians' general understanding: their elders also employed sitar alāp as background music in scenes of pathos (involving mothers, for example). The semiotic chains of culturally constructed and borrowed meanings that resulted in contemporary instrumental conventions (or even those of the 1980s) are difficult, if not impossible, to untangle at this point. An in-depth analysis of musical conventions in the Hindi cinema, however, would make their longevity apparent and might offer insight into their culturally flexible nature.

Although no one now living can recount the earliest years of orchestral convention, oral history can trace aspects of the interactions among arrangers, producers, and music and film directors that helped develop the characteristically large, string-heavy orchestras of Old Bollywood. It can also document their collapse in the late 1990s and the development of digital arranging and composition, called programming, under the dual impact of the innovative technological possibilities and new business models of the twenty-first century.

Early Development of Orchestral Size and Practice

Changing ideas about orchestration and arrangement, a sense that bigger is better on the part of some film directors and producers, and the influence of foreign films all contributed to the gradual expansion of the Mumbai film orchestra. In part I, I discussed the successful integration of song scenes into the formal design of the Hindi cinema. Here, the history of the gradual incorporation of elements of the Hollywood-style background score somewhat parallels that discussion. Although I follow both Indian and foreign scholars in attributing the presence of film songs to indigenous influences, oral accounts suggest that the development of background music was explicitly due to the influence of foreign films. This source might be responsible for what I perceive to be a less successful integration of the background score into Hindi films. Morcom (2007) has hinted at these issues, but the topic requires further research.

Movie musicians often viewed foreign films eagerly and sometimes repeatedly. Specific stylistic elements and occasionally even specific melodies, adapted from a range of sources, appeared in the songs of Mumbai's film composers. In the case of background music, although musical content has certainly been borrowed, the very practice of the background score and accompanying musical-cinematic techniques was novel. Composers made use of the orchestral techniques and practices of the Western symphonic score but often ultimately adopted the content without the structure. Dattaram Waadkar is one of those who watched American films to gain a sense of Hollywood's musical practices:

> Dattaram Waadkar: It used to be that, before the picture started, there would be a symphony, and all the orchestra would play. It would be five minutes or so, and I gained very much knowledge from that. How the music should work, *The Sound of Music,* all those pictures.

It is hardly surprising that Waadkar should recall a film such as *The Sound of Music,* which so readily fits the Indian notion of how a movie should be. For a musician in Waadkar's position, the film may have represented a kind of ideal in which both songs and a symphonic background score are integrated into this late American musical's formal design.

Along with the Western notion of background music as integral to a film's structure and meaning, orchestral practices such as the separation and expansion of instrumental roles and functions—as exemplified in foreign films by distinct bass lines, by harmonies expressed in sections as static chordal lines, arpeggios, and rhythm patterns, or by contrapuntal melodies—were imitated. Perceived by Mumbai's musicians as fundamentally Western procedures, they were generally much slower to emerge than the more straightforward increase in the size of the studio orchestras. I suggest that this was due to the orchestra's fundamental role as an accompanying ensemble for vocal melodies.

In much Indian musical practice an extremely important model of melodic accompaniment for voice is one in which players of a melodic instrument (often bowed; for example, the sārangi or the violin) echo or copy the melodic content performed by a vocal soloist. In genres with a great deal of improvisation, this practice produces an imitative, heterophonic texture, but as improvisation decreases, which it does increasingly as the genres become "lighter" (e.g., dādra, ghazal, and especially film song), this practice of imitative heterophony gives way to virtual unison.

Unison instrumental accompaniment can be heard in recordings of Marathi Sangeet Natak songs and in film songs as well. As the ensembles accompanying orchestras began to grow, the increased timbral range was employed mainly for musical interludes in which there was no singing (and which were often composed by musicians with some degree of theoretical or practical training in Western music), as the majority of songs recorded in the early 1950s demonstrate. A generally low level of understanding of contrapuntal or harmonic practice (as found in much of Western music) helps explain Sagar Movietone's response to Anil Biswas's request for more instruments when Biswas joined the Mumbai studio in 1935:

> ANIL BISWAS: When I came to Sagar, I said, "I must have six violins, a cello, double bass, clarinet, saxophone, plus sarod, sitar, tabla, and flute." But they asked me, "Whatever are you going to do with all these instruments?" Even the recordist said, "You give me one violin, I'll make so much noise just from one." I couldn't make him understand.

A recordist who was used to the Indian model of melodic accompaniment might indeed think that more violins would produce only a louder (not more diverse) melodic line and thus be forgiven for believing that one amplified violin would suffice.

For a number of reasons Anil Biswas frequently appears in musicians' discourse about early orchestral developments. First, Biswas was one of the very first Bengali musicians to join the Mumbai film line. Second, he was associated with the earliest musician named as an arranger in Mumbai, Ram Singh. Finally, Biswas himself has laid claim to being the innovator in this area. Some older musicians, however, have argued that orchestral developments in Kolkata, perhaps fueled by the presence of Western music in the colonial capital, provided the model that the Mumbai film industry copied in the matters of orchestras and orchestration.

Bengali Influences?

The musical, linguistic, and theatrical cultures of the two major Hindi-film-producing centers, Kolkata and Mumbai, were distinctive. Woodfield (2000) has described the beginnings of the relatively stronger presence of Western music culture in Kolkata. In the 1930s Kolkata had ceased to be the political, as well as commercial, center of British India, but still had a functioning symphony orchestra, an abundance of nightclubs, and many amateur and professional foreign musicians. None of these features was absent in Mumbai, but overall, Kolkata's Western music culture appears to have been somewhat more fully developed in 1930. Whether or not these conditions actually encouraged film musicians' and composers' engagement with orchestral playing, Kolkata's music directors (specifically those at New Theatres) acquired a reputation for leadership in film music generally and particularly in orchestration among Mumbai's film musicians in that decade. "Together with Rai Chand Boral, [Pankaj] Mullick was in large part responsible for New Theatres' early adoption of Western instruments" (Arnold 1991, 54).

Naushad Ali was one of a number of older musicians who have argued that the early orchestral developments came from composers and film studios in Kolkata:

> NAUSHAD ALI: In the very early times, the music for films was just *pethi* [harmonium] and tabla and maybe some solo instrument—clarinet, sitar, that sort of thing. Slowly, slowly, the early music directors began to add instruments. [New Theatres' composers] Timur Baran and R. C. Boral, these men are like my gurus because by listening to them I learned to compose with a big orchestra.

Thus, both foreign and Indian sources credit the influence of composers Baran and Boral and, more generally, the film scores of Kolkata's New Theatres for early developments in film orchestration (figure 7.1):

> NAUSHAD ALI: Bengalis were very important. Everybody [in Mumbai] was dressing like a Bengali. Even I was wearing a Bengali dhoti! If you didn't have Bengali dress, you didn't seem like a musician!

The dhoti—an unstitched item of male clothing worn instead of trousers—was also worn by communities other than Bengalis. Nevertheless dhotis were considered to be especially characteristic of male Bengali dress. As unstitched apparel, however, a dhoti would traditionally have been more appropriate for a Hindu than for a Lucknowi Muslim such as

Figure 7.1 Pankaj Mullick directs an exceedingly large orchestra in the last days of New Theatres (Kolkata). The presence of Vistasp Balsara (standing directly behind Mullick) suggests that the photo may be from 1954. Courtesy of Sanjay Chakravarty.

Naushad, who (after this temporary aberration) wore *churidars,* the tightly tapered, stitched trousers, throughout his life.

Vistasp Balsara claimed that it was the influence of New Theatres that led him to leave Mumbai for a new career in Kolkata in 1954; this at least offers a sense of the importance of the Kolkata film-music industry in national terms. Balsara recalls the turning point at an event in Kolkata while both he and Anil Biswas were living and working in Mumbai:

> VISTASP BALSARA: Anil Biswas had one program in Calcutta, so he requested me to come and accompany him. At that time I was settled in Bombay, but from my childhood I used to play all the songs of New Theatres, Pankaj Mullick, Kanan Devi, Jutikar Rai, and all that. I knew all those names. So in the get-together the next day [after the program], I saw everybody whose names I knew, and I was so much overtaken by their presence that I decided that I will come and settle down in Calcutta.

New Theatres, which opened in 1931, might have had this impact on Mumbai film musicians for several good reasons. Boral and Mullick "were especially familiar with Western and Indian light music" because of their prefilm experiences in radio and silent film, and in consequence, "music directors at New Theatres . . . experimented more with Western scale patterns, song forms, and orchestrations" (Arnold 1991, 46). As the first film-production studio in India to be purpose-built for sound films, New Theatres had the best sound technology in the country in the very first years of sound film. Their sound tracks appear to have been technically superior to many of Mumbai's first efforts, which were recorded outdoors in numerous instances. New Theatres also concentrated the best Bengali film talent in a single unit in order to produce quality films in both Hindi and Bengali. Unlike Mumbai, where four or five major studios and at least as many smaller ones were dividing the city's technical and musical talents among themselves, Kolkata in the 1930s appears to have had no more than three major studios: the prolific but musically insignificant Madan Theatres, New Theatres itself, and East India Films.

Finally, New Theatres was crucial in the early career of K. L. Saigal, an extremely popular romantic actor and singer. His was perhaps the most important single voice in Indian cinema until the appearance of Lata Mangeshkar. "Saigal's singing in *Devdas* (1935) surely marked a different mode of voice-production, if not of singing as such. He nearly crooned—softly and slowly" (Ranade 2006, 117); he set the standard for male playback singers such as Mukesh, Talat Mahmood, and even Mohamed Rafi. The film to which Ranade refers (and to which all three of New Theatres' famous music directors contributed) remains one of the great film scores of

Hindi cinema. In light of this impact, Naushad's flirtation with Bengali dhotis seems to have a cultural explanation.

Ironically, at least some of the musicians who left Kolkata to work in the Mumbai music industry were not as assertive about Bengal's musical contributions as was Naushad-saheb. Although he finally moved west in the late 1950s, Salil Chaudhuri paints a relatively basic picture of New Theatres' musical sophistication, arguing that its reputation as the source of Mumbai's orchestral sound may have been exaggerated. He gives credit to colonial India's other major source of Western influence, the Portuguese-trained musicians of Goa:

> SALIL CHAUDHURI: There was no counterpoint in New Theatres. Obbligato, arranging, and all those things were a development of the Hindi film industry [in Mumbai] that came as a result of the Portuguese influence. These are the people who were used as arrangers and orchestrators. Music directors at that time [1930s and '40s], none of them knew about Western music.

Anil Biswas, who arrived in Mumbai from Kolkata during New Theatres' heyday, corroborates Naushad's earlier description of very early film music in Mumbai:

> ANIL BISWAS: When I came to Bombay, I found that the music that was prevalent at that time was being lifted from the stage and used in films, only with *paun pethi* [pump organ] and possibly clarinet or sārangi and with tabla.

Biswas had no background in Western music, but he nevertheless asserts that it was neither Bengalis nor Goans who led the way in orchestration but rather his personal vision:

> ANIL BISWAS: I had an idea of orchestration in my mind, [but] this music was not going on in Bengal at that time. I was one of those persons who started the vogue of orchestration, a little bit of orchestra here and there. I didn't have any idea that I was giving birth to such a big thing that is Indian film music today. I can't really explain where I got my ideas for orchestration.

Early developments in film orchestras undoubtedly took on energy from both of India's major urban centers, among other sources. Nevertheless, it seems that Mumbaikars have been more willing to give credit to Kolkata and to New Theatres than have those composers who left Kolkata for Mumbai:

> ANIL BISWAS: There was a myth in Bombay, you can say, about New Theatres, that it was very expert in the production of film music. But there wasn't much work in Bengal in those days.

Biswas was not the only musician who felt that employment opportunities might be more favorable in Mumbai. In the late 1930s K. L. Saigal himself left New Theatres to work at Ranjit Movietone.

Whether or not the products of New Theatres Studios were more orchestrally developed than those of the Mumbai studios, the Kolkata facilities in general were completely outproduced by Mumbai's faster and more numerous film factories. Kolkata's best showing in terms of output was in 1932, when Madan Theatres and New Theatres together released 22 films (42 percent of the 52 movies released in Mumbai and Kolkata that year). Kolkata's output remained almost unchanged the following year (21 films), but Mumbai's increased from 30 to 48 films in 1933 (70 percent of the total Mumbai-Kolkata production). Mumbai reached 90 percent five years later and never looked back.

At least equally significant is the extent to which Mumbai films dominated recordings of film songs. In 1936, just as playback was being introduced and the sound of Indian films might have been considered still up for grabs, Mumbai-produced songs represented 77 percent of all the film songs released on disc. That percentage was 90 only four years later and climbed to 99 percent in 1946. Leaving aside the handful of films that Lahore and Pune produced, the Kolkata sound, however influential, was simply shouted down by its more prolific rival.

Mumbai's Film Orchestras and Practices in the 1940s

Biswas's proposed studio orchestra at Sagar may have been somewhat on the large side in 1935, but the size of a studio's salaried orchestra depended on that facility's priorities and financial success. Fourteen musicians may have been too much for Sagar in 1936, but two years later Filmistan had between eight and ten musicians:

> VISTASP BALSARA: When I started [at Filmistan in 1938], it was, say, three or four violins, one saxophone, clarinet, mandolin, but they were very good musicians. For mandolin, there was Isaac David. For cello, there was Albuquerque. And for saxophone there was Ram Singh-ji.

Balsara here includes two of the three members of the famous A-R-P group in his list, so it is safe to assume that Peter Sequeira was playing at Filmistan as well. According to Jerry Fernandes, A-R-P's importance lay partly in their ability to help structure the basic orchestration and provide obbligatos on short notice during the recording process. Other than these obbligatos, Fernandes suggests that arrangements were largely nonexistent in the mid-1940s:

JERRY FERNANDES: There was not much arrangement. I think you should say that things were very basic, really only in one voice. Mostly musicians like [Alfonso] Albuquerque were making the obbligatos and recording them then and there only, in the studio.

Kishore Desai also reports that soloists such as Issac David and Goodi Seervai were contributors to the musical content of film songs throughout the 1950s.

Ram Singh was another soloist who participated in this relatively un-structured early process of enriching a song through added countermelody, but as Shyamrao Kemble notes, "he used to arrange for Anil Biswas." Un-like his two colleagues, Singh is also one of the very first named arrangers in the Mumbai studios. According to Anthony Gonsalves, Singh's training was in part a result of his father's career in a band that was attached to a princely state (as the semi-independent kingdoms of British India were often described):

ANTHONY GONSALVES: [Ram Singh's] father was a clarinetist; he played in a state band; he played for Anil Biswas for many years. He also conducted the small orchestra that played for films. There were just a few musicians in those times. There were eight or nine musicians at Bombay Talkies; at Kar-dar there were thirty musicians.

Gonsalves here is describing the late 1930s and the early '40s, but these numbers emphasize the differences in the sizes of various studio orchestras. It may be significant that Naushad Ali, always a proponent of larger or-chestras, was working at Kardar at this time.

Kersi Lord, himself a respected composer and arranger, also notes that Ram Singh "was a very fine arranger." Singh's presence as Biswas's arranger, however, clouds the accurate assessment of the latter's impact on orchestration. "Anil Biswas joined Mehboob's Sagar Movietone and be-came the first composer to use an orchestra of about twelve musicians. Probably he was also the first to use 'part-writing' to get maximum musi-cal input from his instrumental resources" (Ranade 2006, 113). Ranade seems to mean harmony here rather than counterpoint; certainly Biswas's scores demonstrate more harmonic than contrapuntal content. Ultimately, it is not possible to determine what percentage of a Biswas film score should be attributed to his arranger, Ram Singh. The public face of the film industry credited the music directors with all musical agency.

Listening to a Biswas-Singh collaboration such as the score to the film *Arzoo* (1950) suggests that "arranging" here simply means writing out, in staff notation, the parts that Biswas composed and producing solos as needed (Singh's saxophone and clarinet are prominent in this score). Despite the many solos by Ram Singh and Albuquerque, as well as some developed harmony and counterpoint (especially in the introductory music), the absence of developed harmonic arrangements that Jerry Fernandes has described is a characteristic of this score.

The connection between the Panjabi bandsman (as Singh apparently was) and Bengali composer Anil Biswas is one of the earliest instances of a distinctive interculturality embodied in many composer-arranger collaborations in Mumbai, especially in the industry's earlier years. Most music directors in the 1930s and '40s had little or no experience or expertise in Western music.

In the mid-1940s Jerry Fernandes joined the film line at the height of Anil Biswas's fame and may have come just in time to play on the *Arzoo* recordings, although he cannot recall whether in fact he did. He does recall playing for other Biswas recording sessions and reports that, since Biswas's experiences at Sagar Movietone in 1935, the music director had made some progress in expanding his orchestra:

> JERRY FERNANDES: At that time [1944–1945] he had about twenty-five to thirty musicians. We had eight to ten violins, double bass, one saxophone, one guitar, piano, tabla, dholak.

Fernandes obviously omits instruments (even sections since he mentions no cellos).

Goan Arrangers: Integrating the Bengali Sound

Although Naushad Ali acknowledges the composers of New Theatres and Anil Biswas gives credit to himself, others attribute the growth of the film orchestra to Naushad-saheb:

> KERSI LORD: Mr. Naushad started the big orchestras. I joined with him, so what I saw was that Mr. Naushad was having the first large orchestra. The nice thing about Mr. Naushad's music was that it had a good classical base: The songs were traditionally correct—the Indian classical and the Western arrangements.

Lord specifies not only the importance of a classical base but, in Naushad's case, the strength of both the Indian and Western classical content as well. Naushad's scores of the late 1940s (when Lord joined the line) and early 1950s often employ orchestras that sound as though they are larger than anything Anil Biswas used at the time, and occasionally they have a more sophisticated (and at times specifically Western) orchestral approach. I have already noted Naushad-saheb's association with Indian classical music; he has recorded his interests in Western orchestration and his belief that orchestration in the Western sense could make an important contribution to Hindi film music (Ali 2004).

Naushad's enthusiasm for large ensembles and elaborate orchestration may have been his own, and he certainly used his popularity and position to pursue these goals, but the actual arrangements and much of the composed background music are more properly the work of his arrangers, who orchestrated, harmonized, and arranged his song melodies and composed the background music for his films. Naushad's earliest arrangers included Ram Singh and violinist Josique Menzies. Anthony Gonsalves may also have contributed informally to the orchestration and arrangement of Naushad's scores.

After the mid-1960s, jazz pianist Martin Pinto regularly worked with Naushad as his assistant and arranger, as did Kersi Lord a few years later. Neither Menzies nor Pinto (nor Lord) would have required much prompting or the example of external models to take a harmonic, Western approach to Naushad's melodies. Gonsalves, however, points out that his harmonic approach was sensitive to Indian sensibilities:

> ANTHONY GONSALVES: I started arranging in 1948 with Shyam Sunder. He had only a little knowledge about orchestration and harmony, so he allowed me to ornament his melodies with harmony. He had some restrictions because it was a new method, and he had not accepted it, the Western way of orchestration. He thought it was all out of tune. Before, melodies were based on rāga and *tala* (rhythm cycles), but I noticed that they were always in unison, and I did what I could to help that. I did not go for Western harmony. I tried to blend with the rāga and not conflict.

The impact of the Kolkata music directors and the New Theatres' scores may have been quite real, but it appears that it was felt most strongly by Mumbai's music directors, who in turn had to rely largely on the skills of Portuguese-trained Goan arrangers. In the late 1940s and early '50s, Mumbai's orchestral voice reflected the musical heritage of British and Portuguese colonialism as interpreted by a number of prominent composers and arrangers in both Kolkata and Mumbai. It also suggested a fundamentally classical (or at least light classical) aesthetic in both Western and Indian terms. While this characterization may be accurate, it was rather suddenly overtaken by other changes in the Mumbai cinema and its music.

Some Goan musicians such as Gonsalves and Josique Menzies were aligned with classical European music as a result of family and class. This was reflected in their professional activities, including their work in the movies. Another classically trained musician, Maoro Alfonso, notes, "We used to play arias and all string music." These musicians were in fact mak-

ing a living playing classical music and other elite colonial styles in the hotels, clubs, and restaurants of the colonial metropolises (see chapter 3).
There was at the same time a parallel world of jazz musicians and dance
bands, also largely Goan and Parsi, playing in different venues and with a
more popular ideology. Benny Gracias grew up in Bandra, where he played
classical cello in orchestral settings:

> BENNY GRACIAS: We only met those people [who were playing in dance
> bands] when we started playing for films; we had not met them before.
> Those people were not playing for the orchestras. The Gomes brothers,
> George Fernandes, Leslie Godinho—they were not in the classical side. So
> we were a separate group, but we were accepted in the film line because we
> used to play orchestral music, and they knew we were talented.

A unitary notion of "Goan musicians" is therefore misleading.

The decision to give up on the failing dance-band industry after Indian
independence and to work in films instead was mirrored by those in the
more refined hotel/elite music ensembles, although there were relatively
fewer people on this side of the industry. Collectively and increasingly these
decisions resulted in a comparatively abrupt and significant increase in the
population of Goan musicians (jazz and others) in Mumbai after 1948.
The new concentration of musicians in the city was both physical and industrial. As the Godinhos, the Coreas, the D'Souzas, and so on abandoned
the hill-station hotel and dance-band circuit, the impact in Mumbai was of
a sudden availability of more musicians who could read notation and were
used to playing Western music. Most, unlike Josique Menzies and Anthony
Gonsalves, were musicians with popular music experience. Their presence
changed much of the sound (as well as the composition) of the Mumbai orchestras in the 1950s.

Salil Chaudhuri first came to Mumbai to work on the production of
Bimal Roy's Do Bigha Zamin (1953). He suggests that the post–World War
II period witnessed the development of Western-style orchestras in the
Hindi film line:

> SALIL CHAUDHURI: [After World War II] we were in need of good musicians,
> and you could get ready-made musicians only in Goa. That was the time
> when the Western orchestra was being introduced, so we needed musicians
> who could play. We used to use musicians also from the navy band, especially
> for instruments that you would not get, like French horn, tuba, bass clarinet.

John Gonsalves connects developments in arrangement and orchestration with the size of the orchestra:

> JOHN GONSALVES: In those days [early 1950s], the cello used to play songs
> along with the melody. Slowly arrangement started coming. Arrangement

was good for us, for cellos, and violas, and even for violins. You know, before, when I joined, there were eight violins, and they used to play the same
song melody. But you know you cannot play all the same melody together
like that.

After 1947 the Goan presence in the film orchestras grew disproportion-
ately, as did the size of the standard orchestra. Robert Corea learned piano
in Kolkata after his family moved there in the late 1940s. In the late 1950s
he became one of Shankar-Jaikishan's regular pianists and joined the
Shankar-Jaikishan orchestra:

> ROBERT COREA: Shankar-Jaikishan were the best. Other music directors had
> ten people or twelve people coming to their rehearsals, but Shankar-Jaikishan
> had thirty people. Every day!

The changes were not simply matters of size but also of personnel and
levels of experience with Western music of all kinds. This is true for some
of the "new" arrangers who began working in Mumbai in the early 1950s.
Among these was perhaps the most influential arranger of the 1950s and
1960s, Sebastian D'Souza.

Freelance Orchestras and Western-Style Arrangements

Sebastian D'Souza was neither the first nor the only Goan dance-band
arranger in the Mumbai film line. Antonio Vaz and Johnny Gomes were arranging in Mumbai before D'Souza arrived from Lahore. Vaz is especially
associated with music director C. Ramchandra; the results of their collaboration can be heard (and, more unusually, seen) in the 1951 romantic
comedy *Albela*.

D'Souza's dance-band arranging skills first become evident in two 1951
Shankar-Jaikishan films: *Nagina* and the more important R. K. Films release, *Aawara*. Because of the confusion around the credits for these films,
however, which resulted from the behavior of Shankar-Jaikishan's previous
arranger, Sonny Castelino, Ranade can legitimately suggest (based on film
credits) that "Desouza [*sic*] worked for the first time as arranger for O. P.
Nayyar for the film *Asman*" in 1952 (2006, 125). John Pereira, who had a
familial and professional relationship with both men, sheds some light on
the mix-up:

> JOHN PEREIRA: Really it was Sebastian who would arrange, but the moment
> Sonny would come, he would arrange. He would just take over, like that.
> He also used to do the recording.

There was a multiplicity of arrangers and composers who were, in effect,
participating in the project to enhance the size, sound, and (less consis-

tently) Western flavor of the Bollywood orchestra. All were responding in their own way to Western musical styles and the musical structure (and content) of Hollywood films. In video 7.1 [⬤] Anthony Gonsalves recalls S. D. Burman's fascination with a particular bit of Western popular culture.

Despite the broad engagement with Western styles and orchestration, D'Souza's collaboration with highly successful music directors gave him an advantage in terms of influence. Jerry Fernandes argues that, between them, Shankar-Jaikishan and D'Souza led the developments in orchestral size:

> JERRY FERNANDES: I started with *Aawara* [1951], and from that time I played with them always. Before that time, not so many musicians were there. I think they are the people who started using a lot of musicians all the time.

Although he joined much later than Fernandes, Anil Mohile paid special attention to the job that Sebastian did:

> ANIL MOHILE: Shankar-Jaikishan had great orchestration. I am a great fan of Mr. Sebastian. He used to sit with a small, small pencil, and he would write harmony and obbligato just like that. He was so gifted. I never saw him sitting at the piano and composing, "Okay, let's see this chord or that chord." No, he just wrote. I used to watch how Mr. Sebastian composed, how he wrote the countermelody. He never used to compose an obbligato as if it were a filler. Along with the main melody, another melody would come, and it would be so beautiful.

The small pencil is something that many people report, but Dattaram Waadkar provides a broader picture, again emphasizing the integrative aspect of D'Souza's work with Indian materials:

> DATTARAM WAADKAR: There was never another arranger like Sebastian in our industry. He used such a small pencil. And he wrote things so fast. He did such good work. You know our Indian *rāgs?* Well, he was so talented. He could arrange those notes and our English notes so that they sounded like they belonged together.

Anil Mohile also explains that, in the mid-1950s, Sebastian D'Souza's arrangements formalized two aspects of vocal accompaniment practice. The first was the use of what became the standard four-row violin section. The second and perhaps more important development divided the musical tasks among those rows:

> ANIL MOHILE: The first row, twelve to fifteen violins, used to play basic melody; they would play the song. Then the remaining violins would play the countermelody. And sometimes they would play full harmony. It was so rich.

Pyarelal Sharma, who proved to be D'Souza's primary successor in terms of orchestration, nevertheless suggests that the older man's work was relatively simplistic. But simplistic or not, D'Souza's arranging skills were applied to an enormous number of the hit songs of the 1950s and '60s. Since credits are not consistent in listing arrangers, even if one could view all of the films of that period, there would be no definite way to ascertain the actual numbers. Nevertheless, Salil Chaudhuri argues that much of what happened in the 1950s was D'Souza's doing:

> SALIL CHAUDHURI: Sebastian was the arranger for my songs, but also for Shankar-Jaikishan, O. P. Nayyar, Burman-dada, many others. I was always giving his name. He should have credit.

Later Developments in Old Bollywood

The extent of Sebastian D'Souza's contribution was no doubt a result of his work with many important composers. D'Souza dominated the arranging work in many sitting rooms, along with Anthony Gonsalves, Frank Fernand, Johnny Gomes, Martin Pinto, Jerry Amaldev, and others. I have no information on how long Ram Singh continued to work as an arranger. By the time Gonsalves left in 1964, the standard recording orchestra comprised more than fifty freelance musicians; the arranging ranks had been joined by Kersi Lord, Jai Kumar Parthe, Master Sonik, and others. Shortly thereafter, Amar Haldipur, Anil Mohile, Arun Paudwal, Manohari Singh, Vasu Chakravarty, Uttam Singh, and others all appeared as arrangers.

As I have already noted, Pyarelal Sharma was unique to the extent to which he composed and arranged music as part of Laxmikant-Pyarelal. Under his influence, this duo embodies the high point of Bollywood's film-orchestra tradition:

> JERRY FERNANDES: He was the man who introduced the big orchestra. Before him, no one used such a big orchestra. He really loved it. Six cellos, eight violas, fifty violins, brass section, all those things. But it wasn't just for show; he wrote music for all those instruments. Not just for effect.

Amar Haldipur argues that Sharma's truly orchestral style was possible only because Sharma was one of the few composers in Mumbai who had sufficient musical training:

> AMAR HALDIPUR: Pancham was a great composer, no doubt, but as far as orchestra, it was a different style. But L-P, Sonik-ji, Salil Chaudhuri, that was the style of orchestra. I followed Pyare-ji all my life; what he used to do, why he is using this kind of phrase, why the woodwind section is playing like that, why is the brass section like that? Whatever I have done, it is all because of him. He is the only complete music director, and Sonik-ji. They

were the only complete music directors who could write music, who could read music, who could make you understand what is what.

As Laxmikant-Pyarelal's popularity reached enormous proportions, so did their orchestra, which nevertheless continued to combine Indian and Western instrumentation:

> SHANKAR INDORKAR: Pyarelal-ji had woodwinds coming all the time. Two E♭ clarinets, one sopranino saxophone, one oboe, one flute, three Indian flutes, one shahanai. Everyday there were eight or nine guys in that woodwind section.

Pyarelal Sharma was known for his routine (sometimes daily) use of large orchestras. Kartik Kumar is one of many to note Sharma's trademark use of instrumental multiples to produce a very full sound:

> KARTIK KUMAR: For song recordings he used four, five, ten sitars sometimes. He would tell me, "Kartik-bhai, we need five more sitars." Sometimes we had even fifteen sitars, like in that song "Barda dukha dina, O Rama-ji" [*Ram Lakhan,* 1988]. Only Pyarelal did like that.

Pyarelal-ji's use of multiple instruments may well have been innovative in quantitative terms, but the practice as such precedes his career, as J. V. Acharya has suggested.

Sharma emphasizes the depth and breadth of his orchestral scores and, like others, notes the importance of foreign influences:

> PYARELAL SHARMA: By the time of *Agneepath* [1990] and *Khuda Gawah* [1992] we were using a full brass section. That means seven trumpets, three trombones, bass trombones, tuba, and also six synthesizers. I was a big fan of John Williams at that time.

These late scores by Laxmikant-Pyarelal are among some of the last the duo composed. They represent the height of Old Bollywood's orchestral sound and demonstrate (as many other film scores do) the influence of Hollywood's blockbuster orchestral scores.

Joe Monsorate also heard the John Williams connection. However, he notes that, by the time his late scores were being produced, Sharma was increasingly a holdout, using his reputation for commercial success to resist change and maintain his large studio orchestra:

> JOE MONSORATE: The '80s and '90s were very good; we had Pyarelal Sharma, an orchestral man. He didn't believe in synthesizers. He was like John Williams.

Despite his assertions, however, Monsorate, like others, saw synthesizers and other digital technologies as a potential threat to studio musicians' livelihoods.

New instruments, drum sets, electric guitars, and electronic keyboards had been increasingly part of film orchestras since the late 1950s. The new instruments, however, were just new voices, sometimes carrying stylistic meaning as well, but not effecting changes in the way the studio orchestras worked. The reality is that, aside from relatively superficial stylistic advances, very little actually altered in the size and nature of the Bollywood orchestra from the mid-1950s through the early 1980s and, in some ways, for a number of years beyond. The late 1980s, however, form a transition period in which innovations took place beneath a patina of constancy driven by habit, the sheer prosperity of the film (and film-music) industry, and the difficulty in enacting technological progress in the old, established studios. Despite the occasional new instrument, orchestras and recording sessions continued to function in primarily just as they had from the 1950s through the end of Old Bollywood. When changes did come to Mumbai's orchestras, they were driven by the increased presence and sophistication of electronic keyboards.

Keyboards, Synthesizers, and MIDI

Electronic keyboards and their successors—sequencers, synthesizers, and so forth—have always been a source of great interest to musicians in Mumbai, but acquiring such instruments was often a significant challenge in financial and regulatory terms:

> TAUFIQ QURESHI: It became easy to buy these things in the late 1990s. Until then, it was a little difficult; the customs people were creating problems. They would charge so much.

Access to Foreign Music Technology

The recording that provided the earliest and most innovative push for electronic instrumentation in the Hindi film-music industry was created by Kalyanji Shah. The young Shah was assisting music director Hemant Kumar in his work on the score for a film that focused on a fanciful tribe of snake catchers, *Nagin* (1954). The score, composed by Kumar and Shah, included what became one of the most widely known instrumental melodies in the Hindi cinema, performed by Shah on his newly acquired keyboard, called a claviolin:

> ANANDJI SHAH: My brother saw an ad in *Popular Science* about this electronic musical instrument, so he tried to get one. It took us through many things.

"Been music," which is heard as the introduction of the song "Man dole mera tan dole" from *Nagin,* was meant to represent the sound of the double-pipe, free-reed instrument called the *been* (known as a snake charmer's instrument). Despite the title, the film melody was played on the claviolin:

> VIPIN RESHAMMIYA: In those days Kalyanji had one claviolin, and he was playing "been music." That was very popular. He taught me how to play the instrument, so he is my guru. Sometimes he allowed me to borrow that instrument also. He would charge me a small fee to borrow it, but he did not like to lend it.

Reshamiya, like Shah, came from a business family, although he had learned to play Indian classical music on harmonium. Success in a talent contest led to an engagement with the film line that expanded after his exposure to the wonders of electronic instruments, courtesy of Kalyanji Shah. As traditional business families, the Shahs and Reshamiyas both had more experience with the Indian government's import-export and foreign-exchange laws (and the associated costs) than did most film musicians. Reshamiya soon began importing instruments himself:

> VIPIN RESHAMMIYA: In 1959 or 1960 I managed to bring one Claviolin Reverb from London. It was very expensive because the government charged 200 or 300 percent import duty on such things. From then I joined the film orchestra line. I played with Shankar-Jaikishan, and they exploited that instrument very much.

Vipin Reshammiya played electronic keyboards on the Shankar-Jaikishan sound track for *An Evening in Paris* (1967). The electronic sound was appropriate for this extremely popular, modernist vision that featured scenes of actor Shammi Kapoor filmed in Paris, dressed in the latest European fashions. The popularity of these songs and of his electronic contributions to them provided a major boost to Reshamiya's career and may have given a new lease on life to that of Shankar-Jaikishan as well. Reshamiya learned more than keyboard technique from Kalyanji: When he acquired a Yamaha keyboard in the 1960s, he also rented it out from time to time, often to accordionist Sumit Mitra, who played it for Laxmikant-Pyarelal in a film released the same year as *Evening in Paris:*

> SUMIT MITRA: Vipin Reshammiya brought the first Yamaha YC-45 in 1965; it cost 30,000 rupees. I used to play it on commission. It cost 100 rupees per song or 350 rupees for a background session. I first played it on *Farz* [1967]. Then he brought a second one and gave it to the R. D. camp—to Mr. Kersi Lord—in the same way. Then after some time, Kersi and Joe Menezes' daughter together bought one of their own.

Although Kalyanji Shah's claviolin is the first electronic sound most Indians and film musicians remember, it was apparently not the first instrument in the business. The very first electronic sounds in a Hindi film were produced by an instrument called a Univox, played by classical (and film) pianist Lucila Pacheco. No date is given for Pacheco's acquisition of her instrument, which was made possible by her husband's travels in the Indian merchant marine. Furthermore, although those in the field all agree that Pacheco was playing the Univox before Kalyanji Shah made his hit with *Nagin*, no one can name a film on which the earlier instrument is heard.

In addition to having relatives in business or in traveling occupations, musicians acquired electronic keyboards by going abroad with touring shows, which also began taking to the road in the 1960s (see figure 6.5). As Charanjit Singh notes, everyone wanted to be part of the new fad:

> CHARANJIT SINGH: I started playing in 1965, and I had been abroad with [playback singer] Kishore Kumar. While I was abroad, I got that new instrument [an electronic keyboard], so then I started playing with Shankar-Jaikishan. At that time, the hit movie was *Evening in Paris* [1967]. Then other music directors started calling me because I had the latest instrument—because when something is new, everybody wants it. At that time I was so busy, everybody was always calling me for sessions.

Difficulties in acquiring new music technology continued through the mid-1970s, when Kalyanji's son Viju began touring with his Uncle Babla. The younger Shah had the musical training that his famous father lacked and took over the arranging duties for Kalyanji in 1976, when Jai Kumar Parthe, one of Kalyanji's regular arrangers, stopped coming to work. Even though Viju Shah began in the system that had been standard for more than twenty years at that point, he also experienced the power for change that was inherent in the new technologies:

> VIJU SHAH: It was the electronics that changed this. It was a Mini-Korg. I went along with my Uncle Babla for shows [overseas], and we got this synthesizer—I'm talking about 1974. And we used it for this song, "Yeh mera dil," from *Don* [1978]. I used that keyboard, and we got a lot of sounds from it. It was very shocking for everyone that one keyboard can produce all these different sounds. So, of course, it became a wave.

By 1978 electronic keyboards had been a "wave" for quite some time, of course, but each new development made the wave stronger and more clearly demonstrated the potential problems that they and synthesizers represented for acoustic musicians. Sumit Mitra reports the concerns they had, even in the 1960s, regarding the ability of electronic instruments to replace acoustic ones when he first recorded using an electronic organ in another score by Shankar-Jaikishan:

> SUMIT MITRA: I played the first electronic organ—it was a Farfisa—on the film *Brahmachari* [1968]. Robert [Corea] was supposed to play it, but he couldn't control the volume. It would suddenly come very loud, and it was giving very many problems to Minoo [Katrak, the recordist at Famous (Tardeo)]. So Jaikishan-ji said to me, "Okay, you try." So I turned the one volume up and the other down and left them like that, and it worked out. People panicked when they heard that because it sounded like one hundred musicians playing. They were afraid that they would not have work.

Brahmachari again starred Shammi Kapoor, this time as a rather altruistic and nationalistic Good Samaritan, but the score is largely Western pop or rock 'n' roll oriented. The Farfisa figures prominently in many of the songs. Listening to the lullaby "Mai gaoon, tum so jaao," in which the organ dominates the entire song, one can perhaps understand the concerns of some of Mitra's colleagues. Musicians, it seems, were focusing on the matter of volume (as had Sagar Studios' unnamed recordist in responding to Anil Biswas's request for multiple violins in the 1930s). Volume, however, was not the issue. As long as recordings had to be done live, the orchestral musicians could be confident of remaining part of the equation.

Mumbai's film musicians continued to work, but keyboards and synthesizers became a standard part of the ensemble. When Anjan Biswas moved from Kolkata in the 1970s to work in Mumbai's studios, he had just spent six months polishing his violin performance skills so as to keep up with the CMA violinists. He did not remain in the violin section for very long, however. By that time keyboards were available in some of the city's music stores:

> ANJAN BISWAS: For one year I played violin, and then I started playing keyboards. At first I rented keyboards, mostly from Swami, in Dadar. They used to rent keyboards for 200 or 300 rupees per shift.

Sumit Mitra recounts the seemingly endless procession of new models and numbers that Mumbai's studios and sitting rooms enthusiastically embraced:

> SUMIT MITRA: Then the first polyphonic synthesizer came around the time of *Julee* [1975]; that was a Roland SA/H 1000. Then in December 1980 I bought a Jupiter 4 from Chris Perry. He had brought one back from overseas, Singapore, I think. It cost 34,000 rupees. Then the Juno-60 came in 1983 and the DX-7 in 1985; that was very popular. Laxmikant-Pyarelal used it—also Anu Malik. Bappi Lahiri had three keyboard players in his group: There was myself and also Arun Paudwal and Ronnie Monsorate

and also Louiz Banks. Then in 1987 Mr. Kersi bought one Korg M1, a polyphonic multitrack synthesizer. That was the first in the film line.

As with everything else, of course, the particular sequence changed from musician to musician. Viju Shah offers a different technological trajectory:

> VIJU SHAH: See the transition! Mini-Korg to ARP Omni, ARP Omni to Jupiter 4, Jupiter 4 to Jupiter 8 and then Jupiter 6 and then after that DX 7 Yamaha, then Roland D50—this is the transition. ARP had the string sound. People were very thrilled that this keyboard could make such good string sound. And Jupiter 4 was polyphonic four voices. But as yet, no MIDI, even with Jupiter 8 there was no MIDI, but then with Jupiter 6 finally there was MIDI. Then I got that DX7, and on that, I think, I started laying the rhythm tracks for the song. That's how the first sequencing started happening. It was more like rhythm programming. I would put something in, then [push the button], and, "Okay, the rhythm has started. Now you play something live." Then EMU SP1200 came. This was *Tridev* [1989]. I had two of those and one DDD-1 Korg and one Oberheim all connected.

By the 1980s the presence of keyboards in the orchestral mix began to have unexpected economic implications for producers when the musicians who owned this equipment started passing on the costs of their acquisition. Taufiq Qureshi suggests that he made more "renting" his equipment than he did from his actual shift fee:

> TAUFIQ QURESHI: When I was working with Anand-Milind [circa 1989], I was A grade; I got 975 rupees for one and a half [background] shifts. But we realized we had an advantage and started giving hiring charges. I would say, "Okay, I've got one octopad, that means 1,000 rupees; one Mackie mixer, that's 1000 rupees; and one Roland drum machine, that's 2,000 rupees. So I would get an extra 4,000 rupees. We were signing on a voucher one for 975, one for 4,000.

As electronic keyboards developed, they became instruments for music composition rather than simply performance devices. As their capabilities were exploited, they came into conflict with the older processes of film-song composition. However, for producers, they also had the potential to improve the economics of the process. The lush scores, enormous orchestras, and recording methods of late Old Bollywood were often very expensive. But by the time Pyarelal-ji was composing and recording his last monumental scores, a filmmaker who lacked the money to hire Laxmikant-Pyarelal and their one hundred–piece orchestra could take advantage of new, less expensive alternative in the shape of music sequencers and sampling technology. As a composer and arranger, Viju Shah had already demonstrated the possibilities by almost single-handedly producing an entire background score on his own:

> VIJU SHAH: I think *Tridev* [1989] was the first that I did totally electronic. Rajiv [Rai, director] gave me a free hand. He said, "We should experiment with this. I am there with you. Don't worry." We used some live, some flute was there and sometimes violins, but most of it was electronic. We tried to produce an Indian sound through the electronic. Like you can hear the tabla in "Tirchi topi wale"; that's me, all that stuff. I think that worked very well. People were dazed. That was the first film we did background single-handed.

Samplers could replicate the sound of an entire string section or a whole battery of Indian percussion; they were often too tempting as cost-cutting measures:

> SUMIT MITRA: Samplers didn't come until the 1990s. They changed everything. They started using keyboards to cover everything, and acoustic instruments became much less. The violins, cellos, all those things were replaced slowly, slowly.

The tension between enthusiasm for new possibilities and a desire to retain live acoustic music practice was a feature of the late 1980s and '90s, especially for musicians who could see both sides of the situation:

> KERSI LORD: I blame myself actually because I brought the synthesizer here. And I'm not joking. But we used them for so many years, and we never spoiled the music. Even now when some people ask me, can you replace acoustic instruments with these things, I say, "No, never!"

Lord is not the only person who feels that it was musicians themselves who changed the sound of Hindi film music:

> ANNIBAL CASTRO: We were responsible for the downfall of Indian music. We were always searching for some new things, all these foreign instruments. Just because we wanted to make more money, we brought all these keyboards and synthesizers. We ruined it ourselves.

Even more than Castro, Kersi Lord was in the ambiguous position of leading the industry's fascination with the possibilities of new technology while trying to maintain a rearguard action to protect acoustic performance. The results in a profit-driven industry like the film-music business in Mumbai were inevitable.

Programming, Background Music, and the Orchestra

These electronic keyboards, even those with sampling technology, were played live as one of a film orchestra's instrumental resources. They required real musicians with the skills to perform real music in real time. In the hands of a musician-friendly music director such as Pyarelal Sharma, this method had almost no impact on the size of the acoustic orchestra because the keyboard was simply another (if louder and more versatile) instrument in the ensemble and some producers were willing to pay for a large orchestra regardless of the cost.

Multipercussionist Taufiq Qureshi began his film career in the same way as many other keyboardists and, like many of the early ones, had special access to foreign technology, this time through his brother, who was living in the United States:

> TAUFIQ QURESHI: I played on the title song for the film *Deewana Mujhsa Nahi* [1990]. I was playing octopad. I had just asked Zakir-bhai [his brother] to get one for me when he went abroad. I had seen one in a show somewhere, so he brought it. It was very new at that time. Any kind of MIDI was new and especially rhythm MIDI. I bought a Roland R-8, and I would MIDI that to the octopad. I spent almost two years playing with the rhythm section for Anand-Milind.

In other words, Qureshi was playing his electronic instrument, with its MIDIed sampler, as just another voice in midst of the dholaks, congas, tablas, and so on of the orchestra's rhythm section.

Part of the MIDI technology that was available in the 1980s, however, allowed musical information to be entered (and changed) note-by-note as slowly as necessary, outside the technical and physical constraints of real time, rather than performed and recorded. Notes could be entered slowly, one at time, stored, and later played back at any tempo. Products that could store musical input and trigger keyboards to play it back in real time were initially called "sequencers." This way of making music has come to be called "programming" in Mumbai; programming represents an entirely different way of making and playing music, one that requires little by way of instrumental technique and is consequently disparaged by older musicians who have spent their lives acquiring their musical skills. Sumit Mitra comments that he initially had to use a separate unit that triggered a keyboard:

> SUMIT MITRA: The first sequencer in the film industry, I used. That was in 1983, the MS-Q60 attached to the Juno [keyboard]. Then Louiz Banks got the MS-Q100 multitrack sequencer in 1984. Then they brought in this quanta [non-real-time "quantized" data entry]. At that point I knew that now this is anybody's game. Anybody can be a music director. At least before, you had to be able to play the notes. And many of those parts were very difficult; you had to practice. But now, because they just slow it down, anybody can play.

These comments are echoed by other musicians who value the musician-ship skills of Old Bollywood—the need to practice, as Mitra puts it. He im-plies here that the importance of these abilities declined with the ebb in the need for real-time performance. Like others in this transition, guitarist Ramesh Iyer began his career as a recording musician but now makes his living as a programmer and arranger in New Bollywood:

> RAMESH IYER: I am on the audition committee for CMA. Last year twenty guitarists auditioned. This year there were four and only one who was any good. There used to be twenty or thirty violinists every year. This year there was one; keyboard, there were twelve. Everybody wants to buy a key-board—a Roland or a Korg or something—and program it. All right, you are playing the keyboard, fine. You take the Trinity or the Royal College [music certificates] or something, and you can play. But these kids, they play note by note. It will take them a whole day to do anything.

Programmable keyboards required a particularly technological skill set, an understanding of programming concepts rather than musical virtuosity. They also enabled a different system of use. They were not played live, along with other instruments or even other tracks. Instead, the musical content was "dumped" (in the modern terminology used in Mumbai) di-rectly onto tracks that were then synchronized automatically:

> KERSI LORD: I never thought about what might happen. We never meant for it to replace the orchestra. Pancham and I always used it nicely, so it fit with the live instruments. I was just interested in the technology.

Realistically, of course, it is impossible to assign blame in these matters. If Lord had not been the first, someone else would have. The result, how-ever, as Taufiq Qureshi explains, was a mix of live and programmed music:

> TAUFIQ QURESHI: Like, if some action scene was there, I would program some rhythms, but then if Vanraj [Bhatia, background composer] wanted some pakhāwaj or something, we would call Bhavani-ji [Shankar] or some-one who would come. And he would play live, and he might make the music also. I would go out and play some live parts.

In earlier chapters I have noted other aspects of the technology- and eco-nomics-driven transition from the orchestral world of Old Bollywood to the individualized session musicians of New Bollywood. This narrative of the rise of electronic keyboards and synthesizers complements those earlier versions by depicting an industry fascinated with novelty, one that thus put itself out of business without really trying.

Full Circle?

Mumbai's engagement with the technology led to a decline of the film orchestras that had produced the music of Old Bollywood. Younger music directors such as Himesh Reshammiya, Pritam Chakraborty, or M. M. Kreem learned their trade in what was, in effect, a postorchestral world and in studios that were increasingly competitive on an international level.

While working on this project in Mumbai in early 2007, I was called by cellist Sanjay Chakravarty, who told me that he and some other cellists had been requested for a recording session at Yash Raj Studios; Sanjay asked whether I wanted to accompany him and Benny Gracias to the session. When I asked what the recording was for, however, and who else was coming, Chakravarty admitted that he had not been told. We all went to discover what in 2007 passed for a large string section: twenty-four violins, four violas (including my friend Shankar Indorkar), and six cellos (figure 3.1). Nothing, of course, compared to the sections of Laxmikant-Pyarelal fifteen years earlier but large enough for contemporary Mumbai for everyone to be commenting on how nice it was to see so many musicians together.

The session turned out to be a background recording for a film score by the composing trio Shankar-Eshaan-Loy. Parts were distributed, two or three rehearsals or run-throughs took place under the direction of Inderjeet Sharma, and the parts were recorded. Although the group began rather hesitantly, by the end of the session there was a marked improvement in the ensemble playing, intonation, and overall musicality. For most, it was the first time in years they had recorded in such a large group. The players then stood in line for their pay, distributed by Shankar-Eshaan-Loy's music coordinator, and four hours after we had arrived, everyone left for their cars or to catch a bus or train.

Afterward I had a conversation with composers Shankar Mahadevan and Loy Mendonsa, who had been present, overseeing the session. Both were quite enthusiastic about how things had gone. Their remarks provide a suitable final word on the Mumbai film orchestras. Also participating in the conversation was the studio's recording engineer:

> SHANKAR: That was great. That was the first time we've recorded in Mumbai since *Mission Kashmir* [2000]. Everybody said the string section was better in Madras. But you know, in Madras they were always playing; there was no break, you could say. Here there has been a break. This was like a trial run for us to see how it would sound.
>
> RECORDING ENGINEER: People thought they could just use samples. The synthesizers and the samplers replaced these guys. But you never really get that

sound, that emotion using samples of the Vienna Symphony or whatever. Today these guys, by the end, they were really playing.

LOY: But you have to give them good parts, parts they can understand.

SHANKAR: So much music has been rubbish, it's no wonder they didn't play nicely. They now just need some training up. Nothing beats a live section.

LOY: Actually, I'd like the section to be still bigger.

Despite this kind of rhetoric regarding a return to acoustic orchestral recording, Viju Shah expresses doubts that it would in fact be possible in New Bollywood:

VIJU SHAH: It will go this way only. We'll never go back to the live way. In fact, a lot of our acoustic musicians have left the line; they don't get work. It's very sad. They're a thing of the past. I can still remember one hundred musicians coming for sessions, but now it's like one guy coming.

Shah is correct that many musicians have indeed left Mumbai and/or the film business for other places and other jobs that will allow them to support their families.

The process of change is ongoing, of course. It is unimaginable, as Shah suggests, that there could ever be a return to the excesses and enthusiasms of Old Bollywood. Shankar's and Loy's enthusiasm here may simply be an emotional response to the same human aspects of music making that Old Bollywood musicians recall with such nostalgic fondness. More than a year later my friends in Mumbai report that this session remains a one-time event.

8

Issues of Style, Genre, and Value in Mumbai Film Music

Style, genre, value, ideology, and contextual meaning are all issues of concern for studies of popular music (e.g., Frith 1996; Hamm 1995). Hindi film songs as a collective repertoire, however, are unique to the degree to which they are produced by the playback system (cf. Majumdar 2001) and interact with the specific cinematic and popular-culture contexts in which they are located (cf. Booth 2000; Morcom 2007). After some preliminary consideration of the distinctive notions and patterns of style and genre construction in film music, I examine film musicians' representations of and relationships with musical style and the ways they value and relate to the music they play.

Film musicians' comments on style range from an exclusive focus on musical content (sound quality, rhythm patterns, melodic form, and so on) to at least the implication of ideological and cultural content that I associate with genre (Walser 1993). Although musicians frequently use the term "style," I have yet to hear anyone in the film line use the term "genre." The term may simply be too little used in standard English, but Fabbri (1982) suggests another possibility. In historical European musicology, the concepts of style and genre (as well as form) have effectively been conflated. The ethnocentrism and cultural hegemony that characterized European classical music culture in the nineteenth and early twentieth centuries made this possible. The cultural dominance of film music in India may have produced a similar form of conceptual myopia among its listeners and practitioners.

Style, Genre, Ideology, and Film Song

Style, genre, and distinctions between them are matters of considerable contention in classical and popular Western music scholarship (e.g., Dahlhaus 1982; Walser 1993). Theories have advocated musical, ideological, cultural, and still other bases for distinction. Kallberg (1988) and Walser (1993) have explicitly emphasized discursive or rhetorical approaches. The latter also focuses on the distinctions between genre as constructed by fans and by the music industry. "Rigid genre boundaries are more useful to the music industry than to fans, and the commercial strategy of hyping cultural genres while striving to obliterate the differences that make individual choices meaningful often works very effectively to mobilize efficient consumption" (Walser 1993, 5). Hindi film songs, as a source of ready-made and relatively inexpensive popular-music content, represented a windfall for HMV, but one that was not necessarily flexible in the ways that Walser implies.

In the precassette period, film songs were heard in theaters and on the radio or television as singles or as LPs of songs from their film. Despite Walser's arguments about the importance of genre to the music industry, the power of the visual image (as both star and narrative situation) tied HMV's products to the identity, structure, and ideology of the film in a way that was almost inescapable and that makes the application of Western theories of genre in popular music problematic.

Film songs are organized into a wide variety of musical and nonmusical categories by film, star, composer, musical style (in specific cases), and singer, but these groupings routinely overlap. Style and genre themselves cut across each other in Hindi film music and its offshoots (e.g., the "parody" *bhajan*, in which a popular film-song melody—sometimes with quite erotic visual associations—is set to a new devotional Hindu text, thus making it bhajan). As singles and LPs with the collected songs from a given film score, music products could not easily reflect extracinematic genre or even style associations without repackaging. This was relatively rare until the advent of cassettes, when legal and illegal compilations, reorganized on the basis of a range of musical and extramusical commonalities, began appearing in the new format (such as the "ghazals from films" compilations, which appeared on cassette in the 1980s, organized around the poetic and ideological associations of that Urdu literary form).

One exception to this situation that engaged film musicians was the instrumental version recording. "Version" is the term the industry uses to identify a rerecording of a film song more or less as it was originally recorded but not necessarily with the same musicians. This is legal under In-

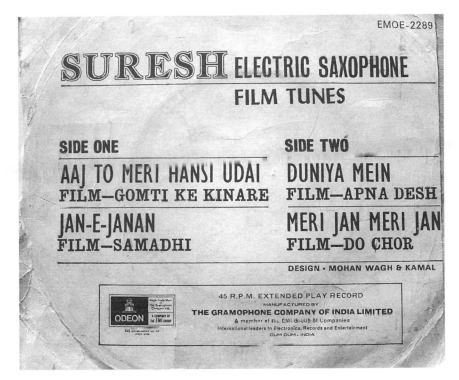

EMOE-2289

SURESH ELECTRIC SAXOPHONE
FILM TUNES

SIDE ONE

AAJ TO MERI HANSI UDAI
FILM—GOMTI KE KINARE

JAN-E-JANAN
FILM—SAMADHI

SIDE TWO

DUNIYA MEIN
FILM—APNA DESH

MERI JAN MERI JAN
FILM—DO CHOR

DESIGN · MOHAN WAGH & KAMAL

ODEON

45 R.P.M. EXTENDED PLAY RECORD
MANUFACTURED BY
THE GRAMOPHONE COMPANY OF INDIA LIMITED
A member of the EMI Group of Companies
International leaders in Electronics, Records and Entertainment
DUM DUM · INDIA

Figure 8.1   A 45 rpm EP cover, showing a version-song release featuring saxophonist Suresh Yadhav.

dian copyright laws. Early instrumental version recordings often featured instrumentalists who had significant careers outside the movie business, such as accordionist Goodi Seervai or the famous clarinetist Master Ebrahim, who were, in a limited way, stars in their own rights. Figure 8.1 shows the content of a 45 rpm EP on the Gramophone Company's Odeon label, released in 1973, featuring "electric" saxophone, that is, amplified saxophone with some added reverb and echo effects. Suresh Yadhav, who played the saxophone on the recording, explains:

> SURESH YADHAV: They were doing an instrumental series, Hawaiian guitar, accordion, all those things, so they thought, why not saxophone? And they asked me to play. And they put in all sorts of modern effects because that was the style at those times. But the music was the same as the original songs, only the orchestra was small. I got a royalty for that—5 percent.

As new recordings, version song compilations gave the record companies an opportunity to repackage and configure songs in ways not necessarily suggested by their cinematic contexts. The songs in this set are from four different films released in 1972, all composed by R. D. Burman. For its Indian audience, the idea and the sound of an "electric" saxophone would carry implications of modernity, contemporary (Western) popular music, and so forth, reinforced by Burman's reputation as a proponent of these concepts. To the extent that it was possible with the technology available in 1973, the Gramophone Company was attempting to shape efficient consumption according to a broad ideological genre loosely defined by notions of modernity, working (to paraphrase Walser) to produce a notion of modern film music that was both inclusive and indiscriminate and that would appeal to a younger, college-age audience. However, this was happening within the context of Hindi film music as the overarching genre, and, other than the instrumental feature and the minimalist electronic effects, there is almost no stylistic difference between these versions of the film songs and the original recordings. Further, the nature of Burman's modernity was tied to a significant extent to the films whose scores he was producing.

Musicians argue that many composers, regardless of the type of song they are composing, have personal styles that distinguish their music:

> DATTARAM WAADKAR: Most composers have a style, one style that they use. And you can tell, "Oh, this is Madan Mohan. This is Sadar Malik. This is Roshan-ji."

Likewise, J. V. Acharya makes similar assertions for O. P. Nayyar but, like many musicians, can verbalize the perceived distinction only with difficulty.

Joe Monsorate argues that this notion of personal style could affect the relationship between song and background music in the same film:

> JOE MONSORATE: It happened to one Subhash Ghai film that L-P [who composed the songs] could not give the background; they had no time. That was *Krodhi* [1981]. So they gave the background to Kalyanji-Anandji, but what was coming in the picture, the flavor was very odd.

For those who could perceive them, the differences in musical style between L-P's songs and Kalyanji-Anandji's background score were aesthetically disruptive.

As with many other things in late Old Bollywood, issues of personal style coalesced around the sounds or styles of R. D. Burman and Laxmikant-Pyarelal. Here, both A. N. Tagore and Kersi Lord consider the relationship between stylistic distinctions and the recording venues and processes. Tagore argues that style was not defined by sound:

> A. N. TAGORE: L-P shifted [to Mehboob Studios] in 1976 or '75, just after I came. They stamped their own sound. Like recording in Film Centre, you

can find out from the song that it's R. D. [Burman]. But any other music director's recording from Film Centre—can you tell it's Film Centre? Or any other music director's recording from Mehboob besides L-P, you can tell [that it's Mehboob Studios]?

Tagore implies the negative in his rhetorical questions. He contends that these two styles were distinctive, reinforced perhaps by the qualities of the two studios and preferred recording methods but nevertheless independent of them. Tagore goes on to suggest that the compositional and orchestral styles of late Old Bollywood were in general aligned with one or the other of these veteran composers.

Kersi Lord, on the other hand, maintains that sound, as a technical feature of the recording, was crucial to the development of style:

KERSI LORD: There are two types of recording. One is where you have a lot of crossover, like if there are four mics and a not properly acoustic room. If you have a loud drum there, it will go in each mic, that plus that plus that, but with a delay of milliseconds. It will be like a delay. L-P were like that. And we, that is, Mr. R. D. Burman, our side, we always tried to avoid that as much as possible. Their songs are like that—it sounds so big because everything was loud.

Lord illustrates the differences in process with an event he attributes to Ashok Shukla. His story reinforces Tagore's suggestion that style was a matter beyond recording space:

KERSI LORD: They were making a recording for L-P with Pancham's group at Film Centre; this was the first time L-P were coming there to record. My friend was the engineer there. He asked me, "What shall I do?" I said, "Don't worry. When you listen to record, put all the mics on and put lots of reverb on the mics." He said, "What are you saying? How can I do that?" So I met him after one week. I said, "How was the recording?" He told me, "You know, we recorded for two hours, and Pyarelal-ji was saying, 'Accha hai, accha hai, lekin mazza nahi aata' " [It's good, but the excitement isn't coming]. So after two hours I remembered your advice, and I put all the reverb on like that. Immediately [Pyarelal said] "Yes! That's it!"

Despite individual constructions, however, personal style did not necessarily interact with one's musical approach. Although some composers were known for their stylistic preferences or expertise (e.g., Roshan's connection to Indian classical music or Lahiri's success with disco), stylistic specialization, in musical terms, was counterproductive in building a successful film-music career. Composing for movies did not allow music directors to specialize. Narrative context, together with the implications of stylistic borrowings from Western music, complicated the possibilities of ideological content and impact that Western scholarship routinely attributes to genre construction, meaning, and preference. The "rigid genre boundaries" that Walser (1993) suggests industries seek to construct were neither rigid nor boundaries in India; they could never connect music as such to ideologies that were solely cultural. Categories based (however loosely) on musical style elements are easily overwhelmed and sometimes effectively replaced by film-star personae and singer identities, often working in tandem. The songs of the Hindi cinema are *of* the cinema and thus largely, if not predominantly, received in a context that includes actors, dance, narrative emotions or tensions, scenery, and so forth, all elements that make up the Indian term "situation."

Film Musicians, Style, and Situation

Although they recognize and may be personally fond of different musical styles (however those are constructed), most musicians grasp that these are dependent on the cinematic context: In other words, the situation usually determines the style of the song they have to compose or record on any given day. This pragmatic view of the industry is encapsulated in the comments of guitarist Sunil Kaushik:

> SUNIL KAUSHIK: Really you can only say that I was jack of all, master of
> none. Why? Because in this industry, sometimes you have to play Indian
> classical kinds of pieces, sometimes Western classical, sometimes this,
> sometimes that. So I knew all kinds of music a little bit. Because you have
> to play. You have to be able to give a touch of anything, you know?

Kaushik makes two different kinds of stylistic distinctions here between musical notions of Indianness and Westernness and, by implication, between classical and other styles. These are some of the most consistent stylistic distinctions made by musicians in the film line.

Composing for Situations

In Hindi film music the composition process is powerfully affected by a song's situation or cinematic context. In contemporary terms, Morcom (2007) considers this matter in depth. This discussion provides some complementary historical perspective on this issue and connects musicians to these issues. Naturally, it is composers who potentially have the most input in stylistic matters. Even they, however, are limited by the tastes of their producer or director (or even the film's investors), the nature of the film and its situations, its star, and (given the Mumbai industry's conservative nature) the musical styles fashionable at any given moment. This was clear to music director Anil Biswas as early as the mid-1930s:

> ANIL BISWAS: Music must belong to the period and to the character [of the film], and that used to give me ideas when I sat to compose.

Biswas's contemporary, Vistasp Balsara, who worked on salary at Filmistan Studios in the 1930s, provides an idea of the details of picturization and situation that informed the composition process.

> VISTASP BALSARA: The director would tell us the situation of the picturization of the song: What would happen when the interlude came, what the actors would do, what should be played, and what would happen when this particular line [of the song] would be played.

Picturization is the cinematic manifestation of a song's situation. Omprakash Sonik expands on the importance of situation for melodic composition:

> OMPRAKASH SONIK: In making the songs, it depends on the film and the situation for the songs. The main thing in the song is the words. So we tell the lyricist, "You compose the words, we'll compose after that." If it's a folk song or a cabaret or a disco, whatever it is, we'll compose the song on that theme.

Morcom's research (2007, 32–48) contributes significantly to our understanding of music directors' perspectives on the importance of situation in film-song composition, a process on which Bablu Chakravarty elaborates:

> BABLU CHAKRAVARTY: The music director calls the director, and we ask, "What is your idea for the first music?" So perhaps he says, "Okay, so song has started, but she [the heroine] is dreaming maybe, so you give me music so that we can go outside, heaven or anywhere, for a dream." Or maybe he says, "This song needs to have the typical sounds of some place." So the director has these ideas. Or sometimes the song is going very nicely, but we see the villain coming from far away, just like *Tezaab,* and we need to give some suitable sound to tell the audience that the villain is coming with villain sound. That will continue throughout the music, whenever the villain is coming.

Bablu-da refers to the hit song "Ek do teen char" from a popular 1988 film in which, as he describes, shots of actress Madhuri Dixit's famous dance are intercut with shots of the villains on their way to kidnap her.

The flexibility required of composers (and musicians) in an industry where such changes could radically affect musical content and style were considerable. Ravi Shankar Sharma offers an extreme example of the perils:

> RAVI SHANKAR SHARMA: I composed the music for *Kaajal* [1965]; the lyrics
> were by Sahir [Ludhianvi], "Yeh zulf agar khul ke." But when I had
> composed the song, then the producer told me, "This song is being sung
> by Helen. She is dancing, so we need *ghunghuroo* [ankle bells] and these
> things." So I changed the tune so it would be suitable for that. And
> Mohamed Rafi was singing that song, but the hero [actor Raaj Kumar]
> was there while we were recording, and he said, "But I'm drunk! I'm
> singing, but I'm supposed to be drunk, and the song doesn't give any idea
> of that." And I said, "But nobody told me!" So then I had to compose yet
> again.

In his comments, Ravi-ji adds to the confusion in this situation by first describing Helen, an actress famous for her cabaret dancing (see Pinto 2006), as singing this song. In fact, the song was sung by Mohamed Rafi as Ravi-ji states later. The song was picturized on Helen (as a dancer) while actor Raaj Kumar was picturized miming the words (and apparently acting inebriated as well). Given the importance of situation in these comments, however, it is little wonder that film musicians are able to conceptualize musical style features as free-floating signifiers of postmodern cultural theory.

In Deepan Chatterji's explanation of how he categorized the tapes he made of Burman's songs, we get a sense of the standardization of situations that many composers kept in mind even if they were composing songs in advance:

> DEEPAN CHATTERJI: I had categorized Pancham-da's compositions according
> to the situation, romantic and all that. In those days, there were some stan-
> dard situations like the romantic song, the sad song, the happy song, the
> duet, and those things. So if Pancham-da had to work on something and
> sometime he would have a mental block, I would play that tape. And some-
> times the tape would go on for hours together, and we'd just be sitting
> there. And then he would suddenly say, "Hey, there's a good one!" So I
> would copy that onto a cassette and keep it.

Anthony Gonsalves worked as an arranger and background music composer throughout the 1950s. Although Gonsalves is Goan, he maintained a lifelong interest in Indian classical music, working to integrate Indian classical style into the movie orchestral scores and develop ways of harmonizing and orchestrating Indian rāgas without destroying their specific modal characters. Gonsalves also correlated situation and style, specifically in the composition of background music. He notes that the fusion of

Indian and Western elements was one of the main aesthetic goals (as he perceived them) in the construction of a film music sound in Old Bollywood. Dattaram Waadkar mentions similar results from Sebastian D'Souza's arrangements, in which classical melodies were orchestrated and harmonized (such as *Basant Bahar,* 1956).

The fusion of Western and Indian elements was not a goal for all composers in the 1950s or even the early 1960s (Ali 2004). Nevertheless, Anthony Gonsalves argues that many music directors "wanted our Hindustani music, but sounding like symphonics." Gonsalves refers specifically to those with whom he was working. Both then and now, he may also be projecting his own interests and goals onto others. Gonsalves did in fact compose a series of extended orchestral works—a number of symphonies and a violin concerto—in the late 1950s (cf. Fernandes 2005). His comments, however, introduce one of the fundamental stylistic distinctions that film musicians routinely express between the collectivities of Indian and Western musical styles.

Musicians' Constructions of Indian and Western Styles

Film musicians unanimously agree that there are indisputable stylistic differences between Indian and Western music. Music director Salil Chaudhuri has gone so far as to suggest that the Mumbai industry's engagement with Western musical style was a part of the process of Indian national integration:

> SALIL CHAUDHURI: Bombay was the national center at that time [after independence], so people came there looking for work and all these things. You should really say that national integration has happened more in films than in politics and that also with the influence of Western music.

In their conversations, musicians may include anything understood as Western or Indian under their respective music labels. Commonly, however, "Western" has an assumed and sometimes unspecified connection to popular music, whereas things Indian more routinely refer to classical or folk traditions. These specificities are by no means absolute. For violinist Jerry Fernandes, it was the presence of harmony, orchestration, and countermelody that distinguished Western and Indian styles. Speaking of the mid-1930s, before orchestral arranging became the norm, Fernandes identifies unharmonized, unison playing with Indian style.

Although referred to as styles, "Indian" and "Western" sometimes come with ideological baggage and tensions similar to those that exist among Western genres. Among other things, there is always an extent to which the use of Western music needed justification:

MANOHARI SINGH: Sometime back, some so-called well-known music director, I think maybe Naushad-saheb and one or two others, made some criticisms of Pancham—that he was making only Western-style music. Then he [Burman] gave music for *Kati Patang* [1970] and *Amar Prem* [1971]. That proved that he could also give Indian-style music.

Burman's major critic, it appears, was fellow composer Naushad Ali, who in the early 1950s (slightly more than ten years into his long career) had begun making a concerted and public effort to associate himself with Indian classical music and to promote classical music through his film scores. In explaining his position, Naushad wrote, "I felt that . . . if the same trend continued [using Western music as the basis for film songs], very few people would follow our own Indian traditional and classical music. I thought, why not make a movie in which music would play a pivotal role, and it would have songs based on Indian classical music?" (Ali 2004, 67). The motivation identified here led to *Baiju Bawra* (1952), but Naushad's scores for *Kohinoor* (1960) and *Mughal-e-Azam* (1960) also used orchestral versions of Indian classical music and engaged classical singers as guest playback singers for key song scenes.

In the film industry, the Indian-Western dichotomy had the potential to be enacted as a divide between Goan musicians (Western) and "Indian" (that is, non-Goan) musicians. Because he played guitar, an instrument stereotypically associated with Goan musicians, Bhupinder Singh was very aware of this possible tension and initially expresses it in Indian-Western stylistic terms. Ultimately, especially with his inclusion of blues guitarist B. B. King as an influence, Singh makes a case for what one could view as a syncretic musical style:

BHUPINDER SINGH: Many guitar players, even Bhanu [Gupta], had a lot of opposition. Because the Goans thought, "These Indians, they cannot play guitar." But we excelled in our own style because we are playing for Indian films and Indian songs. We are not playing jazz music or any other type of music. So we specialized in that—in playing our own style. I created my own style. They [Goans] never used to bend the notes on the guitar. I also created vibrato. I used to see the famous American guitar player B. B. King, his blues, you know. So we started mixing up, and it really helped me a lot. We created our own style. I had an Indian style of playing.

"Our own style" means, if you hear any of the songs from "Dum Maro Dum" [from the film *Hare Rama Hare Krishna*, 1971] to [the songs in the film] *Satte pe Satta* [1981], all these solos have been played in that Indian style.

Despite Singh's somewhat startling assertions regarding the song "Dum Maro Dum," it is clear that within the film-music line, musicians may express the Western-Indian stylistic difference in the context of specific instrumental performance practice. Leslie Godinho makes a similar claim for a unique Indian-Western mix for his famous drum-set solo in *Teesri Manzil* (1966). He offers a unique perspective on the multicultural nature of his rhythmic thinking in the 1960s. [Video 8.1]

In contrast to the explicitly eclectic styles these musicians suggest, others (especially violinists) sometimes describe specialties in either Western or Indian styles. Such orientations might have implications for a musician's career, especially soloists. Ernest Menezes, a violinist in the Western tradition, explained that his uncle, Joe Menezes, was a featured soloist in all of Raj Kapoor's movies throughout the early 1970s, with but one exception, which, as Ernest explains, was based on stylistic needs:

> ERNEST MENEZES: Joe played solos for background music and for songs also, through *Bobby* [1973], but in *Jis Desh Mein Ganga Behti Hai* [1960], Mr. Narvekar played the solos because that film was Indian style. Mr. Narvekar was a great musician; he played all the Indian-style solos.

As it happens, *Jis Desh Mein Ganga Bahti Hai* contains few notable violin solos; the melodic instruments that accompany the film's Indian style are largely and explicitly Indian as well. Sitar and sārangi are frequently heard in the background score and are often supported by shahnāi in appropriate scenes. Many of the song scenes are exuberant dance numbers in which percussion figures prominently.

Narvekar's Indian-style violin playing is audible in the background, however, a little more than two hours and fifteen minutes into the film, during the long, introductory scene leading to the last song, "Aa, ab laut chale." Narvekar's playing uses identifiably Indian notions of ornamentation, elaboration, vibrato, and seamless connections among pitches. In these and other films (certainly, in almost any movie of this period, the Indian solo violin playing was recorded by Narvekar) these stylistic features are distinct from the Western style favored by Joe Menezes, in which discrete pitches and unornamented or unelaborated notes are the norm.

Because violins were in high demand, musicians such as those in the Menezes family could adhere to a single side of the Western-Indian stylistic divide and still have successful careers. Most violinists made small gestures toward the Indian style in their sectional playing through token attempts at ornamentation when compelled to do so, along with everyone else. Ernest Menezes notes that violinist Peter Sequeira (of A-R-P) played in both styles.

More commonly, it was an ability or familiarity with Western styles that helped musicians find work, as Louiz Banks suggests. He compares his keyboard or piano playing to that of others on that basis:

LOUIZ BANKS: Those [piano players] who had come before were very Indian in their styles of playing. I introduced something different, a Western style with different chords, different harmonies. They enjoyed that, so I was very much in demand. Because of my jazz background, my playing was different, so they liked that.

Since the pianists "who had come before" included primarily Goan musicians (such as Robert Corea or Mike Michardo) whose early experience had been in European-style dance and jazz bands, Banks's comments may reveal a historical rather than a cultural basis for his distinction. "Indian" here may in fact mean "colonial." Banks introduced a more contemporary Western feel to keyboard playing in Mumbai.

Musicians who played relatively uncommon or hard-to-find instruments or were in need of any work they could get found they had to adopt Sunil Kaushik's "jack-of-all-trades" attitude, regardless of the difficulties it entailed. This was the case for Shankar Indorkar, whose inability to play Indian style initially imperiled his career as an oboist. Indian musicians often point to the numerous keys on wind instruments as a disadvantage in Indian-music performance. Instruments such as the Boehm-system clarinet and the saxophone, which have few if any finger holes that are not covered by keys, are commonly considered to present special challenges to the performance of Indian-style music (Booth 1997). The oboe also suffers from this "excess." Indorkar explains his notion of Indian style (which he refers to as "our" style, despite his Western instrument) in describing his attempts to perform this style on his instrument. He also differentiates between the technicalities of style as a performance practice and as a broader cultural construct:

SHANKAR INDORKAR: Western classical is one technique, but our film music is a different technique. The music is the same, but the style of playing is different. In our Indian style there are so many grace notes and such things. Every note, you can say, has some grace note. And I didn't know how to do that.

In Western music some note is there, and you go straight to the next note; it comes straight away. But in our Indian music, there is *gamak*, like the shahnāi guys play. But the oboe is hard that way. So when I went for recordings, sometimes people would say, "He doesn't play the way his father did" because I didn't understand about how to make that style, those gamaks and all those things. I talked to my father about this and how I should play and what I should practice. And I practiced a lot. My father would listen; he didn't play the oboe any more, but he would sing to me and say, "This is how it should go. Play it like this." And slowly I understood how to do these things, but it was a big problem.

The importance of the voice as the basis of all Indian music and the fundamental medium of transmission makes a late appearance here in the way that Lallu Ram taught his son to play Indian-style oboe.

Suresh Yadhav was often in charge of the wind section in the Laxmikant-Pyarelal orchestras. The two stylistic approaches and their associated performance practices made his job challenging:

> SURESH YADHAV: I had to do all the checking of the grace notes and all the notations and make sure everyone was playing correctly. That was headache work, I tell you.
>
> Ram Lal, he played shahnāi, but he was a "by-heart" player, so I had to make sure he was playing the notes correctly.
>
> The oboe players, they could read, but they had trouble playing the grace notes. Indian style is very difficult because of the grace notes. So sometimes the grace notes would come, and sometimes they wouldn't.
>
> So I would check and maybe change the grace notes or tell them to use a different fingering because the sound should be good, no? In those tutti sections, everyone must play the grace notes smoothly in the Indian style, not note-by-note like that. That way the sound will be spoiled.

"Note-by-note" and sometimes "note-to-note" are common ways that Indian musicians in general describe the Western style of melodic playing—with clear and absolute distinctions between pitches.

Conversely, musicians whose instruments were specifically Indian seem to have suffered somewhat in the 1980s, when India's fascination with Western popular music reached a peak. Although he does not mention disco by name, one of the industry's leading sitar soloists found that he had to take other measures in order to continue supporting his family.

> J. V. ACHARYA: In 1981, what happened, I was a little bit frustrated. There was no work for me. But I have to support my family. So I phoned one of my friends there in Chennai, Mr. Mani, to say I'd stop and see him, but he said, "No. Don't come like that; bring your instrument. Because here there is only one sitar player, and he's troubling us like anything." So in '81 I went. Right away I was playing three to four recordings a day.

Acharya remained in Chennai until 1988, when Lata Mangeshkar invited him back to Mumbai to rehearse for a foreign tour. It is not entirely coincidental that his absence closely mirrors the period of Bappi Lahiri's prominence and disco's appeal in Mumbai. There may well have been less work for sitārs in those years.

Just what is Western and what is Indian is not always clear and certainly not always agreed upon. As a classical Indian percussionist, Bhavani Shankar played on many film recordings, especially those that required Indian-style music and dance, and acted as rhythm arranger on a number of films as well. Although Shankar is careful not to specifically attribute Westernness to S. D. Burman's son, he suggests here that the musical differences between Burman and his son R. D. were those between Indian style and a more modern, Western approach. Shankar contends that even songs of the elder Burman that include some elements of Western music remain essentially Indian. His argument in this case appears to be based primarily on the song's rhythm track, however:

> BHAVANI SHANKAR: Burman-dada was pure Indian, total Indian, but his son was very creative person. When R. D. came in, then things changed. Sometimes when Burman-dada was sitting to compose, R. D. was not allowed in the room! Burman-dada thought he would confuse the song [i.e., confuse the style so that it sounded Western]. He would say, "I want Indian music. You stay out 'til I'm done." Even a song like "Tadbir se bigdi hui taqdeer" [*Baazi,* 1951], that's not Western, that's completely Indian in its style, that song. Even the arrangement is not Western.

The famous Burman composition to which Shankar refers features a primarily diatonic melody consisting of unornamented pitches. The introduction consists of scalar and chordal material played by Spanish (acoustic) guitarist Boney D'Costa. The main melody is largely unharmonized, however, and is accompanied only by unison strings and tabla until the final phrases, when trumpeter Frank Fernand plays a harmonic accompaniment and a basic harmonic progression is at least implied. Shankar's use of the word "even" in his identification of this song, however, emphasizes his attempt to define these elements as superficial to the song's core content and style. It may also demonstrate his response to the song's situation (an explicitly urban, lower-class bar populated by a host of drinkers in Western clothing), which might well generate some expectation of Westernized music.

Here Shankar suggests indirectly that S. D. Burman's Indianness, as he perceives it, contrasts with his son's more "creative" compositions. However, other musicians argue that even the younger Burman's music was inherently Indian and never directly copied Western music:

> FRANCO VAZ: I would never say "copy" because he took the influence, the inspiration, and used that in his work. Like, we were doing a song, which was inspired by some Western singer. But he used just that one bit of the hook. The song itself was totally different. That was his strong point. He would turn it into a very Indian product that would appeal to most Indian masses. That was his forte. It was fantastic.

Both musicians argue, in effect, that the character of a song is in the song itself (i.e., the setting of the text) and that the Western touches heard in the

music (i.e., the instrumental sections) are somehow less central to the identity of the work as a whole.

Perceptions of Indianness vary. Adding to the ambiguity, Indian musi-
cians use the term "Western" to conflate an enormous range of internal
(Western) stylistic and generic distinctions. They also use terms such as
"jazz," "disco," "Latin," "rock," and so on, however, to identify specific
Western musical styles or film songs that are understood to embody them.
Vaz also refers to specific individual songs, musicians, and bands:

> FRANCO VAZ: I listened to a lot of music whenever I had free time, like even
> when I'm traveling to work, I had my Walkman all the time on, going and
> coming. I listened to Billy Cobham, Phil Collins, a lot of Santana, a lot Stan
> Getz, a lot of pop, Whitney Houston, Mariah Carey—stuff like that.

Although he was only four years older than Vaz, guitarist Ramesh Iyer
identifies a slightly older set of sounds coming out of the United States and
Britain:

> RAMESH IYER: I listened to a lot of Nat King Cole, Elvis, Jim Reeves, Beach
> Boys, Beatles, so much of Beatles, and the Shadows and the Ventures. And
> then jazz—Wes Montgomery, John McLaughlin, Lee Ritenour—all those
> musicians.

In addition to a global stylistic opposition, Mumbai musicians sometimes identify South Asia's various cultural and linguistic regions (or even
neighbors) as centers of discrete musical styles. Kersi Lord contends that
the dynamic was by no means a simple bidirectional matter; the West was
not alone in its interactive influences on Hindi film music. The interaction
between Egyptian and Lebanese composers such as Mohamed Abdel Al-
Wahab (a Shankar-Jaikishan favorite) and the Rahbani brothers has also
been influential in Hindi film music.

Shivkumar Sharma, himself both classical and regional, explains the
polyglot nature of film music based on styles identified with some of India's
regional cultures and languages:

> SHIVKUMAR SHARMA: I think the real fusion music, the original fusion music,
> was film music. First of all, you have music directors coming from different
> places. So O. P. Nayyar brings the Panjabi influence in, or Salil Chaudhuri
> brings in Bengali influence—all these different influences.

This discussion demonstrates that composers were not the only contributors to or determiners of stylistic trends. Nevertheless, together with film
directors and producers, music directors had the greatest control in this
area. These individuals were responsible for the stylistic context in which
the musicians operated. It is clear, however, that many musicians, although

they were usually not formally recognized as contributors, played important roles in stylistic development in film songs.

Musicians and the Creation and Performance of Style

In individual songs, musicians' personal musical interests or professional musical experience sometimes allowed them to act as crucial intermediaries in the creation of the fusion that Shivkumar Sharma refers to. Their ability to do so derived directly from their specialist knowledge of and experience in a particular style or set of styles. This appears to have been consistently true for Indian classical music but only periodically so with regard to those whose special skills lay in Western popular music.

Indian Classical and Folk Musics

Classical music found its way directly and naturally into the Hindi cinema, as sitārist Ustad Halim Jaffar Khan explains:

> HALIM JAFFAR KHAN: The classical music directors were Pankaj Malik, R. C. Boral, and Ustad Jhande Khan. Actually, classical music came into the films naturally. Before, there was classical music in the natak companies [the Marathi music drama troupes].

The two factors that effectively define the presence of classical music for most Indian musicians are the use of identifiable rāgas (most frequently north Indian) and/or distinctively classical instruments. There is a flourishing fan fascination with film songs that use rāga materials (see, for example, "Songs Based on Ragas" at http://www.downmelodylane.com). This discourse extends to musicians as well. Halim Jaffar Khan lists the various rāgas used by different composers as the basis of various film songs:

> HALIM JAFFAR KHAN: Madhan Mohan, he introduced Maru Bihag into films. Then in *Baiju Bawra* [1952], there was Malkauns, Pilu, Bhairo, and others also. But going very far back, in the film *Chitralekha* [1941], Jhande Khan-saheb introduced Bhairavi and also Asavari. This was a very influential film for all the later films.

Like other classical soloists, Halim Jaffar Khan did more than play music composed by others. In background scenes and sometimes for solos in songs, he composed his own music:

> HALIM JAFFAR KHAN: They would say to me, "This is the *bandish,* this is the situation, so from here you just arrange something for five seconds or ten seconds." Then I had to see if there was *komal ga* [flat third scale degree]

or what have you, what was the rāg, you can say, and then I would compose something that would go smoothly without disturbing the main melody. After some time I became famous for sitār; I had a name.

Classical musicians quite often created the solo music they played for background scenes. They frequently consulted with the music directors to get a sense of what was wanted but then based their music on their response to the scene in question. In his explanation of this creative process, sitārist Kartik Kumar refers to the aesthetic theory of *rasa*, which originally established the connection between music and emotional response in the context of classical theater (cf. Rowell 1992):

> KARTIK KUMAR: When I was making background music, you know those *nava rasas* [nine moods/emotions] . . . the music director says, "Kartik-ji, this scene you play with sitār." So after I've seen [the scene], [the heroine is] crying and crying and only very soft dialogue. So the question is, what music should I play for this? I should play something that gives *karuna rasa* [the emotional response of pathos].

Kumar's question is the same one that all background composers and soloists asked themselves in that situation. He frames his answer in terms of classical aesthetic theory, but oddly, his solution is not based on mode (as *rasa* theory is) but on performance practice (the use of alāp):

> KARTIK KUMAR: Karuna rasa we call it. That means I have to play something that is ālāp without rhythm. That will give the right feeling.

Despite this focus on practice, Kumar here argues for the reconnection between dramatic representation, mood, and music, elements that have long been problematic in North Indian classical music discourse.

Like classical music, folk music is aligned with scenes that specifically require Indianness. Vijay Chauhan established a reputation for specialist instrumental skills in Marathi- and Indian-style folk percussion:

> VIJAY CHAUHAN: People call me when they want folk music and maybe rhythm—if they want special rhythm playing or some folk drums or rural sounds. But that is God's gift for me. Fortunately, I established my name on my playing.

Indian classical or folk instruments, the sitars and shahnāis, tend to act as markers, in many cases, of Indian culture. Nevertheless, speaking of music directors Kalyanji-Anandji, tabla player Sharafat Khan argues that the pair also used tabla in Western music, thereby ignoring the traditional associations.

Indian classical traditions and the needs of the film industry were not always easily aligned. Music director Anil Biswas argued that rather strict rules of the classical traditions could be only loosely approached in the film line:

> ANIL BISWAS: I never learned classical music. I didn't want to because I didn't want to have to be concerned with all those rāga rules. I wanted to be free. But I promised myself that I will not do anything that will belittle the Indianism of the music.

Sārangi master Ustad Sultan Khan, who worked as a soloist on many film scores, echoes Biswas's comments:

> SULTAN KHAN: Playing for films I feel is very free. I don't really have to think what is the rāg, how should I approach this note, how can I treat that note, any of those things. I can use the rāg, but I can treat it very freely. Not like classical music.

In his typically assertive way, Anthony Gonsalves offers a detailed description of the difficulties that could arise when the classical rules—as embodied in the person of a dance director whose training was in the classical rhythms, dancing, and drumming of south India—clashed with the pragmatics of film-music composition and production and an orchestra and an arranger who were primarily Western-trained Goans:

> ANTHONY GONSALVES: We were recording some song, and the dance master was a *mridangam* [south Indian barrel drum] player. And [actress] Vyjayanthimala was dancing in that song. Shankar-Jaikishan had written the music, and Lata-ji was singing. But you may know what the dancers and the rhythms are like in Madras; they are very strict but very difficult. When Sebastian wrote [notated] the music, it came out with many different rhythms in it, a bar of seven, a bar of six, a bar of eight, like that. And we would play it, and the dance master would go "Drrrrrrrrrrp" [imitates the drum/rhythm language of south India, called *solukatu*], and then the music would not come [the various musicians would not end together at the right point], and he would say, "No, no!" And we would try again, and again he would go "Drrrrrrrrrrp." It was not coming at all.

Like all classical Indian systems, south Indian rhythms are based on cyclical patterns (tāla) in which subdivision and phrase length can and do change quite frequently (see, for example, Clayton 2000). Sebastian seems to have approached every phrase as if it were a differently metered measure (or bar), ignoring the longer cyclical structure that tied the entire composition together. The difference in rhythmic thinking and the orchestra musicians' unfamiliarity with the challenges of south Indian rhythmic composition precluded what would have been a challenging musical task in any event.

Gonsalves relates here how he finally solved this dilemma. Ironically, not only did he ignore the Indian cyclical structure as Sebastian had done but he also assumed that the task, as set out, was beyond the group's collective abilities. He catered to his orchestra colleagues' habits and provided a straightforward rhythmic structure that they could play accurately, demanding, in effect, that the Indian drummer use his more flexible rhythmic and improvisational skills to simply accommodate himself to whatever the orchestra played:

> ANTHONY GONSALVES: Then Lata-bai came and sat next to me and said to me, "Why don't you help them?" So I went to the dance master and said, "Why don't you play one time?" I wrote all the music in duple rhythm, and then I told the dance master to play with the orchestra. Something had been written, you see, but it was very wrong and had many different rhythms and meters in it. So I just wrote it all out simply in two-four meter. And I told the dance master that he should adjust himself according to how the orchestra was playing. And then it all came very well.

One wonders, of course, whether the dance master would offer quite the same assessment of this cultural interaction (as one might describe it).

Film music was fusion in almost all respects, however one interprets that term, but it is clear that many songs came with intentional stylistic markers and that at least some had an accompanying ideological content, as when Naushad Ali intentionally structured films and scores around Indian classical music. Musicians such as Gonsalves (as well as Halim Jaffar Khan) assert that classical musicians, whom Naushad engaged for specialist playback vocal roles in some of his classically oriented songs, contributed core melodic content to many of those songs. Those musicians, however, such as Ustad Bade Ghulam Ali Khan (heard in some of the songs of *Mughal-e-Azam*, 1960), were located primarily outside the film world.

Among musicians in the film line, classical training was not uncommon (e.g., Zarin Sharma, Kishore Desai, Kartik Kumar). Perhaps more common, however, were backgrounds in Western popular music. Such musicians were often sought out for that expertise, however acquired; they contributed stylistic features to individual songs and film scores as a result of their experience and knowledge.

Western Popular Styles

Some film composers, such as Naushad Ali, S. D. Burman, and Sajjad Hussain, came to the film business with training in Indian classical music. Western popular styles, on the other hand, are those with which Indian film composers have historically had the least experience and, concomitantly, those to which musicians have often contributed most significantly. Most film musicians trace the prominent appearance of Western pop music, that is to say, dance band music, to the impact of composer C. Ramchandra in the late 1940s.

Francis Vaz was a drummer in Mumbai's best-known dance band, led by trumpeter Chic Chocolate. Francis's son explains the relationship:

> FRANCO VAZ: People used to come and listen to the bands, like if they were playing at Greens or the International Cricket Club of India. And the music directors used to come there to listen to the bands to get ideas, to get inspiration and all that. And that's where they met Chic Chocolate and Johnny Gomes and Mike Marchado and my dad. And to make that crossover, they called them over to work with them. They said, "Why don't you come and listen to my song? I have a rock 'n' roll song, and I don't know which way it goes. Please come and arrange it for me."

Vaz was too young to have worked with C. Ramchandra early in his career, but he notes that the composer's interest in Western pop had not diminished even in the 1970s:

> FRANCO VAZ: When I was working for C. Ramchandra, I was seventeen or eighteen. Whenever he knew that I didn't have college or whatever, he would call up and come over to the house. "What is your kind of music? Play me something that you like," that kind of thing. I was into the Hollies at that time. He used to sit and listen to that Hollies tape until it was worn out.

The Antonio Vaz–C. Ramchandra collaboration was an extremely early instance of the incorporation of Western dance band music into film scores, but a much more influential and long-lasting collaboration began at roughly the same time between another Goan arranger, Sebastian D'Souza, and the music-director duo Shankar-Jaikishan. It was not just D'Souza's arranging skills as such that the composers valued; it was his experience in contemporary popular dance music.

Musicians with training in Western theory and experience in Western popular styles were crucial intermediaries in the incorporation of Western popular music into films. Mumbai's music directors were sometimes inspired by the musical content of foreign recordings or films, but again it was often the musicians who made the adaptation possible. Further, C. Ramchandra was not the only composer who spent his leisure time in places where he could encounter Western pop:

> JOE MONSORATE: Jaikishan liked that kind of music [Western jazz and pop]. He had a particular restaurant that he would go to all the time, Gaylord's at Churchgate. He had a table reserved for him only. And he would hear

the latest tunes, like "Come September" and all those things. He knew all the latest songs.

Ironically, perhaps, Indian composers also gradually engaged with Hollywood's emphasis on the orchestral background score as presented in foreign films. Many musicians paid great attention to showings of foreign films, especially the background scores, as composer and arranger Anthony Gonsalves has recalled.

The Regal Cinema in downtown Mumbai showed only foreign films throughout much of the twentieth century. Dattaram Waadkar, who also worked as a composer and music director in his own right, spoke very little English, but he watched foreign films as part of his own education:

> DATTARAM WAADKAR: I studied foreign pictures very much. I didn't understand the words, but I listened very carefully to the music. I saw many, many pictures. Sometimes I would go five times to see the film, just to hear the music.

Although C. Ramchandra's scores may represent the first incorporation of foreign popular music into film music, many other musicians perpetuated and developed that early interest:

> HOMI MULLAN: I used to buy all the long-playing records and listen to what were the new Latin instruments and the new rhythms and all those things. It was not that easy to get those. But I used to go with Mr. Bhupinder Singh to Bombay side. One store was there. He used to keep [the new LPs] completely for us. Whenever we used to go there, he would have something.

The owners of Furtado's and other Goan-owned music shops in or near Dhobi Talao (one of the original Goan neighborhoods of Mumbai) were thus also involved in the transmission of Western music.

Music directors R. D. Burman and Bappi Lahiri had the widest general public association with Western popular music in late Old Bollywood. Although Burman was not the first to engage successfully with rock 'n' roll, his impact was perhaps greater than that of his predecessors:

> KERSI LORD: No one has come close to making such an impact. In my time, the college crowd was never interested in film music. Mr. R. D. Burman brought the college crowd and got them interested in Indian films and film music. Before, Indian film music was for the parents, not their children. There was nothing going on, [just] tabla and dholak, nothing Western, nothing. He made it popular for them; he made something they can dance to.

Burman is still idolized by many film fans for his incorporation of Western popular styles (see, for example, http://www.panchamonline.com or the still more comprehensive http://www.panchammagic.org, two of the more complete websites venerating the composer and his music). However, his role as a mediator of new Western styles for the Indian audience involved the services of Indian musicians who participated directly in that process. Like C. Ramchandra before him, Burman recruited musicians who had learned how to produce that style or were able to engage in a more technical manner with a particular style's musical elements:

> RAMESH IYER: Pancham always was listening to new things. He was more into Latin than anything else. I remember we were making *Rocky* [1981], and he said to me, "I have a new CD. You have to hear it. Come quick!" So we went out to his car; he had a CD player, or maybe it was tape. And he played me Sergio Mendes, which was really great. And he said to me, "You must make a song like this." So we did.

With his technical skills in notation and guitar performance, as well as his familiarity with and enthusiasm for popular music, Iyer is thus another musician who aided in the translation of Western pop in Hindi film song.

Louiz Banks, who defines himself as a Western-style pianist, also worked with both R. D. Burman and Bappi Lahiri, mostly in the 1980s:

> LOUIZ BANKS: R. D. Burman, especially, was such a music director, a visionary, very open minded, very willing to experiment, willing try new stuff all the time. So I fit in nicely in that groove. And Bappi made his name on Western music; I was very much part of that with him. At that time, Western music really flourished in India.

As a percussionist and rhythm programmer, Taufiq Qureshi made the transition to the realities of New Bollywood, some of which he found difficult to accept. Although the fundamentals of the process are no different from those described by Ramesh Iyer, Qureshi implies that the lessened interpersonal and creative aspects of the new process were enough to force him to reevaluate his position:

> TAUFIQ QURESHI: I've gone to sessions where the music director has given me a CD or something and said, "See that guitar part? I want that. You program that." Or maybe it would be the rhythm. And I don't want to do that.

Louiz Banks also acknowledges that the use of Western musical styles has been part of the creative process in Mumbai since the late 1940s, but as Qureshi also implies, the need to physically re-create those Western styles that characterized the process in Old Bollywood has been replaced in the contemporary digital world by direct replication:

> LOUIZ BANKS: They're aping the West like anything and blatantly copying stuff. We're doing that all the time; it's not a new phenomenon. From the

days of Shankar-Jaikishan or C. Ramchandra they copied also. But with sampling it has become so easy to replicate; you can just lift sounds, insert the real thing into a composition, and nobody knows the difference. Digital technology has changed a lot, some for the better, some for the worse.

The comments of both Banks and Qureshi suggest some level of dissatisfaction with the musical aspects of the processes in which they were engaged. Interpersonal issues aside, musicians in the film line have had a range of responses to the music they have recorded. The final section of this chapter returns to the issues of ideology, meaning, and genre, with which the chapter began.

Valuing Hindi Film Music: Musicians' Perspectives

Indian film music "does not emerge from an extensive base of amateur and professional live performance," argues Manuel. "The ability of a musician to make any sort of oppositional statement is thus practically nil, since his or her own contribution is so deeply imbedded in a capitalist production network" (1993, 49). Even more fundamental than the ability to make oppositional statements is musicians' ability to make musical, creative, or personal emotional statements—to find value in the music they are playing. Since financial rewards are not always readily forthcoming in musical professions, personal satisfaction is often the primary compensation. In this respect Manuel is correct to suggest that Hindi film song could be interpreted as missing something in comparison to Western popular music. Although remuneration was often forthcoming, especially during Old Bollywood, musicians' statements about personal, professional, and musical satisfaction are quite variable.

Before considering some of this variation, I note one area of the musical life of the film line from which almost everyone has drawn considerable satisfaction: the quality of the musicianship, the standard of the performances, and the perception of recordings well played:

> SHIVKUMAR SHARMA: What great music it was! There were some very great musicians. And [the music was] very hard also. In classical music, you are free, but in films, everybody had to fit in with each other. I think those orchestras were as good as anything in the West. All those different instruments and Indian and Western—everything. And all playing together, straight through. You couldn't stop or make a mistake.

Interestingly, Sharma takes almost exactly the opposite position from that expressed earlier by Sultan Khan-saheb, who experienced a sense of freedom in film music's weakened rules regarding rāga.

Despite this almost universal satisfaction with what was undoubtedly excellent ensemble playing, not all of the musicians felt this was enough:

> TAUFIQ QURESHI: Lots of good musicians have stagnated in the film industry. They're such good musicians, but they're playing "tak——dun dun—" [i.e., simple rhythmic patterns]. They say it takes discipline to play that. Okay, but what kind of discipline? As a musician you're stagnating. There were percussionists when I joined the line who were playing such great stuff, but ten years later they're still where they were.

Qureshi has been fortunate enough to establish a viable alternative career as a percussionist and so perhaps is in a position to more easily express sentiments that others may share. No doubt the threat of musical or creative stagnation could well be common in many commercial music industries.

Kersi Lord makes a distinction between skills learned in other musical contexts and applied to film music and those learned in the film line itself:

> KERSI LORD: You can't learn from this music. From other types of music, if it's jazz or classical music, you can learn very much. But from film music, you don't really learn. The younger musicians only played in the film line itself. They joined for that only. They don't understand very much about music.

Perhaps the highest levels of satisfaction (and variance) are demonstrated by the musicians who worked closely with R. D. Burman, a music director who considered his musicians' opinions and gave them credit (at least verbally) when he took their advice. While other music directors no doubt had similar attitudes, Burman's behavior and general enthusiasm for the job were exceptional, as drummer Franco Vaz makes clear:

> FRANCO VAZ: The moment he sang the song to you, you would be involved. You would be inspired to give it your own 100 percent. He'd sing it to you, and maybe he's dancing along to it. But everybody was inspired, so when we'd come to the final take, everyone would give it that 101 percent. And he used to come out of the control room screaming, "Yeah, fantastic! We've done it! We've killed it!"

Burman's openness to suggestions and sense of musical adventure offered this group of musicians an opportunity to develop a sense of both enjoyment and satisfaction that was not always easy for other musicians to maintain. This is reflected in the words Deepan Chatterji, Burman's recording assistant:

> DEEPAN CHATTERJI: The whole thing was great fun; we enjoyed whatever we did. What I've heard about other music directors is that the moment they

entered the studio, there was absolute silence. But it was the exact opposite with Pancham-da; the moment he entered, everything lit up.

Manohari Singh also clearly valued both the atmosphere in the Burman sitting room and the quality and quantity of the music this workshop produced. [⬤ Video 8.2]

The experiences and attitudes toward their work of most of those in R. D. Burman's workshop contrast significantly with those of older men (many of whom also played with Burman from time to time) who came to the film line from other musical professions. This is most true of those musicians, mostly Goan, whose musical lives began in the dance and jazz band trade. Here it is difficult to find musicians making statements such as those that immediately precede this section or that focus on stylistic prestige, authenticity, and value or on musical lineage, such as the jazz musicians that Gitler (1985) identifies or the heavy-metal musicians that Walser (1993) mentions.

Live performance was a part of many film musicians' backgrounds, especially throughout the 1960s and even into the 1970s in some cases. However, many younger musicians who had live-performance experience (such as Ramesh Iyer) acquired it while playing film music on stage. In contrast, older musicians' performance careers began in specific nonfilm genres, especially jazz, as well as Indian and European classical musics. All of those styles contributed to film music's stylistic repertoire, but film music's consistent stylistic diversity and its volatility in the face of situational exigencies presented many obstacles to these musicians' attempts to realign (or maintain) any sense of stylistic loyalty.

Saxophonist Joe Gomes makes this clear with regard both to the Western dance band music he played until Indian independence in 1947, with which he still clearly identifies, and to film music, which he came to as a profession:

> JOE GOMES: When the Britishers left, Western music was gone also because that was a British thing. I used to love to play my Western music, but we had to come here [Mumbai] for the film industry because of the money. I had a wife and son.

Gomes and his brother Johnny, as well as many of their dance band colleagues, made significant creative contributions to Mumbai's style of film music, but he had joined a profession in which musicians could not afford to become attached to a single musical style. As guitarist Sunil Kaushik argues at the beginning of this chapter, a high degree of professional neutrality in matters of style had to override personal preference. Film music had an ideological structure and content that were completely different from the popular dance music to which Gomes was attached. Film music was by no means connected ideologically to the country's political and cultural elite (at least not in the 1950s).

As most Goan musicians understood or experienced notions of genre, an even more fundamental problem existed. From their perspective, film song simply had no genre identity at all. Cellist John Gonsalves had an extensive career playing classical and light classical music in trios, quartets, and other small ensembles for hotels and private events; he also played in many film orchestras. At one point in my conversation with him, I asked whether he would consider himself a classical musician or a film musician:

> JOHN GONSALVES: I've never thought that there is film music because I knew the orchestras, this classical music. And I learned from Mr. Verga, this classical music. And film musician is one kind of thing, but even then I was not thinking that I would get a lot of work in the films. I only really knew about classical music. Then when Anthony [Gonsalves, his cousin] took me for some recording with [music director] N. Datta, I sort of realized that this was films. But I only knew music. I hadn't thought about the differences.

Like most of those with whom he worked, Joe Pereira was clear about his motivation for joining movies. Like Gonsalves, he asserts in effect that film music had no clear generic identity. As a jazz musician, he did not find its eclectic, almost nonideological nature appealing:

> JOE PEREIRA: I didn't like the film music. I just did it for the money. Film music was just a copy of Western music but all mixed up. It wasn't Indian music; it wasn't jazz.

The attitudes expressed here by Gomes, Pereira, and Gonsalves are typical of many individuals who had personal or community investments in the ideologies of Western classical music or jazz. Film music used elements of these, as well as Indian, styles. However, the mixture, the Hindi language, and the film orientation meant that, for some musicians who were working hard to establish or maintain their careers in any of the "parent" styles, the aesthetics and the ideology of Hindi film music did not translate. Like many others confronting a weakened market for Western music, Maoro Alfonso began playing for films just after Indian independence. For him, the business was lacking in the respect to which he had become accustomed in the classical or hotel music world. It was, as he describes it, a matter of "you play, take your money, and go."

Unlike some of his elders, Franco Vaz took great pleasure in the music he was playing with R. D. Burman and in the quality of the group's performances in the recording studio. In spite of that, however, Vaz was not a fan of Hindi films or their culture:

FRANCO VAZ: I may have watched one or two Hindi films, just the movies that I have done or something, because it's all the same thing. Some people come and ask me, "This song you have played for R. D. Burman, which film was it from?" I can't tell them.

Like the other Goan musicians here, violinist Joe Pinto paid little attention to the music he was playing for the Hindi cinema. It was only when the film-music industry was collapsing around him that Pinto and his family left India to try his luck in another country and a different profession. There he found that the music he had been playing (but largely ignoring) made him a minor celebrity. Speaking from his new "homeland," Pinto reflects on the cultural irony of his former career:

JOE PINTO: I never used to watch the movies. [But] when you come here, and you mention that you were in the film industry, the Indians go crazy about it. "Oh, did you play in this one? Did you play in that one?" I can never tell them because I don't know. And they don't believe it. They either think you're just lying about the whole thing or that you're playing it down. So I have to ask, "Who was the music director? Was it around this time?" And then I know if I was playing then because if I was playing for that guy at that time, then sure, I'm on that movie. But you know, that culture was not our culture. I have probably heard more Hindi film songs here [outside of India] than I ever heard in India.

Like many immigrants all over the world, Pinto has learned the adaptive strategies necessary to integrate his identity and experience in his old home with the interests and understandings of those in his new home.

Nostalgia

Earlier I referred to nostalgia and its importance in this history. It may be clear by this point why musicians would in fact be nostalgic for the social, musical, and financial pleasures of past. Viju Shah, a keyboardist, composer, and programmer who began working in the 1970s, says with the clarity of hindsight, "I have seen the transition." Shah is clearly his father's son in this since his father, Kalyanji Veerji Shah, is widely identified as the person who introduced electronic keyboards to the film industry:

VIJU SHAH: I could see then that in the future it would be electronics taking over the market. This was my vision. There would be a time when one person would be doing the whole film by himself. And I was right. That is what has happened.

Shah's justifiable pride in his sense of foresight and his family's role in changing the nature of Mumbai film music is tempered, however, by a sense of what those changes have meant for many of his colleagues.

> VIJU SHAH: Of course, it's a sad state for our musician brothers because suddenly they have been sidelined. All the big studios have been shut down; they have all these small studios and people working in a garage or what have you.

Although many of the younger men, like Shah, have made a successful professional transition to the economic and technological practices of New Bollywood, many remain nostalgic for Old Bollywood:

> FRANCO VAZ: Most of the time when I pray, I thank God for involving me in those times and for giving me the opportunity to work with all those great music directors. They were fantastic. I can't believe I have gone through that. Even when musicians used to meet at that time—in the morning—it used to be like a big family; we'd meet, sit in the canteen. It was so friendly.

Annibal Castro is still more explicitly negative:

> ANNIBAL CASTRO: There's no pleasure left in film music. You go in a small room and put on headphones and play. It's not fun. Now we call them "toilet studios" because they are so small.

Sadly, "no fun," "no pleasure," and "no life" are common responses to New Bollywood. Like many of their contemporaries, Sunil Kaushik and Tappan Adhikhari suggest that what they experienced in Old Bollywood was "life." For both men in the new world, there is no life:

> TAPPAN ADHIKHARI: We were all together, and we had fun. It was life. We'd get the tempo just right, and we'd rehearse together, and we'd hear the whole song. Now it's no fun; now we don't meet. You don't see friends for six months. What to do? Play four bars, take your payment. It's a mechanical life.

Indeed, in my work in Mumbai, I found that I had often had more recent contact with many musicians than they had had with each other. It was a common experience for musicians to ask me for the telephone numbers of friends and colleagues with whom they had lost touch. Sunil Kaushik uses almost the same words as Adhikhari:

> SUNIL KAUSHIK: There used to be full orchestra, and everybody would sit together, and it would be life. But now, no more life. It's like somebody's doing his part and going to the studio and playing some part, like that. So, how we used to meet everyday, that is no more.

Kaushik and Adhikhari both realize, however, that even if there is no "life," life must go on. Like many others, Kaushik resigns himself to the changing times:

SUNIL KAUSHIK: But anyway, you have to change according to the times. If
you sit and say, "Oh, what great times those were! Now we have nothing,"
then you will sit at home. So you have to move with the time.

Although Homi Mullan argues that no one can be blamed for the current situation, he is ultimately reduced almost to speechless despair by the
disappearance of "the life":

HOMI MULLAN: What I have played! Now the memory is there only. I see the
old films and hear what I have played, and what can I say? What's the use
of saying anything?

At the close of the first decade of the twenty-first century, whether they
miss the income, the music, or the social life, most Mumbai film musicians
are indeed nostalgic for the past.

Conclusion

Oral History, Change, and Accounts of Human Agency

As part of the research for this volume, I arranged to record some of the musicians' interviews on videotape. Among those filmed was Jerry Fernandes, who, at the end of the session graciously agreed to play his violin for me and my colleagues, who had been recording him with camera and tape recorder. Jerry-saheb (as some in the film line refer to him) played a light classical waltz from his childhood, as well as his favorite jazz tune, George Gershwin's "Lady Be Good," which he had originally learned by listening to a recorded performance by Stéphane Grappelli. He also played the violin solo from the film song "Ek pyaar ka naghma hai," which he had originally recorded as part of the Laxmikant-Pyarelal score for *Shor* (1972). For my colleague, Avijit Mukul Kishore, who had been filming the session, Fernandes's performance of this film song transformed the routine work of filming into a more memorable event. Recalling the session later, Kishore explained that "Ek pyaar ka naghma hai" had been his favorite song when he was a boy:

AVIJIT MUKUL KISHORE: "Ek pyaar ka naghma hai" and its opening refrain on the violin had been my childhood favorite. I remember that although we never possessed a record of *Shor*, it played often enough on the radio; the opening bars on the violin, simple and beautiful, are etched in my memory forever. It was overwhelming when Jerry Fernandes broke into that song. This was the man behind that tune from my childhood. I will never forget that experience.

284

The musicians of Mumbai's film industry were responsible for an enormous number of different childhood (and adulthood) favorites. Their impact and their anonymity, both so clearly demonstrated in this incident, were equally systemic: Their music was, for many decades, India's only widely available popular music, but the faces and names attached to their songs were those of actors, playback singers, and music directors (probably in that order). Most of those who listen to film songs or watch Hindi films have indeed given little thought to the musicians who played the songs, but even if they have, it would have taken enormous effort (and probably a trip to or a contact in Mumbai) to actually put names, let alone faces, to the melodies, as had fortuitously happened that day in Goa. For Avijit, the experience had allowed him to look behind the curtain that continues to separate film musicians from the Indian public. Anecdotal as it is, incidents of this kind justify the importance of this examination of the production of Hindi cinema music to provide a forum for the descriptions and perceptions of the musicians who participated in that production in a range of ways. As an oral history, however, the descriptive content of the preceding chapters presents a unique historical perspective on the matter of human agency in cultural and industrial change.

At the beginning of this book I stated that an oral history could be a difficult historiographic form. In addition to the concerns I set out there, it is clear that an oral history cannot, in one sense, offer a balanced or comprehensive account of its object. The musicians whose voices are in the majority in this account had a specific view of the production of Hindi film songs and an equally specific set of concerns about that process. Some diversity of viewpoint is present here through my inclusion of a small number of music directors, engineers, and others, but it is the musicians who have also defined the shape of this account. Consequently, this book is only one version of film music's history.

As Morcom's (2007) recent research demonstrates and as earlier research implies, that same story, if told by the music directors and film producers, would demonstrate levels of difference ranging from trivial to culturally significant. The same could be said about a narrative of film music generated by engineers, playback singers, or lyricists. Similarly, the description of the music's production varies considerably from that of its reception, as some of the comments in chapter 8 demonstrate. In a field as complex as Hindi films and film music, multiple perspectives are essential. The approach I have chosen nevertheless offers a valid, fundamentally ethnographic account of the socioprofessional and technological creation of Mumbai's film music.

I have focused on musicians' comments on the technological and industrial conditions under which they were working, as well as their economic and structural relationships with film producers and music directors. In addition, some musicians have enunciated a specific place or role for themselves within the industry. A few have been concerned with the place of film music in their own cultural lives and in the culture of India more generally. Accounts that emphasize the industry's exploitation of studio musicians are quite common, but many also argue that the pay was good and work plentiful in many periods of the industry's existence. Almost everyone I have spoken with has expressed some sense of the film line in historical terms.

A sense of history means a sense of change and separation from the past. This volume proposes two major transformations in the Mumbai film and film-music industry: from the studio period to Old Bollywood and from Old to New Bollywood. Both entail a feeling of separation, but in these accounts they appear as very different kinds of transitions.

The end of the studio period was marked by many structural changes in the Mumbai film industry, which achieved its synonymous status with the Hindi film industry only after World War II, Indian independence, and the collapse of its rivals in Lahore and Kolkata. As film musicians experienced it, the studio period lasted a mere twenty years, less than half the length of the remarkable era that followed. There were, no doubt, musicians whose careers were spent working on salary in a studio, but none of those individuals is with us today. Cawas Lord, who joined the line around 1931, at the very beginning of the sound era, would nevertheless go on to spend much more of his life working as a freelancer in Old Bollywood. In an oral history, at least the studio period and its demise must necessarily be painted in broader strokes than later events.

Consequently, in this work, the transition to Old Bollywood appears systemic, driven by large-scale cultural factors unrelated to music. Many of the actual musical changes (such as the new dominance of the Lata-Rafi generation of playback singers or of a more intentionally syncretic group of music directors) that took place more or less simultaneously were parallel rather than interactive. The appearance of actual recording studios, other gradual technological changes, and the economic and human flexibility of the freelance system all seem to have supported the greater demand for films and music, but in terms of the song-production process (salaries for musicians aside), very little changed as Old Bollywood took shape.

The historical transition from the studio period to Old Bollywood was experienced by musicians primarily in terms of the transition from salaried work to freelancing. This period may have been traumatic (musicians have described the gradual disappearance of their salaries even as they continued to report for work every day), but changeovers often are. None of those who lived through that time portray the results negatively. Because of their perspectives and because of the ages of the musicians now living, Old Bollywood, especially after CMA came into existence in 1952, appears as "normal." Musicians who were connected to the dance-band trade experienced the decline in the demand for that music, but the growing size of the orchestras in the 1950s, the increasing importance of (and demand for) the music they were recording, and the improving employment conditions (again, after 1952) must have had some compensating effect even for those who felt the way Joe Gomes did ("I used to love to play my Western music").

However challenging the transition to Old Bollywood may have been for film musicians, its demise was (and continues to be) more distressing. For these musicians, however, even for those too young to have lived through it, the earlier shift was experienced as the beginning of normality, while that to New Bollywood has for most represented the end of "the golden time." In oral histories, endings appear more personal and more important—but perhaps less natural—than beginnings.

What is more, unlike the earlier set of changes and because of the changes in music technology, the growth of New Bollywood has had more serious implications for music production and recording processes and for musical content. When they specify the differences between Old and New Bollywood, musicians point specifically to technological advances in sound recording for film (e.g., the track system, punching, synthesizers, programming) and the economic modifications that were, to a great extent, made possible by those technological innovations (e.g., lump sum contracts with music directors, the inability of CMA to enforce its rates). In this instance, the digital technologies that affected the musicians and the music-production process were equally and simultaneously affecting other parts of film production and reception. In contrast, no major technological modernization accompanied (let alone drove) the demise of Mumbai's producing studios in the late 1940s.

Technological progress, although affected by governmental changes that simply made new technology more available, produced radical alterations in the ways that music was recorded in the late 1990s. Despite arguments to the contrary (especially in Arnold 1991), there were no comparable developments at the beginnings of Old Bollywood. Although economics and governmental regulations played a role in both periods, the specific mix of factors that determined the course of those transitions was distinct in each case.

As a result of the transformations that began in the mid-1990s and their impact on film-music production, most of the musicians in this volume see themselves as speaking from the other side of an irreparable, systemic divide. Violinist Francis D'Costa is here recalling a prediction made by trumpeter, arranger, and composer Frank Fernand, who worked with many of Mumbai's music directors. D'Costa's comments illustrate this sense of permanent historical change:

> FRANCIS D'COSTA: You know, Frank Fernand said it thirty years back. He told us, "The time will come when everybody will have to put headphones on and play. Studios will become very small; musicians will become very few; nobody will meet each other." And we all said, "What are you saying?" At that time [the late 1970s], it seemed impossible. We couldn't believe it.

In the 1970s, with film production up to 120 or more films a year, D'Costa and his colleagues might be forgiven for their skepticism. The plentiful work and a system that had, at that point, been in place for at least twenty years made it difficult *not* to believe that Old Bollywood would last forever. Even the beginnings of the technological and industrial changes that I encapsulate under the label "New Bollywood" were more than ten years away. As Blacking (1990) has so accurately noted, however, it is musical continuity rather than change that should be understood as remarkable. Eventually, innovations did take place in Old Bollywood. A few (like Fernand) saw them coming, but many perceived little difference in their day-to-day professional existence. For every Joe Pinto who noted, "Even by 1993 we could see it going," there appear to have been two or three Joe Monsorates: "We never thought this kind of change would come."

They all may not have seen fundamental transformation coming, but from the other side of it, most musicians agree about what actually happened and when. Accounts of the 1990s are offered here. Musicians' understandings of causality, however—matters such as why things altered or who was responsible—are more varied and deserve brief attention by way of conclusion.

For certain musicians, change appears to be simply a part of the system or (without being too philosophical about it) simply part of life. They do not attribute agency to any individual or even any particular group. It is not people who become different; it is time itself:

> BHAVANI SHANKAR: What happened, the times changed. No one has any time any more. Musicians, singers, producers, music directors—no one has any time.

For Shankar, everyone in the industry, from the paymasters on down, is a victim of changing times. Homi Mullan specifically argues that "you can't blame anyone" for change.

Other musicians attribute historical agency to humans and to members of their own profession, although at various levels and with differing attitudes toward the quality of that agency. A number of the Laxmikant-Pyarelal regulars implicitly depict Pyarelal-ji as heroically holding back the tide of musical change in the early 1990s. Shankar Indorkar is one such musician. He thus implies that the power for change was located in the hands of key music directors who managed the process or employed technology in particular ways. In addition to Pyarelal, Indorkar suggests that at least one other music director, A. R. Rahman, had the power to modify the industry significantly:

SHANKAR INDORKAR: He's the one who changed [the sound and the production process of film music] because if you see *Roja* [1993], there's hardly any acoustic instrument and hardly any Indian instrument also. And that was his first picture.

Indorkar's personal experience of Rahman's approach to technology and music may lead him to emphasize the power that this particular composer was able to exert in the production of musical/historical change. His perceptions are nevertheless valuable:

SHANKAR INDORKAR: I got called to Madras to his studio. In his studio there were so many keyboards, [it was as if] every keyboard that ever came to India, it ended up in his studio. Like, you know that claviolin that Kalyanji-Anandji used? I used to see that in their music room a long time ago. From that instrument to the latest instrument, he had everything. He was a keyboard director.

Indorkar's colorful imagery carries the usual element of truth. Rahman's music can, at the very least, be said to embody a culmination of the incremental changes that began with Kalyanji's claviolin solo in 1954 (especially since that instrument was used to synthesize a sound that was understood to be specifically Indian and has come to *be* specifically Indian).

Still other musicians are more critical of their own individual roles in the process. As Annibal Castro says of himself and his colleagues, "We were responsible for the downfall of Indian music." Like Kersi Lord and others, Castro sees decisions made by Mumbai's musicians as contributing to the collapse of the system that had supported them and that had produced "Indian music," by which Castro means film music (this is in itself an interesting characterization). In his conclusion, Castro, like Lord, appears to have realized the extent of the impact of his actions only after the fact. Nevertheless, they see themselves and other musicians as acting rather than as acted upon, empowered at least to influence the rate and direction of musical change in Mumbai's film music.

From this oral history, then, emerge three or more views of the role of human agency in musical or cultural change. Bhavani Shankar and Homi

Mullan are among those whom Sahlins (2004, 142) might call "leviatha-
nologists": The system (the times) changed, and humans were helpless (and
blameless) in the face of the economic and technological determinants at
work. Annibal Castro takes the more radically individualist view that musicians themselves, as individuals, had power and were agents of change.

In the end, however, it is Shankar Indorkar who, while blaming A. R.
Rahman for recent innovations and joining those who valorize Pyarelal-ji
for his resistance to them, gives us the clearest account of the complexities
of the process of cultural and musical evolution. Shankar reports that,
knowingly or unknowingly, he himself participated in this process by al-
lowing Rahman to sample his oboe playing for use in later projects:

> SHANKAR INDORKAR: He [Rahman] says, "Just you play something. Play
> anything. Just open the cor anglais and play something." I didn't under-
> stand. I say, "What key? At least tell me something!" But he says, "Play
> anything, whatever you want." So I played something, nothing, just some-
> thing. Maybe half an hour. From low to high on both instruments (oboe
> and English horn). Whatever I could think. And he just recorded every-
> thing. So it got to be about two o'clock in the morning, and then he says,
> "Okay, pack up." I didn't understand what was going on. He paid me, and
> I went back [to Mumbai]. And after that he never called me. Because he
> had all my sounds. So you could say he has me.

Human agency, which is hard enough to clarify in matters of political
history, seems to me to be still more complex in cultural history. The implications of Indorkar's account for a symbiotic and interactive notion of
agency in the process of cultural transformation stand out clearly.

In this story, although the power for change may not be evenly distributed, Rahman and Indorkar are both participating in the process. The shift
that is taking place is personal on one side: Indorkar will not be asked
to future Rahman recording sessions because Rahman "has him" on his
sampler. This represents a difference in Indorkar's income stream. On the
other side, the development is systemic and musical: By repeating this process with other musicians, Rahman frees himself and anyone else with
whom he shares his digital files from the necessity of writing out parts for
oboes or other instruments, from having to schedule rehearsals and recordings, and from the expense of hiring orchestral musicians. Furthermore, a
sampled oboe sound can play in ranges and at speeds that oboe players
cannot. Indorkar and Rahman occupy different positions in the system
after all, and they accordingly have more or less power to produce musical
or cultural change.

Nevertheless, to a certain degree Indorkar was participating in an altered situation that was detrimental to him. Whether in fact he did not

understand or simply did not wish to understand what was happening, he, like many musicians in this study, was accustomed to doing what music directors asked. Like many of his colleagues, Indorkar was used to viewing music directors (especially Burman and Pyarelal-ji, with whom he worked regularly) as supporters and elder brothers, not as people who would take advantage of him. In the midst of the experience, confronting an important figure of Rahman's caliber, grasping the implications of Rahman's actions may have been beyond him.

Finally, there is the matter of competition (cultural and economic) as a driver of change. Rahman's use of samplers in the 1990s was both personal choice and technological and/or economic compulsion. Since the technology was available and being used by others, Rahman was making a decision and pursuing a practice that benefited him in his competition for work with other music directors. In turn, his use of that technology no doubt added momentum to the impetus for innovation, as those who saw him as either competition or a role model sought to imitate his success.

Technology—in this case the samplers that were used to record and store the sounds of Indorkar's oboe and English horn—altered the limits of what was possible, but those modifications could be pursued only through human action, motivated by a range of personal and systemic issues. Individual human agency, personal and cultural motivations, economics and competition, power relationships, and technological possibilities all merge in the oral histories presented in this volume. They make abundantly clear the complex interaction of factors that have produced music and musical change in the twentieth and twenty-first centuries.

Notes

Notes to Introduction

1. Titles of Hindi films are italicized and spelled following common English usage in the Hindi film industry. Titles of songs are given in double quotes but are not italicized.

2. Unless otherwise noted, all quotations from musicians in this book are personal communications made to me in various locations in India between 2004 and 2007. Many of the original recordings are held in the Archive and Research Centre for Ethnomusicology (ARCE, located in Gurgaon, Haryana state), which is part of the American Institute for Indian Studies, New Delhi.

3. Copies of the interviews are held in the ARCE.

Notes to Chapter 1

1. Among expert sources there is some confusion about this matter. Ranade (2006) reports *Dhoop Chaon* as the original Bengali version and *Bhagychakra* as the Hindi remake (although directed by Devaki Bose). Rajadhyaksha and Willemen (1995) list the two as 1935 films, but they reverse the languages. Singh (1988), on the other hand, lists *Dhoop Chaon* as 1935 in his Hindi film-song dictionary. He lists *Bhagychakra* as the product of an unnamed Mumbai studio, released in 1933.

2. All Hindi words are italicized on first use only.

3. The song is the second one in the film, a film-style *qawwali* [a choral, respon-

sorial Muslim devotional song form] titled "Kab aaoge . . . Tere na ho jaayen, kahe der na ho jaayen." The interlude Jog refers to is "sung," that is, mimed, by the heroine. It is an excellent example of a musical convention in which percussion accompanying an unmetered vocal (alāp) signifies internalized reflective commentary that stands aside from the main body (and sometimes meaning) of the song.

Notes to Chapter 2

1. Most musicians abbreviate microphone as "mic" (pronounced "mike"). I spell the abbreviation in this way throughout.

Notes to Chapter 5

1. Madan Mohan in *Legends: Madan Mohan: The Instinctive Genius*, vol. 4 (track 10). Sa Rē Gā Ma India, Ltd.

References

Abbas, Khwaja Ahmad. 1985. "Art and Commerce in Indian Cinema." In 70 Years of Indian Cinema (1913–1983), ed. T. M. Ramachandran, 237–43. Mumbai: CINEMA India-International.

Agarwal, Amit. 1993. "Movies for Music's Sake." India Today (January 31): 94–95.

Ali, Naushad. 2004. "The Magical Music of Baiju Bawra." In Notes of Naushad, ed. Shashikant Kinikar, 65–72. Mumbai: English Edition Publishers and Distributors.

Altman, Rick. 1985. "The Evolution of Sound Technology." In Film Sound: Theory and Practice, ed. Elisabeth Weis and John Belton, 44–53. New York: Columbia University Press.

Arnold, Alison. 1991. "Hindi Film Git: On the History of Commercial Indian Popular Music." PhD. diss., University of Michigan.

Aziz, Ashraf. 2003. Light of the Universe: Essays on Hindustani Film Music. Delhi: Three Essays Collective.

Bali, Karan. n.d. "Evolution of the Hindi Film Song, Parts 1–6," http://www.upperstall.com/hindisong1.html.

Barnouw, Erik, and S. Krishnaswamy. 1980. Indian Film. New York: Columbia University Press.

Blacking, John. 1990. "Some Problems of Theory and Method in the Study of Musical Change." In The Garland Library of Readings in Ethnomusicology, vol. 6. Musical Processes, Resources, and Technologies, ed. Kay Kaufman Shelemay, 259–84. New York: Garland.

Booth, Gregory D. 1995. "Traditional Content and Narrative Structure in the Commercial Hindi Cinema." Asian Folklore Studies 54: 169–90.

———. 1997. "Socio-musical Mobility among South Asian Clarinet Players." Ethnomusicology 43 (Fall): 489–516.

———. 2000. "Religion, gossip, narrative conventions, and the construction of meaning in Hindi film songs." *Popular Music* 19(2): 125–46

———. 2007. "Musicking the Other: Orientalism in the Hindi cinema." In *Music and Orientalism in the British Empire, 1780s to 1940s: Portrayal of the East,* ed. Martin Clayton and Bennett Zon, 315–38. Burlington, Vt.: Ashgate.

Bose, Derek. 2006. *Brand Bollywood: A New Global Entertainment Order.* New Delhi: Sage.

Braudel, Fernand. 1972/1973. *The Mediterranean and the Mediterranean World in the Time of Phillip II.* 2 vols. Trans. Siân Reynolds. New York: Harper and Row.

———. 1984. *Civilization and Capitalism 15th–18th Century,* vol. 3. *The Perspective of the World.* Trans. Siân Reynolds. New York: Harper and Row.

Chakravarty, Sumita. 1993. *National Identity in Indian Popular Cinema, 1947–1987.* Austin: University of Texas Press.

Chatterjee, Biswanath. 1991. *Hindi Film Geet Kosh, 1971–1980,* vol. 5. Kanpur, India: Mrs. Satinder Kaur.

Chatterjee, Gayatri. 1992. *Awāra.* New Delhi: Wiley Eastern L.

Chopra, Anupama. 2000. *Sholay: The Making of a Classic.* New Delhi: Penguin.

Clayton, Martin. 2000. *Time in Indian Music: Rhythm, Metre, and Form in North Indian Rāg Performance.* New York: Oxford University Press.

Dahlhaus, Carl. 1982. *Esthetics of Music,* trans. William W. Austin. New York: Cambridge University Press.

Das, Gurcharan. 2001. *India Unbound.* New York: Knopf.

Dayal, John. 1983. "The Role of the Government: Story of an Uneasy Truce." In *Indian Cinema Superbazaar,* ed. Aruna Vasudev and Philippe Lenglet, 54–61. New Delhi: Vikas.

de Certeau, Michel. 1988. *The Writing of History.* New York: Columbia University Press.

Dissanayake, Wimal, and Malti Sahai. 1988. *Raj Kapoor's Films: Harmony of Discourses.* New Delhi: Vikas.

Dwyer, Rachel. 2002. *Yash Chopra: Fifty Years in Indian Cinema.* New Delhi: Roli Books.

Fabbri, Franco. 1982. "A Theory of Musical Genres: Two Applications." In *Popular Music Perspectives: Papers from the First International Conference on Popular Music Research, Amsterdam, June 1981,* ed. David Horn and Philip Tagg, 55–59. Gothenburg, Sweden: International Association for the Study of Popular Music.

Fernandes, Naresh. 2005. "In Search of Anthony Gonsalves." *Man's World* (December): 108–14.

Frith, Simon. 1996. *Performing Rites: On the Value of Popular Music.* Cambridge, Mass.: Harvard University Press.

Gitler, Ira. 1985. *From Swing to Bop.* New York: Oxford University Press.

Gopal, Sangita, and Moorti, Sujata. 2008. *Global Bollywood: Travels of Hindi Song and Dance.* Minneapollis: University of Minnesota Press.

Gopalan, Lalitha. 2002. *Cinema of Interuptions: Action Genres in Contemporary Indian Cinema.* London: British Film Institute Publishing.

Guha, Ramachandra. 2007. *India After Gandhi : The History of the World's Largest Democracy.* London: Macmillan.

Gujral, I. K. 1985. Interview. In *70 Years of Indian Cinema (1913–1983),* ed. T. M. Ramachandran, 185–92. Mumbai: CINEMA India-International.

Gupt, Somnath. 2005. *The Parsi Theatre: Its Origins and Development,* trans. and ed. K. Hansen. Kolkata: Seagull Books.

Hamm, Charles. 1995. "Genre, Performance, and Ideology in the Early Songs of Irving

Berlin." In *Putting Popular Music in Its Place*, 370–80. New York: Cambridge University Press.

Henry, Edward O. 1988. *Chant the Names of God: Music and Culture in Bhojpuri-speaking India*. San Diego: San Diego State University Press.

Hughes, Stephen. 2007. Music in the Age of Mechanical Reproduction. *Journal of Asian Studies* 66(1) (February): 3–34.

Kallberg, Jeffrey. 1988. "The Theory of Genre: Chopin's Nocturne in G Minor." *19th-Century Music* 11(3) (Spring): 238–61.

Kaur, Harpreet. 2004. "Churning Out Classics." *Jetwings* (March): 166–69.

Kinnear, Michael S. 1994. *The Gramophone Company's First Indian Recordings, 1899–1908*. Mumbai: Popular Prakashan.

Lastra, James. 2000. *Sound Technology and the American Cinema: Perception, Representation, Modernity*. New York: Columbia University Press.

Majumdar, Neepa. 2001. "The Embodied Voice: Song Sequences and Stardom in Popular Hindi Cinema." In *Soundtrack Available: Essays on Film and Popular Music*, ed. Pamela Robertson Wojcik and Arthur Knight Durham, 161–84. Durham, N.C.: Duke University Press.

Malik, Saeed. 1998. *Lahore: Its Melodic Culture*. Lahore: Sang-e-Meel.

Manuel, Peter. 1993. *Cassette Culture: Popular Music and Industry in North India*. Chicago: University of Chicago Press.

Marre, Jeremy, and Hannah Charlton. 1985. "There'll Always Be Stars in the Sky." In *Beats of the Heart: Popular Music of the World*, 137–54. New York: Pantheon.

Mishra, Vijay. 2002. *Bollywood Cinema: Temples of Desire*. New York: Routledge.

Morcom, Anna. 2001. "An Understanding between Bollywood and Hollywood: The Meaning of Hollywood-Style Music in Hindi Films. *British Journal of Ethnomusicology* 10(1): 63–84.

Morcom, Anna. 2007. *Hindi Film Songs and the Cinema*. Burlington, Vt.: Ashgate.

Nadkarni, Mohan. 1985. "Magnificent Obsession." *Illustrated Weekly of India* (May 26): 43–45.

Neuman, Daniel. 1980. *The Life of Music in North India*. Detroit: Wayne State University Press.

O'Brien, Charles. 2005. *Cinema's Conversion to Sound: Technology and Film Style in France and the U.S.* Bloomington: Indiana University Press.

Pinto, Jerry. 2006. *Helen: The Life and Times of an H-Bomb*. New Delhi: Penguin.

Prakash, Sanjeev. 1983. "Music, Dance, and the Popular Films: Indian Fantasies, Indian Repressions." In *Indian Cinema Superbazaar*, ed. Aruna Vasudev and Philippe Lenglet, 114–18. New Delhi: Vikas.

Prasad, Madhava. 2003. "This Thing Called Bollywood," Unsettling Cinema: A Symposium on the Place of Cinema in India, May 2003, no. 525; http://www.india-seminar.com/2003/525.htm.

Premchand, Manek. 2003. *Yesterday's Melodies, Today's Memories*. Mumbai: Jharna Books.

Raina, Raghunath. 1983. "The Context: A Socio-cultural Anatomy." In *Indian Cinema Superbazaar*, ed. Arun Vasudev and Phillippe Lenglet, 3–18. New Delhi: Vikas.

Rajadhyaksha, Ashish. 1995. Introduction. In *Encyclopaedia of Indian Cinema*, ed. Ashish Rajadhyaksha and Paul Willemen, i–xviii. New York: Oxford University Press.

———. 2004. "The 'Bollywoodization' of the Indian Cinema: Cultural Nationalism in a Global Arena." In *City Flicks: Indian Cinema and the Urban Experience*, ed. Preben Kaarsholm, 113–39. Kolkata: Seagull Books.

———, and Paul Willemen, eds. 1995. *Encyclopaedia of Indian Cinema.* New York: Oxford University Press.

Ranade, Ashok. 1984. *On the Music and Musicians of Hindoostan.* New Delhi: Promilla.

———. 1986. *Stage Music of Maharashtra.* New Delhi: Sangeet Natak Akademi.

———. 2006. *Hindi Film Song: Music beyond Boundaries.* New Delhi: Promilla.

Rangoonwalla, Feroze. 1983. *Indian Cinema Past and Present.* New Delhi: Clarion.

Rowell, Lewis. 1992. *Music and Musical Thought in Early India.* Chicago: University of Chicago Press.

Sahlins, Marshall. 2004. *Apologies to Thucydides: Understanding History as Culture and Vice Versa.* Chicago: University of Chicago Press.

Said, Edward. 1991. *Orientalism.* London: Penguin Books.

Shope, Bradley. 2003. "The Anglo-Indians Were the Gate Keepers: Intimate *Lucknowi* Musical Histories." Ph.D. diss., Indiana University.

———. 2007. " 'They Treat Us White Folks Fine': African American Musicians and the Popular Music Terrain in Late Colonial India." *South Asian Popular Culture* 5 (October): 97–116.

Singh, Harmandir. 1980. *Hindi Film Geet Kosh, 1951–1960,* vol. 3. Kanpur, India: Sumer Singh Sachdev.

———. 1984. *Hindi Film Geet Kosh, 1941–1950,* vol. 2. Kanpur, India: Sumer Singh Sachdev.

———. 1986. *Hindi Film Geet Kosh, 1961–1970,* vol. 4. Kanpur, India: Sumer Singh Sachdev.

———. 1988. *Hindi Film Geet Kosh, 1931–1940,* vol. 1. Kanpur, India: Mrs. Satinder Kaur.

Skillman, Teri. 1986. "The Bombay Hindi Film Song Genre: A Historical Survey." *Yearbook for Traditional Music* 18: 133–44.

Srivastava, Sanjay. 2006. "The Voice of the Nation and the Five-Year Hero: Speculations on Gender, Space, and Popular Culture." In *Fingerprinting Popular Culture,* ed. Vinay Lal and Ashis Nandy, 122–55. New York: Oxford University Press.

Turino, Thomas. 1999. "Signs of Imagination, Identity, and Experience: A Peircian Semiotic Theory for Music." *Ethnomusicology* 43(2): 221–55.

Uberoi, Patricia. 2001. "Imagining the Family: An Ethnography of Viewing Hum Aapke Hain Koun." In *Pleasure and the Nation: The History, Politics, and Consumption of Popular Culture in India,* ed. Rachel Dwyer and Christopher Pinney, 309–29. New Delhi: Oxford University Press.

Valicha, Kishore. 1998. *Kishore Kumar: The Definitive Biography.* New York: Penguin.

Vijayakar, Rajiv. 2004. "Lata Mangeshkar: From Golden to Platinum." *Screen* (October 1): 24.

Virmani, Ashish. 2004. "The Prodooser Is Dead! Long Live the Producer!" *Man's World* (February): 77–79.

Wade, Bonnie. 1979. *Music in India: The Classical Traditions.* Englewood Cliffs, N.J.: Prentice-Hall.

Walser, Robert. 1993. *Running with the Devil: Power, Gender, and Madness in Heavy Metal Music.* Hanover, N.H.: University Press of New England.

Waterman, Christopher. 1990. *Jùjú: A Social History and Ethnography of an African Popular Music.* Chicago: University of Chicago Press.

Weis, Elisabeth, and John Belton, eds. 1985. *Film Sound: Theory and Practice.* New York: Columbia University Press.

White, Hayden. 1987. *The Content of the Form*. Baltimore: Johns Hopkins University Press.

Winston, Brian. 1996. *Technologies of Seeing: Photography, Cinematography, and Television*. London: British Film Institute.

Woodfield, Ian. 2000. *Music of the Raj: A Social and Economic History of Music in Late Eighteenth-century Anglo-Indian Society*. New York: Oxford University Press.

Filmography

Note: I translate these film titles so as to convey in English a sense of their meaning. In some cases this means that my translations are not literal. A handful of Hindi films have come to have conventionally accepted English titles; I use these when they are known. Titles that consist solely of proper nouns are not translated.

1942: A Love Story. 1993. Director: Vidhu Vinod Chopra. Music: R. D. Burman. Vinod Chopra Productions, Mumbai.

Aah [Sigh]. 1953. Director: Raja Navathe. Music: Shankar-Jaikishan. R. K. Films, Mumbai.

Aashiqui [Lover]. 1990. Director: Mahesh Bhatt. Music: Nadeem-Shravan. S. C. Independent and Vishesh Films, Mumbai.

Aasman [Sky]. 1952. Director: C. M. Pancholi. Music: O. P. Nayyar. Pancholi Productions, Mumbai.

Abhiman [Vanity]. 1973. Director: Hrishikesh Mukherjee. Music: S. D. Burman. Amiya Productions, Mumbai.

Achhut Kanya [Untouchable Girl]. 1936. Director: Franz Osten. Music: Saraswati Devi. Bombay Talkies, Mumbai.

Agnipath [Trail of Fire]. 1990. Director: Mukul S. Anand. Music: Laxmikant-Pyarelal. Dharma Productions, Mumbai.

Albela [A Jolly Person]. 1951. Director: Bhagwan. Music: C. Ramchandra. Bhagwan Arts Productions, Mumbai.

Amar, Akbar, Anthony. 1977. Director: Manmohan Desai. Music: Laxmikant-Pyarelal. M. K. D. Pictures, Mumbai.

Amar Prem [Immortal Love]. 1971. Director: Shakti Samanta. Music: R. D. Burman. Shakti Films, Mumbai.

Andaaz [Estimate]. 1949. Director: Mehboob Khan. Music: Naushad Ali. Mehboob Productions, Mumbai.

Anuraag [Affection]. 1972. Director: Shakti Samanta. Music: S. D. Burman. Shakti Films, Mumbai.

Arzoo [Tears]. 1950. Director: Sahid Latif. Music: Anil Biswas. Indian National Pictures, Mumbai.

Awaara [Loafer]. 1951. Director: Raj Kapoor. Music: Shankar-Jaikishan. R. K. Films, Mumbai.

Ayodhya ka Raja [The King of Ayodhya]. 1932. Director: V. Shantaram. Music: Govindrao Tembe. Prabhat Films, Kolhapur.

Baazi [Indulgence]. 1951. Director: Guru Dutt. Music: S. D. Burman. Navketan, Mumbai.

Baazigar [Trickster]. 1993. Director: Abbas-Mustan. Music: Anu Malik. United Seven Creations, Mumbai.

Baiju Bawra. 1952. Director: Vijay Bhatt. Music: Naushad Ali. Prakash Pictures, Mumbai.

Barsaat [Rainy Season]. 1949. Director: Raj Kapoor. Music: Shankar-Jaikishan. R. K. Films, Mumbai.

Basant Bahar [Springtime]. 1956. Director: Raja Navathe. Music: Shankar-Jaikishan. Sri Vishwabharati Films, Mumbai.

Begum [Queen]. 1945. Director: Sushil Majumdar. Music: Hari Prasanta Das. Taj Mahal Pictures, Mumbai.

Betaa [Son]. 1992. Director: Indra Kumar. Music: Anand-Milind. Maruti International, Mumbai.

Bhaagyachakra [Circle of Fate]. 1933–1935. Director: Devaki Bose. Music: R. C. Boral and Pankaj Mallik. New Theatres, Kolkata.

Bluff Master. 1963. Director: Rajendra Krishan. Music: Kalyanji-Anandji. Subash Pictures, Mumbai.

Bobby. 1973. Director: Raj Kapoor. Music: Laxmikant-Pyarelal. R. K. Films, Mumbai.

Brahmachari [Follower of Brahma]. 1968. Director: Bhappi Soni. Music: Shankar-Jaikishan. Sippy Films, Mumbai.

Chal Chal Re Naujawan [The Young Man Making Progress]. 1944. Director: Gyaan Mukherjee. Music: Ghulam Haider. Filmistan, Mumbai.

Chaudvin ka chand [Four Quarters of the Moon]. 1960. Director: M. Sadik. Music: Ravi. Guru Dutt Films, Mumbai.

Chitralekha. 1941. Director: Kedar Sharma. Music: Ustad Jande Khan. Film Corporation of India, Kolkata.

Chitralekha. 1964. Director: Kedar Sharma. Music: Roshan. Pushpa Pictures, Mumbai.

Chupke Chupke [Quietly]. 1975. Director: Hrishikesh Mukherjee. Music: S. D. Burman. Rupam Pictures, Mumbai.

Dastaan [Story]. 1950. Director: A. R. Kardar. Music: Naushad Ali. Musical Pictures, Mumbai.

Deewana mujhsa nahi [No One Is Crazier than Me]. 1990. Director: Y. Nageshwar Rao. Music: Anand-Milind. Vandana Productions, Hyderabad.

Devdas. 1935. Director: P. Barua. Music: Timir Baran. New Theatres, Kolkata.

Devdas. 1955. Director: Bimal Roy. Music: S. D. Burman. Bimal Roy Productions, Mumbai.

Dhoop Chaon [The Sun's Shadow]. 1935. Director: Nitin Bose. Music: R. C. Boral and Pankaj Mullick. New Theatres, Kolkata.

Dilwale Dulhania Le Jayenge [He with a Heart Wins the Bride]. 1995. Director: Aditya Chopra. Music: Jatin-Lalit. Yashraj Films, Mumbai.

Disco Dancer. 1982. Director: B. Subash. Music: Bappi Lahiri. B. Subash Movie Unit, Mumbai.

Do Bigha Zamin [Two Acres of Land]. 1953. Director: Bimal Roy. Music: Salil Chadhuri. Bimal Roy Productions, Mumbai.

Do Shatru [Two Enemies]. 1976. Director: Kewal Mitra. Music: Kalyanji-Anandji. Kewal Art Productions, Mumbai.

Don. 1978. Director: Chandra Barot. Music: Kalyanji-Anandji. Nariman Films, Mumbai.

Dostaanaa [Friendly]. 1980. Director: Raj Khosla. Music: Laxmikant-Pyarelal. Dharma Productions, Mumbai.

Dosti [Friendship]. 1964. Director: Satyen Bose. Music: Laxmikant-Pyarelal. Rajshri Productions, Mumbai.

Evening in Paris. 1967. Director: Shakti Samanta. Music: Shankar-Jaikishan. Shakti Films, Mumbai.

Farz [Duty]. 1967. Director: Ravi Nagaich. Music: Laxmikant-Pyarelal. Vijaylaxmi Pictures, Chennai.

Hare Rama Hare Krishna [Hail Rama, Hail Krishna]. 1971. Director: Dev Anand. Music: R. D. Burman. Navketan International Films, Mumbai.

Heer Raanjha. 1970. Director: Chetan Anand. Music: Madan Mohan. Himalaya Films, Mumbai.

Hello Brother. 1999. Director: Sohail Khan. Music: Himesh Reshammiya, Sajid-Wajid. G. S. Entertainment, Mumbai.

Henna. 1991. Director: Randhir Kapoor. Music: Ravindra Jain. R. K. Films, Mumbai.

Hum Dil De Chuke Sanam [I've Already Given My Heart, Sweetheart]. 1999. Director: Sanjay Leela Bhansali. Music: Ismail Darbar. Bhansali Pictures, Mumbai.

Hum Saath Saath Hai [We Stand United]. 1999. Director: Suraj R. Barjatya. Music: Ram-Laxman. Rajshri Productions, Mumbai.

Humayun. 1945. Director: Mehboob Khan. Music: Ghulam Haider. Mehboob Productions, Mumbai.

Jeewan Yatra [The Journey of Life]. 1946. Director: Vinayak. Music: Vasant Desai. Rajkamal Kalamandir, Mumbai.

Jhanak Jhanak Payal Baje [Jangle Jangle, Sound the Ankle Bells]. 1955. Director: V. Shantaram. Music: Vasant Desai. Raj Kamal Kala Mandir, Mumbai.

Jis Desh Mein Ganga Behti Hai [The Country Where the Ganga Flows]. 1960. Director: Raghu Karmaarkar. Music: Shankar-Jaikishan. R. K. Films, Mumbai.

Julee. 1975. Director: K. S. Sethumadhuvan. Music: Rajesh Roshan. Vijaya Productions, Chennai.

Kaajal [Eyeshadow]. 1965. Director: Ram Maheshwari. Music: Ravi. Kalpanalok, Mumbai.

Kabhi Khushi Kabhie Gham [Sometimes Happy, Sometimes Sad]. 2001. Director: Karan Johar. Music: Jatin-Lalit. Dharma Productions, Mumbai.

Kati Patang [Unfettered Kite]. 1970. Director: Shakti Samanta. Music: R. D. Burman. Shakti Films, Mumbai.

Khel Qismat Ka [The Game of Fate]. 1977. Director: S. K. Luthera. Music: Kalyanji-Anandji. Carrier Films, Mumbai.

Khuda Gawah [Divine Witness]. 1992. Director: Mukul S. Anand. Music: Laxmikant-Pyarelal. Glamour Films, Mumbai.

Kismat [Fate]. 1943. Director: Gyaan Mukherjee. Music: Anil Biswas. Bombay Talkies, Mumbai.

Kohinoor [Mountain of Light]. 1960. Director: S. U. Sunny. Republic Films Corporation, Mumbai.

Kraanti [Revolution]. 1981. Director: Manoj Kumar. Music: Laxmikant-Pyarelal. V. I. P. Films, Mumbai.

Krodhi [Angry]. 1981. Director: Subash Ghai. Music: Laxmikant-Pyarelal. Ranjit Films, Mumbai.

Lamhe [Moments]. 1991. Director: Yash Chopra. Music: Shiv-Hari. Lyrics: Anand Bakshi. Yashraj Films, Ltd., Mumbai.

Leader. 1964. Director: Ram Mukherjee. Music: Naushad Ali. Lyrics: Shakeel Badayuni. S. M. K. Syndicate, Mumbai.

Love in Tokyo. 1966. Director: Pramod Chatterjee. Music: Shankar-Jaikishan. Pramod Films, Mumbai.

Maasoom [Unfortunate]. 1960. Director: Satyen Bose. Music: Rabin Banerjee. B. R. Chitra, Chennai.

Madhumati. 1958. Director: Bimal Roy. Music: Salil Chaudhuri. Bimal Roy Productions, Mumbai.

Madhuri. 1932. Director: R. S. Chaudhuri. Music: Pransukh Nayak. Imperial Film Company, Mumbai.

Mahal [Mansion]. 1949. Director: Kamal Amrohi. Music: Kemchand Prakash. Bombay Talkies, Mumbai.

Mard [Man]. 1985. Director: Manmohan Desai. Music: Anu Malik. M. K. D. Films and Aasia Films, Mumbai.

Mela [Festival]. 1999. Director: Dharmesh Darshan. Music: Anu Malik, Leslie Lewis, Rajesh Roshan. Venus Records and Tapes, Mumbai.

Meri Jung [My Battle]. 1985. Director: Subhash Ghai. Music: Laxmikant-Pyarelal. N. N. Sippy Productions, Mumbai.

Milan [Meeting]. 1967. Director: S. Subbarao. Music: Laxmikant-Pyarelal. Prasad Productions, Chennai.

Mission Kashmir. 2000. Director: Vidhu Vinod Chopra. Music: Shankar-Eshaan-Loy. Vinod Chopra Productions, Mumbai.

Mughal-e-Azam [Leader of the Mughals]. 1960. Director: K. Asif. Music: Naushad Ali. Aarooyatmak Starlight International Corporation, Mumbai.

Muqqadar ka Sikandar [Sikander's Destiny]. 1978. Director: Prakash Mehra. Music: Kalyanji-Aanandji. Prakash Mehra Productions.

Nagin [Female Serpent]. 1954. Director: Nandulal-Jaswantlal. Music: Hemant Kumar. Filmistan, Mumbai.

Nagina [Female Serpent]. 1951. Director: Ravindra Dave. Music: Shankar-Jaikishan. Pancholi Productions, Mumbai.

Nanhaa Shikari [Small Hunter]. 1973. Director: R. L. Desai. Music: Bappi Lahiri. Mukherjee Brothers, Mumbai.

Naya Sansar [New World]. 1941. Director: N. R. Acharya. Music: Saraswati Devi. Bombay Talkies, Mumbai.

Pardes [A Foreign Country]. 1997. Director: Subhash Ghai. Music: Nadeem-Shravan. Mukta Arts, Mumbai.

Prem Nagar [City of Love]. 1940. Director: M. Bhavnani. Music: Naushad Ali. Bhavnani Productions, Mumbai.

Pukar [Sacrifice]. 1983. Director: Ramesh Behl. Music: R. D. Burman. Rose Movies, Mumbai.

Purab aur Pachhim [East and West]. 1970. Director: Manoj Kumar. Music: Kalyanji-Anandji. Vishal International Productions, Mumbai.

Pyaasa [Thirst]. 1957. Director: Guru Dutt. Music: S. D. Burman. Guru Dutt Pictures, Mumbai.

Qayamat Se Qayamat Tak [From Age to Age]. 1988. Director: Mansoor Khan. Music: Anand-Milind. Nasir Husain Films, Mumbai.

Rajdhani [Capital]. 1956. Director: Ramesh Sahegal. Music: Hansraj Bhel. N. C. Films, Mumbai.

Ram aur Shyam [Ram and Shyam]. 1967. Director: Chanakya. Music: Naushad Ali. Vijaya International, Chennai.

Rishte Naate [Close Relationship]. 1965. Director: K. S. Gopalakrishna. Music: Madan Mohan. Amar Jyoti Films, Chennai.

Rocky. 1981. Director: Sunil Dutt. Music: R. D. Burman. Nalanda, Mumbai.

Roja (also known as *Roza*) [Daily]. 1993. Director: Mani Rathnam. Music: A. R. Rahman. Hansa Pictures, Chennai.

Saathi [Companion]. 1968. Director: Shridar. Music Director: Naushad Ali. Venus Pictures, Chennai.

Sanyasi [Monk]. 1975. Director: Sohanlal Kanwar. Music: Shankar-Jaikishan. Filmnagar, Mumbai.

Satte pe Sataa [Seven on Seven (also known as Seven Brides for Seven Brothers)]. 1981. Director: Raj N. Sippy. Music: R. D. Burman. Uttam Chitra, Mumbai.

Satyam Shivam Sundaram [Truth, Godliness, and Beauty]. 1978. Director: Raj Kapoor. Music: Laxmikant-Pyarelal. R. K. Films, Mumbai.

Shalimar. 1978. Director: Krishna Shah. Music: R. D. Burman. Laxmi Productions, Mumbai.

Sholay [Flame]. 1975. Director: Ramesh Sippy. Music: R. D. Burman. Sippy Films, Mumbai.

Shor [Noise]. 1972. Director: Manoj Kumar. Music: Laxmikant-Pyarelal. VIP Films, Mumbai.

Soormaa Bhopali. 1988. Director: Jagdeep. Music: Silip Sen-Sameer Sen. J. N. Entertainer, Mumbai.

Teesri Manzil [Third Floor]. 1966. Director: Vijay Anand. Music: R. D. Burman. Nasir Hussain Films, Mumbai.

Tezaab [Acid]. 1988. Director: N. Chandra. Music: Laxmikant-Pyarelal. N. Chandra Productions, Mumbai.

Tridev [Three Deities]. 1989. Director: Rajiv Rai. Music: Kalyanji-Anandji. Trimurti Films, Mumbai.

Umrao Jaan. 2006. Director: J. P. Dutta. Music: Anu Malik. J. P. Dutta Productions, Mumbai.

Vidyapati [Learned Man]. 1937. Director: Devaki Daas. Music: R. C. Boral. New Theatres, Kolkata.

Index

Page numbers in **bold** refer to illustrations.

Aashiqui (1990), 80, 115
Aawara (1951), 241, 242
Abbas, K. A. 29, 96, 97, 99
accordion players, 140, 182, 193, 257
Acharya, J. V., 93, 105, 130, 156, 168,
    181, 200, 207, 208, 244, 258
  and Cine Musicians Association,
    209, 210
  sitār playing, 267
actors
  singing, 42–43, 44, 45, 56, 285
  "star system," 99, 104, 218
Adhikhari, Tappan, 85, 113, 151–52,
    163, 282
advertising jingles, 64–65, 205, 214
Agneepath (1990), 244
Agra, 148
Ahmad, Nisar, 50–51, 130
Ajit Recording, 80
Albela (1951), 48, 241
Albuquerque, Alphonso, 33, 54, 93,
    193, 236, 238
Alfonso, Maoro, 54, 124–25, **125**,
    145, 152, 204, 239, 280

Ali, Abbas, 29, 102
Ali, Naushad, 32, 50, 52, 54, 88, 106,
    126, 135–36, 156, 170, 172, 196,
    208
  associations with other musicians,
    197
  and background music, 94, 199
  and Indian classical music, 264, 273
  move from Lucknow to Mumbai,
    129
  and orchestral developments, 232,
    237, 238–39
  payment to musicians, 211
  and playback, 43
  recordings, 67
  rehearsals, 192–93, 194
All-India Radio, 13, 29
Altman, Rick, 34, 39, 45
Alvarez, Vincent, 201
Al-Wahab, Mohamed Abdel, 269
Amaldev, Jerry, 243
Amar, Akbar, Anthony (1977), 3, 5, 6,
    226
Amar Prem (1971), 264

Anand, Chetan, 163
Anand-Milind, 176, 177, 249, 251
Andaaz (1949), 99, 197
Andheri, 84
Anil-Arun, 178
Arnold, Alison, 15, 16–17, 28, 38, 42,
    44, 63, 88, 114, 121, 130, 199,
    232, 234, 287
A-R-P, 93, 141, 185, 236
arrangers (assistants), 70, 146, 163,
    185, 201, 226–27, 231, 243
  fees, 109, 179, 181
  Goan, 238–41
  impact of technological changes, 77,
    84, 175–79
  1940s, 236–38
  relationship with music
    directors/composers, 168–75,
    179–81, 238
  Western-style arrangements, 241–43
  See also names of specific arrangers
Arzoo (1950), 237, 238
Australia, 52
Awaara (1951), 114, 206
Ayodhya ka Raja (1932), 35–36
Aziz, Ashraf, 15, 213

Baazi (1951), 268
Bachchan, Amitabh, 3–4, 5, 104, 220,
    227
background music, 7, 23–24, 73, 130,
    228–29
  composing and arranging, 154, 161,
    162, 168, 169, 170–71, 172, 198,
    227, 228–29
  costs of, 109, 111
  digital technology, 81, 83, 202, 250
  increase in, 58, 89
  Indian classical, 271
  influence of foreign films, 230
  integration of Indian and Western
    elements, 262–63
  payment for, 214
  recording, 94, 154, 169, 185, 186,
    198–202, 204, 211, 214
  relationship with song, 258
Badayuni, Shakeel, 197
Baiju Bawra (1952), 264, 270
Bakshi, Anand, 3, 5

Bali, Karan, 89
Balmohan Sangeet Company, 132
Balsara, Vistasp, 52, 123–24, 134,
    137, 160
  arranging, 91–92, 171, 179, 181
  composing, 171, 261
  conducting, 92, 169
  Filmistan Studios, 61, 91–92, 94,
    236
  move from Mumbai to Kolkata,
    138–39, **233**, 234
  payment, 207–208, 209, 212
bands. *See* dance bands; military and
    police bands
Bangalore, 116, 210
Banks, Louiz, 64, 111–12, 116–17,
    122, 150, **180**, 249, 251, 265–66,
    276–77
Baran, Timur, 232
"Barda dukha dina, O Rama-ji,"
    244
Barnouw, Erik, 14, 29, 38
Barsaat (1949), 45, 50, **51**
Batanagar, 142
Bengali language, 30, 38, 133, 134,
    135, 137, 138, 139, 234, 293
Bhagychakra (1935), 38, 293
bhajan, 256
Bhapat, Ulhas, **180**
Bharve, Mohan, **203**
Bhatia, Vanraj, 202, 252
Bhosle, Asha, 46, 47, 85
Bihag, Maru, 270
Biswas, Anil, 15, 43, 92–93, 134,
    176–78, 202, 231, 234, 235,
    237–38, 248, 261, 271–72
Blacking, John, 288
Bluff Master (1963), 171
Bobby (1977), 200–201
Bollywood, 7, 18, 87
Bollywood, New, 7, 18, 87, 114–18,
    172, 199, 282, 288
  new systems of production, 116–18,
    176, **177**, 179, 189, 190, 216,
    254, 287
  and Western-style music, 276–77
Bollywood, Old, 7, 18, 23, 87, 88, 89,
    95, 100–13, 118, 119, 136,
    220–21, 252, 287, 288

cottage industry model, 41, 102,
    104, 108, 118, 154–55, 179,
    181–82, 187, 191, 208
fusion of Indian and Western elements
    in film music, 262–63
independent producers and new
    funding model, 102–104
late Old Bollywood, 91, 107–13,
    172, 185, 213, 243–45, 249, 258,
    259, 275
nostalgia for, 282–83, 284
star programs, 218
transition from studios to music
    directors, 105–107, 191, 208
transition to New Bollywood, 17,
    106, 214, 252, 286, 287
Bombay Labs, 78, 80, 205
Bombay Sound, 66, 67, 69, 80
Bombay Talkies, 92, 93, 95, 237
Boral, R. C., 33, 37, 232, 234, 270
Bose, Hiren, 134
Bose, Mukul, 37
brass instruments and players, 213,
    228, 244. See also saxophonists;
    trumpeters
Braudel, Fernand, 18–19, 56–57, 89
Britain, 91, 220, 222, 269. See also
    London
Burman, R. D., 4, 64, 82, 88, 91, 106,
    115, 150, 156, 180, 215, 220,
    221, 291
    arrangers, 168, 174, 178, 181, 243
    categorization of songs, 262
    composing, 108, 258
    inspiration to musicians working
        with, 278–79
    music room, 159, 160–61, 166
    nickname Pancham, 21, 23
    orchestra, 185, 197, 198, 243
    recordings, 66, 67, 71, 107, 164,
        180, 280
    sitting musicians, 182–83, 188, 198,
        278–79
    and strike in Kolkata, 212
    style, 258, 259, 264, 268, 275–76
    use of technology, 71–75
Burman, S. D., 42, 44, 88, 134, 160,
    168, 174, 178, 197, 227, 242,
    268, 273

Carvalho, Bridget, 126
cassette industry, 16, 88, 108, 133,
    163, 184, 256
Castelino, Sonny, 146, 147, 241
Castro, Annibal, 250, 282, 289
cellos and cellists, 74, 139, 197,
    240–41. See also names of specific
    cellists
Central Studio, Tardeo, 160
Certeau, Michel de, 8
Chakraborty, Pritam, 253
Chakravarty, Bablu, 138, 178, 228–29,
    261
Chakravarty, Devi, 180
Chakravarty, Sanjay, 113, 123,
    125–26, 135–36, 170, 217, 253
Chakravarty, Sumita, 15
Chakravarty, Vasudeo, 73, 74, 125–26,
    135, 138, 168, 170, 180, 243
Chal Chal Re Naujawan (1944),
    171
Chand, Devi, 180, 182, 220, 221
Chandrakant, 180
Charlton, Hannah, 14
Chatterjee, Bishwadeep, 61, 63–64,
    71, 76–77, 82, 83, 84, 114–15
Chatterjee, Gayatri, 66, 206
Chatterjee, Robin, 62, 69
Chatterji, Deepan, 65, 66, 67, 71–72,
    82, 160–61, 180, 262, 278–79
Chaudhuri, Salil, 15, 134, 135–36,
    235, 240, 243, 263, 269
Chaudvin Ku Chand (1960), 225–26
Chauhan, Deepak, 188
Chauhan, Vijay, 133, 271
Chaurasia, Hariprasad, 227
Chaurasia, Rakesh, 112
Chennai, 30, 133, 181, 210, 267
Chic Chocolate (Antonio Vaz), 48,
    140, 148, 150, 196, 241, 274
Chitralekha (1964), 127, 270
Chitramandir Studios, 95, 96
Chopra, Anupama, 72
Chopra, Yash, 91, 101, 113
Chopra family, 104
Cine Musicians Association (CMA),
    11, 105, 150–51, 152, 187, 189,
    209–15, 217–18, 287
Cine Musicians Union, 210

classical music
    Indian, 122, 127–28, 129–32, 152,
        174, 231, 238, 239, 246, 260,
        263, 264, 270–73, 279
    Western, 4, 124–25, 141, 145, 152,
        238–40, 255, 256, 260, 279
claviolin, 245–46, 247, 289
Clayton, Martin, 272
"click tracks," 85, 86, 188
colonial music culture, decline of,
    143–48
Columbia, 30, 34, 101
composers. *See* music directors
Corea, Alec, 144
Corea, Louis, 106, 129
Corea, Mickey, 144
Corea, Robert, 106, 141, 193, 241,
    248, 266
Corea's Optimists Band, 144
Cotton, Rudy, 146
creative process, 159–75
    narrative music, 226–29
    and programming, 175–79
crystal motors, 70–71, 80, 81

Dalhouse, Carl, 256
dance bands, 122, 125, 140, 144–47,
    150, 191, 194, 209, 240, 241,
    266, 274, 279, 287
Darjeeling, 150
Das, Gurcharan, 60
Das, Hari Prasitra, 171
David, Isaac, 193, 236, 237
Dayal, John, 97
D'Costa, Boney, 193, **203**, 268
D'Costa, Francis, 158, 287–88
"Deewana Yeh Parwana," 48
De Ghatak, Anupam, 218, 220
"Dekh ke tumko dil dhola hai," 226
Desai, Kishore, 60, 138, 148, 167,
    237, 273
Desai, Manmohan, 3, 5
Desai, Vasant, 93, 130, 156
Devdas (1935), 234
Devdas (1955), 226
Devi, Kanan, 234
Devi, Saraswati (Khursheed Mancher-
    shah), 126
Devi, Sri, 104

Dhawan, David, 202
dholak and dholak players, 124, 132,
    162, 164, **173**, 174
Dhoop Chaon (1935), 38, 293
digital technology, 7, 75, 77, 83–86,
    117, 217, 229–30, 287–88, 290–91
    hard-disc recording systems, 83
    home computer, software-driven
        systems, 83–84, 176
    See also Dolby digital noise reduc-
        tion; electronic instruments;
        MIDI; programmers; samplers;
        synthesizers
"Dil ki kahani rang layi hai," 226
Dil Padosi Hai, 72
directors. *See* film directors; music
    directors
disco, 113, 115, 163, 267, 269
Disco Dancer (1981), 115
Dissanayake, Wimal, 14, 206
Dixit, Madhuri, 261
Do Bigha Zamin (1953), 240
Dolby digital noise reduction, 81
Don (1978), 227, 247
Dostaana (1980), 171
Dosti (1964), 172
Dourado, A. P., 125, **203**
Dourado, Martin, 193
drama. *See* music drama
drama sets, 30, 31
drums and drummers, 50, 60, 107,
    140, 146, 161, 213
    drum machines, 188, 249
    See also dholak and dholak players;
        khol; tabla and tabla players; and
        names of specific drummers
D'Souza, Sebastian, 116, 146, 147,
    156, 158, 168, 185, 193, 200,
    241–43, 263, 272, 274
D'Souza, Victor, 146
dubbing, 77, 80, 81, 84–85, 176
dubbers. *See* optical dubbers; repro-
    ducers
Dubey, V. K., 63, 101–102
"Dum Maro Dum," 264
Dwyer, Rachel, 104

Eastern Art Syndicate, 92
East India Films, 234

Ebrahim, Master, 257
Egyptian composers, influence of, 269
"Ek do teen char," 261
"Ek pyaar ka naghma hai," 284, 284
electronic instruments, 60–61, 117,
    216, 257–58
  and creative process, 175–79, 202
  drum machines, 188, 249
  keyboards, 60, 201, 245–49, 252,
    281, 289
  See also sequencers; synthesizers
EMI, 65
Empire Studio, 84, 85, 201
Europe, 31, 33, 41, 220
An Evening in Paris (1967), 156, 246,
    247

Fabbri, Franco, 255
Famous Film Laboratories (Tardeo),
    54, 66, 67, 80, 81, 82, 84, 173,
    196, 203, 205, 248
Famous Film Studios and Laboratories
    (Mahalaxmi), 67, 160
Fernand, Frank, 228, 243, 268, 288
Fernandes, George, 188, 240
Fernandes, Jerry, 158, 236–37, 284,
    284
  and Anil Biswas, 238
  Indian and Western music styles,
    263
  and jazz, 136–37
  and orchestras, 106, 107, 187, 242,
    243
  payments, 207, 208, 212
  recordings, 201
  rehearsals, 191, 193
  sitting musician, 164
Fernandes, Mario, 185, 214–15
Fernandes, Naresh, 3, 263
Filmalaya, 52
Film and Television Institute of India
    (FTII), 58, 64, 80
Film Centre, 54, 66, 67, 69, 70, 72,
    74, 78, 79, 80, 81–82, 84, 107,
    164, 167, 180, 205, 258, 259
film directors, 40–41, 50, 91, 162,
    163, 179, 202, 225, 229, 230,
    269
Film Federation of India (FFI), 210

film industry, French, 34, 41, 102–103
film industry, Hindi
  artisanal nature of, 105–106
  changing structures of, 87–91
  film output, 236
  global market for, 116, 117–18
  history of, 17–19
  investment in, 93–94, 115
  Mumbai centers, 51–52, 53, 54–55
  perception that films vehicles for
    songs, 163
  scholarship on, 12–17
  See also Bollywood; Studio Period of
    Mumbai film industry
film industry, Hollywood, 40, 104, 116
  early sound films, 33–34
  influence on Hindi film industry, 57,
    89, 115, 242
  orchestral scores, 35, 230, 242, 244,
    275
  playback, 33–34, 37, 45
  recorded popular songs in films, 35
film industry, Indian, 89, 91
  early sound films, 33–37
Filmistan Studios, 61, 67, 92, 97, 169,
    171, 207, 236
film music, Hindi
  distinctions between songs and, 168,
    170
  scholarship on, 12–17
  stylistic elements, 108, 255–77
  valuing: musicians' perspectives,
    277–83
  See also background music; film
    musicians; film songs, Hindi;
    orchestras
film musicians, Indian
  before sound in films, 32–33
  impact of playback, 39
  See also names of specific musicians
film musicians, Mumbai, 68, 75, 90, 91
  anonymity, 5–6, 153, 168, 285
  attracted to growing field of Mumbai
    film industry, 133–36
  auditions, 150–52
  classical and music drama back-
    grounds, 122, 127–28, 129–33
  community backgrounds, 121–22,
    123–28

film musicians, Mumbai (*continued*),
  creative process, 159–75
  friends and family connections,
    122–23, 148–50, 151, 156–57
  groupings, 196–98
  headphone use, 74–75, 85, 288
  impact of government policy, 60–61,
    76
  impact of playback, 39, 42–51
  impact of technological changes, 86,
    114–15, 116–18, 189, 190, 202,
    215, 216–17, 290–91
  money laundering by, 97, 99, 115
  reaction to digital technology, 84–85
  salaried, 91–93, 95, 96, 99, 105,
    106, 157, 190, 207, 208, 286
  sitting musicians, 159, 164–67, 172,
    174, 181–83, 185, 188, 198
  strikes, 212–13
  training, 122, 136–43
  travel to studios, 52, 54–55, 186
  See also actors, singing; arrangers;
    freelance musicians; music direc-
    tors/composers; orchestras; pay-
    ment and pay rates; playback
    singers; rehearsals; recordings;
    and names of specific musicians
film-music industry, Mumbai
  communities in, 123–28
  costs of production, 108–13,
    117–18
  documentary, *There Will Always
    Be Stars in the Sky*, 14
  geography of, 51–52, 53, 54–55
  historical influences, 30
  oral history, 6–8, 9–12, 284–91
  periodization of, 26, 88–89
  relationships with recording industry
    32, 41–42, 63
  scholarship on, 14, 15, 17
  structuring a history of, 17–19
  See also Bollywood; Studio Period of
    Mumbai film industry
film processing, 66, 67–68, 94
films, nonmusical, 29
film shows, 135
film songs, Hindi
  composing as melodies without
    words, 163

constructions of Indian and Western
  styles, 263–70
costs of production 108–13, 117
creation and performance of style,
  270–77
demand for, 105, 106
dependence/independence on films,
  40, 102, 156
distinct form of, 37
distinctions between film music and,
  168, 179
evolution of, 89
importance and dominance of, 14,
  41, 51, 64, 100–101, 255
increase in numbers released. 236
industrial reasons for continued use
  of, 35
instrumental version recording,
  256–58, **257**
picturization, 42, 102, 261, 262
prerelease, 42
scholarship on, 13, 14–15, 16, 17
song situations, 41–42, 160–61,
  225–26, 260–63
style and genre ideology, 13, 16,
  255, 256–60
stylistic redefinition by playback
  singers, 57
See also arrangers; composers;
  lyrics and lyricists; music
  directors
film songs, Indian
  assumption that films must have
    songs, 29, 35, 37, 51
  before sound film, 28–33, 88
  early sound films, 33–35, 88
  impact on popular Indian culture,
    27, 37, 38, 40
film studios, 51–52, 53, 54–55,
  67, 91–102, 234, 236. *See also*
  Studio Period of Mumbai film
  industry; and names of specific
  film studios
folk music, Indian, 17, 108, 133,
  270–73
France. *See* film industry, French
freelance musicians, 89, 92, 99,
  100–101, 105–107, 114, 155–56,
  207, 286–87

arrangers, 168
messengers, 186–87
music directors, 92, 99, 100, 155, 207–208
orchestral musicians, 93, 106–107, 110, 112, 114, 115–16, 115–16, 186, 191, 194, 241–43
pay rates, 207–209
Frith, Simon, 255

Gangawane, Lala, 132
Ganguli, Ram, 122
Gazmer, Ranjit, 180
Germany, 62, 69
Ghai, Subash, 258
"Ghar aya mere pardesi," 206
Gitler, Ira, 279
globalization, music television, 7
Goa and Goan musicians, 52, 121, 126, 137, 139, 141, 197, 279
arrangers, 238–41
and genre, 280
source of Western influence, 122, 124–25, 137, 138, 143–48, 235, 264, 266, 272
women instrumentalists, 126
See also names of specific Goan musicians
Godinho, Leslie, 50, 60, 146, 193, 218, 240, 265
Gomes, Joe, 145, 146, 204, 209, 240, 279, 287
Gomes, Johnny, 129, 146, 240, 241, 243, 274, 279
Gonsalves, Anthony (arranger and composer), 4–5, 4, 6, 48, 49, 139, 190, 237, 239, 243, 280
and classical Indian music, 272–73
correlation of situation and style, 262–63
Kardar Studios, 172
and Western music, 228, 239, 242
Gonsalves, Anthony (film character), 3–4, 5, 6
Gonsalves, John, 139, 240–41, 280
Gonsalves Clarinet Quintet, 49
Gopal, Sangita, 27
Gopalan, Lalitha, 15
Gorakh, 171

Goregaonkar, Datta, 131, 179
government policy, 59–60, 76, 96, 97, 100, 114–15, 287
Gracias, Benny, 100, 197, 198, 206, 211, 240, 253
Gramophone Company of India, Ltd, 22, 29, 30, 36, 52, 101, 257
Guha, Ramachandra, 60
Guild, 210
guitars and guitarists, 33, 60, 78, 137. See also names of specific guitarists
Gujarati language, 137
Gujral, I. K., 97
Gupta, Bhanu, 97, 99, 163, 166, 198, 214, 264
Gupta, Satish, 80
Gupt, Somnath, 29

Haider, Ghulam, 92, 95, 134, 160, 171, 179, 181, 207–208
Haldipur, Amar, 243–44
Hamm, Charles, 255
Hare Rama Hare Krishna (1971), 264
harmoniums, 32, 33, 81, 129, 132, 161, 165, 172, 175, 232, 246
headphones, 74–75, 77, 85, 288
Henna (1991), 47
Henry, Edward, 14
Hindi film industry. See film industry, Hindi
Hindi film music. See film music, Hindi
Hindi film songs. See film songs, Hindi
Hindi language, 133, 137, 234
history, distinction between oral history and, 8–9, 10
HMV (His Master's Voice), 22, 34, 130, 256
Kolkata, 13, 139
Mumbai, 36, 37, 40, 42, 52, 55, 63, 64, 65, 72, 80, 93, 101–102, 108, 130, 207
Hollywood. See film industry, Hollywood
Hughes, Stephen, 30
Humayun (1945), 92
Hum Dil De Chuke Sanam (1999), 202

Hussain, Sajjad, 50–51, 129–30, 273
Hussain, Zakir, 13
Hyderabad, 133

Imperial Movietone studios, 91, 94
Indian and Western styles, musicians'
    constructions of, 263–70. *See also*
    classical music; Western music
Indian Film Enquiry Committee, 103
Indian film industry. *See* film industry,
    Indian
Indian film music. *See* film music,
    Indian
Indian film songs. *See* film songs,
    Indian
Indian independence, 7, 56, 88, 89,
    122, 133, 146, 209, 240, 263,
    279, 280, 286
Indian Motion Pictures Producers'
    Association (IMPPA), 181, 210,
    213
Indorkar, Lallu Ram, 142–43, 149,
    266–67
Indorkar, Shankar, 112, 115, 142–43,
    149, 157, **205**, 244, 253, 266–67,
    289, 290–91
instrumental accompaniment
    melodic, 231
    to silent films, 32–33
    unison, 231
Irani, Adeshir, 94
Iyer, Ramesh, 55, 60, 75, 137, 149–51,
    220, 252, 269, 276, 279

Jahan, Noor, 43, 44
Jaikishan, **165**, **173**, 194, 196, 199–200.
    See also Shankar-Jaikishan
Jain, Ravindra, 47, 108
Jaitin-Lalit, 177
Jaora, 129
jatra, 30
jazz, 6, 48, 108, 122, 136, 140, 143,
    144, 145, 146, 147–48, 150, 152,
    240, 266, 269, 279
Jish Desh Mein Ganga Behti Hai
    (1960), 265
Jog, Prabhakar, 47–48, 190, 294
Joshi, G. N., 130
Jyoti Film Studios, 132

Kadam, Sudhir, 156–57
Kallberg, Jeffrey, 256
Kalyanji-Anandji, 88, 106, 108, 148,
    150, 157, 213, 289
    arrangers, 227, 247
    background music, 258
    Laxmikant-Pyarelal as assistants to,
        172
    music rooms and sitting musicians,
        164–65, 174
    recordings, 67, 79, 107
    star shows and tours, 220
    use of tabla in Western music, 271
Kandivali, 84
Kapoor, Manohar, 129
Kapoor, Raj, 14, 50, 95, 114, 132,
    173, 200, 201, 206, 265
Kapoor, Shammi, 50, 246, 248
Karachi, 144
Kardar, A. R., 93
Kardar Studios, 172, 237
Karim, Abdul, 127
Karnad, Gajanan, 190
Kathaks, 174
Kathuria, Suresh, 68–69, 80, 81
Kati Patang (1970), 264
Katkar, Amrut, 159, 165, 166, 186,
    188
Katrak, Minoo, 66, 82, 248
Kaur, Harpreet, 97, 99
Kaushik, Anil, 66
Kaushik, Sunil, 78, 209, 260, 266,
    282–83
Keer, Maruti Rao, 174, **180**
Kemble, Shyamrao, 132, 139–40, 141,
    152, 171–72, 199, 237
Khan, Bade Ghulam Ali, 273
Khan, Halim Jaffar, 103, 105, 131–32,
    270–71, 273
Khan, Imrat, 127, 128
Khan, Jhande, 129, 270
Khan, Kadim Hussain, 148
Khan, Mehboob, 67, 92, 95, 197
Khan, Sharafat, 5, 165, 213, 271
Khan, Sultan, 131, 218, 272, 277
Khanna, Usha, 108, 126
khol, 151–52
Khuda Gawah (1992), 244
King, B. B., 264

Kinnear, Michael S., 22, 30, 101
Kishore, Avijit Mukul, 284, 285
Klangfilm Company, 69
Kohinoor (1960), 264
Kolhapur, 51
Kolkata, 21, 37, 44, 45, 125, 138–39,
    140, 145, 150, 170
  fees in, 179
  film production, 51, 91, 94–95, 133,
    134, 236, 286
  musicians' relocation from Mumbai
    to, 142, 179
  musicians' relocation to Mumbai
    from, 92, 122, 125, 128–29, 134
  music drama, 30
  orchestras, 185–86, 231–32, **233**,
    234–46, 239
  strike, 1970s, 212
  Western music culture, 231–32
Kreem, M. M., 253
Krishna Studio, 84
Krishnaswamy, S., 14, 29, 38
"Kuch na kaho," 166
Kudalkar, Laxmikant, 5
Kumar, Arun, 43
Kumar, Ashok, 21, 42, 43
Kumar, Dilip, 95, 197
Kumar, Gulshan, 80, 108
Kumar, Hemant, 134, 245
Kumar, Kartik, 130–31, 244, 271, 273
Kumar, Kishore, 42, 220, **221**, 247
Kumar, Raaj, 262

Lahiri, Bappi, 108, 113, 160, 178,
    227, 267
  sittings, 163–64
  use of electronic instruments, 248
  use of large orchestra, 113
  and Western popular music, 163,
    259, 267, 275, 276
  workshop and working process,
    198, 201, 213–14, 215
Lahore, 51, 92, 95, 122, 133, 134,
    146, 241, 286
Lala-Sattar, 132, 213
Lal-Ji, Pandit Babu, 174
Lastra, James, 34, 38
Laxmikant-Pyarelal, 156–57, 215
  composing, arranging and directing

music, 3, 5, 67, 88, 91, 107, 108,
    110–11, 115, 160, 171, 172, 196,
    199, 258
  dominance of stylistic trends, 161,
    258–59
  electronic instruments, 246, 248,
    251
  music assistants, 171–72, 174, 205
  music rooms, 160, 161–62, 166
  orchestra, 185, 196, 198, 199, 200,
    215, 210, 243–44, 249
  recordings, 79, 84, 164, 259
  rehearsals, 196
  star status, 112
  See also Sharma, Pyarelal
Lebanese composers, influence of, 269
Lobo, Tiny, 146
London, 66, 73, 74, 76, 246
Lord, Bhuji, **221**
Lord, Cawas, 94, 123, 140, 142, 193,
    209, 286
Lord, Kersi, **v**, 18, 103, 123, 150, 157,
    289
  arranging, 170–71, 173–74, 237,
    239, 243
  and Cine Musicians Association,
    209
  composing, 199, 200, 202
  conducting, 169
  electronic instruments, 175, 176,
    182, 249, 250, 252
  and influences on Hindi film music,
    269, 275
  and Naushad Ali, 238, 239
  pay rate, 208
  performing skills, 182
  recordings, 59, 61, 62, 66–67, 72,
    80, 82, 93–94, 130, 183, **203**
  rehearsals, 190, 194, 200
  and style, 258, 259, 278
  tours, 220
A Love Story (1993), 82, 166
Lucknow, 32, 51, 129, 145
Ludhianvi, Sahir, 262
lyrics and lyricists, 14, 15, 37, 39, 42,
    95, 109, 162, 163, 164

Madan brothers, 51
Madan Theatres, 91, 94, 234, 236

Madhubala, 42
Madhumati (1958), 135
Madhuri 34
magnetic tape, 58, 59, 62–64, 68–71
   inch system, 61, 62, 63–64, 65–66,
      70, 72
   multitrack, 58, 65, 69–70, 72–73,
      73, 76, 77
   single-track, 65, 69, 77, 82
   synchronizable, 62, 66, 68
   35 mm, 61, 62–63, 64, 65, 68, 72,
      73, 75, 77, 81, 82, 206
   See also tape recorders
Mahabharata, 35
Mahadevan, Shankar, **205**, 253, 254
Mahmood, Talat, 234
"Mai gaoon, tum so jaao," 248
Majumdar, Neepa, 42, 45, 46, 255
Malik, Anu, 133, 162, 174, 177, 248
Malik, Pankaj, 270
Manchershah, Khursheed (Saraswati
   Devi), 126
"Man dole mera tan dole," 246
mandolin and mandolinists, 60, 130,
   148, 193, 236
Mangeshkar, Lata, 4–5, 13, 44, 45,
   46, 47–48, **49**, 105, 160, **165**,
   194, 234, 267, 272, 273
Manuel, Peter, 16, 17, 22, 28, 46, 60,
   88, 101, 133, 277
Marathi language and music, 30, 35,
   132–33, 137, 270, 271
Marchado, Mike, 274
Marre, Jeremy, 14
Martins, Micael, **49**
Mehboob Studios, 62, 66, 67, 68, **68**,
   92, 127, 128, 192–93, 205
   former main recording studio, **219**
   Laxmikant-Pyarelal's use of, 79,
      161–62, 164, 196, 258, 259
   recording technology, 69, 70, 76,
      78, 79, 82, 84
Mehrani, Indu, 104
Mehta, Melli, 140
Mendes, Bosco, 112, 116, 213
Mendonsa, Loy, **205**, 253, 254
Menezes, Ernest, 50, 54, 93, 100, 106,
   114, 148, 196–97, **219**

and Cine Musicians Association,
   210, 211
and Indian/Western styles, 174, 265
and recording technology, 86, 217
and rehearsals, 191–92
Menezes, Isobel, 126
Menezes, Joaquim (Joe), 50, **51**, 126,
   148, 193, 265
Menzies, Josique, 239
Menzies, Myra (Shroff), 126
Meri Jung (1985), 79
messengers, 185–89
Michardo, Mike, 266
microphones, 34, 38, 57–58, 59, 61,
   62
MIDI, 251
military and police bands, 141,
   142–43, 144, 145
Minerva Studios, 130
Mishra, Vijay, 15
Mitra, Sumit, 135, 140, 151, 156, 192,
   193–94, 211, **219**, 246, 247–49,
   250, 251
Mitsubishi, 77
mixers, 58
mobile vans for sound recording, 62
Modi, Sohrab, 95
Mohan, Madan, 4, 106, 156, 157,
   163, 196, 197, 200, 270
Mohan Studio, 97
Mohile, Anil, 138, 178, 201, 227, 228,
   242, 243
Monsorate, Joe, 76, 111, 151, 187–88,
   200–201, 212–13, 218, 222, 244,
   258, 274–75, 288
Monsorate, Pete, 151, 188
Monsorate, Ronnie, 248
Moorti, Sujata, 27
Morcom, Anna, 17, 27, 28, 31, 35, 57,
   72, 89, 101, 102, 121, 163, 168,
   172, 199, 225, 230, 255, 260,
   285
Mughal-e-Azam (1960), 264, 273
Muhammad, Ghulam, 156
Mukesh, 44, 46, 234
Mukherjee, S., 92
Mullan, Homi, 138–39, 140, **180**,
   182, 187, 275, 283, 288, 289–90

Mullick, Pankaj, 33, 170, 232, **233**, 234
Mumbai
  power line electrical frequencies, 78
  professional geography of, 51–52,
    53, 54–55
  See also film-music industry, Mumbai;
    film musicians, Mumbai
Muqqadar ka Sikander (1978), 226
musical instruments, 60–61, 226–29,
    244, 245
  Indian, 124, 270
  learning to play, 139–40, 142–43,
    144–45, 148
  See also classical music, Indian; elec-
    tronic instruments; instrumental
    accompaniment; orchestras; and
    specific instruments
music directors/composers 10, 12, 37,
    40–41, 44, 66–67, 72, 88, 89, 92,
    103, 152, 185, 285, 286
  arrangers' relationship with,
    168 75, 179–81, 238
  background music, 198–99, 200,
    201
  charges to producers, 108–13, 114,
    162, 179
  and Cine Musicians Association,
    210
  composing for situations, 260–63,
    261
  costs of song production, late Old
    Bollywood 108–13
  effect of characteristic sound of
    studios, 67
  freelance, 92, 99, 100, 155,
    207–208
  impact of electronic instruments, 77,
    83, 84, 175–76, 249–50
  importance of hit films, 50–51, 102
  interactions with sitting musicians,
    164–67, 181–83
  and "lump sum" payment system,
    117, 216–18, 287
  musicians' association with,
    105–107, 152, 155–58, 179–83,
    194, 196–98, 286, 291
  New Bollywood, 179
  Old Bollywood, 108, 155–58, 179

pairs of, 21
salaried, 92, 99
and scheduling of musicians, 186,
    196
and stylistic context, 269–70
total films, producers and directors,
    98
women, 126
See also arrangers; music rooms;
    sittings; and names of specific
    composers/music directors
music drama
  early sound films, 34, 35–36
  film musicians' backgrounds in, 122,
    132–33
  history, 29–32
  relationship with recording industry,
    30–32, 40
musicians. *See* film musicians
music rooms, 159–62, 191–92. *See
    also* sittings
"My Name is Anthony Gonsalves,"
    3–4

Nadeem-Shavran, 81, 163, 176
Nadkarni, Mohan, 50
Nagari, Ratna, 189
Nagin (1954), 245–46
Nagra recorders, 65, 66, 70–71, 80
Nargis, 50, 99
narrativization, 8–9, 11
Narvekar, Harishchandra, 190, 265
Natak, Marathi Sangeet, 231
Nathan, **167**
national identity, Indian, 60
National Studio, 92
Naushad. *See* Ali, Naushad
Navketan Films, 104, 168
Nayyar, O. P., 22, 23, 88, 89, 106,
    136, 146, 157–58, 192, 206, 241,
    243, 258, 269
Neuman, Daniel, 14, 119
New Bollywood. *See* Bollywood, New
New Delhi, 52
New Theatres Studios, 37, 38, 51, 61,
    94, 232, **233**, 234, 235, 236, 238,
    239
Newman, Joseph, 142

nonfilm recording, 36, 64, 65, 72, 76, 80, 83, 102
nostalgia, 11–12, 281–83
notation, 168
    European (staff), 4, 137, 138, 139, 140, 141, 144, 171, 237, 240
    Indian (sagam), 137–39, 141
Nuendo, 84

Oak, Avinash, 64, 65, 73, 75, 84, 85
oboists, 142–43, 149, 266–67, 290
O'Brien, Charles, 34, 37, 41, 102, 103
Odeon label, 101, 257
Old Bollywood. See Bollywood, Old
optical dubbers, 38, 42, 88
optical film, 34, 36, 62, 63, 68–69, 72, 82, 84, 91, 93
    drawbacks of, 59
    single-track, 58, 61
optical transfer machines, 63, 64
oral history
    distinction between history and, 8–9, 10
    and human agency, 285–91
    nostalgia in, 11–12, 281–83
orchestras, 17, 35, 36, 77–78, 89, 92, 108, 116, 185, 225–30
    conductors/conducting, 168–69, 200
    and costs of song production, 109, 110, 111, 112, 113, 114
    early development of size and practice, 230–45
    freelance members, 93, 106–107, 186–89, 191, 194, 241–43
    Goans in, 124, 125–26
    Hollywood orchestral scores, 35, 230, 242, 244, 275
    impact of technological changes, 117, 175, 216–17, 244, 245–54, 290–91
    Kolkata, 185–86, 231–32, **233**, 234–36, 239
    large, 57, 75, 82, 89, 109, 113, 116, 136, 186, 188, 191, 201, 206, 220, 226, 229, 230, 232, **233**, 238–39, 240–41, 243–44, 251, 287
    later developments in Old Bollywood, 243–45

members playing from memory, 137, 139, 190
narrative music, 226–29
1940s, 236–38
salaried members, 92, 93, 185, 186, 236
sectional playing, 168, 214, 230–31
supplementary members, 185, 186–89, 190
women in, 126–28
See also instrumental accompaniment; musical instruments; rehearsals; recordings

Pacheco, Lucila, **49**, 126, 247
Pakistan, 135
Pancham. See Burman, R. D.
Pancholi Studios, 95
Panjabi language, 228
Parasmani (1963), 172
Parsi musicians, 121–22, 123–24, 125, 126–28, 137, 138
Parsi Theater, 30
Parthe, Jai Kumar, 243, 247
Patwardhan, Vinayakrao, 34
Paudwal, Arun, 178, 201, 243, 248
payment and pay rates, 12, 179, 181–83, 184, 191, 192, 201, 206, 207–14, 286
    Cine Musicians Association, 209–15, 287
    "lump sum" system, 117, 216–18, 287
    overtime, 109, 114, 208, 210–11, 215
    "set payment" system, 212
    star shows and tours, 220
    See also film musicians, salaried; freelance musicians
percussion and percussionists, 76, 77, 218, 220, 265, 271
    Latin-style percussion, 140
    side percussion, 159, 188
    See also drums and drummers; and specific percussionists
Periera, Dominic, 145
Periera, Joe, 116, 144, 147–48, 280
Pereira, John, 145, 146, 188, **195**, 241
Perry, Chris, 248

pianos and pianists, 139, 140–41. *See also* specific pianists
Pinto, Joe, 84, 115–16, 163, 188–89, 239, 281, 288
Pinto, Martin, 106, 243
playback, 18, 26, 27–28, 37–41, 88, 89, 94, 189, 236, 255
  Hollywood, 33–34, 37, 45
playback singers, 43–48, 56, 57, 109, 110, 135, 209, 218, 234, 273, 285, 286
Polydor, 101
popular culture, Indian, 33
  impact of film song, 27, 37, 38, 40, 64, 184, 255
  impact of playback, 38, 40
popular music, Indian, 234, 285
  before sound film, 28–33
popular music, Western, 108, 136, 152, 161, 163, 256, 258, 263, 267, 269, 287
  comparison with film song, 16
  Goan association with, 137, 240
  New Theatres, 234
  Parsi association with, 123, 137, 240
  styles, 273–77
  See also dance bands; disco; jazz
Prabhat Films, 35
Prakash, Kemchand, 129, 134
Prakash, Sanjeev, 28, 29
Prasad, Madhava, 18, 87
Premchand, Manek, 15, 88, 89
Prithivi Theatres, 122
producers, 7, 12, 16, 17, 31, 32, 35, 47, 51, 59, 97, 99, 286
  and Cine Musicians Association, 210
  and costs of electronic instruments, 249
  and costs of song production, 108, 109–13, 114, 162, 179, 181–82, 191, 209, 210, 212, 213–14, 215, 217
  fees and royalties, 30–31, 34
  independent, 7, 88, 99, 100, 101, 102–104, 216
  "lump sum" payment system, 117, 216–18, 287

  in music rooms and sittings, 162, 163–64
  new systems of production, 116–18
  small, 115
  total films, producers and directors, 98
  See also names of specific producers
programmers, 175, 176–78, 202, 251–52, 287
Pro Tools, 83, 176
punching, 76, 81, 84, 85, 297
Pune, 51, 58, 1332
Pyaasa (1957), 61

Qayamat Se Qayamat Tak (1988), 80, 176
Qureshi, Taufiq, 75–76, 177, 202, 245, 249, 251, 252, 276, 277, 278

Rafi, Mohamed, 44, 46, 110, 194, 206, 234, 262
rāga, 270, 271, 272, 277
Rahbani brothers, 269
Rahman, A. R, 71, 289, 290, 291
Rai, Jutikar, 234
Rai, Rajiv, 250
Raina, Raghunath, 91, 103
Raj, Shyam, 219
Raj, Sumant, 132, 156, 193, 209
Rajadhyaksha, Ashish, 13, 14, 60, 88, 89, 100, 293
Rajkamal Kalamandir, 207
Raj Kamal Studio, 73, 93, 212
Ram, Parsu, 209
Ramchandra, C. (Anna), 44, 93, 106, 132, 140, 145, 150, 156, 160, 192, 196, 241, 274
Ranade, Ashoke, 15, 29, 34, 35, 36, 37, 40, 42, 46, 89, 234, 237, 241, 293
Rang Mahal Studio, 62, 95
Ranga Rao, V. A. K., 101
Rangoonwalla, Firoze, 14, 37
Rani, Buloo C., 156
Ranjit Movietone, 95, 96, 99, 129, 207, 208, 236
rasa, 271
Ravi (Ravi Shankar Sharma), 110, 197

RCA equipment, 77, 82
recording industry
    relationship with film industry, 32,
        34–35, 40, 41–42, 63
    relationship with music dramas,
        30–32, 40
    songs as staple product of, 34, 37, 40
recordings, 184–85, 202–206, **203**,
        205, 215, 220
    background music, 199, 200–201,
        202, 204, 253–54
    and Cine Musicians Association,
        211
    decline in, 189, 190, 221, 253–54
    isolation booths, 189–90
    live-performance environment,
        75–76, 84, 184–85
    musicians' earnings based on, 192,
        207–209
    and rehearsals, 192, 193
    socializing after sessions, 204
recording studios, 52, **53**, 54–55, 60,
        61–62, 66–68, 76–77, 80–83,
        109, 154–55, 234, 286
    decline of studio system, 94–99,
        190, 208, 286, 287
    home studios, 83–84
    See also music rooms; sound-
        recording technology; Studio
        Period of Mumbai film industry;
        and names of specific studios
recordists, 26, 57, 67, 69–71, 75–76,
        83–84. *See also* names of specific
        recordists
rehearsals, 67, 107, 108, 109, 110,
        185, 190–202, 207, 208, 211–12
reproducers, 70
Reshammiya, Himesh, 253
Reshammiya, Vipin, 107, 156, 246
rhythm arrangers and programmers,
        163, 172–75, 202, 249
R. K. Film and Studios, 45, 51, 52,
        241
Rocky (1981), 276
Roja (1993), 289
Rosario, Benny, 113, 213–14
Roshan, Rajesh, 108
Roshan (Roshan Lal Nagrath), 106,
        127–28, 156, 259

Rowell, Lewis, 271
Roy, Bimal, 240
royalties, 34, 102, 184

Sagar Movietone, 92, 134, 231, 236,
        237, 238
Sahai, Malti, 14, 206
Sahlins, Marshall, 290
Said, Edward, 10
Saigal, Kundan Lal, 43, 44, 234, 236
samplers, 249, 250, 251, 253, 277,
        290, 291
Sangeet Natak, 30
Sa Rē Gā Ma, 22, 163
Sattar, **173**
saxophonists, 144, 168, 257, 258
Sayani, Ameen, 43
Seervai, Goodi, 193, 194, **195**, **203**,
        237, 257
Sequeira, Peter, 93, 265
sequencers, 249, 251
Shah, Anandji, 59, 123, 157, 164–65,
        227, 228. *See also* Kalyanji-
        Anandji
Shah, Babla, 174, 247
Shah, Chandulal, 95
Shah, Kalyanji, 123, 148, 157, 245,
        246, 281. *See also* Kalyanji-
        Anandji
Shah, Viju, 48, 69–70, 78, 79, 81, 205,
        206, 247, 249–50, 254, 281–82
Shalimar (1977), 74, 182
Shankar, Bhavani, 161, 174, 214, 215,
        252, 267–68, 288, 289–90
Shankar-Eshaan-Loy, **205**, 253
Shankar-Jaikishan, 21, 88, 196
    arrangers, 146, 148, 156, 241, 243
    background music, 199–200
    composing, 122, 136, 170, 199, 272
    electronic instruments, 246, 247, 248
    harmonizing, 170
    orchestra, 106–107, 125–26, 156,
        197, 241, 242
    payment to musicians, 182, 211
    recordings, **173**, 206
    rehearsals, 67, 160, 191–92,
        193–94, 211
    sittings, **165**, 172–73
    Western music, 274–75

Shantaram, V., 130
Sharma, B. N., 80
Sharma, Inderjeet, **205**, 253
Sharma, Naresh, 176
Sharma, Pandit Shivkumar, 130, 229
Sharma, Pyarelal, 5, 68, 95, 99, 126,
    151, 157, 243, 289, 290, 291
  background in Western music, 171
  and background music, 199,
    200–201, 204, 214, 227
  changes to way of working, 198
  composing, 198, 199, 243
  concern for welfare of musicians,
    149, 187
  and costs of composition and
    orchestration, 111, 112–13
  goals of sittings with producers/
    directors, 162
  introduction of big orchestra,
    243–44
  recordings, 185, 198, 204, 214, 259
  See also Laxmikant-Pyarelal
Sharma, Ramprasad, 126, 142
Sharma, Ravi Shankar, 216, 225–26,
    262
Sharma, Shivkumar, 131, 269, 277
Sharma, Zarin, 126–28, 152, 200, 273
Shashikant, 171
Shetty, Ramanand, 187, 189
Shiv-Hari, 65
Sholay (1975), 72–74, **74**, 75, 161, 212
Shope, Bradley, 122, 143, 145
Shor (1972), 284
Shukla, Ashok, 66, 69, 70, 74, 75,
    80–81, 83, **85**, 201, 259
Sikh musicians, 137, 141
silent films, 88, 234
  live musical accompaniment, 32–33
Silsila (1981), 65
Sindh, 51
Singapore, 33
"singer's cabin," 189
Singh, Bhupinder, 168, **221**, 264, 275
Singh, Binoy, **180**
Singh, Charanjit, **221**, 247
Singh, Harmandir, *Hindi Film Geet
    Kosh*, 15, 23, 44, 293
Singh, Hazara, 95, **96**, 99
Singh, Manmohan, 228

Singh, Manohari, 128–29, 134, 135,
    142, 150, 168, **180**, 181, 243,
    264, 279
Singh, Raju, 176
Singh, Ram, 93, 141, 231, 236,
    237–38, 239, 243
Singh, Uttam, 243
Sinha, Satrughan, 165
Sippy, G. P., 73
Sippy, Ramesh, 73
Sircar, B. N., 51
Siri Sound, 94
sitār and sitār players, 93, 124, 127,
    128, 130, 228, 229, 244, 265,
    267, 271
sittings, 157, 162–64, **165**, 221
  sitting musicians, 159, 164–67, 172,
    174, 181–83, 185, 188, 198
  virtual, **177**
  See also music rooms
Skillman, Teri, 15, 88
Sodi, Surender, 201
Sondor equipment, 81, 82
song banks, 163
songs. *See* film songs
Sonik, Omprakash (Master), 199, 200,
    226, 243, 261
Sonik-Omi, 108, 109, 110
Sood, Daman, 38, 58–59, 65
sound engineers. *See* recordists
sound-recording technology, 10,
    56–58, 91
  discs, 30, 36, 42, 62, 63
  double tracking, 216–17, 287
  early sound films, 33–34, 35–37,
    87–88
  editing, 59, 75–76
  live-performance environment,
    75–76, 84, 184–85
  1935–1985, 58–75
  1985–2005, 75–86
  nonfilm, 36, 64, 65, 72, 76, 80, 83,
    102
  nonsynchronous formats, 63, 65–66
  synchronizable formats, 62, 63, 64,
    65, 66, 68–69, 81, 87, 88
  See also digital technology; dubbing;
    magnetic tape; microphones; mix-
    ers; optical dubbers; optical film;

sound-recording technology (*continued*)
  playback; punching; recording
  industry; recordings; recordists;
  reproducers; stereo recording; tape
  recorders
South Asia, 13, 17, 31, 51, 88, 95,
  121, 123, 143, 145, 269. *See also*
  specific countries
Spectral Harmony recording studio,
  61, 83
Srivastava, Sanjay, 46
star shows, 218–20, **221**, 222, 247
stereo recording, 72–75
  track tuning, 77–79, 80
Studer recorders, 80–81
Studio Period of Mumbai film industry, 87, 89, 91–99, 169, 190–91,
  286
  decline of studio system and transi-
    tion to Old Bollywood, 94–99,
    190, 208, 286–87
  studio investments, 93–94
studios. *See* film studios; recording
  studios
subtitles, English, 7, 13
Sudeep Studio, 80, 81, 84
Sunder, Shyam, 239
Sunny Super Sound, 81, 84
Super Cassettes, 80
Suraiya, 43
synthesizers, 60, 77, 175, 244, 247,
  248–49, 250, 252, 253, 287,
  289

tabla and tabla players, 5, 32, 33, 127,
  157, 159, 162, 164, **165**, 174,
  271. *See also* names of specific
  tabla players
"Tadbir se bigdi hui taqdeer," 268
Tagore, A. N., 69, 79, 82–83, 258–59
Tagore, Dakina Mohan, **180**
Tamil Nadu, 30
tape recorders, 64–6, 69–71, 77, 80,
  81. *See also* magnetic tape; and
  specific brands
Teesri Manzil (1966), 50, 265
"Tirchi topi wale," 250
tours, 218–20, **221**, 222, 247
track tuning, 77–79, 80

trumpeters, 76, 79, 145, 151, 187–88
T-Series label, 29, 80, 163
Turino, Thomas, 31

Uberoi, Patricia, 40
Umrao Jaan (2006), 174
United States, 27, 31, 33, 41, 47, 52,
  62, 91, 220, 222, 251, 269. *See
  also* film industry, Hollywood
Upperstall, 89

Varma, Devi Lal, 95, **96**, 99, **203**
Varma, Prakash, 77, 95, **167**, 176,
  177, 192–93, 216, **219**
Vasu-Manohari, 168. *See also*
  Chakravarty, Vasudeo; Singh,
  Manohari
Vaz, Antonio (Chic Chocolate), 48,
  140, 148, 150, 196, 241, 274
Vaz, Dennis, **49**
Vaz, Franco, 107, 148, 151, 196, 268,
  269, 274, 278, 280–81, 282
Verga, Edigio, **49**, 139–40
Vijayakar, Rajiv, 46
violins and violinists, 33, 106–107,
  149, 151, 197, 225, 226, 241,
  243
  impact of technological changes,
    216–17, 248, 250, 252
  in Goan community, 136–37, 139,
    144, 145
  in large orchestras, 110, 115, 193,
    226, 242
  learning and teaching to play, 4, 5,
    125, 126, 148
  recording, 77, 84, 86, 232, 248
  song violin, 189–90
  specialties in Western or Indian
    styles, 265
  See also names of specific violinists
Virmani, Ashish, 7, 87, 89, 104, 116

Waadkar, Dattaram, v, 124, 196
  and composers' style, 258, 263
  and Gangawane, 132
  influence of foreign films, 275
  and orchestras, 226, 230
  payment, 182, 210, 211, 215
  recordings, 160, 185, 188, 193, 206

rehearsals, 160, 185, 196
rhythm arranger, 172–73, **173**
and Sebastian D'Souza, 242
sitting musician, 165, **165**, 188
Wade, Bonnie, 14
Wadia Movietone, 91
Walser, Robert, 255, 256, 260, 279
Waterman, Christopher, 16
Western music, 91, 136, 137, 143,
    168, 171, 231–32, 234, 235, 260
decline of colonial music culture,
    143–48
integration of Indian and Western
    elements, 17, 262–63
musicians' constructions of Indian
    and Western styles, 263–70
Western-style arrangements, 241–43
See also military and police bands;

classical music, Western; nota-
    tion, European; popular music,
    Western
Western Outdoor Advertising, 59,
    63–64, 65
Westrex equipment, 69, 77, 82
White, Hayden, 8, 9
Willemen, Paul, 14, 293
Williams, John, 244
Winston, Brian, 43
women music directors and instrumen-
    talists, 126–28
Woodfield, Ian, 232

Yadhav, Suresh, 86, **221**, 257
Yash Raj Studios, **90**, 91, 253
"Yeh mera dil," 247